From Instruments to

STRATEGIES

How Derivatives Are Used in Practice

From Instruments to STRATEGIES

How Derivatives Are Used in Practice

Frank J. Fabozzi
Johns Hopkins University, USA

World Scientific

NEW JERSEY • LONDON • SINGAPORE • BEIJING • SHANGHAI • HONG KONG • TAIPEI • CHENNAI • TOKYO

Published by

World Scientific Publishing Europe Ltd.
57 Shelton Street, Covent Garden, London WC2H 9HE
Head office: 5 Toh Tuck Link, Singapore 596224
USA office: 27 Warren Street, Suite 401-402, Hackensack, NJ 07601

Library of Congress Cataloging-in-Publication Data
Names: Fabozzi, Frank J. author
Title: From instruments to strategies : how derivatives are used in practice /
author, Frank J. Fabozzi.
Description: London ; Hackensack, NJ : World Scientific Publishing Europe Ltd, [2026] |
Includes bibliographical references.
Identifiers: LCCN 2026006130 | ISBN 9781800619395 hardcover |
ISBN 9781800619401 ebook for institutions | ISBN 9781800619418 ebook for individuals
Subjects: LCSH: Derivative securities
Classification: LCC HG6024.A3 F197 2026
LC record available at https://lccn.loc.gov/2026006130

British Library Cataloguing-in-Publication Data
A catalogue record for this book is available from the British Library.

For any available supplementary material, please visit
https://www.worldscientific.com/worldscibooks/10.1142/Q0570#t=suppl

Desk Editors: Nambirajan Karuppiah/Cian Sacker Ooi

Typeset by Stallion Press
Email: enquiries@stallionpress.com

Preface

This book is the product of decades spent watching, teaching, and debating derivatives in boardrooms, classrooms, and training programs. My perspective is shaped by over 35 years on the board of BlackRock fund complexes, where I interacted directly with portfolio managers as they explained how derivatives fit into their strategies. I have also worked alongside investment banking and asset management firms in their training programs, gaining a front-row seat to the practical realities of how derivatives are used. Add to that more than half a century of teaching derivatives, and the result is a book informed not just by academic theory but by lived experience across multiple corners of the financial world.

The focus of this book is unapologetically on applications. Derivatives may appear in textbooks as abstract concepts, but in practice, they are tools used daily by asset management firms, corporations, pension funds, commercial banks, and investment banks. I intend to show what they actually do, not just what the formulas say they should do. This is not a book about turning every reader into a valuation expert; rather, it is about equipping future users of derivatives with the knowledge to understand why they matter and how they are employed.

Students often find derivatives to be the most challenging course in a finance curriculum, and rightly so. The reasons are twofold. First, derivatives cut across domains of finance that students may not yet have studied before taking a derivatives course. For instance, appreciating why certain derivatives are used in asset management is challenging without a full grasp of asset allocation, fixed income, or currency management. I add footnotes and brief asides to explain the background when it is missing, like a guide pointing out landmarks along the way. Without context, derivatives can look like the dashboard of a car to someone who has never driven—lights flashing, gauges moving, and buttons everywhere. To the uninitiated, it seems confusing and maybe even alarming. But once you know the purpose of each dial and switch, it becomes clear that the dashboard is simply a tool for managing the journey.

The second reason is that derivatives courses are too often taught as if every student were destined to be a quant. Complex equations are marched across the blackboard; before long, even the most attentive students are left staring into the mathematical abyss. Yet in practice, commonly traded derivatives are priced in broadly efficient markets, with the mathematics embedded in online tools available at the click of a mouse. When exotic or highly structured products are involved, portfolio managers turn to what I affectionately call the "quant geeks"—the PhDs in physics, mathematics, or quantitative finance whose job it is to wrestle with the formulas. Let the quant geeks wrestle with the partial differential equations (those sprawling formulas with multiple variables, second derivatives, and enough Greek letters to make a fraternity jealous); the rest of us should focus on whether a derivative actually solves a financial problem. No fund manager is going to hand the pricing of complex instruments to someone who took one derivatives course in business school. That's why every serious asset management firm has a cadre of quants—PhDs in math, physics, or finance—whose job is to live in the weeds of models and calibration. Even commercial and investment banks keep armies of these specialists on staff because no responsible institution will trust the valuation of exotic products to a generalist.

I have developed this perspective on education over many years and formalized it in my article, "Transforming Derivatives Education: Bridging the Gap Between Theory and Practice," published in *The Journal of Derivatives*. In that piece, I argue that courses should shift emphasis away from emphasizing pricing models toward teaching applications that reflect what students will encounter in practice.

In this spirit, the book emphasizes application over abstraction. Yes, the valuation frameworks are covered; they have to be, but always with an eye toward their place in practice rather than as intellectual exercises detached from the real world. I hope that this blend of experience, context, and practicality will demystify derivatives and show them for what they are: not villains or saviors, but powerful tools whose impact depends entirely on how they are used.

How to Use This Book

Because derivatives cut across many areas of finance, this book can be approached in different ways depending on purpose. Some courses or users will want the full sequence, while others may emphasize applications, valuations, or institutional practices.

Before considering different pathways, two elements should always be addressed. Chapter 2, which explains when and why derivatives are used, is essential reading. It sets out the strategic motivations for derivatives and frames their role across corporations, commercial and investment banks, and asset managers. In addition, the chapters in Part 2 on derivative instruments—forwards, futures, swaps, options, structured products, and credit derivatives—should be reviewed unless the audience is already well-versed in these contracts. Together, these form the foundation upon which every other part of the book depends.

With those anchors in place, several pathways described as follows are possible. Whichever path is chosen, the unifying theme of the book remains the same: Derivatives are best understood through their applications. Whether the emphasis is on valuation models, strategic use, or institutional practice, the aim is to show how these instruments function as tools for solving real financial problems.

Comprehensive course path

The full sequence (Parts 1–5) works best for a semester-long university course. Beginning with motivations and classifications, then moving into instruments, strategies, institutional applications, and valuation, this approach provides a complete framework that balances practice with theory.

Applications-first path

For practitioners or courses focused on real-world use, begin with Part 3 (Strategies) and Part 4 (Institutional Applications). These sections show how derivatives are used in portfolios, corporations, and banks. Once the practical applications are clear, return to Chapter 2 and Part 2 for the foundational motivations and instruments, and consult Part 5 for valuation frameworks as needed.

Valuation-focused path

The natural entry point for quantitative finance or advanced programs is Part 5 (Valuation Frameworks). Chapters 11 and 5 provide useful background on option features and insurance-type derivatives. Even here, Chapter 2 and the relevant contract chapters in Part 2 are recommended to connect valuation models with their practical purposes.

Institutional case path

MBA courses, executive education, and professional training programs may find it most helpful to focus on Part 4 (Institutional Applications). These chapters illustrate how derivatives are integrated into corporate treasury, commercial banking, and investment banking. Selected chapters from Part 3 can be added to emphasize strategies in action. Once again, Chapter 2 and the overview of instruments in Part 2 provide the necessary anchor.

Selective module path

For short courses or focused training, specific combinations can be chosen:

- Corporate treasury programs: Chapters 2, 4, and 16.
- Asset management programs: Chapters 2, 3, and 10–14.
- Banking programs: Chapters 2, 7, 9, 17, and 18.

Self-study path

Independent learners may wish to begin with the real-world cases in Chapter 1 (Introduction) and then follow their interests. Because the book is modular, individual chapters can stand alone, whether the focus is on hedging strategies, institutional practices, or valuation. Even for self-study, Chapter 2 and the instrument chapters in Part 2 are indispensable for context.

About the Author

Frank J. Fabozzi is a professor of practice in finance at the Carey Business School at Johns Hopkins University. He is the editor of *The Journal of Portfolio Management*, coeditor of *The Journal of Financial Data Science*, and an editorial advisor for *The Journal of Derivatives*. Frank has served on the boards of directors for BlackRock Fixed Income Funds, BlackRock Equity-Liquidity Funds, BlackRock BCIA Funds, and Guardian Mutual Funds and Guardian Annuity Funds. In his 55-year teaching career, he has taught at the Massachusetts Institute of Technology (MIT), Yale, Princeton, EDHEC Business School, New York University, Rutgers University, and Carnegie Mellon University. Over several decades, he has authored and edited books on derivatives, including *Stock Index Futures* (1984), *Interest Rate Futures and Options* (1990), *Treasury Securities and Derivatives* (1998), *Valuation of Fixed Income Securities and Derivatives* (3rd ed., 1998), *Derivatives and Equity Portfolio Management* (1999), *Credit Derivatives: Instruments, Applications, and Pricing* (2004), and *Subprime Mortgage Credit Derivatives* (2008). He is the recipient of the CFA Institute's 2007 C. Stewart Sheppard Award and the 2015 James R. Vertin Award. In 2002, Frank was inducted into the

Fixed Income Society's Hall of Fame. He has a doctorate in economics from the Graduate Center of the City University of New York and an honorary doctorate of Humane Letters from Nova Southeastern University. He has earned the designations Chartered Financial Analyst (CFA) and Certified Public Accountant (CPA).

Contents

Part 1

Foundations

Chapter 1

Introduction

Derivatives are among the most talked-about yet least understood instruments in modern finance. To some, "derivatives" suggests complexity, hidden risks, and even financial disaster. To others, derivatives are indispensable tools that make today's global financial system possible. The truth, of course, lies somewhere in between. Derivatives are neither inherently dangerous nor inherently safe. At their core, they are contracts whose value is linked (i.e., "derived from") something else, whether an individual stock, a stock index, a bond, a commodity, an interest rate, or even the weather.

When most people hear "derivatives," they think of crises and disasters. Barings Bank, brought down in 1995 by a single trader's unauthorized bets in a derivative instrument (a futures contract), became the archetype of rogue speculation. The 2007–2008 Global Financial Crisis (GFC), in which a derivative instrument (a credit default swap), amplified exposures to subprime mortgages and transmitted losses across the banking system. More recently, the collapse of Archegos Capital in 2021 showed how another derivative instrument (a total return swap) could be used to build massive, leveraged stock positions outside normal disclosure rules, leading to billions in losses for global banks when the trades unraveled. These high-profile failures dominate headlines and shape public opinion, casting derivatives as villains—symbols of hidden leverage and financial engineering gone wrong. I understand that perception and have seen how easily it can overshadow everything else. But that is only half the story because for every spectacular failure that makes front-page news, there are countless quiet successes where derivatives deliver stability, efficiency, and opportunity without fanfare, such as Coca-Cola's long-standing use of futures and options to keep commodity costs in check or the New England Patriots' creative use of interest rate swaps to finance Gillette Stadium on favorable terms.

In my experience, what makes derivatives important is not their structure but how they are used. Like any tool, they can be misapplied, sometimes with dramatic consequences, but they can also be used responsibly to solve problems no other financial instrument can address. A hammer can build a house or break a window. Similarly, derivatives can destabilize markets when misused. Still, they can also help corporations stabilize costs, pension funds meet long-term obligations, municipalities finance infrastructure, and investors manage risk more effectively than is possible.

That perspective is the driving force behind this book. My objective is not to overwhelm readers with abstract formulas or to explain derivatives in an abstract way. I start from practice: The most effective way to build understanding is to examine how real organizations use derivatives to make concrete decisions.

I also want to make clear why this approach matters. Exchanges, textbooks, and training manuals contain stylized examples showing how a particular derivative could be applied. But those are illustrations, not practices. I want to show real-world instances where companies, pension funds, municipalities, and asset managers have employed derivatives in meaningful ways. These stories are difficult to find outside of SEC filings or occasional disclosures; successful derivative programs rarely make news. And that makes sense: Smooth earnings, lower financing costs, or a hedge that quietly works as intended are not dramatic headlines. Disasters make the front page; successes are buried in the footnotes. The same is true in other fields. Air travel, for example, is one of the safest forms of transportation, yet we hear about crashes, not the millions of safe flights.

In the following section, I present cases drawn from practice: Coca-Cola managing commodity costs, AB InBev hedging raw materials and currencies, Nestlé stabilizing agricultural inputs, Madison and Vontobel using options to generate income, and pension funds like CalPERS and Ontario Teachers' aligning long-term liabilities with assets. These are not theoretical "could be" scenarios; they are documented uses of derivatives by organizations facing real challenges. My purpose in beginning here is simple: Before we dive into mechanics, models, and classifications, I want you to see derivatives as they genuinely are—tools being used every day in boardrooms, trading desks, and treasurer's offices around the world.

1.1 Derivatives in Action: Real-World Usage

The following examples are not hypothetical illustrations or classroom exercises. They are drawn from real organizations that have turned to derivatives to solve specific problems, whether managing commodity costs, stabilizing financing, or aligning investment portfolios with long-term obligations. These cases demonstrate that derivatives are not abstract constructs or mere teaching tools, but contracts used daily in boardrooms, treasury offices, and investment committees to manage risk and improve financial outcomes.

It is important to acknowledge, however, that information about successful programs is often limited. Other than in SEC filings or occasional disclosures, most effective derivative strategies go unnoticed. Companies rarely highlight that a well-timed hedge stabilized earnings or that a financing deal worked because a certain derivatives instrument removed uncertainty. Quiet successes, as I just pointed out, generally remain buried in technical notes, not front-page news.

The cases that follow are meant to correct that imbalance. They show how derivatives are essential risk control tools and contribute to financial stability across industries and institutions, even if their contributions rarely make headlines.

1.1.1 *Futures, options, and forward contracts in practice*

Futures, forwards, and options are some of the most widely used derivatives in corporate finance and institutional asset management. These instruments are often the first line of defense against cost volatility, interest-rate shifts, and currency risk, and far from being theoretical, these contracts are embedded in the day-to-day operations of global corporations, asset managers, and pension funds. The following cases illustrate how household names and leading financial institutions employ futures, options, and forwards.

Coca-Cola Company: Hedging input costs with commodity futures and options

Coca-Cola has long relied on futures and options markets to manage volatility in the costs of sugar, corn, and aluminum, commodities critical to its beverages business. In 2020, the company increased its commodity hedging exposure by 70%, with the notional value of contracts[1] equal to 10.7% of its cost of goods sold.[2] By locking in input prices through commodity derivatives, Coca-Cola ensured that even as inflation in sweetener and aluminum markets surged, the impact on its reported production costs was described by management as "benign." Derivatives provided a stabilizing anchor for margins and pricing power.

What makes Coca-Cola's approach especially notable is how it contrasts with some of its peers. As reported in 2021, Procter & Gamble (P&G), another consumer goods giant facing similar input cost pressures, chose not to employ commodity hedges at that time. Instead, P&G managed rising raw material costs through pricing adjustments and operational strategies.[3] The difference between Coca-Cola's reliance on derivatives and P&G's decision to forego them highlights the diversity of approaches companies take in managing commodity risk. Some opt for financial instruments to lock in costs, while others rely on their ability to adjust operations or pass costs on to consumers.

---

[1]The notional value of a derivative contract refers to the total underlying amount upon which the contract's payments are based. It is not an amount actually exchanged but a reference figure used to calculate gains, losses, or cash flows. For example, in a commodity futures contract, the notional value is tied to the quantity of the commodity covered by the contract. Thus, when Coca-Cola discloses the notional value of its hedges as a percentage of cost of goods sold, it signals the scale of production costs being economically covered, not the cash amount spent on derivatives.

[2]Anmol Singh, "Commodity Inflation Puts Consumer Goods Giants' Hedging To The Test." *EuroFinance*, 2021. https://www.eurofinance.com/news/commodity-inflation-puts-consumer-goods-giants-hedging-to-the-test/.

[3]Singh, "Commodity Inflation Puts Consumer Goods Giants' Hedging To The Test."

Anheuser-Busch InBev: Forward contracts on raw materials and currencies

Anheuser-Busch InBev (AB InBev), the world's largest brewer, faces ongoing exposure to barley, corn, and packaging inputs and currency risks in its global markets. The firm follows a strict 12-month forward hedging policy. During the commodity rally of early 2021, AB InBev reported that derivatives offset 56% of its raw-material cost increases. CEO Carlos Brito highlighted that this program of forward contracts and related derivatives gave the firm 12-month visibility into its transaction foreign exchange (FX) and commodity exposures, making financial planning more predictable.[4]

Nestlé: Multi-commodity futures, options, and forwards

Nestlé, one of the largest global food companies, hedges its input exposures across coffee, cocoa, cereals, dairy, and packaging. In 2020, it disclosed open commodity hedges with a notional value of CHF 917 million. Nestlé combines futures, options, and forward contracts in a layered program designed to cushion sudden spikes in global agricultural and packaging costs. These instruments helped the company absorb sharp increases in dairy and cereal prices, limiting the impact on operating margins and ensuring greater stability for investors.[5]

Madison Investments: Covered call strategies

Madison Investments operates the Madison Covered Call & Equity Income Fund, a portfolio of 30–50 growth stocks with systematic covered-call writing.[6] The strategy involves selling call options on stocks the fund already owns. By doing so, Madison collects option premiums upfront, which provides an additional and predictable source of income for shareholders. This income stream helps cushion returns when the underlying equities move sideways or experience modest declines. The trade-off is that this strategy gives up some potential gains if stock prices rise sharply. However, that exchange can be attractive for investors who value steady income and reduced volatility. Instead of relying only

---

[4] Singh, "Commodity Inflation Puts Consumer Goods Giants' Hedging To The Test."

[5] *Ibid.*

[6] Madison Covered Call & Equity Income Fund Strategy Overview. Madison Investments, 2025. https://madisoninvestments.com/assets/img/investment-strategies/MadisonCoveredCallEqtyIncFund-StrategyOverview.pdf.

on dividends or stock appreciation, the portfolio generates an extra cash flow stream by writing options in a disciplined and repeatable way. By systematically writing single-stock calls, Madison enhances yield while moderating volatility—a practical example of how options can be used not for speculation, but for income generation and risk control. The approach reflects a disciplined use of derivatives to align portfolio outcomes with the needs of income-focused investors.

BlackRock: Treasury futures in fixed-income portfolios

BlackRock, the world's largest asset manager, routinely uses U.S. Treasury futures across its bond funds. These futures provide quick and liquid exposure to government bonds, making them a practical tool for portfolio adjustments. One everyday use is to manage duration, which measures how sensitive a bond portfolio is to changes in interest rates. By adding or reducing Treasury futures, BlackRock can fine-tune that sensitivity without directly trading the underlying bonds.

Treasury futures are also used to implement yield-curve positions, that is, to express views on how interest rates may change across short-, medium-, and long-term bond maturities. For example, suppose the portfolio manager expects short-term rates to rise faster than long-term rates. In that case, they can adjust their exposure accordingly using futures rather than buying and selling dozens of individual bonds. Another application is to *equitize cash*. Large bond funds often hold cash temporarily, perhaps because of investor inflows or pending trades. Holding cash can drag down returns if markets move, so managers use Treasury futures to give that cash "bond-like" exposure until it is fully invested. In this way, the portfolio stays aligned with its benchmark and avoids performance gaps.

BlackRock's fixed-income disclosures show that these practices are not occasional but routine. Standardized Treasury futures are core tools for portfolio construction, providing flexibility and efficiency while ensuring that large-scale funds remain tightly managed against their objectives.

Vanguard: Futures and forwards for index tracking

Vanguard, one of the world's largest asset managers and a pioneer in index investing,[7] makes strategic use of Treasury futures and FX forward contracts across its bond index funds and active fixed-income strategies.

[7] Index investing is a passive strategy that aims to match, rather than beat, the performance of a benchmark (such as the S&P 500) by holding the same securities in the same weights.

These derivative instruments play a vital role in managing tracking error (i.e., the tendency for a fund's returns to deviate from its benchmark). Because the bond market is vast and less liquid than equities, Vanguard often cannot buy every bond in an index without incurring excessive costs or distorting markets. Instead, portfolio managers use a combination of sampling (i.e., holding a representative subset of bonds), risk-factor modeling, and optimization tools to align key exposures, such as duration, credit quality, and sector weightings, with those of the benchmark. Futures and forwards then fill the gaps by providing precise exposure to interest rates or currencies without having to trade the full bond or FX universe, helping to keep tracking error tightly controlled while minimizing transaction costs.

In practice, Treasury futures allow Vanguard fund managers to quickly adjust duration (interest-rate sensitivity) or "equalize" cash flows when there are large inflows or outflows, delivering bond-like exposure without buying or selling individual securities. Meanwhile, currency forwards offer a straightforward way to hedge or manage FX risk in international bond holdings, again without swapping large quantities of foreign bonds in and out. Vanguard's disclosures and research make clear that these derivative tools are indispensable in enabling large fixed-income funds to track their benchmarks efficiently and cost-effectively.[8]

Teucrium Soybean Fund: Hedging and price exposure through futures
The Teucrium Soybean Fund (SOYB) is an exchange-traded fund (ETF)[9] designed to provide investors, commercial users, and producers with exposure to the daily price movements of soybean futures contracts, specifically those traded on the Chicago Board of Trade (CBOT). SOYB achieves this by holding a diversified portfolio of soybean futures, typically split across three different CBOT contracts: the next-to-expire, the second-to-expire, and the third-to-expire. This laddered approach allows the fund to capture price dynamics across the crop cycle, smoothing delivery-related volatility and minimizing the costs of rolling contracts.

---

[8] https://corporate.vanguard.com/content/dam/corp/public-policy/pdf/CFTC_Use%20of%20Derivatives%20by%20Registered%20Investment%20Companies%20and%20BDCs.pdf.

[9] An ETF is a pooled investment vehicle that holds a basket of assets (e.g., stocks, bonds, commodities) and seeks to track a specified index or strategy. Shares trade on exchanges throughout the day at market prices, like a stock.

Unlike physical soybean storage or forward contracting, SOYB does not handle actual commodities. Instead, it manages its assets exclusively in futures positions, which are mark-to-market daily.[10] For commercial participants, such as processors, merchandisers, and agribusinesses, SOYB offers a transparent and accessible vehicle to hedge against adverse moves in soybean prices. This means users can directly offset risk from unsold inventory or anticipated purchases simply by buying or selling shares in SOYB, which align with the value of soybean futures.

In regulatory disclosures and investor materials, Teucrium emphasizes that the fund is built for real risk management: helping stakeholders lock in prices, protect margins, and respond dynamically to global market developments. This is accomplished through actual futures contracts, without recourse to physical soybeans or over-the-counter derivatives.[11]

Pension funds: CalPERS, Ontario Teachers', and Dutch funds

Large pension funds also rely on futures and forward contracts as part of *liability-driven investment* (*LDI*) *programs*. LDI is an investment framework that begins not with pursuing maximum returns but with the pension plan's obligations (i.e., its liabilities to current and future retirees). Because those liabilities are highly sensitive to long-term interest rates and inflation, funds must structure their portfolios to move in tandem with the value of those obligations. Derivatives such as stock and interest rate futures and currency forwards allow plans to fine-tune exposures and hedge risks cost-effectively and flexibly, ensuring that the fund's assets remain aligned with its liabilities even as markets shift.

Examples include CalPERS, the largest U.S. public pension plan, and the Ontario Teachers' Pension Plan (OTPP) in Canada, both of which disclose the use of derivatives in their LDI frameworks. The Netherlands is a critical reference point, where pension funds have long been global leaders in liability-driven investing. Dutch funds such as ABP, the civil service pension fund, and PFZW, the healthcare workers' fund, are among the largest pension plans in the world and are managed by the investment organization APG. These funds use derivatives extensively to match their long-dated liabilities, employing interest rate futures to manage duration

[10]"Mark-to-market" (fair value) means revaluing an asset or liability to its current market price at each measurement date. When reliable market prices do not exist, firms may rely on models or comparable quotes ("mark-to-model"), which introduces estimation uncertainty.

[11]https://teucrium.com/etfs/soyb.

risk, stock index futures for efficient portfolio adjustments, and currency forwards to reduce exchange-rate volatility across their globally diversified holdings.

In all these cases, derivatives are integral to ensuring that pension portfolios remain tightly aligned with funding obligations, while also giving fund managers the flexibility to adjust exposures quickly and efficiently in changing markets.

1.1.2 *Swaps as advanced derivatives in practice*

Up to this point, the focus has been on the more fundamental derivative contracts: futures, forwards, and options. Swaps take the concept further. Swaps allow two parties to exchange cash flows over time instead of simply betting on or hedging the price of a single asset. These arrangements have become a cornerstone of modern finance, with applications ranging from managing borrowing costs to hedging currency risk to tailoring portfolio exposures.

There are many forms of swaps, each serving different purposes. Interest rate swaps allow borrowers to transform floating-rate debt into predictable fixed payments. Currency swaps help global companies and institutions borrow in one currency while effectively repaying in another. Total return swaps (TRSs) give institutional investors synthetic exposure to stocks, indexes, or bonds without directly owning them. Credit default swaps (CDSs) function like insurance against the risk of borrower default.

Swaps are especially powerful because they can be customized. This flexibility has produced remarkable successes and costly failures. In the cases that follow, we see swaps used to finance stadiums, stabilize pension funds, manage global corporate cash flows, and, in some instances, generate crises that made headlines.

The lessons from the cases that follow are twofold. First, swaps demonstrate how flexibility can be a strength: When matched carefully to revenues, liabilities, or investment mandates,[12] they can reduce uncertainty, lower borrowing costs, and align risks with financial goals.

[12]An investment mandate is the formal set of objectives, constraints, and guidelines that govern how a portfolio is managed (e.g., target return or benchmark, eligible asset classes, risk limits, liquidity needs, and any regulatory requirements). It is typically documented in an investment policy statement or manager agreement and binds decisions on allocation among asset classes, instruments (including derivatives), and leverage. Performance is evaluated relative to the mandate's benchmark and risk parameters.

For example, Denver International Airport and Canada's CPP Investments show how swaps can stabilize finances and free resources for long-term investment. Second, the same flexibility can introduce new vulnerabilities if contracts are poorly structured, mistimed, or misused. The experiences of Wembley Stadium, Italian municipalities, and Archegos Capital illustrate how swaps can lock borrowers into costly obligations or concentrate hidden risks that only surface during crises.

These cases show that swaps are not inherently stabilizing or destabilizing. Instead, they are powerful financial tools whose impact depends entirely on context, governance, and execution. Readers should approach the examples that follow not merely as stories of success or failure, but as evidence of the fine line between swaps as instruments of stability or as sources of fragility.

1.1.2.1 *Interest rate swaps*

Interest rate swaps are among the most widely used derivatives in large-scale financing. Their appeal lies in managing exposure to fluctuating borrowing costs: issuers with variable-rate debt can use a swap to lock in fixed rates, providing predictable future payments and budget certainty. This has made swaps especially common in stadium finance, infrastructure projects, and municipal debt programs.

Why not simply issue fixed-rate bonds from the outset? There are several reasons. First, investor demand often favors floating-rate debt, making placing bonds in that market easier or cheaper. Second, the fixed-rate bond market may require higher term premiums than the swap market, meaning a synthetic fixed rate (floating debt plus a swap) can be less expensive than issuing a conventional fixed bond. Third, swaps provide flexibility that standard bonds cannot easily replicate. Their structure can be tailored to match expected revenues, construction schedules, or refinancing plans. For these reasons, many issuers choose floating-rate financing combined with swaps rather than relying solely on fixed-rate debt.

Gillette Stadium: The New England Patriots: In the early 2000s, Robert Kraft and the New England Patriots planned a new stadium in Foxborough, Massachusetts. The team needed a reliable financing structure to fund the construction, which would cost several hundred million dollars. Rather than issuing traditional fixed-rate bonds, Kraft's team issued auction-rate securities. These are similar to short-term bonds that periodically reset their interest rates through an auction process and were especially accessible at the time. The team entered a long-term interest rate swap with Salomon Smith Barney to convert the resulting floating payments into fixed-rate obligations. This swap transformed volatile, auction-based payments into a steady, fixed-rate schedule.

Because the financial markets were favorable at the time, the team locked in historically low fixed rates via the swap. This meant that over the life of the financing, the stadium authority paid less in interest than it would have under a conventional fixed-rate bond structure. Reports suggest the swap arrangement saved the Patriots tens of millions of dollars over 25 years while preserving the flexibility and favorable terms of the auction-rate market at issuance.

The Gillette Stadium financing stands out because the swap arrangement delivered a lower all-in cost than a direct fixed-rate bond issuance while also providing stability with flexibility. Using the swap to convert auction-rate debt into predictable fixed payments, the Patriots organization could secure a steady repayment schedule without sacrificing the upfront advantages of auction-rate funding. Just as importantly, the team's timing proved advantageous: Interest rates did not collapse after the swap was executed. This allowed them to avoid the significant losses that later plagued projects such as MetLife Stadium and Wembley Stadium, as described in the following. In this way, Gillette Stadium illustrates how an interest rate swap, combined with creative debt structuring, can achieve a cost-effective and durable financing solution when matched with favorable market conditions.

MetLife Stadium: The New York Giants and Jets: In 2005, the New York Giants and New York Jets agreed to build a new stadium in New Jersey at a cost of roughly \$1.6 billion. Giants Stadium LLC issued about \$650 million in bonds to finance its share. Because these bonds carried floating interest rates, the teams faced the risk that debt payments could spike in future years if interest rates increase. To protect against this uncertainty, starting around 2007, the teams entered into interest rate swap agreements with investment banks such as Lehman Brothers. These swaps converted their floating-rate obligations into fixed payments, which meant the teams could match debt service to more predictable ticket and concession revenues.

The timing, however, proved difficult. After the GFC, interest rates fell sharply. The swaps required the teams to continue paying fixed rates much higher than prevailing market levels, leaving them disadvantaged. Matters worsened when Lehman Brothers collapsed in September 2008, creating disputes over how the swap contracts should be settled. What began as a strategy for financial stability became a long-running legal and financial challenge, showing both the promise and pitfalls of using swaps for large-scale infrastructure financing.

Wembley Stadium (England): When the new Wembley Stadium was being redeveloped in the early 2000s, the English Football Association (FA) borrowed heavily to fund the project, taking on about £426 million of debt. To make the debt service more predictable, the FA entered into a large interest rate swap that locked in a fixed rate of 6.92%. At first, this looked like prudent management because the FA could plan for steady annual payments without worrying about fluctuations in the interest rate markets.

But when interest rates began to fall in the mid-2000s, the swap became costly. By 2009, the FA reported losses of about £38 million on the arrangement, a significant financial strain on an already expensive stadium project. The Wembley case is often cited in Europe as a cautionary tale: Swaps can provide stability. However, if market conditions move in the wrong direction, the "insurance" they provide can become an expensive burden.

Denver International Airport: Denver's experience shows that interest rate swaps can be constructive when used carefully and with clear objectives. In the early 2000s, Denver International Airport faced a major financing challenge: It needed to fund expansion and modernization projects, including runway improvements and terminal upgrades. However, issuing conventional fixed-rate bonds would have been costly. Instead, the city opted for a structure that combined floating-rate bonds with interest rate swaps. The swaps converted the floating payments into predictable fixed costs at a lower rate than the market demanded for straight fixed-rate bond issuance. Over time, this approach saved Denver tens of millions of dollars in debt service costs, freeing resources for airport investment without raising taxes or cutting services. The key to Denver's success was that the swap was straightforward, aligned with the city's financing goals, and did not expose the airport to undue market volatility. Unlike other municipalities, Denver locked in a structure that matched its needs and avoided speculative elements.

City of Richmond, California: Richmond's experience with swaps tied to pension obligation bonds illustrates how well-intentioned financial engineering can backfire. City officials were persuaded that entering swaps would reduce borrowing costs compared with issuing traditional fixed-rate bonds. Instead, when interest rates shifted, the city was locked into higher-than-expected payments and steep termination fees. By 2025, the frustration had boiled over into litigation: Richmond sued JPMorgan Chase, Royal Bank of Canada, and its financial advisors, alleging the swaps were mis-sold and violated state law. For Richmond, what began as a strategy to manage pension debt became a protracted legal and financial burden.

Orlando, Florida (Central Florida Expressway Authority): The Central Florida Expressway Authority entered swap contracts with several major banks, expecting them to hedge against interest rate risks and support funding for regional infrastructure. Instead, the swaps siphoned millions that could have been used for new roads and highway improvements. The Authority eventually challenged the deals in court, arguing that the contracts were presented as risk-reducing tools when introducing additional costs and volatility. Orlando's case highlighted how financial complexity can undermine a public mission when oversight and risk management are insufficient.

Italian Municipalities: Across Italy, dozens of municipalities, including Venice and Cattolica, entered swaps that were promoted as cost-saving measures for local budgets. The agreements backfired, producing losses that many towns could not absorb. Litigation spilled into English courts, where judges ultimately required banks such as Intesa Sanpaolo and Bear Stearns to return payments. These rulings were significant because they underscored two principles: Banks must disclose risks more clearly when marketing swaps, and municipalities may lack full legal authority to engage in such complex contracts. The Italian cases became international precedents, shaping how swaps are regulated in the municipal sector.

Toll roads: Toll road financing provides some of the clearest illustrations of both the benefits and the risks of using swaps. A prominent example is the Indiana Toll Road, whose privatization financing included a nine-year bullet loan[13] paired with a 20-year accreting swap.[14] The swap was designed to smooth debt service by gradually stepping up fixed payments, anticipating that toll revenues would grow over time. While this structure initially offered predictability, it backfired when interest rates declined significantly. The project remained locked into higher fixed obligations, which produced substantial mark-to-market losses and strained finances.

Colorado's E-470 toll road faced similar challenges. Local officials entered swaps to convert floating-rate debt into fixed obligations, intending to stabilize financing for the highway system. However, as interest rates shifted unfavorably, the costs of these swaps rose, leaving the project with less financial flexibility. Both cases highlight a central tension: While swaps can insulate toll road projects from volatility, they can also entrench costly positions when market conditions evolve unexpectedly.

Airports: Airports have likewise used swaps to manage financing for large-scale capital improvements. Facilities such as Charlotte Douglas International, Miami-Dade, Sacramento, Salt Lake City, and Detroit Wayne County Airports issued floating-rate bonds. Still, they then converted them into synthetic fixed-rate obligations through swap agreements. This approach was particularly appealing because airports typically generate relatively stable revenue streams from landing fees, parking, and concessions. Matching predictable income with fixed debt service obligations reduced uncertainty and allowed management to plan long-term expansion confidently.

Yet, the strategy carried the same vulnerability seen in stadium and toll road financings. When rates fell below expectations, airports were locked into above-market payments. While the swaps reduced exposure to rate spikes, they limited participation in the benefits of declining interest costs. In addition, these arrangements exposed airports to counterparty credit risks, as the bankruptcy of Lehman Brothers demonstrated. Thus, while

---

[13] A bullet loan is a non-amortizing loan—meaning no principal is repaid during the term—in which the entire principal is paid in a single "bullet" at maturity, with interest typically paid periodically (or accrued) beforehand.

[14] An accreting swap is a derivative, often an interest rate swap, whose notional amount increases on a preset schedule to match a growing underlying exposure (e.g., a construction drawdown or ramp-up in funding). It is used instead of a standard, flat-notional swap to avoid overhedging early in the project's life, reduce unnecessary carry costs, and improve hedge effectiveness by aligning the hedge notional with the exposure profile over time.

swaps offered a tool to align airport finances with predictable revenues, they introduced risks that were not always fully appreciated at the outset.

Ports: Major U.S. ports have also integrated swaps into their borrowing programs to support modernization and expansion projects. The Port of Los Angeles and the Port of San Francisco both relied on swaps to convert floating-rate debt into fixed obligations, stabilizing borrowing costs for capital projects such as terminal upgrades and infrastructure improvements critical to trade flows. For ports competing in a global shipping environment, steady debt service is essential to maintaining investment capacity and operational reliability. The use of swaps helped these ports stabilize borrowing costs during periods of rate volatility.

The use of swaps allowed ports to avoid sudden increases in financing costs that could disrupt capital programs. At the same time, these strategies carried familiar risks. Falling interest rates left ports paying more than market levels, while exposure to bank counterparties added layers of financial and legal uncertainty. The experience of ports underscores the broader theme: Swaps can be highly effective in stabilizing funding for long-term infrastructure, but they also commit issuers to paths that may not prove advantageous in all market conditions.

1.1.2.2 *Currency swaps*

A currency swap is a financial agreement in which two parties exchange a specified amount of two different currencies at the outset, make payments to each other over time—often trading periodic interest payments—and ultimately return the original amounts at maturity. These swaps are designed to help organizations deal with the risks of fluctuating FX rates. Crucially, currency swaps are used for borrowing in foreign currencies and help companies manage cash flows and revenues from currencies other than their home currency.

In essence, currency swaps allow businesses to "trade" currency exposures, whether from loans, operational costs, or incoming sales, and lock in future payments regardless of how exchange rates change. This enables firms to budget confidently, control funding costs, and protect profits from unexpected currency movements, whether those risks arise from debt or international revenue streams.

IBM and the World Bank: In the 1980s, IBM, needing U.S. dollars for its primary operations, had borrowed in Swiss francs and German marks due to previous business in those countries. At the same time, while borrowing in dollars, the World Bank needed French francs and German marks to fund its European projects. By entering a currency swap, the two institutions exchanged debt: IBM made interest payments in dollars (its key operating currency), while the World Bank paid in francs and marks (matching its project needs). At maturity, they swapped the principal back. This maneuver lowered borrowing costs and shielded both parties from unfavorable currency fluctuations related to debt repayments or funding international activities.

Apple Inc.: Apple earns revenues globally in euros, yen, and many other currencies, while its reports and spending are in U.S. dollars. Fluctuations in those foreign currencies can threaten Apple's profits when converted back to dollars. To guard against this, Apple uses currency swaps: By swapping future receipts of, for instance, euros into dollars at a fixed rate, Apple ensures it knows how much dollar revenue it will get, stabilizing its earnings and simplifying its financial planning. This "locks in" exchange rates and shields Apple from currency risk.

Toyota Motor Corporation: Toyota sometimes borrows money by issuing bonds in dollars, but its operations and costs are largely in Japanese yen. If the dollar moves unfavorably against the yen, paying back those bonds could become unexpectedly costly. Toyota uses currency swaps to convert its dollar-based obligations into yen-based ones. Toyota pays and receives yen instead of dollars through annual exchanges, making its costs predictable despite market volatility. Currency swaps thus ensure stable borrowing costs and protect Toyota's bottom line from exchange rate surprises.

Thames Water: Thames Water is the largest water and wastewater services provider in the U.K., responsible for supplying clean water and managing sewage for millions of customers in London and the surrounding region. As a critical public utility with vast infrastructure and long-term investment needs, Thames Water relies heavily on external financing, issuing debt in both sterling and other major currencies and taking on complex obligations linked to interest rates and U.K. inflation.[15]

---

[15] "Liquidity Extension Update 13 December." Thames Water, December 13, 2024. https://www.thameswater.co.uk/media-library/home/about-us/investors/liquidity-extension/liquidity-extension-update.pdf; "Debt information | Investors | About us—Thames Water." Thames Water, September 30, 2024. https://www.thameswater.co.uk/

Thames Water maintains a substantial derivatives portfolio that includes interest rate swaps, index-linked (inflation swaps), cross-currency swaps, and currency swaps to manage these risks and provide greater financial stability. These instruments serve several key purposes:

- *Interest rate swaps*: These allow Thames Water to fix or manage the variability of interest payments on its floating-rate loans, protecting the company if benchmark rates (such as Sterling Overnight Index Average, SONIA, a benchmark interest rate) rise unexpectedly.
- *Index-linked swaps*: These tie portions of Thames Water's interest or principal payments to the U.K. RPI inflation index to match cash flows with inflation-linked revenues and liabilities.
- *Cross-currency and currency swaps*: These swaps let Thames Water convert foreign currency debt into pounds sterling and manage both currency and interest rate risk over very long timeframes. For example, suppose the company borrows in euros or dollars because market rates are cheaper or investor appetite is stronger. In that case, it can swap those cash flows into sterling, ensuring it will not be exposed to sudden exchange rate movements between the currencies.[16]

For a utility like Thames Water, derivatives, particularly swaps, play a central role in managing financial risks and stabilizing long-term obligations. Interest rate fluctuations are a constant concern: Without swaps, the company could face significantly higher debt costs if market rates rise. Inflation is another critical factor, as regulated water bills and other revenues are often tied to inflation indices. By employing index-linked swaps, Thames Water can better align debt service with inflation-linked revenues, reducing margin volatility. Currency exposure adds further complexity since borrowing in non-sterling currencies, such as euros, yen, or dollars, would leave the company vulnerable to adverse FX rate movements. Currency swaps address this by locking in repayment rates, allowing the company to focus on its core operations rather than

---

media-library/home/about-us/investors/debt-investors/thames-water-utilities/thames-water-utilities/Investors-reports/investor-report-30-september-2024.pdf.

[16]A currency swap involves exchanging principal and interest payments in two different currencies, typically to hedge currency and funding risks. A cross-currency swap, a more advanced version, also swaps regular interest payments and often involves differing interest rate structures (such as fixed for floating) in each currency, providing comprehensive management of both currency and interest rate exposures for long-term debt.

speculating on currency markets. Finally, swaps give Thames Water the flexibility to structure and diversify its debt in ways that align with both its cash flow profile and regulatory requirements, extending obligations decades into the future, sometimes as far out as 2060.

In sum, Thames Water's extensive use of these derivatives reflects both the scale of its financial needs and the risk management challenges of a modern, internationally active public utility. The swaps portfolio is a cornerstone of its financial strategy, designed to shield the company from shocks in interest rates, inflation, and FX, ensuring that it can invest long-term in reliable infrastructure without putting its financial health or customers at risk.

1.1.2.3 *Total return swaps*

A TRS allows an investor to get the full economic ride of a stock, index, or basket (price moves plus dividends) without owning it directly. A bank holds (or references) the shares and passes the "total return" to the investor; in exchange, the investor pays a financing fee and posts margin. TRSs are popular because they are flexible, can be scaled quickly, and may delay or reduce disclosure in some jurisdictions compared with outright share ownership. The trade-off is clear: Leverage and discretion also mean sharper losses and dependence on bank financing if markets move the wrong way.

Lone Pine Capital: Lone Pine Capital is a well-known long/short equity hedge fund[17] based in Greenwich, Connecticut. Public filings show a large, research-driven equity program with extensive use of equity instruments and prime broker relationships typical of major hedge funds. In practice, managers at this scale commonly use equity derivatives,

[17] A long/short hedge fund takes long positions in securities expected to rise and short positions in those expected to fall, aiming to generate alpha while managing market (beta) exposure. Net exposure can range from market-neutral to net long or net short, and gross exposure often exceeds 100% due to leverage. The strategy emphasizes security selection and relative-value views over broad market direction. A long position means owning (or having positive exposure to) a security to increase its value when the underlying price rises. A short position means selling a borrowed security to profit if the price falls, with the obligation to repurchase or deliver later; short sales typically require margin, may incur borrow/dividend costs, and can have theoretically unlimited loss if the price rises sharply.

including TRSs, to size positions efficiently, rebalance exposures, and manage financing without always buying or selling the underlying shares in the market. While specific TRS positions are generally not itemized in public forms, Lone Pine's structure, filings, and operating model are consistent with the standard toolkit used by peer long/short managers. For a stock-picking fund, TRSs can provide quick, scalable exposure (or de-risking) during earnings seasons and corporate events, help manage borrow constraints on hard-to-short companies, and centralize financing through prime brokers instead of moving large blocks in the cash market.

Viking Global Investors: Viking Global Investors is a multibillion-dollar hedge fund based in Greenwich, Connecticut. The firm has consistently ranked among the largest hedge funds globally, managing tens of billions of dollars in assets. Like other top equity long/short managers, Viking seeks to generate alpha[18] through concentrated bets on stocks, often taking significant positions in technology, healthcare, consumer, and financial companies.

To build these positions, Viking has employed TRS as a core tool. A TRS allows the fund to gain synthetic exposure to a stock, capturing all gains, losses, and dividends without purchasing the shares outright. Instead, the fund contracts with a bank which holds the stock on its balance sheet and passes through the "total return" to Viking. In exchange, Viking pays the bank a financing cost (a reference interest rate plus a spread). This structure offers several advantages:

- *Leverage*[19]: Viking can control large positions with less capital by posting collateral rather than the full notional value.
- *Discretion*: Because the shares remain on the bank's balance sheet, Viking does not always have to disclose ownership immediately in

[18] Alpha is a portfolio's risk-adjusted excess return, that is, the part of performance left over after accounting for market (and other factor) exposures defined by a benchmark or model. It is measured net of fees and trading costs.

[19] Leverage refers to using borrowed funds (or derivative exposures) to increase a portfolio's size relative to its equity. When the asset's realized return exceeds the cost of borrowing (including financing rates, fees, and margin costs), leverage amplifies gains; when returns fall short of that cost, it destroys value.

public filings such as 13F reports,[20] giving it a strategic advantage in building or unwinding trades quietly.

- *Capital efficiency*: TRS usage allows Viking to allocate freed-up capital to other opportunities, increasing portfolio flexibility.

While Viking's use of TRSs is consistent with the broader hedge fund industry practice, it highlights the *regulatory blind spots* that became evident in cases such as Archegos Capital Management. In contrast to Archegos, which collapsed under the weight of its leveraged TRS positions, Viking has managed its exposures within more conservative risk parameters, maintaining its reputation as one of the more disciplined hedge funds.

Both Viking Global Investors and Lone Pine Capital have turned to TRSs as part of their investment toolkit. In each case, the swaps enabled the funds to accumulate significant equity exposures while avoiding immediate disclosure, making building positions discreetly and managing capital more flexibly easier. Yet there are important differences. Lone Pine has at times pursued more aggressive, growth-oriented positions, relying on TRSs to scale exposure quickly. In contrast, Viking has generally earned a reputation for more disciplined risk management and tighter portfolio controls. The collapse of Archegos, discussed next, underscored how reliance on swaps can lead to catastrophic outcomes if risk is mismanaged; by contrast, firms like Viking and Lone Pine demonstrate how the same instrument, when handled with adequate oversight, can serve as a practical tool for leverage, efficiency, and discretion rather than a source of existential risk.

Archegos Capital Management: Archegos used TRSs with multiple banks to build massive, leveraged exposures to a handful of U.S. media and technology stocks without holding the shares directly. When prices fell in March 2021, margin calls (i.e., putting up additional cash to maintain a derivatives position) cascaded and the unwind triggered multi-billion-dollar losses at

---

[20]Form 13F is a quarterly report that U.S. institutional investment managers (e.g., hedge funds, mutual funds, advisers, and banks) must file with the SEC if they exercise investment discretion over $100 million in "Section 13(f) securities." It discloses long positions held at quarter-end, primarily U.S.-listed equities and certain related instruments (e.g., listed options), with share counts and market values, and is due within 45 days after each quarter.

several prime brokers (approximately $5.5 billion at Credit Suisse and $2.85 billion at Nomura, among others), making Archegos a global case study in how TRSs can concentrate risk in opaque ways. Subsequent coverage and court proceedings underscored the disclosure, leverage, and counterparty risk lessons for both investors and banks. Archegos shows the other edge of the sword: When TRSs are used to take very concentrated, leveraged bets, losses can propagate quickly through the banking system.

Canada Pension Plan (CPP) investment board: One of the world's largest institutional investors, CPP Investments, oversees hundreds of billions in assets to secure Canadians' retirement. In its disclosures and annual reports, the fund describes its use of TRSs as part of mainstream, transparent portfolio management, distinct from the leverage-driven strategies sometimes associated with hedge funds. CPP uses both equity TRSs and fixed-income TRSs to help shape and manage the risk profile of its portfolios. These swaps allow CPP Investments to:

- *Match exposures*: TRS can be used to quickly and flexibly align portfolio allocations with strategic benchmarks or desired exposure levels, such as gaining synthetic exposure to a stock index or a bond portfolio without buying (or selling) all the physical securities at once.
- *Run overlays*: By using TRSs, CPP can implement overlay strategies[21] for managing risk, adjusting asset allocation, or hedging against market moves without constantly trading the underlying instruments, making daily portfolio management more efficient and cost-effective.
- *Manage liquidity*: TRSs provide a way to gain or reduce market exposure rapidly without needing to buy or sell large blocks of securities. This is especially valuable for a large fund, where direct trades could cause market disruption or require significantly more time and resources.

CPP Investments is a model for mainstream institutional use of derivatives such as TRSs. Unlike hedge funds or family offices that may use TRSs for maximum leverage or to obscure their market activities, CPP's

---

[21] An overlay strategy is a separate layer of positions, typically using derivatives, placed on top of an existing portfolio to adjust exposures without trading the underlying assets. Common examples include currency overlays (hedging FX), duration overlays (altering interest-rate sensitivity), and equity beta overlays (raising or lowering market exposure).

approach is deliberate, well-governed, and fully disclosed to the public. Its swaps are building blocks for efficient management, risk control, and asset allocation, representing the institutional best practice for modern portfolio management.

TRSs enable CPP Investments to maintain a nimble, transparent, and closely aligned portfolio, with long-term objectives—an approach scrutinized and reported in its official annual reports and risk disclosures. This clear, responsible use contrasts sharply with cases where TRSs have contributed to market instability or hidden risk.[22]

1.1.2.4 *Credit default swaps*

CDSs are derivative contracts that operate much like insurance on debt. In a CDS, one party pays a regular premium to another in exchange for protection against the risk that a borrower defaults on a bond or loan. If the borrower experiences a credit event such as bankruptcy, failure to pay interest, or a forced restructuring, the protection seller compensates the buyer for the loss.

The market has two principal sides. On one side are buyers of protection, typically bondholders, banks, or portfolio managers who want to hedge against the possibility of default. By purchasing a CDS, they shift the credit risk of their holdings onto another party while continuing to earn interest on the bonds they hold. On the other side are sellers of protection, which include banks, insurance companies, hedge funds, and other investors willing to assume credit risk in exchange for the steady income from premiums.

Goldman Sachs Asset Management: This asset management firm has long integrated CDSs into its credit strategies. Before the GFC, GSAM used CDSs to hedge exposures in structured products[23] and to implement relative

---

[22] "CPP Investments F2025 Annual Report." CPP Investments, 2025. https://www.cppinvestments.com/wp-content/uploads/attachments/CPP-Investments-F2025-Annual-Report-English.pdf.

[23] A structured product is a pre-packaged investment, typically a note issued by a bank, whose payoff is engineered with derivatives to link returns to one or more underlyings (e.g., an index, stock, basket, rate, or commodity). Designs can target outcomes such as principal protection, yield enhancement, or conditional upside/downside (barriers, caps, or buffers).

value trades in corporate credit. By taking long or short positions through CDSs, GSAM could adjust portfolios more efficiently than buying or selling cash bonds. After the GFC, GSAM remained an active user of CDSs, particularly in sovereign and investment-grade corporate markets, employing them as liquid instruments to fine-tune credit exposure while maintaining portfolio flexibility.

Citadel: This hedge fund is widely regarded as one of the most sophisticated players in credit derivatives. Even before the GFC, Citadel was active in trading CDS indexes and single-name contracts to hedge risks in its multi-strategy portfolios and speculate on shifts in credit spreads. In subsequent years, Citadel became a major liquidity provider in the CDS market, helping to establish its role as one of the world's largest hedge funds with strong credit-trading expertise. The firm's use of CDSs spans hedging, arbitrage, and directional positioning, making it one of the most consistent institutional participants in this space.

BlueMountain Capital Management: This asset management firm rose to prominence during and after the GFC through its involvement in the CDS market. BlueMountain actively trades CDSs on corporate and sovereign entities, often taking contrarian positions (i.e., positions that run against prevailing market consensus). The firm's expertise in navigating CDS contracts in routine trading and crisis management distinguished it from its peers.

PIMCO: Best known for its vast bond funds, PIMCO has long employed CDSs to complement its traditional fixed-income strategies. The firm has used corporate and sovereign CDSs to hedge downside risks, to take tactical views on credit sectors, and to enhance liquidity in portfolios that might otherwise be concentrated in cash bonds. PIMCO's fund disclosures regularly highlight CDS positions, demonstrating how deeply embedded these instruments are within the firm's risk management framework. By blending bond holdings with CDS overlays, PIMCO can precisely shape credit exposure, reduce transaction costs, and react quickly to credit market shifts while maintaining the long-term focus of its fixed-income mandates.

Third Point: This hedge fund has frequently used CDSs to implement directional views on credit markets. Known for its opportunistic and activist style, the firm has disclosed positions in CDSs both as hedges and speculative trades, often tied to distressed companies or sectors. For example, Third Point has taken CDS positions on corporate issues, which it viewed as overleveraged, profiting when spreads widened. These trades reflect this hedge fund's broader strategy of combining fundamental analysis with tactical use of derivatives, using CDS as a flexible instrument to express high-conviction views on creditworthiness.

1.2 Roadmap of the Book

To close this chapter, I provide a guided overview of the chapters that follow. This roadmap is not meant to replace the substance of each chapter but to provide a sense of the structure and flow of the book. Derivatives touch a wide array of topics, from foundational principles to the instruments themselves, strategies, and applications across institutions, and finally to valuation frameworks. By briefly summarizing each chapter, I want to highlight how the material builds step by step, starting with the basic motivations for using derivatives, moving into the specific contracts and markets in which they trade, then exploring their applications, and concluding with the methods used to value them.

The summaries that follow serve two purposes. First, they highlight the book's logical progression, ensuring that each chapter is contextually understood. Second, they underscore the central emphasis on applications, showing how derivatives are actually employed by asset managers, corporate treasurers, procurement managers, pension funds, commercial and investment banks, and governments.

1.2.1 *Part 1: Foundations*

In this part, the groundwork is laid for understanding both the rationale behind the use of derivatives and the frameworks used to categorize them. Chapter 2 examines the strategic motivations and decision-making processes that lead organizations to adopt derivatives. It explores how asset managers employ derivatives to enhance portfolio efficiency, manage liquidity, and improve capital deployment, and how corporate treasurers use them to stabilize earnings, hedge exposures, and align risks with business planning. The discussion distinguishes between the motivations driving derivative use, such as risk control, liquidity management, capital efficiency, and return enhancement, and the constraints imposed by regulation, operational capacity, and governance.

Chapter 3 turns to the classification of derivatives, showing how they can be organized by function, trading venue, structure, and underlying exposure. The analysis demonstrates that the same instrument can serve different purposes depending on the context: An option may represent insurance for one participant and speculation for another. Real-world examples involving pension funds, corporations, and infrastructure projects illustrate both the versatility of derivatives and the trade-offs that practitioners face when balancing cost, customization, and risk.

Taken together, Part 1 establishes both the strategic motivations for using derivatives and the conceptual frameworks for understanding them, setting the stage for the detailed exploration of specific contracts and markets in Part 2.

1.2.2 *Part 2: Derivative instruments and market structures*

This part of the book moves from the foundations into the instruments themselves, showing how different types of derivatives are structured, traded, and applied. Chapter 4 introduces linear contracts (forwards, futures, and swaps) whose payoffs move in direct proportion to the underlying market variable. These contracts are portrayed as tools for risk-sharing.

Chapter 5 contrasts these with nonlinear, insurance-type contracts, where one party pays a premium to transfer specific risks. Their asymmetric payoff structures explain options, caps, floors, and CDSs, emphasizing the logic of paying for downside protection and the trade-offs between cost and coverage.

Chapters 6 and 7 focus on the market structures in which derivatives trade. Chapter 6 examines exchange-traded derivatives, emphasizing standardization, liquidity, transparency, and the role of clearinghouses in mitigating counterparty risk. Chapter 7 turns to the over-the-counter (OTC) markets, where bilateral negotiation provides flexibility but introduces greater complexity and legal, credit, and collateral management challenges.

Chapters 8 and 9 conclude Part 2 by exploring more advanced products. Chapter 8 addresses structured and exotic derivatives, such as structured notes, convertible bonds, and path-dependent options, showing how institutions use them to achieve specialized objectives while accepting greater valuation and liquidity risks. Chapter 9 turns to credit derivatives, examining instruments that isolate and transfer credit risk, from single-name CDSs and indexes to credit-linked notes and TRSs on credit assets.

Part 2 offers a comprehensive map of the instruments, markets, and structures that define the modern derivatives landscape. It illustrates the wide range of available tools and the constant trade-offs among efficiency, customization, and complexity.

1.2.3 *Part 3: Derivative strategies and portfolio applications*

This part shifts the focus from instruments to how asset managers apply them in practice. Chapter 10 examines the operational backbone of derivative strategies, emphasizing margin management, collateral practices, and rolling mechanics across futures, options, and swaps. Chapter 11 develops the conceptual foundations for option strategies by clarifying the role of moneyness, time value, and sensitivity measures in shaping their use.

Chapter 12 explicitly turns to speculation, reviewing directional and non-directional strategies while highlighting how leverage, volatility, and behavioral dynamics influence outcomes. Chapter 13 reframes derivatives as risk control tools, showing how futures, options, and swaps are deployed to hedge exposures, stabilize performance, and manage portfolio volatility. Chapter 14 expands the lens to asset allocation, illustrating how derivatives function as building blocks in strategic and tactical positioning for multi-asset portfolios. Finally, Chapter 15 addresses backtesting, outlining how strategies are evaluated through historical and simulation-based methods, while warning against overfitting and misplaced confidence.

Part 3 emphasizes the move from classification to implementation. The overlap with earlier material is deliberate, as concepts introduced in the foundations and instrument sections are here reinterpreted through the lens of strategic design, execution, and performance evaluation within institutional settings.

1.2.4 *Part 4: Institutional and corporate applications of derivatives*

This part explores how derivatives are embedded in the operations of major financial and corporate institutions. Chapter 16 examines corporate treasury management, showing how companies use derivatives to stabilize earnings, manage currency and interest rate exposures, and hedge input costs. The analysis situates these practices within broader governance frameworks, emphasizing how treasurers weigh financial hedging against operational adjustments.

Chapter 17 turns to commercial banking, where derivatives are integrated into asset-liability management, capital optimization, and regulatory compliance. Here, swaps, caps, and credit derivatives are examined as market instruments and balance sheet tools that influence net interest margins and long-term financial stability.

Chapter 18 focuses on investment banking, highlighting how derivatives are used in client advisory and deal structuring. Equity collars for executives, swaps in underwriting, CDS indices for sovereign risk, and FX overlays in cross-border issuance illustrate how derivatives serve as risk transfer instruments and as building blocks for financial innovation.

Part 4 shows that while the same instruments (swaps, options, and credit derivatives) are encountered throughout the book, their meaning and function shift depending on the institutional setting. What appears in earlier parts as abstract categories or market structures reemerges here as central elements of corporate policy, bank balance sheet management, and investment banking strategy.

1.2.5 *Part 5: Valuation frameworks for derivatives*

Part 5 turns to the analytical backbone of derivatives, the frameworks that allow contracts to be valued consistently across markets. Chapter 19 introduces the core logic of valuing forwards and futures through the principles of no arbitrage and the law of one price. Replication arguments and cash-and-carry strategies are explained, along with the practical issues, such as daily mark-to-market in futures, which create differences between theoretical and observed prices.

Chapter 20 lays out the quantitative foundations of option pricing, explaining stochastic processes, lognormal distributions, and the principle of risk-neutral valuation. These concepts provide the unifying language of modern option theory while underscoring the assumptions and limitations that motivate alternative approaches.

Chapter 21 presents lattice models, particularly the Cox–Ross–Rubinstein binomial option pricing model, as flexible discrete-time frameworks capable of handling features such as American exercise rights, discrete dividends, and path dependence. These models serve as both practical tools and a bridge to more advanced continuous-time methods.

Chapter 22 explains the Black–Scholes–Merton framework, situating it as a landmark achievement in finance. The model's elegance lies in its closed-form solution, linking option values to observable market inputs. Yet, its assumptions (constant volatility, frictionless markets, and no jumps) also highlight the need for extensions, including dividend adjustments, stochastic volatility, and jump-diffusion models.

Chapter 23 concludes the section by turning to swap valuation. It shows how interest rate, currency, equity, and TRS can be decomposed into legs of cash flows and valued by discounting with appropriate curves. The discussion ties back to earlier chapters on swap mechanics but advances the analysis by embedding those contracts in rigorous valuation frameworks.

Part 5 thus combines the book's various strands into a coherent analytical toolkit. It builds from simple replication arguments to the probabilistic foundations of option pricing, moves through discrete- and continuous-time models, and culminates in the valuation of swaps. This progression equips the framework needed to understand how derivatives function in practice and how their prices are determined and compared across markets.

Chapter 2

Adopting Derivatives in Practice: Decision Drivers for Managers and Treasurers

In this chapter, I discuss the decision-making process behind using derivatives in practice. While derivatives are often introduced as technical instruments for hedging, speculation, or arbitrage, their adoption in real-world settings is rooted in deeper strategic, operational, and regulatory considerations. I place this discussion early in the book because understanding why different types of institutions use derivatives provides the essential foundation for the following chapters. Before explaining individual derivative instruments or specific applications, it is crucial to see how derivatives function as deliberate choices shaped by organizational goals, risk management needs, and market constraints.

To frame the discussion, I focus on two domains where derivatives are especially central yet distinctly motivated: asset management and corporate treasury management. These two areas capture the contrast between derivatives as investment strategy tools and financial risk management instruments. For institutional investors such as mutual funds, pension funds, and insurance companies, derivatives are integral to portfolio efficiency, capital deployment, and market access. For corporate treasurers, derivatives serve a different purpose: stabilizing cash flows, protecting operating margins, and aligning exposures with business planning. Together, these perspectives illustrate the breadth of derivative use in practice and establish the baseline decision frameworks underpinning the chapter to follow.

This emphasis also complements the structure of the book. The later chapters examine how derivatives are applied in other domains such as commercial banking and investment banking, where the focus shifts to client intermediation, trading activities, and balance-sheet management. Beginning with asset managers and corporate treasurers, I show how derivatives are first employed by institutions that use them to support their own investment or corporate objectives before turning to intermediaries whose roles extend to servicing clients and facilitating markets.

For institutional investors, the decision to use derivatives reflects long-term portfolio management frameworks. Derivatives allow them to control risk, fine-tune exposures, optimize capital usage, and, in many cases, enhance returns without disrupting strategic allocations. Corporate treasurers, by contrast, approach derivatives with a focus on managing financial risks related to business operations, such as interest rate variability, foreign exchange movements, and commodity price fluctuations. In these settings, derivatives support the firm's broader financial strategy by stabilizing cash flows, safeguarding earnings, and aligning its financial exposures with corporate planning.

Although the objectives differ, both perspectives show that the use of derivatives is not an isolated financial maneuver but a strategic choice shaped by institutional goals, constraints, governance, and regulatory requirements. These distinctions provide the foundation for the remainder of this chapter, where I examine how capital efficiency, regulatory treatment, operational capacity, and risk appetite influence the decision to use derivatives in practice.

2.1 Strategic Drivers of Derivative Use by Asset Managers

The decision to use derivatives, whether in an asset management context or within a corporate treasury function, is rarely made on a purely tactical basis. "Tactical," in this context, refers to short-term, opportunistic decisions that react to market conditions or funding needs. In contrast, the choice to use derivatives typically reflects longer-term strategic objectives. These objectives may include improving portfolio efficiency, controlling risk exposures, optimizing capital usage, meeting regulatory requirements, or enhancing returns in a controlled and cost-effective manner. In many institutions, these decisions are embedded in the organization's investment philosophy or financial risk policy.

While specific applications may differ across organizations, four primary motivations are nearly universal: risk control, capital efficiency, liquidity management, and return enhancement. In the asset management industry, derivatives allow fund managers to take on or hedge exposures without disrupting their underlying asset allocations, making them essential for managing inflows and outflows, rebalancing portfolios, or achieving desired asset-class exposures.

From a capital efficiency standpoint, derivatives can be particularly attractive under current regulatory regimes. Portfolio managers can use derivatives to gain exposure to equities or fixed income with a smaller initial capital outlay than purchasing the physical assets outright. This frees up capital for use elsewhere in the portfolio, facilitating smoother transitions between strategies.

Derivatives are also instrumental in improving liquidity management. Instead of buying or selling securities in bulk, which may incur transaction costs or market impact, portfolio managers can use derivatives to manage exposures or hedge risks efficiently. This is especially important for large institutional portfolios that must remain nimble without disrupting their long-term positioning.

Return enhancement is another crucial strategic motivation. Derivatives can generate incremental yield through volatility harvesting, curve positioning, or cross-market arbitrage strategies. These approaches allow portfolio managers to seek returns from structural features of the derivatives market, such as the volatility risk premium or mispricings across instruments. Importantly, these strategies are often designed to operate with defined downside risk, making them more palatable within risk-constrained institutional mandates.

Derivatives also provide access to otherwise hard-to-reach exposures, such as, volatility strategies, inflation expectations, or commodity curves. This makes derivatives essential for sophisticated active strategies or overlay mandates.

These strategic motivations lay the foundation for understanding how and when derivatives are employed in asset management. However, the decision to implement derivatives is not made in a vacuum. It must account for various practical constraints that vary by investor type, mandate, regulatory environment, and institutional capability. Asset managers must navigate operational limitations, regulatory requirements, and internal policies to determine whether derivatives are a viable and appropriate solution. I examine these in detail in what follows, illustrating how they impact the structure, scope, and scale of derivative usage across institutional portfolios.

2.1.1 *Constraints and limitations*

Incorporating derivatives into portfolio strategies also requires navigating operational complexities that shape how these instruments can be used effectively and responsibly. Defining these constraints allows portfolio managers to assess whether derivatives will enhance portfolios or introduce undue risks. Constraints help determine whether derivatives align with a portfolio's objectives, structure, and client expectations, ensuring they serve as supportive tools rather than potential sources of instability.

The primary constraints in derivatives use include risk tolerance, liquidity needs, operational complexity, regulatory compliance, and ethical considerations. Regulatory compliance introduces additional constraints that can affect which derivatives are selected and how they are implemented. Each of these constraints presents unique challenges, as they often dictate the types of derivatives, transaction frequency, and exposure levels a portfolio can reasonably sustain. For instance, while derivatives can offer tailored risk management solutions, their use must fit within established risk limits to avoid magnifying exposure beyond acceptable levels. Similarly, liquidity needs affect which derivatives are feasible, as portfolios with high liquidity requirements might favor exchange-traded instruments over less liquid over-the-counter (OTC) derivatives. Regulatory considerations can also affect instrument choice, particularly when derivatives introduce reporting, capital, or margin implications.

By addressing these constraints in a structured manner, portfolio managers can build a foundation for derivative use that aligns with regulatory standards and investor values. The following sections detail each constraint, examining how they influence the selection and implementation of derivative strategies in institutional portfolios.

2.1.2 *Risk tolerance*

Risk tolerance is one of the most fundamental constraints in portfolio management. It defines the level of risk a portfolio can endure without compromising its primary objectives or client expectations. This tolerance is typically quantified through various risk measures that differ by asset class and portfolio structure. For instance, in a bond portfolio, risk tolerance can be represented by duration, which gauges the portfolio's sensitivity to changes in interest rates. A low-duration portfolio, indicating limited sensitivity to interest rate fluctuations, reflects a lower tolerance for interest rate risk.

Different portfolio risk measures. such as beta, duration, and tracking error, are directly affected by how derivatives influence portfolio exposures. Risk tolerance is often expressed in equity portfolios through beta, which measures the portfolio's sensitivity to broad market movements. A high-beta portfolio implies a higher risk tolerance, as it tends to fluctuate more in line with the market. In contrast, a low-beta portfolio reflects a preference for stability and lower exposure to market volatility. In multi-asset portfolios, tracking error may represent risk tolerance by measuring the portfolio's deviation from a benchmark. A low tracking error suggests limited risk tolerance, as the portfolio aligns closely with the benchmark. In contrast, a higher tracking error indicates greater flexibility to deviate and take on greater risk.

Derivative strategies must align closely with these defined risk tolerance parameters, avoiding highly leveraged instruments that could amplify exposure beyond acceptable limits. For example, a portfolio with a low-risk tolerance would avoid speculative derivatives, which could add excessive volatility. Instead, it might employ more conservative derivatives to cap potential downside risk and support a stable risk profile.

2.1.3 *Liquidity needs*

Liquidity needs are crucial considerations when selecting derivative instruments and strategies. This is because the ability to access cash or adjust positions quickly can significantly impact portfolio management. Portfolios that require high levels of liquidity, including mutual funds or open-ended investment vehicles with frequent redemption requests, may find derivatives with longer settlement times, such as certain OTC derivatives, less suitable. OTC derivatives, such as customized swaps or forward contracts, typically have extended settlement periods and may require complex documentation and negotiation. This settlement structure can limit flexibility in adjusting or exiting positions, making it challenging for portfolios needing quick cash access or predictable liquidity. For example, an open-ended mutual fund with daily redemption requirements might prefer exchange-traded derivatives, such as options and futures, which are more liquid and can be readily bought or sold to meet investor redemptions. These exchange-traded derivatives benefit from standardized terms, centralized clearing, and shorter settlement times, aligning well with the fund's need for liquidity and operational flexibility.

Other institutional investors, including defined benefit pension plans and insurance companies, also have critical liquidity needs. Defined benefit plans, for instance, must meet ongoing cash flow demands to pay retirees and may be impacted by unexpected changes in cash flow needs, such as a wave of retirements or pension rollovers. Given these liquidity obligations, pension plans may avoid using derivatives with restrictive exit terms or lengthy settlement periods. Insurance companies also operate with strict liquidity requirements, as they must be prepared to pay claims when they arise. Regulatory standards often require insurers to maintain certain liquidity levels; as such, many insurers prioritize highly liquid assets or derivatives that can be readily converted to cash. Insurers are also subject to stress tests that assess their ability to meet policyholder obligations under adverse conditions. Both pension plans and insurance companies may prefer exchange-traded derivatives, such as futures, over OTC derivatives, as these offer the liquidity and predictability needed to effectively manage liabilities.

Liquidity requirements for regulated investment companies, such as mutual funds, are defined by the Securities and Exchange Commission (SEC) in the U.S. Under the SEC's liquidity risk management rule, mutual funds must classify investments, including derivatives, based on how quickly they can be converted to cash without significantly affecting market prices. The SEC mandates that at least 10% of the portfolio be held in highly liquid investments, which can be readily sold or settled within one business day. Additionally, mutual funds must limit their holdings of illiquid investments (including certain OTC derivatives) to no more than 15% of the portfolio's net assets. This rule aims to ensure that mutual funds can meet redemption requests promptly, even during periods of market stress. Consequently, mutual funds will likely favor exchange-traded derivatives that align with these liquidity requirements, as they are easier to liquidate than customized OTC instruments.

For institutional investors, balancing the need for derivative exposure with the ability to meet liquidity demands is essential to ensuring financial stability. By selecting derivatives that match their liquidity profiles—favoring exchange-traded options or futures over less liquid OTC contracts—portfolio managers can better align their strategies with the operational and regulatory constraints unique to their portfolios.

2.1.4 *Operational issues and costs*

Managing a derivatives program within an asset management firm requires substantial operational infrastructure and specialized processes to ensure derivative positions are effectively monitored and controlled. The operations team must coordinate across various functions to manage trade execution, settlement, collateral management, and daily monitoring of exposures. Given the complexity and rapid market movements associated with derivatives, this team is responsible for establishing systems that provide real-time data on portfolio exposures, ensuring derivative positions align with the portfolio's investment guidelines and risk limits.

In most asset management firms, the risk management and compliance departments play a central role in overseeing the use of derivatives. Risk management monitors market, credit, and liquidity risks associated with derivative positions, continuously assessing how these positions impact overall portfolio risk. Compliance ensures the derivatives program adheres to internal policies, client mandates, and regulatory requirements, such as leverage limits and reporting obligations. These departments work closely with portfolio managers to verify that derivatives are used in the investment strategy and within predefined risk tolerance levels. Monitoring risk exposure for derivatives in a standalone format and globally for the portfolio is essential. If a portfolio is in breach, in that it has exceeded certain risk tolerance levels, for example, the source of the breach must be traceable to take corrective action: Does the derivatives overlay or the portfolio holdings need adjustment, or a combination of both? The governance between teams responsible for specific segments is crucial.

Operations teams also handle collateral management for derivatives. Collateral management is a critical aspect of operating a derivatives program, especially OTC transactions, where the absence of a centralized clearinghouse introduces substantial counterparty risk. Collateral acts as a form of security or guarantee between parties to a derivative contract, reducing the risk that one party will default on its obligations. Effective collateral management requires careful monitoring of collateral levels, adjusting them as market conditions change, and ensuring accurate, timely settlement, all of which help maintain financial stability and trust between counterparties.

The need for collateral management arises from the highly dynamic nature of derivative valuations. As market prices fluctuate, the value of derivative contracts can shift significantly, potentially increasing one party's exposure to the other. For instance, if the value of a derivative position moves adversely for one party, that party's counterparty may require additional collateral to cover the heightened exposure. This mark-to-market process ensures collateral levels reflect the latest market values and risk exposures. Adjustments may be made daily or even intraday to maintain adequate collateral, thereby reducing potential losses in case of default.

Collateral management begins with setting initial collateral requirements, or "initial margin," at the inception of the derivative contract. This initial collateral is calculated based on the perceived risk of the transaction, considering factors such as the volatility of the underlying asset and the contract's term. As market values shift, collateral levels are adjusted through variation margin, where additional collateral is posted or released to account for these changes. This step requires operations teams to conduct regular mark-to-market evaluations, ensuring that collateral remains aligned with current real-time exposures.

To support effective collateral management, operations teams must provide regular valuation reports detailing the derivative contract's current value and any adjustments to collateral requirements. Accurate reporting is crucial to avoid discrepancies between counterparties and to prevent disputes. When a derivative contract is closed or the exposure it presents decreases, any collateral held is partially or fully released. Operations teams coordinate these settlements, ensuring the accurate transfer of collateral and proper documentation.

Disputes may arise between counterparties regarding collateral requirements, often due to differences in valuation or interpretation of contract terms. Operations teams are responsible for resolving these issues efficiently, frequently involving legal or compliance departments to ensure resolutions adhere to internal policies and regulatory requirements.

The operations and back-office functions are essential in facilitating the smooth flow of information between portfolio managers, risk management, and counterparties. They handle logistical requirements for collateral transfers, ensuring secure and timely collateral movement between accounts while maintaining comprehensive documentation. This coordination helps to minimize errors, reduce operational risks, and maintain compliance with regulatory standards, which is increasingly critical as regulatory oversight of derivatives grows.

The operational costs of managing derivatives extend far beyond transaction fees, encompassing staffing, technology investments, compliance infrastructure, and collateral management processes. One significant operational cost involves the need for specialized personnel across various functions, including compliance, risk management, and collateral operations. Regulators have raised similar points. For example, as the Bank for International Settlements highlighted, regulatory requirements such as the Dodd–Frank Act and the European Market Infrastructure Regulation have driven firms to expand their compliance and operational teams to manage tasks such as daily margining, collateral management, and real-time reporting of exposures.[1] According to an International Swaps and Derivatives Association (ISDA) report, firms using OTC derivatives commonly hire additional legal and compliance personnel to meet documentation and reporting standards, which are particularly intensive for non-centrally cleared derivatives.[2]

Beyond specialized staff, monitoring derivatives positions requires specialized data processing platforms or complementary modules within the regular platforms in place for traditional assets, which often come with additional data feeds and calculations.

2.1.5 *Regulatory and compliance constraints*

Regulatory requirements can impose strict limitations on derivative use, especially for institutional investors. The objective of these regulations is threefold: to reduce systemic risk, enhance transparency, and ensure that derivatives are employed in ways that align with each institution's risk tolerance and fiduciary responsibilities.

For example, an insurance company might be limited by regulatory caps on derivative exposure to maintain solvency and meet risk-based capital requirements. It may be restricted to using derivatives for hedging purposes only, with strict limits on speculative positions that could introduce excessive risk. Failure to comply with such regulations could lead to

---

[1] Bank for International Settlements. "Regulatory Reform and Collateral Management," BIS Working Papers, 2020. https://www.bis.org/publ/work859.htm.

[2] International Swaps and Derivatives Association. *ISDA Margin Survey*, 2020. https://www.isda.org/a/fgGTE/ISDA-Margin-Survey-Year-End-2020.pdf.

penalties or even legal action, so portfolio managers must carefully select derivatives that meet regulatory standards while achieving the desired investment objectives.

Moreover, some investment mandates or client agreements set clear restrictions on the types of derivatives permitted in a portfolio. For example, a pension fund's investment policy statement (IPS) may explicitly prohibit derivatives involving complex credit structures or exotic options, as these instruments carry heightened risk and may not align with the fund's conservative mandate. In such cases, portfolio managers are typically limited to using straightforward, transparent derivatives, such as index futures or vanilla options, which provide necessary market exposure or hedging benefits while maintaining compliance with the fund's guidelines and risk tolerance. This approach ensures the fund adheres to its regulatory and fiduciary responsibilities while minimizing exposure to potentially volatile or speculative instruments.

2.1.6 *ESG and sustainability constraints in socially responsible investing*

ESG and sustainability constraints increasingly shape derivative strategies within portfolios managed for institutional or socially responsible investors. These guidelines reflect the priorities and values of clients who integrate ESG principles alongside financial returns, aligning their investments with a commitment to social responsibility and sustainable practices. Socially responsible investing (SRI) frameworks often restrict the use of derivatives tied to sectors conflicting with ESG principles, such as fossil fuels or gambling, ensuring investments align with wider sustainability objectives and responsible business practices.

For example, an SRI fund may prohibit derivatives linked to industries inconsistent with its ESG standards, such as fossil fuels or weapons manufacturing. This restriction might limit the use of commodity derivatives like oil futures or sector-specific equity options, helping the fund maintain its ESG integrity while reducing reputational and environmental risks. By excluding these instruments, SRI funds uphold their sustainability commitments and mitigate potential negative social impacts, aligning their investments with investor and stakeholder values.

Another illustration comes from university endowments, which areoften driven by rising demands for transparency in asset management.

Many university endowments with firm ESG commitments may avoid derivatives associated with companies with poor ESG practices, such as those with high carbon emissions. Instead, they may choose derivatives supporting sustainability objectives, such as carbon credit futures, which help offset emissions and contribute to global environmental goals. By selectively choosing derivatives that advance their mission, these endowments align their investment practices with their community's sustainability priorities.

In addition to excluding non-ESG-aligned derivatives, some funds and institutional investors actively incorporate ESG-specific derivatives to support sustainability objectives. ESG-linked derivatives, such as sustainability-linked derivatives, credit default swaps (CDSs) tied to ESG metrics, and emissions trading derivatives, are increasingly common. For instance, a sustainability-linked interest rate swap can adjust payment terms based on whether a company meets predefined ESG targets, such as emissions reduction goals.[3] This structure incentivizes sustainable practices and aligns financial obligations with ESG performance. Siemens Gamesa, for instance, engaged in such a swap, where meeting sustainability targets led to contributions to environmental charities.[4]

ESG-related derivatives also include instruments based on ESG indices tracking high-performing companies in areas such as renewable energy. Funds gain exposure to sectors advancing sustainability by using these index-linked derivatives while hedging against financial risks. Derivatives based on ESG indices allow investors to support what they believe to be responsible companies and sectors, such as renewable energy, using financial mechanisms aligned with their ESG criteria.[5]

Integrating ESG constraints with derivative strategies further allows socially responsible investors to align financial performance with sustainability goals. ESG-specific derivatives provide institutional investors with new avenues to support environmental and social progress while meeting portfolio objectives.

---

[3] International Swaps and Derivatives Association, "Overview of ESG-related Derivatives Products and Transactions." January 2021. https://www.isda.org/2021/01/11/overview-of-esg-related-derivatives-products-and-transactions/.

[4] "Overview of ESG-related Derivatives Products and Transactions."

[5] "ESG Derivatives Today: Regulatory Inconsistencies, Data Issues, But A Clear Opportunity." DerivSource, 2021. https://derivsource.com/2024/06/20/esg-derivatives-today-regulatory-inconsistencies-data-issues-but-a-clear-opportunity-catherine-arias-barrera/.

2.2 Strategic Drivers of Derivative Use by Corporate Treasurers

While asset managers primarily use derivatives to manage portfolio-level risk, enhance returns, or improve tactical asset allocation, corporate treasurers approach derivative use with different objectives and constraints. For treasurers, derivatives are financial instruments that stabilize operating cash flows, ensure budget predictability, and align financial risk exposures with corporate strategy. In contrast to asset managers, who may view derivatives as tools for alpha generation (i.e., return enhancement) or market exposure, corporate treasurers focus on risk control, particularly in managing exposures to interest rates, currencies, and commodities that can directly impact the firm's operating margins and funding costs.

In this section, I examine the strategic rationale behind corporate treasurers' decisions to use derivatives, organized around four key drivers: strategic alignment, financial resilience, governance and accountability, and operational readiness. These drivers help determine whether derivatives are appropriate, how they should be implemented, and how their usage aligns with the broader corporate mission. In doing so, I emphasize that the derivative decision isn't a simple yes-or-no choice. Instead, it's really about weighing the organization's priorities, the level of risk it's willing to take, and the type of systems and resources it has in place.

2.2.1 *Strategic alignment with corporate objectives*

The decision to use derivatives in a corporate treasury setting must begin with a precise alignment to the firm's strategic objectives. Derivatives are not standalone instruments; they are financial tools whose value emerges from supporting broader corporate goals. For many firms, this means stabilizing cash flows, safeguarding earnings predictability, supporting capital budgeting decisions, and enhancing long-term competitiveness. When properly integrated into the corporate planning process, derivatives can enable strategic execution, reducing financial uncertainty and allowing operational plans to be pursued more confidently.

This alignment necessitates a comprehensive understanding of how financial risks intersect with the firm's business model. For example, a company exposed to foreign-denominated revenues or expenses may face substantial foreign exchange (FX) translation risks. Treasury decisions to hedge that exposure must be driven by the company's approach to consolidating financial results, setting pricing policies, and managing investor expectations. The derivative strategy must reflect the desired balance between risk reduction and financial flexibility. Before a company adopts derivatives, it must ensure that the appropriate governance structures are in place. In practice, this means establishing a robust system of checks and oversight, which is one of the key prerequisites for responsible derivative use.

Senior financial leadership, often including the chief financial officer and board-level oversight, must be involved in approving and periodically reviewing the use of derivatives to ensure that the instruments remain consistent with evolving business goals. In some firms, this oversight is codified through a treasury policy that formally articulates which exposures should be hedged, which instruments may be used, and what metrics define success. For example, a strategic goal might be to limit interest rate exposure to a maximum of 25% floating-rate debt, which would justify entering a derivative, such as an interest rate swap. When derivative use is tied directly to corporate goals, the treasury team can ensure its actions support the company's broader strategy rather than working at cross-purposes with it.

2.2.2 *Financial resilience and risk absorption capacity*

Financial resilience refers to a company's ability to withstand adverse shocks and maintain operations without distress. In this context, derivatives can play a vital role in helping a firm absorb volatility in cash flows, financing costs, or revenue streams. When corporate treasurers evaluate whether to deploy derivatives, they must ask whether such instruments enhance the firm's ability to weather market disruptions, unexpected rate movements, or sudden changes in input costs. If used prudently, derivatives transfer unwanted risks to the financial markets, thereby strengthening internal financial predictability.

However, derivatives can also introduce new forms of complexity or exposure, particularly if leverage or exotic structures are used. Financial resilience is not simply about reducing volatility; it is about doing so in a way that preserves capital, liquidity, and credit quality. For example, using FX forwards to hedge foreign currency receivables may reduce revenue volatility but simultaneously introduce counterparty risk with a financial institution. The treasury team must be equipped to assess whether the net effect of derivative use is to enhance or erode resilience. This requires scenario analysis, stress testing, and an understanding of how derivatives interact with other elements of the firm's capital structure.

To answer the question "Will the use of derivatives improve our financial resilience?" treasurers must adopt a holistic lens. They should consider the firm's existing balance sheet capacity, earnings volatility, funding flexibility, and risk appetite. Derivatives are most effective when they absorb shocks that would otherwise threaten the firm's strategic investments, debt covenants, or stakeholder confidence. In this way, derivatives become instruments of corporate resilience, not instruments of speculation. Ensuring that this role is clearly defined in the policy framework helps avoid misuse or misunderstanding of derivatives within the organization.

2.2.3 *Governance, accountability, and stakeholder oversight*

A robust governance framework is one of the most critical prerequisites for effectively using corporate derivatives. This framework encompasses board oversight, clear lines of accountability, and a disciplined approval process. Unlike asset management firms, which often have trading desks, corporate treasuries must demonstrate that derivative decisions are subject to strong internal controls and serve a business purpose. Governance practices help ensure that derivative use is legal, compliant, and aligned with the company's risk culture and ethical standards. Ethical considerations require clear accountability structures, particularly in organizations subject to public scrutiny or mission-aligned mandates.

Accountability begins with the designation of responsible personnel. This typically includes the treasurer, risk manager, and, sometimes, the CFO. They must ensure that decisions regarding derivatives are supported by documentation, scenario analysis, and justification tied to the firm's objectives. For publicly traded firms, there is also the requirement to comply with financial reporting standards, which impose documentation and effectiveness testing criteria for hedge accounting treatment. These standards emphasize the importance of clear governance, as failure to comply may lead to income statement volatility or reputational damage.

Stakeholder oversight extends beyond the treasury department. Board committees, such as audit or risk committees, often review the use of derivatives periodically to confirm consistency with approved policies. External auditors may examine whether hedge relationships are valid, and credit rating agencies (e.g., Moody's Investors Service, Standard & Poor's, and Fitch) may scrutinize derivative positions to evaluate the firm's financial risk. In this environment, transparency is paramount. Treasurers must be able to explain how derivative positions support business objectives and demonstrate that controls are in place to prevent misuse. Effective governance ensures that derivatives are technically sound and institutionally supported.

2.2.4 *Operational readiness and execution capabilities*

A firm must evaluate its operational readiness before engaging in derivative transactions, even when the strategic rationale is clear. Derivative use requires systems, processes, and personnel capable of handling trade execution, valuation, margining, and risk monitoring. Firms risk operational errors, financial misstatements, and regulatory non-compliance without this infrastructure. Therefore, assessing operational capability is necessary for the derivative decision-making process.

Operational readiness encompasses accurately valuing derivatives, reconciling positions, managing collateral, and complying with regulatory reporting requirements. For example, a derivative such as an interest rate swap must be valued on a mark-to-market basis and may require daily variation margin under central clearing rules. FX forwards may require coordination with accounting systems to ensure cash flow hedge documentation is in place. If a firm lacks this capacity, it may need to work with external providers or limit its derivative use to simple instruments until capabilities are strengthened.

Another key consideration is the sophistication of the treasury team. Treasury professionals must understand the mechanics of their instruments, interpret market data, and evaluate hedging effectiveness. Training and staffing have become essential components of readiness. Some firms also invest in treasury management systems or integrate their enterprise resource planning platforms to streamline derivative workflows. Operational readiness is not a static condition; it must evolve with the complexity of the firm's derivative strategies. Firms not operationally prepared to manage derivatives should defer usage or proceed with significant caution.

2.3 Summary

In this chapter, I examine how asset managers and corporate treasurers decide to use derivatives. My goal is to move beyond traditional explanations of hedging, speculation, and arbitrage and instead explore the deeper strategic, operational, and regulatory factors that drive the use of derivatives in real-world settings.

I discuss how asset managers utilize derivatives as strategic tools to enhance portfolio efficiency, mitigate risk, maintain liquidity, and pursue incremental returns. I explain how derivatives offer flexibility to adjust exposures precisely without disrupting long-term allocations and how they can access markets or risk premia that are otherwise difficult to reach. I also explain how risk tolerance, liquidity constraints, operational infrastructure, compliance requirements, and ESG mandates influence the practical application of derivatives within investment portfolios. Throughout the chapter, I provide detailed examples of how these constraints translate into decisions about whether and how derivatives should be used.

I also turn to corporate treasurers, who use derivatives with a very different objective: protecting the business's financial health. Their primary concern is managing risks arising from operating exposure (e.g., foreign currency, interest rate variability, or commodity costs), not outperforming benchmarks. I explain how the decision to use derivatives in corporate treasury depends on strategic alignment with business goals, the company's capacity to absorb financial shocks, a robust governance framework, and adequate operational readiness. I organize this analysis around four key drivers: strategic alignment, financial resilience, governance and accountability, and execution capabilities.

Rather than viewing derivative use as a binary decision, I emphasize that it's a nuanced judgment shaped by institutional priorities, regulatory mandates, financial infrastructure, and risk appetite. The analysis in this chapter reveals that while asset managers and corporate treasurers operate in different contexts, they share a need for a disciplined framework when deciding whether to use derivatives.

By presenting both perspectives in parallel, I show how derivative use is always contextual: What makes sense for a pension fund may not work for a corporate treasury, and vice versa. This distinction sets the stage for the following chapters, where I explore how specific types of derivatives are applied in various asset classes and investment strategies. Understanding the decision framework is the first step before assessing implementation, effectiveness, or performance outcomes.

Chapter 3

Classifying Derivatives: Structures, Functions, and Markets

Derivatives are among the most versatile instruments in modern finance, used across asset classes, markets, and institutional settings. They enable market participants to transfer, reshape, or assume risk in ways traditional securities cannot. A single derivative can serve as a hedge, provide insurance against extreme outcomes, enable speculation with leverage, or offer a customized exposure that aligns precisely with an institution's objectives. Because derivatives can serve multiple purposes, often simultaneously, classifying them is both challenging and essential.

This chapter is the first in the book to present a broad view of derivative instruments, offering a quick glimpse of the many types that appear in financial markets. While Chapter 1 introduced derivatives in general terms and Chapter 2 examined whether to use them, this chapter focuses on how derivatives are grouped in market practice. These high-level classifications by function, trading venue, and structure provide the foundation for the more detailed discussion of contract mechanics, valuation, and applications that will follow in later chapters.

Derivatives are commonly organized along several dimensions:

- *Economic function*: whether a derivative is primarily used for hedging, insurance, speculation, or customization.
- *Trading venues*: whether the contract trades on a centralized exchange or is negotiated bilaterally in over-the-counter (OTC) markets.

- *Contract structure*: whether the payoff is linear, nonlinear, or path-dependent, reflecting how gains and losses evolve with the underlying asset.
- *Underlying exposure*: which market or risk factor the derivative references, including equities, fixed income, commodities, credit, currencies, or multi-asset combinations.

These dimensions interact in practice. For example, a derivative such as a total return swap (TRS) on a corporate loan portfolio might be OTC, linear, and speculative for a hedge fund but hedging-oriented for a bank managing its credit exposure. Similarly, an option may be insurance-like for one party while speculative for another. Understanding derivatives, therefore, requires both the instrument's structure and the context of its use.

In keeping with the book's applied focus, this chapter illustrates how derivatives are employed in real-world scenarios, from pension funds hedging equity market risk to infrastructure developers managing cross-currency and inflation exposures. These examples highlight the diversity of derivative applications while emphasizing the trade-offs between cost, risk, and customization that practitioners face.

This functional and structural overview prepares the ground for subsequent chapters, explaining these instruments' mechanics, valuation, and applications in detail. By the end of this chapter, the principal ways derivatives are classified will be clear, providing a solid foundation for interpreting their role in asset management, risk management, investment banking, commercial banking, and corporate treasury management.

3.1 Classification by Function

The most intuitive and instructive way to classify derivatives is by their economic functions. While many contracts may blur boundaries or simultaneously serve multiple purposes, most derivatives are designed or repurposed primarily to hedge risk, insure against extreme events, speculate on price movements, or customize financial exposure.

3.1.1 *Hedging: Reducing financial exposure*

At their core, derivatives are tools for managing risk. Hedging involves using a derivative to offset the financial exposure of an underlying position. A wheat farmer may use futures contracts to lock in a selling price before harvest; a pension fund may use interest rate swaps (IRSs) to hedge against rising rates that would devalue its portfolio of fixed-income assets. The goal of hedging is not to eliminate all risk but to reduce specific sources of uncertainty that could materially affect cash flows, asset values, or funding needs.

Relatively symmetric payoffs often characterize hedging derivatives commonly used in exchange-traded and OTC markets. A "hedge ratio," or "delta hedge," is central to practice and theory, as it connects derivative pricing to underlying asset sensitivities.

3.1.2 *Insurance: Managing asymmetric and extreme risks*

Some derivatives serve a more protective role by mimicking the structure of insurance contracts. These instruments typically involve an asymmetric payoff: The buyer pays a premium to transfer tail risk (i.e., the low-probability but potentially severe losses in extreme market conditions) to the seller. Credit default swaps (CDSs), catastrophe bonds, and equity put options all fall into this category. In each case, the derivative buyer seeks to limit downside risk, often paying a recurring premium or up-front cost in exchange for a payout that only occurs under adverse conditions.

Insurance-type derivatives are critical for credit risk transfer, tail-risk hedging, and regulatory capital management. They raise unique questions around pricing, default correlation, adverse selection, and moral hazard, which have been historically explored in insurance and financial economics.

3.1.3 *Speculation: Gaining exposure with leverage*

Derivatives also provide a low-cost, high-leverage way to speculate on price movements without transacting in the underlying asset. A directional trader (i.e., a trader who takes positions based on the expectation that an asset's price will rise or fall) might buy call options to profit from a stock rally or enter into a TRS to gain equity exposure without owning shares. In speculative use, the derivative itself represents the market bet rather than a hedge or an insurance policy.

What distinguishes speculation is the intent: The trader accepts risk in pursuit of gain, often without offsetting that exposure. Leverage amplifies profits and losses, and margin and collateral requirements are central to market stability. For this reason, regulators scrutinize speculative derivatives more closely than hedging or insurance activity.

3.1.4 *Customization: Engineering bespoke risk-return profiles*

A fourth and increasingly important function of derivatives is customization (i.e., the engineering of contracts to fit client needs, regulatory constraints, or portfolio mandates). These bespoke derivatives may combine features of hedging, insurance, and speculation. They often appear in OTC markets and include non-standard terms: exotic options, structured notes, index-linked swaps, and multi-factor payoffs.

Customized (bespoke) derivatives are particularly common in institutional settings where exposure cannot be obtained through standard exchange-traded derivatives. A pension fund may enter a longevity swap to hedge the risk that retirees live longer than expected. An insurance company might use a catastrophe-linked derivative to transfer extreme weather risk. A multinational corporation may arrange a cross-currency IRS tailored to its specific debt profile. Similarly, a sovereign wealth fund may use structured equity swaps to replicate benchmark exposure under tax constraints.

This functional classification (i.e., hedging, insurance, speculation, and customization) will recur throughout the book. It serves as an interpretive guide: The same instrument may appear in multiple contexts, but its purpose and structure may differ. Understanding the *why* behind a derivative's use is as important as understanding the *what* of its terms.

3.2 Classification by Trading Venue: Exchange-Traded vs. OTC Markets

Another foundational way to classify derivatives is by the market structure in which they trade: centralized exchanges or decentralized OTC markets. This distinction shapes nearly every aspect of a derivative's life cycle, including its standardization, transparency, counterparty risk, and regulatory oversight.

3.2.1 *Exchange-traded derivatives: Standardized and transparent*

Exchange-traded derivatives (ETDs) are listed on formal markets such as the CME, Eurex, or ICE. These instruments—futures, listed options, and volatility contracts—are standardized regarding contract size, expiration dates, and tick size. Because they trade through centralized platforms with continuous price discovery, they benefit from liquidity, price transparency, and uniform clearing mechanisms.

A critical feature of ETDs is central counterparty (CCP) clearing. In OTC markets, two counterparties trade bilaterally, meaning each is exposed to the risk that the other might fail to perform. ETDs eliminate this direct bilateral exposure because the clearinghouse interposes itself as the legal counterparty to both sides of every trade, guaranteeing performance and standardizing the handling of default risk. This structure reduces counterparty credit risk and allows for multilateral netting, so offsetting positions across participants reduces overall exposures. Most contracts are marked to market daily, and margining is also simplified because requirements are set and monitored centrally.

The standardized nature of ETDs makes them ideal for short-term hedging, tactical speculation, and benchmark exposure. However, they are less valuable when exposures are particular or the underlying asset is illiquid or idiosyncratic.

3.2.2 *Over-the-counter derivatives: Flexible and customized*

OTC derivatives, by contrast, are privately negotiated contracts between counterparties that dealers often mediate. These include IRSs, currency forwards, CDSs, equity swaps, TRSs, and more esoteric structures such as commodity-linked options and basket derivatives.

OTC markets allow for customization in notional size, maturity, reference asset, payment frequency, and embedded features. This flexibility enables institutions to tailor exposures to particular risks, such as credit exposure on a single borrower, correlation between commodities, or synthetic replication of complex benchmarks. However, this customization comes with trade-offs. Because OTC derivatives are not traded on a centralized exchange, they typically involve counterparty credit risk, require bilateral collateral agreements (e.g., via Credit Support Annexes), and are less liquid. Since the 2007–2008 Global Financial Crisis (GFC), regulators have pushed for greater central clearing of standardized OTC contracts and mandated reporting to trade repositories.

3.2.3 *Hybrid evolution and regulatory convergence*

The boundary between ETD and OTC markets is no longer absolute. Some once-OTC products, such as IRSs, are now centrally cleared and increasingly standardized. Meanwhile, electronic platforms have emerged for specific OTC contracts, blurring the distinction further.

Today, the choice between ETD and OTC contracts is not simply about trading venue; it also reflects institutional preferences, regulatory constraints, and portfolio objectives. Understanding how market structure affects pricing, liquidity, and operational complexity is critical to selecting the right instrument for a given application.

3.3 Classification by Contract Structure: Linear, Nonlinear, and Path-Dependent Instruments

Beyond function and trading venue, derivatives can also be grouped by their payoff structure, that is, the mathematical and contractual form of determining gains and losses. This classification helps distinguish between basic building blocks and more complex instruments that embed optionality, timing risk, or contingent features.

3.3.1 *Linear derivatives: Direct exposure to price movements*

Linear derivatives yield payoffs that change proportionally with the underlying asset's value. The most common examples are futures, forwards, and plain-vanilla swaps (such as fixed-for-floating interest rate or currency swaps). If the underlying asset rises by \$1, the derivative's value increases by a fixed amount, often determined by the notional size and hedge ratio.

These contracts are widely used for hedging and speculation, particularly when the goal is to gain or offset delta exposure, which is the directional sensitivity to price changes. Linear derivatives are typically easier to value, margin, and replicate, making them the backbone of many hedging programs and macro trading strategies.

3.3.2 *Nonlinear derivatives: Embedded optionality and asymmetry*

Nonlinear derivatives, most notably options, have payoffs that depend on the value of the underlying but in a non-proportional manner. For example, a call option only pays off when the underlying exceeds the strike price. This introduces convexity, asymmetry, and discontinuity in payoffs, valuable features for hedging extreme events or expressing views on volatility.

Nonlinear structures can be found in exchange-traded options, structured products, exotic derivatives, and hybrid instruments. Many insurance-type derivatives, such as put options, fall into this category because they offer protection against downside risk in return for an upfront premium or yield concession.

Pricing and managing nonlinear derivatives require more sophisticated models and hedging techniques—often relying on delta, gamma, and other so-called "Greeks" that measure sensitivity to various factors.

3.3.3 *Path-dependent derivatives: Outcomes shaped by history*

Some derivatives are defined not only by the terminal value of the underlying but also by how the underlying behaves along the way. These are known as path-dependent instruments. Examples include:

- *Asian options*, where payoffs depend on the average price over time;
- *barrier options*, where knock-in or knock-out triggers are activated during the contract life;
- *lookback options*, which reference the maximum or minimum price over a period.

Path dependence introduces additional complexity in valuation and hedging, often requiring lattice models, Monte Carlo simulations, or dynamic programming approaches. While such features add to modeling difficulty, they also allow for more precise tailoring of exposures, particularly in structured product design and liability-driven investing.

This structural classification helps clarify why two derivatives on the same asset might behave very differently under stress or why one can be easily hedged with linear instruments while another requires dynamic risk management. As the book progresses, many chapters will refer to these distinctions to explain contract behavior, pricing techniques, and market uses.

The following section will provide a concise set of examples that map real-world derivatives into the classifications introduced so far—by function, market venue, and structure—to solidify the multidimensional nature of derivative classification.

3.4 Illustrative Examples: Mapping Derivatives Across Classifications

In this section, I walk through real-world examples showing how different derivatives fit into the classifications I introduced earlier in this chapter (i.e., function, trading venue, and structure). I highlight how these instruments are actually used by pension funds, insurers, hedge funds, and corporations, as well as the trade-offs each strategy involves. The contracts here are only briefly introduced; their mechanics, valuation, and advanced applications are covered in later chapters. These illustrations connect the framework to real market decisions, precisely what this section is designed to do.

3.4.1 *Index futures for strategic hedging and tactical speculation*

Consider a pension fund that holds a diversified portfolio of U.S. equities. Ahead of a potential market downturn (e.g., after an unexpectedly high inflation report), the fund manager may temporarily reduce its equity exposure. Rather than selling securities that could trigger capital gains, violate internal limits, or disrupt portfolio balance, the fund manager sells E-mini S&P 500 futures (derivatives described in Chapter 6) on the CME. These contracts are standardized, exchange-traded, and marked to market daily through a CCP. Using the futures, the fund can effectively "go flat," meaning it offsets its market exposure and neutralizes directional risk for a period without liquidating its physical holdings.

In a different context, a hedge fund manager might buy those same futures after interpreting the inflation report as overblown and expecting a quick rebound. Here, the contract serves a speculative function. The hedge fund manager uses the futures to gain leveraged beta (market) exposure to a broad equity index without tying up the entire amount of capital required to buy the stocks directly since only a margin deposit is needed. The same linear, standardized contract performs a hedging function for one party but a speculative function for another. This dual role is central to the success of ETDs: They attract both hedgers and liquidity-providing speculators.

3.4.2 *Credit default swaps as tail-risk insurance*

A portfolio manager overseeing a corporate bond fund becomes increasingly concerned about the financial health of a high-yield issuer in the portfolio. Rather than liquidate the position, which might trigger poor execution or violate yield mandates, the portfolio manager enters a CDS contract, described in Chapter 9. In this agreement, the portfolio manager pays a fixed spread to a counterparty in exchange for protection: If the issuer defaults, the counterparty pays out the face value of the bond. The CDS is an OTC derivative, usually governed by ISDA documentation, and is settled either physically (by delivering the bond) or in cash (using an auction-based recovery rate).

CDS contracts are nonlinear and insurance-like in their payoff: The protection buyer pays a premium regularly but receives a large payoff under specific adverse conditions. As with any insurance product, pricing depends on default probability, loss given default, and market-implied spreads. Importantly, CDSs can be used by investors who do not hold the bond, turning it into a vehicle for speculative credit bets, a point of controversy during the GFC.

3.4.3 *Interest rate swaps for balance sheet risk-sharing*

Suppose a regulated utility has issued $500 million in 10-year fixed-rate bonds outstanding but receives floating revenues from electricity sales indexed to wholesale market prices. Over time, the utility becomes concerned about rising rates: If short-term interest rates increase, its revenues will rise, but its debt service costs will remain fixed. To better align its cash flow, the firm enters an IRS in which it pays floating and receives fixed.

This plain-vanilla IRS is an OTC derivative but increasingly subject to central clearing, especially in the U.S. and EU. The contract has a linear payoff: Cash flows are exchanged periodically based on a notional amount, but no principal changes hands. The structure allows the utility to synthetically convert its fixed-rate debt into floating-rate exposure, reducing the mismatch between liabilities and revenues.

IRS contracts represent a classic risk-sharing case between counterparties with opposing exposures. One may want to fix cash outflows; the other may want to float them.

3.4.4 *Barrier options in corporate foreign exchange risk management*

Imagine a U.S.-based manufacturing firm with a major export contract in Japan. The firm expects to receive ¥1 billion in revenue in six months and worries that a yen depreciation will reduce its dollar-equivalent revenue and lower the firm's earnings. Suppose the current USD/JPY spot exchange rate is 140, meaning $1 equals ¥140. If the yen weakens, the rate rises (for example, $1 = ¥145), and the firm receives fewer dollars for the same yen. Standard practice might involve buying a yen put (USD call) to protect against this risk, but the firm's CFO faces a tight hedging budget. To lower the upfront premium, the firm chooses a knock-in barrier option, which becomes active only if the exchange rate reaches a specified level during the option's life. Suppose that the barrier is set at 145, meaning the option provides protection only if the yen first weakens to that level (USD/JPY = 145) before expiration.

Barrier options are path-dependent: Their value depends on where the exchange rate ends up and whether it breaches a pre-agreed level along the way. These contracts are OTC, nonlinear, and highly customized. They allow firms to hedge only against "worst-case" scenarios without paying the full premium of a standard (vanilla) option. However, the conditional nature of the payout introduces risk: If the barrier is never reached, the option never activates, leaving the firm fully exposed (i.e., the firm remains unhedged and bears the entire impact of any adverse currency movement).

This structure highlights the tension between cost and coverage. Firms operating across borders must constantly balance accounting treatment, hedge effectiveness, and budget constraints, all of which can be navigated through barrier features embedded in OTC FX derivatives.

3.4.5 *Catastrophe-linked derivatives in reinsurance and risk transfer*

A global reinsurer is exposed to severe hurricane risk in the southeastern U.S. The firm issues a catastrophe bond (or "cat bond") to transfer a portion of that risk to capital markets. A catastrophe bond is a type of insurance-linked security that allows investors to earn a high yield in exchange for agreeing to absorb losses if a specified catastrophic event occurs. In this example, the bond has a parametric trigger, meaning the payout depends on a measurable event, such as wind speed or storm category, rather than the insurer's actual losses. Investors purchase the bond and receive attractive interest payments if no qualifying disaster occurs. However, suppose a Category 4 or stronger hurricane strikes the defined region with wind speeds above the preset threshold. In that case, the bond's principal is partially or fully forgiven and used to cover the reinsurer's claims. If no trigger event occurs during the bond's term, investors receive their principal back at maturity, earning a high-yield return for taking on event risk.

Although issued as a bond, the embedded trigger makes this a derivative in economic terms—the payoff is contingent on a defined event, not default or issuer solvency. These instruments are nonlinear, insurance-like in function, and typically placed through capital market intermediaries rather than exchanges. They attract catastrophe-focused hedge funds, insurers, and pensions seeking uncorrelated return streams.

Catastrophe derivatives represent one of the clearest examples of financial engineering for societal risk, where market tools are used to smooth fiscal shocks and improve disaster resilience. Pricing, however, is far more challenging than the pricing models described in Part 5, relying on probabilistic models, historical storm tracks, and exposure data that remain far from standardized.

3.4.6 *Total return swaps for synthetic exposure and balance sheet efficiency*

A hedge fund manager wants exposure to a portfolio of high-yield loans (i.e., loans issued to below-investment-grade borrowers who pay higher interest rates to compensate for their elevated credit and default risk). Holding these loans directly can be capital-intensive and operationally complex because they are often illiquid, involve extensive documentation, and require active servicing. Instead of purchasing the loans, the hedge fund negotiates a TRS with a bank that owns the portfolio. Under the TRS, the hedge fund receives the full economic return of the loans: All interest payments and any capital appreciation if the market value of the loans rises. In exchange, the hedge fund pays the bank a floating rate, such as Secured Overnight Financing Rate (SOFR), plus a negotiated spread. This structure allows the hedge fund manager to gain leveraged credit exposure without placing the loans on its balance sheet, while the bank transfers the market and credit risk of the loans to the fund without selling them outright.

The TRS is an OTC linear derivative that acts as a synthetic asset holding. The fund achieves full economic exposure without booking the assets, and the bank offloads return risk while retaining the loans on its balance sheet. For regulatory and tax reasons, this can be more efficient for both parties than a sale.

TRSs are widely used in structured credit, private markets, and equity finance. They illustrate how customized derivatives blur the line between ownership and exposure and how derivatives can be used not only for trading or hedging but for structuring capital and economic claims across institutional boundaries.

3.4.7 *Overperformance options in retail structured products*

A private bank is designing a structured note for high-net-worth clients who want selective exposure to the S&P 500 but prefer to benefit only if the index meaningfully outperforms the Nasdaq-100. To achieve this, the bank embeds an outperformance option, also sometimes referred to as a relative performance or spread option, into the note. This derivative pays off if the S&P 500 exceeds the Nasdaq-100's performance by more than 10 percentage points over a six-month observation period. For example, if the Nasdaq gains 5% but the S&P 500 gains 18%, the 13% outperformance exceeds the 10% threshold. The option then pays the corresponding premium return to the investor. If the threshold is unmet, the investor only receives the principal back at maturity, earning no additional return.

Overperformance options are nonlinear and relative, meaning their value depends on directional movement and the spread between two benchmarks. These options are always traded OTC and are typically offered via structured notes, a type of debt security issued by a bank or broker-dealer that embeds a derivative payoff into the note's return profile. The note exposes investors to the derivative's performance, often including features such as principal protection or enhanced upside, without requiring them to trade derivatives directly. Structured notes are especially popular in retail and private wealth channels that market "smart exposure" strategies with some form of capital protection.

These contracts serve a speculative and customized function, offering asymmetric payouts tied to investor narratives (e.g., "tech is overbought; value will rebound"). Pricing is complex and depends on correlation assumptions between indices, implied volatilities, and path dependency. Institutional desks rarely use these derivatives despite their conceptual simplicity because they embed structural complexity into a non-fungible instrument.

3.4.8 *Commodity forwards in agricultural price risk management*

A grain cooperative in Iowa agrees to deliver 250,000 bushels of corn to a cereal manufacturer in five months. To stabilize income for its farmer members, the cooperative enters a forward contract with the buyer to lock in today's price. Unlike a futures contract, this agreement is bilateral, not standardized, and negotiated to reflect actual delivery schedules, crop grades, and local transportation costs.

Commodity forwards are linear, OTC derivatives, among the oldest derivative forms still in use. Their primary purpose is hedging, allowing producers and consumers to lock in future prices and manage the risk of adverse price movements tied to real-world production and processing schedules. Unlike exchange-traded futures, forwards are privately negotiated, not standardized, and generally are not mark-to-market daily. Because settlement occurs at maturity and collateral practices vary, they can carry significant counterparty credit risk.

Despite their simplicity, these contracts underpin billions in global agricultural trade and serve as the foundation for more complex hedging structures involving options and basis contracts. Their continued relevance reflects the importance of customization and bilateral trust in commodity supply chains.

3.4.9 *Inflation and cross-currency swaps in infrastructure project finance*

Consider a European infrastructure developer awarded a 30-year concession to build and operate a toll road in Latin America. The project is financed with euro-denominated equity and local-currency revenue bonds. However, the road will collect tolls in local currency, while construction costs and debt service are partly in euros. Moreover, some cash flows are linked to the country's inflation index, which is volatile and politically sensitive.

To manage this complex mix of exposures, the developer enters two long-dated, customized derivatives: a cross-currency basis swap and an inflation-linked IRS. In the first contract, the developer pays local-currency interest and receives euros, synthetically matching its future toll revenue to euro-denominated debt obligations. In the second contract, the developer receives a floating rate tied to the local inflation index and pays a fixed nominal rate, effectively transforming inflation-linked cash inflows into predictable debt service streams.

These contracts are OTC, negotiated with large international banks or multilateral development institutions, and often extend beyond 20 years. Structurally, they are a mix of linear and path-dependent instruments. Their function is not speculation but risk-sharing and cash flow engineering, essential for making the project bankable under multiple regulatory and market conditions.

This example underscores how infrastructure derivatives are not commoditized but customized to reflect local inflation indices, sovereign credit risk, and bilateral exposure limits. It also illustrates how derivatives can enable mobilizing capital for development projects where conventional funding would be infeasible without risk transformation.

3.4.10 *Revenue hedges and proxy hedges in renewable energy finance*

A U.S.-based independent power producer (IPP) is developing a 100-megawatt (MW) solar facility in Texas. An independent power producer is a private company that builds and operates power plants to sell electricity into wholesale markets rather than to a utility that owns the generator. The facility will deliver its electricity to the Electric Reliability Council of Texas (ERCOT) wholesale market. ERCOT manages most of Texas's electricity grid and its competitive power market. Prices in ERCOT are highly volatile because they fluctuate every five minutes based on real-time supply and demand and are not supported by long-term, fixed-price contracts by default. Without a guaranteed buyer, the project faces uncertain cash flows, which makes it difficult to attract lenders and equity investors who require predictable revenues for financing.

Traditionally, renewable developers secure stability through a physical power purchase agreement (PPA), a contract where a utility or large corporate buyer agrees to purchase the electricity at a fixed price for 10–20 years. A physical PPA is unavailable in this case, so the developer enters a virtual PPA (also called a financial PPA). A virtual PPA does not involve physically delivering power to the buyer. Instead, it is structured as a fixed-for-floating electricity swap tied to a regional market price (called the hub price). In this arrangement, the developer continues to sell its electricity to ERCOT at floating market prices while simultaneously receiving a fixed price from the financial counterparty and paying the floating price to them. If market prices fall below the fixed price, the counterparty pays the developer the difference, thereby stabilizing revenues. If market prices rise above the fixed price, the developer pays the counterparty the difference, giving up some upside in exchange for revenue certainty.

This structure allows the IPP to create a predictable cash flow profile, which is crucial for securing project financing, even though the electricity is still sold in the volatile spot market. Virtual PPAs are widely used in renewable energy because they hedge against price risk while meeting lender requirements for revenue stability.

This agreement, often called a revenue hedge or contract for differences (CfD), allows the IPP to receive a fixed price per megawatt-hour while paying the spot market price for actual electricity sold. If spot prices are above the fixed price, the IPP pays the difference; if below, it receives the shortfall. Importantly, there is no physical delivery under the contract; it is a pure financial derivative that synthetically replicates the economics of a PPA.

These contracts are customized, OTC, and linear in structure, but their valuation depends on complex modeling of renewable output, locational marginal prices, and congestion risk. They serve a hedging function, enabling renewable energy developers to transform stochastic cash flows into fixed financeable revenue streams.

In many jurisdictions, these derivatives are underpinned by long-term risk appetites from utilities, corporates (e.g., Amazon, Google), or commodity trading houses that seek green power exposure. Their emergence reflects how derivatives are now integral to decarbonization efforts, not just capital markets, linking financial innovation to climate finance.

3.4.11 *Credit-linked notes in structured credit and yield enhancement*

A European private bank serves a set of yield-hungry private clients who are frustrated by persistently low government bond yields. To enhance returns without directly allocating to lower-rated credit, the bank's structured products desk creates a credit-linked note (CLN) tied to a basket of investment-grade corporate issuers.

The CLN is legally a debt instrument issued by the bank, but economically it embeds a CDS. The investor in the note receives an above-market coupon. However, if any of the referenced entities default during the life of the note, the investor's principal is reduced by a pre-defined loss amount. The payoff is nonlinear and contingent, and the risk exposure is synthetic. Investors are not lending directly to the referenced companies.

This instrument is an example of derivatives embedded in structured securities, often classified as OTC, nonlinear, and insurance-like in function. The issuing bank offloads credit risk to investors and may retain or hedge its exposure through back-to-back CDS trades with dealers. CLNs are also used by banks to manage regulatory capital by moving credit exposure off-balance sheet without selling assets outright.

From the investor's point of view, the CLN is a yield-enhancing product with asymmetric risk. From the issuer's point of view, it is a credit risk transfer tool. These dual functions reflect the derivative's role as a bridge between structured credit engineering and portfolio optimization, where derivative logic is embedded in a security to appeal to a particular client's need or regulatory outcome.

CLNs also illustrate how credit derivatives were widely repackaged and scaled in the years leading up to the 2007–2008 GFC. During that period, banks and structured credit desks bundled credit exposures into notes that could be sold to investors, often with limited transparency and significant leverage. Today, CLNs are structured under much stricter collateral, disclosure, and regulatory capital frameworks, reflecting lessons from the GFC and the need to better align risk with investor understanding.

3.5 Summary

In this chapter, I explain how derivatives can be classified and why those classifications matter. I examine what derivatives do in practice: how they can hedge risk, provide insurance against extreme events, enable speculation with leverage, or deliver customized exposures when off-the-shelf solutions don't work. I show how the same contract can serve different purposes depending on who uses it and why.

I then explain the difference between exchange-traded and OTC markets, highlighting how central clearing, standardization, and margining shape exchange-traded derivatives. At the same time, OTC markets allow for flexibility and customization but bring more counterparty risk. From there, I break down derivatives by their structure: linear instruments such as forwards and swaps, nonlinear instruments such as options, and path-dependent contracts such as barrier or lookback options.

Throughout the chapter, I include real-world examples to keep the discussion practical. I show how pension funds, insurers, hedge funds, and corporations actually use these tools, whether it's selling E-mini S&P 500 futures to temporarily neutralize market exposure, hedging with credit default swaps, using virtual PPAs in renewable energy, or transferring hurricane risk through catastrophe bonds. These examples are meant to connect the classifications to real market decisions.

In this chapter, I explain how derivatives are grouped, why those groupings matter, and how they appear in real financial strategies. This sets the stage for the following chapters, where I will explain the mechanics, valuation, and more specialized applications of the instruments introduced here.

Part 2

Derivative Instruments and Market Structures

Chapter 4

Risk-Sharing with Linear Derivatives: Forwards, Futures, and Plain Vanilla Swaps

In this chapter, I focus on a category of derivatives whose primary purpose is to redistribute risk between two counterparties through symmetric arrangements. These instruments (futures, forwards, and swaps) are often called risk-sharing derivatives because they are designed to allocate exposure to uncertainty in underlying market variables, such as interest rates, exchange rates, commodity prices, or equity indexes. Rather than transferring risk entirely to one party, these contracts expose both sides to potential market outcomes. Gains and losses are shared linearly, depending on how the underlying variable evolves.

This symmetric risk-sharing contrasts with the derivatives discussed in the following chapter, which function more like insurance. In those cases, one party pays a premium to transfer a specific risk and receives a payout only under defined adverse conditions. That difference in payoff structure (symmetric versus asymmetric) is central to distinguishing these two broad classes of derivatives.

While how these contracts allocate gains and losses is their defining characteristic, they also vary in terms of their degree of standardization and the venues on which they are traded. The institutional mechanics (clearing, collateralization, and documentation) are discussed in depth in Chapters 6 and 7. The emphasis in this chapter remains on the economic role of risk-sharing derivatives rather than the operational infrastructure. Some, like futures, are highly standardized and traded on organized exchanges. Others, like many swaps, are customized and negotiated directly between institutions in the over-the-counter (OTC) market. A typical structure unites all these contracts: Both parties agree to exchange cash flows based on changes in a referenced market variable.

In this chapter, I do not dwell on every contractual detail. Instead, I emphasize the economic purpose and structure of these agreements. While important, topics such as margin requirements, counterparty risk, and clearing arrangements are covered in later chapters. My goal is to explain how symmetric derivatives work, how they differ from insurance-like agreements, and why they remain central to modern risk management and capital allocation. Concrete examples throughout the chapter demonstrate how these instruments are used in real-world settings to manage financial exposures across commodities, interest rates, equities, and currencies.

4.1 Linear Versus Nonlinear Risk Transfer

A central idea for understanding how different types of derivatives function lies in the payoff concept. In the context of derivatives, a payoff refers to the amount of money one party receives or must pay at the end of the contract, depending on how the value of some underlying variable (such as a price, interest rate, or index level) has changed over time. The payoff represents the financial outcome of the contract. Some derivatives produce payoffs that move in lockstep with the underlying variable, while others produce payoffs only under certain conditions. This distinction leads us to the difference between *linear* and *nonlinear* derivatives.

A *linear payoff* is one in which the gain or loss changes directly with the change in the underlying variable. For every unit increase (or decrease) in the underlying, the amount received or paid under the derivative changes by a constant amount. Linear derivatives expose both parties to the full range of market outcomes, meaning either side can gain or lose depending on how the underlying behaves. These contracts do not contain any asymmetry in the rights or obligations of the parties; both participants assume the risk of loss in exchange for the potential gain.

To better understand this, consider a simple example involving two companies: A crude oil producer and an industrial manufacturer that uses oil as an input. Suppose both parties want to reduce the uncertainty they face from oil price fluctuations over the next six months. To do so, they agree today that the producer will sell, and the manufacturer will buy

10,000 barrels of oil in six months at a fixed price of $70 per barrel. This agreement is an example of a forward-style arrangement that locks in the price today for a future transaction. Even without prior knowledge of forward contracts, it provides a helpful conceptual foundation for understanding linear derivatives. The structure and mechanics of forward contracts will be explored more fully in a later section of this chapter.

Now, suppose that six months from now, the market price of oil (i.e., the price at which oil can be bought or sold immediately, known as the *spot price*) is $75 per barrel. As agreed, the manufacturer still pays $70, even though it could buy oil in the open market for $75. The manufacturer has gained $5 per barrel relative to the spot price, resulting in total savings of $50,000. The producer, in turn, delivers oil at $70 when it could have sold it for $75, resulting in a loss of the same amount. If the spot price had fallen to $65 per barrel, the outcome would be reversed: The manufacturer would overpay relative to the market, losing $50,000, while the producer would benefit.

The key feature of this arrangement is that the financial gain of one party is exactly equal to the loss of the other, and both are determined in direct proportion to the change in the market price of oil. There is no upfront payment for the agreement, and no one is shielded from unfavorable outcomes. Each side fully shares in the risk of the price moving against it. This linear, risk-sharing arrangement reallocates price risk between the parties without eliminating it.

In contrast, some derivatives are structured to protect one party from losses beyond a certain point, much like an insurance policy. These are *nonlinear derivatives*, and they will be the focus of the next chapter. In a typical example, one party pays a fee, or premium, in exchange for the right to receive a payment if the market moves unfavorably. The other party receives the premium and agrees to compensate the first party only if certain conditions are met. Unlike linear contracts, these arrangements do not equally expose both parties: One party's losses are limited by the contract design, while the other assumes potentially greater risks.

For instance, a manufacturer concerned about rising oil prices might buy an option that gives it the right, but not the obligation, to purchase oil in six months at $70 per barrel. If the market price rises to $75, the manufacturer can exercise the option and buy at $70, gaining $5 per barrel. If the price falls below $70, the manufacturer can let the option expire and buy oil at the cheaper spot price. By contrast, the party that sold the option must honor the agreed price if the option is exercised but receives no benefit if the price moves in the buyer's favor. This type of arrangement creates an *asymmetric payoff*, or nonlinear risk transfer.

These structural differences have significant implications for the practical application of derivatives. Linear derivatives such as forwards, futures, and swaps are typically employed to hedge exposures by rebalancing those exposures that bear the underlying market risk. Meanwhile, nonlinear derivatives such as options allow market participants to insure against specific adverse outcomes. The remainder of this chapter describes the first category: risk-sharing derivatives with linear payoffs. Understanding this structure is essential before turning to the more complex design and payout structures of insurance-like contracts, which are explored in the following chapter.

4.2 Overview of Risk-Sharing Derivatives

Risk-sharing derivatives comprise a family of contracts in which both parties agree to exchange cash flows based on the evolution of an underlying market variable over time. These contracts enable each party to assume certain market risks while transferring others, allowing them to adjust their financial exposures to better align with their economic needs or preferences. The most widely used instruments in this category are forward contracts, futures contracts, and swaps. While these instruments differ in how they are traded, settled, and regulated, as explained in later chapters, they are unified by a key characteristic: Their payoffs are linear, and both sides are exposed to gains and losses depending on how the underlying market moves.

A *forward contract* is an agreement between two parties to buy or sell an asset at a specified price on a future date. Forwards are typically customized, negotiated directly between institutions, and settled at maturity without intermediate payments. Because they are privately negotiated, forwards expose both parties to credit risk, an issue examined in greater depth later in the book.

A *futures contract* is similar in economic purpose to a forward contract. Still, it is traded on an organized exchange and standardized in terms of contract size, expiration dates, and other key terms. Futures differ from forwards in their trading venue and operational structure: They are exchange-traded, standardized, and supported by centralized clearing institutions. The specific margining, daily settlements, and clearing processes are examined in detail later in the book.

A *swap* is a more flexible derivative in which two parties agree to exchange a series of cash flows over time, typically tied to interest rates, currencies, or equity returns. Although a swap can be considered a bundle of forward contracts, structuring exposure using a single, longer-term swap agreement is often more efficient than replicating the same outcome through a sequence of individual forwards. Most swaps are negotiated, though in recent years, some types have become eligible for centralized clearing to reduce counterparty risk, a topic examined in greater detail later in the book.

I examine these instruments in more detail in the following sections, emphasizing their economic purpose, structural features, and typical applications. I defer the discussion of institutional mechanics such as margin posting, clearing arrangements, and legal documentation to later chapters of the book, where I expand on the operational and legal infrastructure that underpins derivatives markets. Detailed applications also appear in chapters focused on implementation.

4.3 Forward Contracts

A forward contract is a bilateral agreement between two parties to buy or sell an asset at a specified price on a specified future date. The terms of a forward contract are customized, including the quantity and type of asset, the delivery date, and the agreed-upon transaction price. Unlike exchange-traded instruments, forward contracts are typically negotiated OTC, meaning they are privately arranged without the involvement of an exchange or clearinghouse. This flexibility makes them especially useful for institutions seeking to hedge very specific exposures or to structure agreements that are not available in standardized form.

At its core, a forward contract allows two parties to lock in a price today for a future transaction. This eliminates price uncertainty for both sides, but does not eliminate risk. Instead, it reallocates risk by fixing future terms of trade and exposing both parties to potential gains or losses depending on how actual market conditions evolve. If the underlying asset's market price differs from the transaction price at the time of delivery, one party will benefit while the other incurs a loss. The payoff is linear: The profit or loss for each party changes in direct proportion to the difference between the agreed-upon transaction (delivery) price and the actual market price at the time of settlement.

To begin with a simple example, suppose an agricultural cooperative agrees to sell 100,000 bushels of wheat in six months to a food manufacturer at $6.00 per bushel. If the spot price of wheat (the market price for immediate delivery) falls to $5.50 at settlement, the cooperative gains $0.50 per bushel compared to selling at market prices. Conversely, the buyer pays more than the current market value and incurs a loss. If the price rises to $6.25 instead, the buyer benefits while the seller forgoes profit relative to the market. The payoff for each side moves proportionally with the change in the underlying wheat price.

Forward contracts are not limited to commodities. A second everyday use case involves foreign exchange (FX) risk. Consider a U.S.-based company expecting to receive €10 million from a European sale in six months. It faces uncertainty about the euro-to-dollar exchange rate at the time of conversion. To eliminate this uncertainty, the firm enters a forward contract with a bank to exchange €10 million for U.S. dollars at a fixed rate of 1.10 USD/EUR. If the market exchange rate at settlement turns out to be 1.08, the company benefits because it receives more dollars than it would have at market rates. If the rate is 1.12, the company receives fewer dollars than the spot market would have offered. Again, both parties fully participate in the exchange rate movement; neither is protected from adverse shifts, and both are exposed to symmetric outcomes.

Forward contracts also appear in equity markets. Suppose an institutional investor agrees to buy exposure to a stock index, such as the S&P 500, three months from now at a fixed level of 4,200. This could be structured through a total return equity forward, where the buyer will pay 4,200 and receive the actual index level at settlement. If the index rises to 4,300, the investor gains 100 index points; if it falls to 4,100, the investor incurs a loss of 100 points. These forwards are often used to manage temporary restrictions on direct stock purchases or to implement exposure without committing the full capital upfront.

The forward contract creates certainty about the transaction's terms but leaves both parties vulnerable to market fluctuations. No money changes hands when the contract is initiated, so both parties are exposed to the risk that the counterparty may default. This risk is typically addressed in institutional markets using standardized legal and collateral arrangements.

While the most intuitive form of settlement for a forward contract involves physical delivery of the underlying asset, in practice, many forwards are settled in cash. In a cash-settled forward, the parties compare the agreed-upon delivery price with the actual market price on the settlement date and exchange the difference in value. This allows for economic exposure to be realized without requiring the actual exchange of the underlying asset, which can reduce transaction costs and logistical complications.

Forward contracts are widely used in commodities, currencies, and interest rate markets, where institutions often seek to hedge exposures tied to future cash flows, procurement needs, or financing costs. Their flexibility and customizability make them valuable tools for corporate risk management, even though they lack the liquidity and counterparty protections of standardized exchange-traded instruments.

In the following section, we turn to futures contracts, which serve a similar economic purpose as forwards but differ significantly in standardization, trading infrastructure, and risk management mechanisms.

4.4 Futures Contracts

Futures contracts are among the most widely used instruments for managing financial risk. Like forwards, they provide a way to lock in future prices and share exposure to market uncertainty, but they do so within a structured and standardized framework. In this section, I explain how futures differ from forward contracts, describe their key operational features, and illustrate how they are applied across asset classes.

4.4.1 *Structure and standardization*

Like forward contracts, futures contracts are agreements to buy or sell an asset at a predetermined price on a specified future date. While the essential economic purpose is similar—locking in future prices to manage uncertainty—futures differ substantially in their structure, trading, and management. Unlike forwards, which are customized and privately negotiated, futures contracts are standardized and traded on organized exchanges. This makes it easier to buy and sell in active markets, contributing to their widespread adoption across various asset classes.

Every futures contract comes with a set of standardized features, including the underlying asset (such as oil, corn, a stock index, or a bond), contract size (e.g., 1,000 barrels of oil or $100,000 par value of Treasury bonds), the contract's expiration date, and how the final price is determined.

These terms are established by the exchange where the contract is traded. Standardization enables buyers and sellers to enter or exit positions quickly without needing to negotiate terms and ensures that all parties trading a particular contract are dealing with the same product.

The role of clearinghouses and the mechanics of novation are examined in greater detail later in the book. Instead, each participant faces the clearinghouse, which serves as the buyer for every seller and the seller for every buyer. This structure significantly reduces counterparty risk (i.e., one party may fail to fulfill its obligations at settlement). These protections make futures especially attractive for institutions that need reliability and transparency in high-volume trading environments.

4.4.2 *Trading and operational features*

Although futures' economic function is similar to that of forwards, their trading infrastructure introduces important differences. One distinguishing feature of futures contracts is their daily price adjustment process. Chapter 10 examines these operational mechanisms in detail and discusses the specifics of margining, daily settlement, and variation margin more comprehensively.

Another distinction is that most futures contracts are not held to expiration. Instead, participants typically close their positions by entering an offsetting trade. For example, someone who bought a futures contract to gain exposure might sell an identical contract to exit the position. However, if a contract is held to expiration, it may be settled either by physical delivery of the underlying asset or by cash settlement, depending on the specific contract's terms.

Futures contracts offer a highly efficient means of transferring risk. Their liquidity, transparency, and low counterparty risk make them ideal for short- and medium-term hedging, speculative strategies, or tactical asset allocation. In the following section, I turn to swaps, which offer greater flexibility and are often used for more complex or long-dated exposures that cannot be easily addressed with either forwards or futures.

4.4.3 *Applications for futures contracts*

Having established the structural features and economic purpose of futures contracts, we now consider how these instruments are used in practice. Futures are central to portfolio management, risk mitigation, and short-term asset allocation across all major asset classes. While their standardized design and exchange-based trading make them versatile tools, how futures are deployed varies depending on the user's strategic objectives.

This section provides an overview of three typical applications of futures contracts in institutional and professional investment settings. The goal is to illustrate the practical logic and motivation behind these uses, focusing on how futures operate as risk-sharing instruments rather than pure price bets. In each case, futures enable users to reallocate or reshape their exposure to future market outcomes without necessarily owning or selling the underlying asset.

Later chapters dedicated to the applications of derivatives provide more detailed discussions, including step-by-step calculations, risk considerations, and implementation techniques but the focus is on the strategic rationale behind these futures-based approaches. Each use case demonstrates how futures function as risk-sharing instruments, enabling participants to transfer or reshape financial exposures while remaining fully sensitive to underlying market movements. These examples also illustrate how futures complement, rather than replace, direct ownership of the underlying assets, allowing for more flexible and efficient implementation of investment objectives.

4.4.3.1 *Hedging future purchase commitments*

One of the most fundamental applications of futures contracts is to hedge the price risk associated with a planned future purchase of an asset. This is common for manufacturers and producers who rely on raw materials subject to market price volatility. By locking in a purchase price in advance using futures, a firm can protect itself against unfavorable price movements and budget with greater certainty.

To illustrate, consider a jewelry manufacturer that relies heavily on gold as a raw material. Suppose it is March, and the manufacturer expects to purchase 1,000 ounces of gold in June for use in its production processes. Concerned that gold prices may rise before the purchase, the firm seeks to lock in today's price to protect its future input costs.

To do so, the manufacturer enters a gold futures contract with a June expiration. Each standard gold futures contract traded on the COMEX[1]

---

[1]COMEX, short for the Commodity Exchange Inc., is a division of the CME Group and is a major marketplace for trading futures and options on metals such as gold, silver, copper, and aluminum.

represents 100 ounces of gold. To hedge the full quantity needed, the manufacturer buys 10 contracts at a futures price of $4,000 per ounce.

Now, consider two possible outcomes at the time of purchase in June. If the spot price of gold (i.e., the current market price for immediate delivery) has risen to $4,200 per ounce, the manufacturer must pay more for the physical gold. However, the futures position has gained value; the contracts can now be sold at $4,200, resulting in a gain of $200 per ounce, or a total of $200,000 across the 1,000 ounces. This offsets the increased cost of purchasing the gold at the higher market price. If the spot price has declined to $3,250 per ounce, the manufacturer benefits from the lower purchase price in the physical market. However, it will realize a $750 per ounce loss on the futures position. The savings on physical purchases offset the loss in the hedge.

In both scenarios, the firm can stabilize its input costs and avoid being adversely affected by fluctuations in the gold price. The futures contract effectively shifts price risk to other market participants willing to take the opposite side of the trade, perhaps because they expect prices to fall or seek speculative exposure. This use of futures as a cost hedge is common in industries that rely on commodities, including metals, energy products, and agricultural goods.

4.4.3.2 *Equitizing cash holdings*

Another important application of futures contracts is equitization of cash, a strategy institutional investors use to maintain full market exposure when temporarily holding uninvested cash. Large investment funds, such as pension plans, endowments, or mutual funds, may have incoming contributions, redemptions, or strategic reallocations that result in cash sitting idle for a short period. Leaving this cash uninvested exposes the fund to what is referred to as *cash drag*, which occurs when portfolio returns underperform a benchmark due to unallocated capital.

Futures contracts provide an efficient solution. Because they require only a small deposit rather than full capital outlay, they allow portfolio managers to gain immediate exposure to an asset class without tying up cash. In particular, equity index futures, such as those based on the S&P 500, are widely used to replicate stock market exposure until the underlying securities can be purchased.

Consider a portfolio manager who expects a significant cash inflow of, say, $50 million in one month from new client contributions. The manager wants to maintain continuous exposure to the equity market during the waiting period, rather than allow the portfolio's equity weight to fall below target. To bridge the gap, the portfolio manager purchases E-mini S&P 500 futures contracts, which are described in greater detail later in the book. These contracts track the performance of the S&P 500 index and are traded on the CME, offering a low-cost, liquid means of simulating the equity market's performance.

If the S&P 500 rises during the month, the futures position gains value, capturing the market's performance as if the portfolio manager had fully invested. Once the cash arrives, the manager sells the futures and uses the funds to purchase actual stocks. If the market declines, the futures position would incur a loss, mirroring the outcome if the manager had invested in the index. In either case, using futures reduces tracking error or deviation from benchmark returns by preserving full market exposure during the interim.

This process of temporarily using futures to maintain asset class exposure is known as *equitization* and is an essential tool for portfolio managers operating under daily performance benchmarks. While the illustration above demonstrates the core logic, later chapters provide a more detailed treatment of equity derivatives, including specific contract sizing and risk considerations.

4.4.3.3 *Adjusting asset class exposures*

Futures contracts are also widely used to adjust asset class exposures, temporarily or as part of a more strategic reallocation. This application is essential for portfolio managers who need to respond quickly to changes in market conditions, investment outlooks, or asset allocation targets.

Some fund managers specialize in a single asset class, such as equities, fixed income, or commodities, and use futures to fine-tune their exposures within that class. Others manage multi-asset portfolios, allocating capital across several asset classes such as stocks, bonds, and cash equivalents to achieve a diversified risk-return profile. For these multi-asset fund managers, futures offer a flexible tool for implementing tactical or strategic shifts in portfolio exposures without buying or selling the underlying securities.

Consider a multi-asset fund manager overseeing a balanced portfolio of equities and fixed-income securities, such as bonds. Suppose the manager currently holds a 60/40 equity/bond allocation but, based on evolving macroeconomic data, expects equities to outperform over the next three months. Rather than selling bonds and buying stocks—an approach that could trigger transaction costs, tax consequences, or operational delays—the portfolio manager can temporarily use equity index futures to increase the fund's equity exposure. For instance, by going long in E-mini S&P 500 futures, the manager can synthetically adjust the portfolio's allocation toward a 70/30 mix without altering the underlying holdings.

Similarly, suppose the portfolio manager anticipates a short-term rise in interest rates and wants to reduce the portfolio's sensitivity to bond price declines. In that case, they might use Treasury bond futures to create a partial hedge. By selling bond futures, the manager reduces interest rate exposure marginally, helping to protect the portfolio from potential losses in a rising-rate environment.

This strategy is not limited to equities and fixed income. Investors can use commodity futures to gain or reduce exposure to inflation-sensitive assets or use currency futures to manage foreign exchange risk in global portfolios. In each case, fine-tuning risk exposures without permanently changing the underlying asset allocation is a key benefit.

In practice, this use of futures supports *tactical asset allocation* (short- to medium-term shifts based on market outlook) and *strategic overlays* (longer-term adjustments made with minimal portfolio disruption). Because futures are marked to market daily and require only a modest initial margin, they are particularly well-suited for overlay programs run by institutions such as pension funds.

This application of futures emphasizes their value in hedging or replication, portfolio construction, and risk budgeting.[2] Futures give

---

[2]Risk budgeting is allocating a portfolio's overall risk across various asset classes, strategies, or positions deliberately and measuredly, like how capital is allocated in traditional budgeting. Rather than focusing solely on capital invested, the emphasis is on how much volatility or tracking error each position contributes to the portfolio. Futures allow fund managers to fine-tune these risk contributions with precision. For example, a manager might use futures to increase exposure to an underweighted asset class without disrupting core holdings, or to temporarily reduce exposure to keep the portfolio's overall risk within target limits. The ability to adjust exposures quickly, efficiently, and without large capital outlays makes futures an indispensable tool for implementing risk-aware investment strategies.

managers the flexibility to adapt exposures with precision, liquidity, and cost efficiency advantages that explain their widespread use in modern investment strategies.

4.5 Swaps

A swap is an agreement in which two parties agree to exchange one set of future cash flows for another over a specified period, based on mutually agreed-upon terms.[3] The primary purpose of a swap is to transform or tailor financial exposures, such as interest rate risk, currency risk, or equity market risk, without requiring the actual purchase or sale of the underlying assets. This makes swaps especially useful for institutions seeking to reallocate risk efficiently while maintaining their existing portfolios or liability structures.

What makes swaps particularly powerful is their flexibility. They enable firms to manage risk exposures symmetrically: Both parties agree to share gains and losses based on future market outcomes. These are still linear instruments, meaning that the cash flows are proportional to changes in an underlying variable (e.g., interest rates or index levels). Unlike futures and forwards, which generally involve a single payment or delivery on a specific future date, swaps typically involve a series of periodic payments over the contract's life. These payments are calculated using a notional principal amount, which serves as the basis for computing cash flows. For example, in an interest rate swap described as follows, each party pays interest calculated on the same notional amount, such as $100 million, but neither party transfers that principal. Instead, the notional serves as the basis for computing the interest payments to be swapped.[4]

---

[3]Not all instruments labeled as "swaps" have the linear, symmetric payoff structures described in this chapter. For example, credit default swaps (CDSs), described in Chapter 9, function more like insurance contracts than traditional swaps: One party pays a premium in exchange for a contingent payout if a credit event such as default occurs. Due to their nonlinear and asymmetric structure, CDS contracts are typically discussed in the context of nonlinear derivatives or credit derivatives and are not covered in this chapter.

[4]In some types of swaps (notably currency swaps), the notional amounts are exchanged at the beginning and end of the contract. This reflects that the two parties are funding themselves in different currencies and using the swap to manage currency exposure alongside interest payments.

To better understand how swaps function in practice, it is helpful to examine three widely used types: interest rate swaps, currency swaps, and equity swaps. Each serves a distinct purpose, tailored to the type of financial exposure a party wishes to modify, whether it's stabilizing borrowing costs, managing foreign currency obligations, or replicating equity market returns without owning the underlying securities.

4.5.1 *Interest rate swap: Transforming fixed and floating payments*

One of the most common type of swap is the interest rate swap, which converts fixed-rate liabilities to floating-rate ones, or vice versa.

To illustrate this type of swap, suppose a corporation issues $100 million in bonds that pay a fixed interest rate of 5% per year. After issuing the bonds, the company decides it would rather have floating-rate debt (e.g., tied to a short-term benchmark such as the Secured Overnight Financing Rate, SOFR)[5] to benefit from declining interest rates. At the same time, a bank with floating-rate liabilities would prefer to receive fixed-rate income to stabilize its interest margin. The two parties agree to enter an interest rate swap:

- The corporation agrees to pay SOFR (the floating rate) on a notional amount of $100 million.
- The bank agrees to pay 5% fixed on the same notional amount.

Payments are exchanged semi-annually, and only the net difference is exchanged.

If SOFR is 4.5% at the payment date, the bank pays the corporation the 0.5% difference. If SOFR rises to 5.2%, the corporation pays the bank 0.2%. Neither party exchanges the $100 million notional; it's only used to calculate the cash flows. This allows both parties to share interest rate risk mutually beneficially.

---

[5] SOFR is a benchmark interest rate based on actual transactions in the U.S. Treasury repurchase (repo) market, reflecting the cost of borrowing cash overnight secured by Treasury collateral. It has become the preferred replacement for the London Interbank Offered Rate (LIBOR), once the dominant short-term interest rate in derivatives and lending contracts globally. LIBOR lost credibility following manipulation scandals and has been phased out in most major markets. Due to its transparency and robustness, SOFR is the principal alternative in U.S. dollar-denominated instruments.

4.5.2 *Equity swap: Gaining exposure without direct ownership*

An equity swap allows one party to receive returns linked to an equity index or specific stock, while paying a fixed or floating rate in exchange. These are often used when investors want equity exposure without directly holding the underlying asset due to regulatory restrictions, tax considerations, or leverage preferences.

For example, suppose a hedge fund wants exposure to the total return of the S&P 500 index over the next year but prefers not to buy the stocks directly. The hedge fund enters a swap with a dealer. The fund agrees to pay the dealer SOFR + 0.5% on a notional amount of $10 million. The dealer agrees to pay the fund the total return on the S&P 500, including dividends.

If the S&P 500 rises 8% over the year, the dealer pays the fund $800,000. If the index falls by 5%, the fund pays the dealer $500,000. Meanwhile, the hedge fund pays interest on the notional value, regardless of the equity performance. This creates synthetic exposure to equity performance, which helps manage leverage, capital constraints, or jurisdictional rules.

4.5.3 *Currency swap: Managing foreign currency obligations*

A currency swap allows two parties to exchange both principal and interest payments denominated in different currencies. A distinguishing feature of currency swaps is that they typically involve the exchange of notional amounts at both the start and end of the contract, making them an exception to the general structure used in most other swaps.[6] These instruments are commonly used by multinational corporations or governments that need to raise funds or finance operations in a foreign currency but wish to avoid exposure to foreign exchange risk. By locking in the exchange rate and interest payments upfront, each party can effectively borrow in its home currency while gaining access to foreign capital at known costs.

For example, imagine a U.S. company that needs €50 million to build a facility in Europe. In comparison, a European company needs $55 million to expand in the U.S. Each company can borrow more

[6]This distinction is examined in greater detail later in the book, as part of the broader discussion on swap mechanics and notional exchange.

cheaply in their home currency, but they need access to the other. They agree to a currency swap:

- The U.S. company borrows $55 million at home, and the European company borrows €50 million.
- On the start date, they exchange the principal amounts.

Over the next five years, the U.S. company pays the European company interest in euros (say, 3%), while the European company pays the U.S. company interest in dollars (say, 4%). At maturity, they re-exchange the principal amounts at the original exchange rate.

The swap eliminates exchange rate uncertainty for both parties. They each receive and pay in their local currency while accessing foreign capital. This is a powerful example of risk-sharing, especially in volatile currency markets.

Swaps, like forwards and futures, are tools for reshaping exposures in a mutually balanced way. Both parties face gains or losses depending on how the underlying variables evolve, and no one party is guaranteed to benefit. This makes swaps ideal for reallocating financial risks in sophisticated, often long-term arrangements.

While the economic logic of swaps is straightforward, their implementation involves a range of technical and legal details, including valuation, collateralization, and documentation, which are examined more fully later in the book. For now, it is crucial to recognize that swaps allow for precise tailoring of risk exposures across interest rates, currencies, and equity returns without the need to physically own or issue the underlying instruments.

4.6 Summary

In this chapter, I introduce the core category of risk-sharing derivatives, focusing on forwards, futures, and swaps. These instruments allow two parties to share uncertainty about future market outcomes, such as prices, interest rates, or returns, without guaranteeing that either side will benefit. My goal was to show how these derivatives serve as tools for adjusting, rebalancing, or managing exposures in a mutual and symmetric manner, rather than in a one-sided way.

I distinguish between linear derivatives, which generate proportional gains and losses, and nonlinear derivatives, such as options, which I will cover in the following chapter. I explain how linear payoffs preserve the entire risk of the underlying exposure and how that structure is central to the design of forwards, futures, and swaps.

I demonstrate how forward contracts create obligations to transact in the future at a fixed price and how futures contracts, as standardized and exchange-traded instruments, offer similar functionality but are implemented through formal infrastructure and centralized trading venues. I then walk through three practical use cases of futures (hedging input costs, equitizing cash, and adjusting asset class exposures) to demonstrate how they are applied in real portfolios.

From there, I turn to swaps, which allow for the ongoing cash flow exchange over time. I illustrate how interest rate swaps convert fixed-rate exposures to floating (and vice versa), how currency swaps facilitate funding in different currencies while mitigating FX risk, and how equity swaps can replicate index returns without direct ownership. In each case, I highlight the role of the notional amount in determining cash flows, noting that while it is usually a reference value, some contracts, such as currency swaps, involve notional exchanges—a structural feature discussed in greater depth elsewhere.

Throughout the chapter, I emphasize that these instruments do not eliminate risk; they redistribute it. They are not guarantees of safety, but frameworks for mutual exposure to uncertain financial outcomes. In the following chapters, I will shift to nonlinear derivatives, where the payoff structure can be reshaped to favor one side or protect against extreme events, transforming risk exposure and the entire distribution of outcomes.

Chapter 5

Insurance-Type Derivatives: Options, Caps, Floors, and Credit Default Swaps

In the previous chapter, I introduced derivatives whose payoffs are linear, meaning that gains and losses are shared symmetrically between two parties in direct proportion to changes in an underlying variable, such as a commodity price, interest rate, or equity index. These instruments—forward contracts, futures contracts, and swaps—allow both sides to participate fully in market risk and are typically used to reshape or rebalance exposures.

This chapter shifts focus to a different class of derivatives: those designed not to share risk symmetrically but to reallocate it asymmetrically, typically through the payment of a premium in exchange for protection against adverse outcomes. These "insurance-type derivatives" include options, interest rate caps and floors, credit default swaps (CDSs), swaptions, and options on futures contracts. Their defining feature is a nonlinear or asymmetric payoff structure, where one party pays an upfront amount (a premium or spread) for the right to receive compensation under specified conditions. In contrast, the other party receives the payment but bears the risk of making large contingent payments.

The primary aim of this chapter is to explain the economic rationale, structure, and core applications of these derivatives. I begin with a detailed examination of options, including call and put structures, payoff profiles, and their applications. Next, I explain how options are embedded in bonds and loans, such as callable or puttable bonds, or as caps and floors in floating-rate instruments. These embedded features alter cash flow and risk exposures without requiring separate contracts. I then turn to standalone caps and floors, which are used not only in interest rate markets but also in commodities, inflation-linked instruments, and structured products. The section includes detailed numerical illustrations to show how these instruments work.

In the latter part of the chapter, I introduce CDSs, a form of insurance against borrower default that transfers credit risk. I also explain swaptions (i.e., options on interest rate swaps) and options on futures contracts, which institutional investors widely use. While many of these derivatives are based on simple option logic, their institutional use cases are diverse and their structures are often complex.

As in the previous chapter, the goal here is not to provide an exhaustive treatment of legal or regulatory specifics but to provide a unified conceptual foundation for understanding how these instruments function and why they matter. Pricing models, margin requirements, and institutional infrastructure for these derivatives are addressed in later chapters. For now, this chapter explains how financial professionals utilize insurance-type derivatives to protect against extreme outcomes, tailor risk exposures, and construct payoff profiles that would otherwise be difficult to achieve with linear instruments alone.

In subsequent chapters, I will revisit these instruments within the context of specific asset classes such as equity options, bond options, and options on currencies and explain how they are priced using no-arbitrage principles and probabilistic models. This chapter serves as a conceptual foundation for those later discussions by showing how insurance-type derivatives differ from the linear derivatives and why they are essential to modern financial risk management.

5.1 Asymmetric Risk Transfer: A Defining Feature

Insurance-type derivatives are defined by their asymmetric payoff structures. Unlike the linear instruments covered in the previous chapter, where gains and losses are proportionally shared, these derivatives offer a *nonlinear transfer of risk*, often designed to protect one party from unfavorable outcomes while allowing them to retain upside potential. This feature makes them especially valuable for hedging specific risks or structuring limited-exposure investment strategies.

The key idea behind these contracts is that one party pays a premium in exchange for the right, but not the obligation, to benefit from favorable market movements or to receive compensation when adverse events occur. This right is not free; it comes at a cost, and that cost reflects both the probability of the protected outcome occurring and the magnitude of potential losses or gains.

Consider a basic illustration of how insurance-type derivatives work. Suppose one party wants protection against the possibility that the value of an asset they own might fall over the next few months. Rather than selling the asset, they enter a derivative contract that will compensate them if the asset's price declines below a certain threshold. In exchange for this protection, they pay a premium to a counterparty who agrees to absorb the loss if the asset's value drops significantly. If the asset's price stays stable or increases, the buyer lets the contract expire, having lost only the premium. But if the price falls, the buyer receives a payout that helps offset the loss in value. This contract structure limits the buyer's downside risk while exposing the seller (the "writer") to potentially substantial losses in exchange for the premium received.

This type of contract is known as an option, and specific forms such as put options and call options are explored in detail later in this chapter. The key takeaway is that insurance-type derivatives allow one party to limit its losses while another accepts the risk in return for a fixed, upfront payment.

This asymmetry is what gives insurance-type derivatives their power. The buyer obtains downside protection and a known maximum loss (the premium), while the seller accepts a potentially large but uncertain loss in return for the fixed premium. These instruments enable precise tail-risk management, allowing investors to hedge exposures that might otherwise be unmanageable through linear contracts alone.

Importantly, this structure is not limited to equity markets. For example, interest rate caps and floors are option-based structures that borrowers and lenders use to manage uncertainty in floating-rate debt. Similarly, CDSs function as insurance against borrower defaults, with the seller of protection agreeing to make a payment if a specified credit event occurs.

In the following sections, I explain the structure and applications of each of these derivatives, beginning with the most fundamental instrument in this category: the option.

5.2 Options

An *option* is an agreement that gives the buyer the right, but not the obligation, to buy or sell an underlying asset at a predetermined price, known as the *strike price* or *exercise price*, on or before a specified expiration date. The buyer pays the seller (the option writer) a premium for this right. In return, the seller assumes the obligation to fulfill the contract's terms if the buyer exercises the option.

The defining feature of options is their asymmetric payoff: The buyer of the option has limited downside (the premium paid) and potentially significant upside. At the same time, the seller receives a fixed premium but may incur substantial losses depending on how the market evolves.

There are two basic types of options:

- A *call option* gives the buyer the right, but not the obligation, to buy the underlying asset at the strike price.
- A *put option* gives the buyer the right, but not the obligation, to sell the underlying asset at the strike price.

Options can be written on various underlying instruments, including individual stocks, stock indexes, interest rates, foreign currencies, and commodities. Regardless of the underlying asset, all options share a set of common features that define their structure:

- *Underlying asset*: the instrument on which the option is based, such as a share of stock, an index, or a bond.
- *Strike price* or *exercise price*: the price at which the buyer of the option may choose to buy or sell the underlying asset.
- *Expiration date*: the date on which the option expires and can no longer be exercised.
- *Premium*: the upfront payment made by the buyer to the seller for the rights conveyed by the option.
- *Exercise style*: the rules governing when the option can be exercised. Most commonly, options are either European-style, which can be exercised only at expiration, or American-style, which can be exercised at any time up to expiration.

Options are used for many purposes, including risk control, income generation, and speculation. For example, an investor who owns a stock may purchase a put option as insurance against a sharp decline in the stock's price. If the stock drops below the strike price, the investor can exercise the put and sell the underlying at the higher strike price, offsetting losses. Alternatively, a trader may buy a call option to speculate on a price increase without buying the asset outright. The option gives them exposure to potential gains while limiting losses to the cost of the premium.

From the seller's perspective, options can generate income but come with significant risk. The writer of a put option would be obligated to buy the asset at the strike price if its value falls. The writer of a call option may be required to deliver the asset if its price rises above the strike, incurring a loss if they do not already own it. Because of this risk, option sellers must often post margin or collateral, a topic addressed in later chapters.

Understanding the structure of options is crucial for comprehending how more complex insurance-type derivatives function. In the following sections, I provide examples of option payoffs and demonstrate how options are utilized in various financial settings to manage risk or structure investment strategies with defined outcomes.

5.2.1 *Option payoffs and profit/loss*

At the core of every option contract is a distinct asymmetric structure of outcomes known as the option's payoff profile. The term *payoff* refers specifically to the option's value at expiration, depending on the underlying asset's price. It excludes the cost (or premium) paid to acquire the option. Profit, by contrast, is the net financial outcome: the payoff minus the premium paid by the buyer or the premium received minus the payoff to the seller.

Let's begin with call options. A call option gives the buyer the right, but not the obligation, to purchase the underlying asset at the strike price. In Figure 5.1, we depict the profit diagram for a long call option with a strike price of $100 and a premium of $5. If the underlying asset finishes below $100 at expiration, the option expires worthless. The buyer's loss is limited to the $5 premium. If the price exceeds $100, the buyer profits from the difference between the market price and the strike but only after recovering the $5 premium. The breakeven point is $105. Beyond that, the profit rises linearly.

Figure 5.2 presents the corresponding short call option. Here, the seller (writer) of the option receives the $5 premium upfront. If the

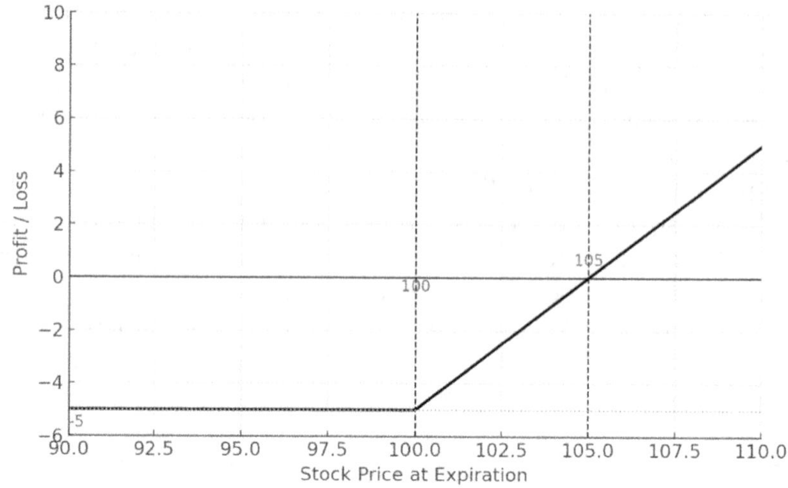

Figure 5.1. Profit Diagram of a Long Call Option with Strike = \$100 and Premium = \$5

Notes: The long call option has limited downside (equal to the premium paid) and unlimited upside as the underlying asset's price rises. The breakeven point is the strike price plus the premium. If the asset finishes below the strike price, the option expires worthless price.

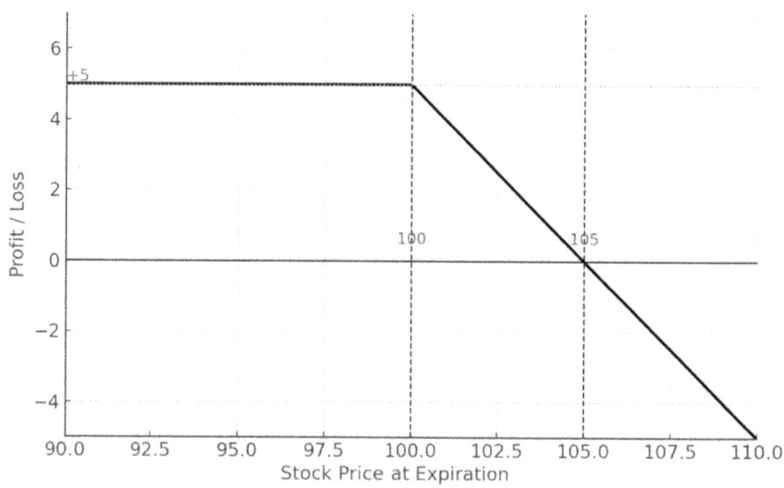

Figure 5.2. Profit Diagram of a Short Call Option with Strike = \$100 and Premium = \$5

Note: The short call position receives the premium upfront but has unlimited downside if the asset price rises above the strike price.

underlying asset remains at or below $100, the option expires worthless, and the seller keeps the full $5 as profit. However, if the price rises above $100, the seller must deliver the asset at $100, even though it is worth more on the market. Losses grow as the price increases, with no cap. The breakeven for the seller is also $105; beyond that, the position becomes increasingly loss-making.

Now turn to put options. A put option gives the buyer the right, but not the obligation, to sell the underlying asset at the strike price. Figure 5.3 shows the long put option with a strike of $95 and a premium of $3. If the underlying asset finishes above $95, the put expires worthless, and the buyer loses the $3 premium. If the price drops below $95, the option is exercised. The breakeven point is $92, and profits increase as the asset price continues to fall. For $80, the payoff is $15; after subtracting the $3 premium, the profit is $12.

Figure 5.4 shows the short put option. The seller collects the $3 premium upfront. If the price stays above $95, the put expires worthless, and the seller keeps the premium. If the price falls below $95, the seller must buy the asset at the strike price, even though the market price is lower.

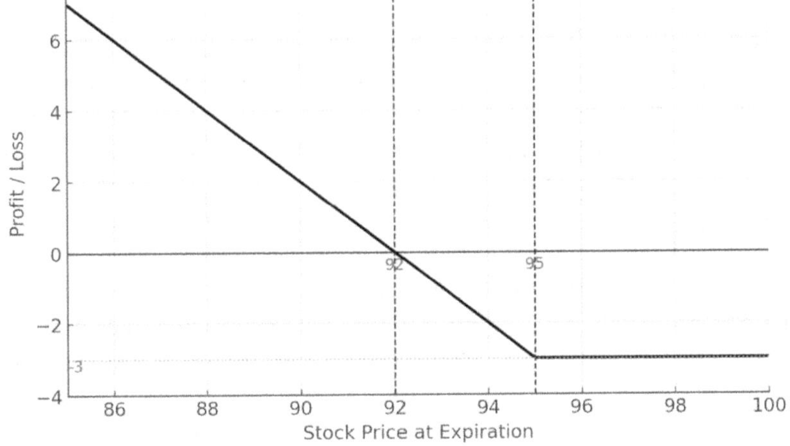

Figure 5.3. Profit Diagram of a Long Put Option with Strike = $95 and Premium = $3

Notes: The long put option becomes profitable as the price of the underlying asset falls below the strike price. Losses are limited to the premium paid. The maximum profit occurs if the underlying asset falls to zero (or near zero), and the breakeven point is the strike price minus the premium.

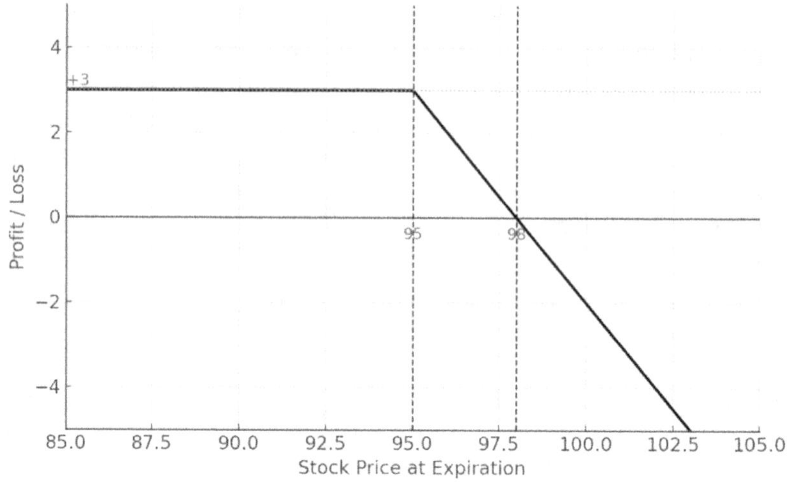

Figure 5.4. Profit Diagram of a Short Put Option with Strike = $95 and Premium = $3

Notes: The short put writer profits if the price of the asset stays above the strike. However, if the asset price falls, losses grow—potentially significantly—though they are capped at the full strike price (i.e., if the asset falls to zero).

The seller's losses increase as the asset price declines. The breakeven is $92, and losses accumulate beyond that.

These four examples illustrate the defining feature of options: nonlinear payoffs. Option payoff diagrams typically exhibit flat segments, indicating no payoff, and angled lines beyond the strike price where the profit or loss increases. They differ sharply from linear instruments such as forwards or futures, where the gain or loss changes dollar-for-dollar with the underlying price.

From a strategic perspective, options provide powerful tools to reshape the distribution of outcomes. The buyer accepts a known, limited loss (the premium) in exchange for uncertain, potentially large gains. The seller, by contrast, assumes a non-trivial risk in return for a fixed reward. Unlike in the linear case where exposure is symmetric, this transfer of risk is asymmetric and depends on market movements beyond the strike price.

These figures help illustrate why options are considered nonlinear derivatives. The slope of the payoff is either zero (flat) or positive/negative, depending on the direction of the asset price movement and the structure of the contract.

5.2.2 *Exercise styles of options*

In addition to understanding the basic structure and payoff profiles of options, it is essential to understand when an option can be exercised. The contract's exercise style defines this. Exercise style determines the timing flexibility granted to the option holder, which can significantly impact the option's value and application in trading strategies.

The two most common types are the European and American exercise styles. A European-style option can only be exercised at expiration, not before. This means that even if it becomes highly profitable before the expiration date, the holder must wait until the end of the contract term to realize the option's value through exercise. Because the holder cannot exercise early, the option valuation models used to price these options (as described in Chapter 21) are simpler and assume exercise only at the expiration date.

An American-style option, by contrast, can be exercised at any time up to and including the expiration date. This flexibility allows the holder to capitalize on favorable market movements before maturity. Most exchange-traded equity options in the United States are American-style. However, this early exercise feature introduces additional complexity into option valuation and strategy because, as explained in Chapter 21, it must account for the optimal exercise decision at each point in time.

At this stage of the book, where we focus on understanding profit diagrams and the economic intuition behind options, we assume that early exercise does not occur. This assumption allows us to construct clear, unambiguous profit diagrams, as shown in Figures 5.1–5.4 for long and short call and put options. These diagrams are valid under the assumption that options are European-style. This simplifying assumption will be revisited in later chapters, particularly when pricing models and strategy design are discussed, where the potential for early exercise in American-style options must be incorporated.

As we delve further into real-world applications, it will become clear that exercise style has strategic importance. For instance, whether an option can be exercised before a dividend is paid (as in the case of American-style calls on dividend-paying stocks) may influence whether it should be exercised early. Likewise, hedging strategies and pricing methodologies must explicitly account for the timing rules embedded in the contract.

Beyond these two core types, another exercise style is the *Bermudan-style option*, which allows exercise on specific, predetermined dates before expiration. This option can only be exercised on specific predetermined dates or periods up to the expiration date.

The key insight is that an option's timing flexibility is not merely a contractual detail; it directly influences the option's value, its optimal use in a strategy, and the mathematical tools used for its pricing. We continue to assume no early exercise, but the distinction between exercise styles will become increasingly relevant as we turn to more advanced option structures and pricing techniques.

5.2.3 *Embedded options in bonds*

In addition to standalone option contracts, option features are frequently embedded in traditional fixed-income instruments, most notably in callable and puttable bonds. These embedded options provide the bond issuer or investor with specific rights that alter the bond's cash flow structure and market behavior, without requiring either party to enter a separate derivatives contract.

A *callable bond* includes an embedded call option that gives the issuer the right, but not the obligation, to redeem the bond before its scheduled maturity, typically at a specified call price and after a predetermined lockout period. Issuers include this feature when they expect interest rates to decline. If rates fall, the issuer can refinance its debt at a lower cost by calling the outstanding bond and reissuing new bonds at a lower interest rate. Because this flexibility benefits the issuer and imposes reinvestment risk on investors, callable bonds typically offer higher yields to compensate bondholders for the risk of the bond being called.

On the other hand, a puttable bond includes an embedded put option that gives the bondholder the right to return the bond to the issuer at a predetermined price before maturity. This feature is attractive to investors in environments with rising interest rates or periods of credit deterioration. If the bond's value falls due to an increase in market rates or issuer risk, the holder can exercise the put and recover par (or the contractual put price). Since the put option protects the investor, puttable bonds usually offer lower yields than similar non-puttable ones.[1]

[1] These embedded call and put features are fundamentally different from option-based structured products described later in this chapter. In the case of callable and puttable bonds, the option is part of the bond's design—not a separate contract purchased from a

Embedded options in bonds significantly affect valuation, risk exposure, and expected cash flows. Investors must consider the likelihood that the issuer will call the bond or that they might benefit from exercising a put.

5.3 Caps and Floors: General Structure and Applications

A *cap* and a *floor* are types of option-based derivatives that place an upper or lower limit, respectively, on the value of a variable that determines future payments. These instruments are not tied to a specific asset class; they are flexible structures that can be applied to any underlying reference variable, such as interest rates, commodity prices, inflation indices, or even asset returns.

The purpose of a cap is to ensure that a payment obligation does not exceed a pre-specified maximum, while a floor guarantees that it will not fall below a specified minimum. In both cases, these instruments constrain the range of possible financial outcomes, creating bounded exposures that help entities (financial institutions or corporate treasury departments) manage risk more precisely. They are useful when the risk being hedged is not the full volatility of a market variable but rather its extreme movements, either upward or downward.

A cap is structured as a series of call options on the reference variable. Each time the reference value is observed (e.g., monthly or quarterly), the buyer of the cap receives a payment if the reference value exceeds the cap level. A floor, conversely, is structured as a series of put options and provides payment when the reference value falls below the floor level. Each option is referred to as a *caplet* or *floorlet*, and the entire series defines the cap or floor contract.

To enter a cap or floor contract, the buyer must pay a premium to the seller (writer) of the contract. This premium is typically paid upfront at the

---

third-party derivatives dealer. There is no standalone option premium paid upfront; instead, the effect of the embedded option is reflected in the bond's yield, pricing, and sensitivity to interest rate changes. The issuer or investor does not transact with a commercial or investment bank to hedge or offset the option; the bond's terms are fixed at issuance, and the embedded option is exercised (or not) by the relevant party based on prevailing market conditions.

initiation of the agreement. It compensates the seller for assuming the risk of making future payments if the reference variable moves beyond the agreed threshold. A cap or floor is a notional contract,[2] meaning that while the payments are calculated based on a specified notional amount, the notional itself is not exchanged between the parties. The size of the premium depends on contract terms such as the level of the cap or floor, the notional amount, the contract term, and the frequency of potential payouts. Once this premium is paid, the buyer will receive payments under the contract if and when the reference value breaches the agreed-upon threshold. At the same time, the seller is obligated to make those payments when triggered.

Although caps and floors can be written on any measurable variable, the most common and standardized use is in the interest rate market. In this context, the underlying variable is a reference interest rate used to reset payments on a floating-rate loan or bond.

5.3.1 *Interest rate caps and floors*

Caps and floors are widely used to manage interest rate risk in floating-rate financial instruments. When borrowers or lenders are exposed to changes in a reference rate such as the Secured Overnight Financing Rate (SOFR), they may want to limit how much their payments rise or fall over time. This is where interest rate caps and floors come into play.

An *interest rate cap* provides the buyer with protection against rising interest rates. It sets a maximum interest rate (the cap rate) on a floating-rate loan. If the reference rate exceeds the cap rate on a reset date, the seller of the cap compensates the buyer for the difference. Conversely, an *interest rate floor* guarantees the buyer a minimum interest rate, ensuring they receive a floor-level payment even if market rates fall.

To obtain this protection, the cap or floor buyer pays a premium to the seller upfront at the inception of the contract. The premium reflects

---

[2]A notional contract is a derivative agreement where the specified principal amount—called the "notional"—is used solely for calculating payments but is not exchanged between the parties. This concept was discussed in the previous chapter in the context of swap contracts, where the notional amount determines cash flow amounts without changing hands.

the expected likelihood and magnitude of future payments made under the cap or floor.

Let's examine two detailed numerical illustrations—one for a cap and one for a floor—to see how they work in practice.

Example 1: Interest Rate Cap (Borrower Perspective)

A company has a $10 million floating-rate loan that resets quarterly based on three-month SOFR. Worried that rates might rise, the firm's treasurer buys a one-year interest rate cap with a cap rate of 4% to ensure its interest payments don't exceed this threshold. The cap covers four reset periods, and the company pays an upfront premium of $50,000 for this protection.

Contract Terms:

- *Notional*: $10,000,000
- *Cap rate*: 4.00%
- *Premium*: $50,000
- *Reference rate*: three-month SOFR
- *Settlement frequency*: quarterly
- *Day count convention*: actual/360[3]
- *Protection periods*: four quarters

Assume the observed three-month SOFR rates at each reset as shown in Table 5.1.

Table 5.1. Illustration of Quarterly Payments Under an Interest Rate Cap

Quarter	Observed SOFR (%)	Payment Triggered?	Payout Formula	Payment ($)
Q1	3.8	No	N/A	0
Q2	4.5	Yes	$10,000,000 × 0.005 × 90/360	12,500
Q3	4.7	Yes	$10,000,000 × 0.007 × 90/360	17,500
Q4	3.9	No	N/A	0

[3] Interest rate cap and floor payments are calculated using a day count convention, commonly actual/360, which assumes 360 days per year and uses the actual number of days in the interest period. This convention is standard in money market instruments and affects the precise cash flow calculation.

The cap functioned as an insurance policy. The company limited its exposure to rising rates and was reimbursed when SOFR exceeded 4%. Although the premium exceeded the payouts in this scenario, the company benefited from the certainty and protection that would have been provided in case rates had risen further.

Example 2: Interest Rate Floor (Lender/Investor Perspective)
Now, consider a pension fund with a $20 million floating-rate note linked to three-month SOFR in its portfolio. Concerned that falling interest rates might reduce its income, the fund manager purchases a one-year interest rate floor with a floor rate of 2.50%, covering four reset periods. The premium paid is $60,000.

Contract Terms:

- *Notional*: $20,000,000
- *Floor rate*: 2.50%
- *Premium*: $60,000
- *Reference rate*: three-month SOFR
- *Settlement frequency*: quarterly
- *Day count convention*: actual/360
- *Protection periods*: four quarters

Assume the observed SOFR rates shown in Table 5.2.

In this case, the floor ensured the fund's yield did not drop too low. Although the premium was slightly more than the protection received, the fund secured predictable cash flows and avoided steeper income losses if rates had declined further.

Table 5.2. Illustration of Quarterly Payments Under an Interest Rate Floor

Quarter	Observed SOFR (%)	Payment Triggered?	Payout Formula	Payment ($)
Q1	2.3	Yes	$20,000,000 × 0.002 × 90/360	10,000
Q2	2.1	Yes	$20,000,000 × 0.004 × 90/360	20,000
Q3	2.7	No	N/A	0
Q4	2.2	Yes	$20,000,000 × 0.003 × 90/360	15,000

5.3.2 *Caps and floors in other markets*

Beyond the domain of interest rates, caps and floors are used in various markets to serve the same fundamental purpose: to limit potential outcomes by placing a ceiling (cap) or a floor on a variable that determines payment or value. These structures are instrumental in nonlinear payout situations where market participants want to limit exposure to extreme values of prices, indices, or rates.

5.3.2.1 *Commodity markets*

In commodity markets, caps and floors are frequently used to manage price volatility for both buyers and sellers of physical goods. A *price cap* ensures that a buyer of a commodity, such as oil or wheat, pays no more than a pre-agreed maximum. Conversely, a *price floor* ensures that a producer receives a minimum price for selling the commodity.

To illustrate, consider a grain processor whose management expects to purchase 100,000 bushels of corn in six months. To guard against rising prices, it purchases a corn price cap with a strike of $5.50 per bushel, paying a premium to a counterparty. If, at the time of purchase, the market price rises to $6.10 per bushel, the processor receives a payment of $0.60 per bushel × 100,000 = $60,000, offsetting the higher purchase cost. If the market price remains below $5.50, no payment occurs, and the processor absorbs only the cost of the premium.

On the producer side, a corn grower could enter a price floor agreement at $5.00 per bushel. If prices fall to $4.40, the floor pays the farmer $0.60 per bushel, cushioning the impact of unfavorable price movements. Depending on the terms, these agreements can be physically settled (by delivering or accepting the commodity) or cash-settled.

Unlike standardized exchange-traded options, most commodity caps and floors are customized and traded OTC. They require negotiation of notional amounts, strike levels, settlement terms, and counterparties, and the terms are customized to the specific needs of the parties.

5.3.2.2 *Caps and floors in structured products*

In addition to being used as standalone derivatives, caps and floors are also embedded directly in investment instruments, particularly in bonds and loans, to limit the variability of future cash flows. These embedded features are commonly found in floating-rate bonds and loans, where interest payments reset periodically based on a reference interest rate. The inclusion of a cap ensures that the interest paid does not exceed a specified ceiling, protecting the issuer from rising interest expenses. A floor, conversely, guarantees a minimum interest rate, benefiting the investor by protecting against falling rates.

In these cases, the embedded cap or floor is part of the bond's or loan's contractual terms. The issuer does not enter a separate derivatives contract with a third party; instead, the presence of the cap or floor is reflected in the security's pricing through a higher or lower yield, depending on which party holds the embedded option, as in the case of callable and puttable bonds.

This approach differs from medium-term notes (MTNs) issued with structured payoff features. In MTNs, the issuer typically enters into a derivatives transaction with a commercial or investment bank to replicate a desired exposure, such as a cap on equity returns or a floor on commodity prices. For example, a corporation issuing an MTN linked to the performance of a commodity index might purchase a floor from a dealer to ensure minimum cash flows. In these cases, the derivative is sourced externally and embedded in the note's design, with its cost being incorporated into the instrument's pricing.

Structured investment products, such as *principal-protected notes* or *equity-linked notes*, also rely on externally sourced caps and floors. These instruments are designed to provide investors with bounded exposure, typically offering complete downside protection (a floor at 0%) and limited upside potential (a return cap). The issuer hedges this payoff by using appropriate option strategies with a derivatives dealer, embedding the net cost into the product's structure.

Whether embedded internally in a bond's terms or externally structured through a derivatives overlay, caps and floors serve the same economic purpose: They define the range of possible outcomes, allowing issuers and investors to manage exposure to volatility, interest rates, or market-linked returns in a more targeted way.

5.3.2.3 *Inflation-linked instruments*

Pension funds, insurers, and inflation-sensitive investors frequently use caps and floors on inflation indices, such as the Consumer Price Index (CPI), to control exposure to unpredictable changes in inflation.

A pension plan promises beneficiaries inflation-adjusted payments linked to the CPI. To avoid excessive increases in liabilities during surges in inflation, the fund buys an inflation cap at 4%. If the CPI rises to 6%, the cap pays the fund the difference on the notional exposure, helping offset the higher cost of benefits. Conversely, the fund may use a floor of 1% to guarantee a minimum adjustment in periods of low inflation or deflation, thereby protecting beneficiaries' purchasing power.

These instruments are often embedded in inflation-linked bonds (called "linkers") or structured contracts and may be transacted bilaterally or through dealers in specialized OTC markets. National governments issue linkers. In the United States, these bonds are issued by the U.S. Department of the Treasury and are called Treasury Inflation Protection Securities (TIPSs).

While caps and floors outside the interest rate space are often less liquid and less standardized, their purpose remains to limit uncertainty and shape the distribution of possible outcomes. Whether protecting cash flows from inflation surprises, stabilizing commodity prices, or engineering bounded returns in structured notes, these tools play an essential role in modern risk management and investment design.

5.4 Credit Default Swaps: Protecting Against Credit Risk

Among the most widely used instruments for managing credit risk is the CDS. While often referred to as a derivative, a CDS is, in functional terms, an option-like instrument. It protects the buyer against adverse credit events of a particular borrower—typically a corporation or sovereign government—without requiring the buyer to own the underlying bond.

A CDS is a contract between two parties: a protection buyer and a protection seller. The buyer of protection pays a periodic premium (known as the CDS spread) to the seller. In exchange, the seller agrees to compensate the buyer in the event of a credit event, such as default, bankruptcy, or a debt restructuring, affecting a specified reference entity (the bond issuer). If no such event occurs during the term of the contract, the seller keeps the premium and no payment is made.

This type of arrangement is economically similar to a put option: The buyer gains the right to receive payment if there is a credit event covered by the agreement, while the seller assumes this risk in exchange for compensation. However, CDS contracts do not follow the payoff structure of traditional exchange-traded options. While CDS contracts resemble options in their payoff logic, they are negotiated according to standardized templates and terms. Their structural and legal features are addressed later in this book.

CDSs are widely used by institutional investors, banks, and hedge funds to hedge credit risk in bond portfolios or to speculate on changes in creditworthiness. For example, a fund holding corporate bonds may purchase CDS protection to guard against potential defaults, or a trader may buy CDS on a firm perceived to be at increasing risk of a downgrade.

This section provides a simplified overview. Chapter 9 provides a more detailed discussion of CDSs, including their mechanics, pricing, settlement, and regulatory treatment.

CDSs illustrate how derivatives can be used to manage price risk or interest rate risk and isolate and trade credit risk. While the name implies a derivative, their design and purpose align more closely with contingent claims, and they are best understood as part of the broader category of insurance-like, option-based instruments within the derivatives family.

5.4.1 *Illustration: Using a CDS to hedge corporate bond risk*

Suppose a pension fund owns \$10 million in five-year bonds issued by Company A, a large industrial firm. While the fund expects to receive interest payments and the full principal at maturity, it is concerned that a deterioration in Company A's financial condition could lead to default before the bonds mature.

The fund enters into a five-year CDS with a large bank to hedge this credit risk. Under the terms of the CDS contract:

- The pension fund pays the bank a CDS spread of 150 basis points (1.5%) per year, or \$150,000 annually for five years.
- In return, the bank agrees to compensate the fund if Company A defaults on its bonds during the contract term.

If no credit event occurs, the pension fund pays the annual premiums and receives no other cash flows from the swap. But if Company A defaults in year three, the bank compensates the fund, typically by paying the difference between par value and the post-default recovery value of the bonds. For instance, if the bonds are now worth only 40% of face value, the bank would pay 60% of the \$10 million notional, or \$6 million.

This contract has allowed the pension fund to insure against the risk of default without selling the bonds or changing the composition of its portfolio.

5.5 Swaptions: Options on Interest Rate Swaps

A *swaption* is a type of option that gives the holder the right, but not the obligation, to enter into an interest rate swap at a specified future date with predetermined terms. It combines elements of both swaps and options, allowing the buyer to decide later whether to initiate a swap agreement depending on how interest rates evolve.

There are two basic types of swaptions:

- A *payer swaption* gives the holder the right to enter into a swap where they will pay a fixed rate and receive a floating rate.
- A *receiver swaption* gives the holder the right to enter into a swap where they will receive a fixed rate and pay a floating rate.

Swaptions are most commonly used by institutions seeking to hedge or manage future interest rate exposure. For example, a company planning to issue fixed-rate debt in six months might buy a payer swaption. If interest rates rise during that period, the company can exercise the swaption to lock in a favorable fixed rate and reduce borrowing costs. If rates fall, the firm can let the option expire and benefit from lower market rates.

Similarly, pension funds and insurance companies use receiver swaptions to hedge the risk of falling rates, which could lower the value of their fixed-income assets or reduce expected investment income.

This section introduces only the basic concept of swaptions. Swaptions are a crucial tool within the broader category of interest rate derivatives, enabling institutions to incorporate flexibility into their hedging and investment strategies by retaining the option to manage interest rate risk without committing to a swap at present.

5.6 Options on Futures Contracts

Another important class of derivative instruments is the *option on a futures contract*. As the name suggests, this option gives the holder the right, but not the obligation, to buy or sell a specific futures contract at a predetermined price (the strike price) on or before a specified expiration date. Options on futures are used in a wide range of markets, including interest rates, commodities, equity indexes, and currencies.

Like other options, there are two types:

- A call option on a futures contract gives the holder the right to enter into a long position in the underlying futures contract.
- A put option on a futures contract gives the holder the right to enter into a short position in the underlying futures contract.

5.6.1 *The institutional preference for futures options*

Options on futures have become the dominant form of listed options across many asset classes, displacing options written directly on physical instruments. This preference reflects a combination of structural, operational, and strategic advantages that futures-based options offer, particularly in terms of standardization, liquidity, pricing efficiency, and risk management.

A primary factor is the standardization of futures contracts. Futures are exchange-traded instruments with uniform contract terms, including the size, quality, delivery date, and pricing conventions, ensuring that all market participants trade the same product. This uniformity promotes deep, liquid markets ideal for supporting the secondary market in options. In contrast, physical assets such as bonds, commodities, or equities can differ, making them harder to package into uniform option contracts. Illiquidity, varying quality grades, and non-standard settlement practices reduce the effectiveness of physical-based options.

In addition to improving liquidity and transparency, futures options help prevent market manipulation and delivery squeezes, a key concern for institutional investors. A squeeze occurs when the party obligated to deliver the underlying asset under an option or futures contract cannot easily obtain it because it has become scarce or illiquid in the market.[4]

---

[4]The Hunt Brothers (Nelson and William) began aggressively buying physical silver and silver futures in an attempt to corner the market. By early 1980, the price of silver had skyrocketed from around $6 per ounce to nearly $50, largely due to their concentrated buying. Their positions forced others—particularly short sellers in futures contracts—to scramble for delivery, driving prices even higher in what became a classic short squeeze. A notable example of a squeeze in the bond market occurred in the early 1990s, when Salomon Brothers attempted to dominate a U.S. Treasury bond auction by submitting bids

This scarcity can drive up the underlying price, forcing the delivering party to incur substantial losses or fail to meet its obligations. Physical markets—particularly in commodities or off-the-run bonds—are more susceptible to such squeezes due to limited float or fragmented supply. Because futures contracts have ample deliverable supply and are backed by a broad basket of deliverable instruments, options on futures are less vulnerable to such risks. This makes them a safer and more predictable structure for institutional hedging.

Pricing efficiency also favors futures options. Futures prices are quoted continuously during exchange trading hours and benefit from real-time price discovery. This makes the underlying value used to price the option visible and reliable. In contrast, physical assets, especially thinly traded bonds or specialized commodities, may not have continuously updated pricing data, making the valuation of options on those assets more challenging and less precise.

Operationally, futures options are cleaner and simpler to manage. Upon exercise, a futures option creates a futures position at the strike price, which is then marked to market. There is no need for physical delivery, no accrued interest adjustments (as in the case of bond options), and no logistical complexities. Options on physicals, by contrast, can involve complicated delivery procedures, settlement risk, and significant transaction costs. For many institutions, these factors make physical-based options operationally burdensome.

Moreover, the extensive risk management infrastructure surrounding futures contracts—central clearing, daily margining, and regulatory oversight—extends naturally to options on futures. Market participants can manage exposure more efficiently and with greater transparency. The alignment between how hedgers already use futures and how futures options are structured makes these instruments ideal for layering optionality onto existing hedge positions.

For these reasons, futures options have become the preferred vehicle for institutional investors seeking to manage price risk flexibly and precisely. While options on physicals still have a role in specific markets, particularly for equities and certain physical commodities, they are far less common in interest rate, fixed income, and energy markets, where the

---

under multiple customer names. This led to a temporary shortage of deliverable bonds and caused major disruptions in the Treasury market, ultimately resulting in regulatory penalties and changes to auction procedures.

structure of futures options is better suited to institutional scale and complexity.

5.6.2 *Mechanics of exercising a futures option*

Unlike options on physical securities, futures options do not involve delivering an underlying security or commodity when exercised. Instead, when a futures option is exercised, it establishes a futures position at a price equal to the option's strike price. The position is then immediately marked to market, meaning that the buyer and seller of the option are credited or debited with the difference between the current market price of the futures contract and the option's strike price. This process ensures that both parties now hold a futures position at the prevailing market value, rather than at the strike price, but with the appropriate economic benefit of the option built in as an initial gain or loss on the newly created futures position.

To illustrate the mechanics of exercising a futures option, consider a generic commodity futures option, such as one written on crude oil futures. The principles described here apply across various asset classes, including commodities, equities, interest rates, and currencies, wherever options on futures are utilized.

Assume the following:

- *Underlying contract*: crude oil futures
- *Contract size*: 1,000 barrels
- *Option type*: call option
- *Strike price*: $75 per barrel
- *Current futures price*: $78 per barrel
- *Option holder*: buyer of the call
- *Option writer*: seller of the call

Because the current futures price ($78) is higher than the strike price ($75), the option holder chooses to exercise the call futures option. Upon exercise, the option holder is granted a long position in crude oil futures at $75. This is the agreed-upon strike price in the futures option contract.

Immediately after the position is created, it is marked to market against the current price of $78. The difference between the two prices is $3

($78 – $75). Because each futures contract represents 1,000 barrels, the total mark-to-market gain is $3,000 ($3 × 1,000). This $3,000 gain is credited to the buyer of the futures option, and the same amount is debited from the seller (writer) of the futures option, who is now short the futures contract at $75 while the market is trading at $78.

Both parties are now active participants in the futures market. The option holder holds a long position in the futures contract at a price of $75 but has already received the $3,000 difference in cash and is effectively holding the position at market. The option writer holds the opposite short position and has already realized a $3,000 loss through the mark-to-market process. From this point forward, both are subject to daily variation margins, just like any other futures contract participant.

This procedure ensures that futures options are exercised cleanly and efficiently, which is one reason why institutional traders prefer them over options on physical assets that may be illiquid, include interest adjustments, or be prone to settlement complications.

5.7 Summary

In this chapter, I introduced insurance-type derivatives—financial instruments that enable one party to protect against adverse movements in a reference variable by paying a premium in exchange for a potential payout. Unlike the linear, symmetric payoff profiles of forwards, futures, and swaps, the instruments I discussed here, including options, caps, floors, CDSs, swaptions, and options on futures, feature asymmetric payoffs. These allow market participants to transfer risk selectively rather than entirely or proportionally.

I began by explaining the foundational structure of options, distinguishing between calls and puts, and showing how each functions as a contract that grants a right but not an obligation. I illustrated how these contracts allow investors or firms to insure against downside risk or preserve upside opportunity. To ensure accessibility, I deferred technical pricing or modeling discussions to later chapters and focused instead on how options function as practical tools for risk management.

Next, I explored embedded options in bonds and loans, such as callable and puttable bonds, and explained how these options alter the issuer's or holder's exposure to interest rate changes. I emphasized the distinction between these embedded features and externally sourced derivatives in structured products, where issuers use caps, floors, or equity options to create customized return profiles.

I then introduced standalone caps and floors and showed how they operate as a series of option-like payoffs. I walked through several basic numerical illustrations, including interest rate caps and commodity floors, to show how these contracts are structured, how payments are determined, and how they help institutions manage exposure to extreme outcomes. I also described how caps and floors are used beyond interest rate markets, including in inflation-linked instruments and structured investment products.

I explained several advanced but widely used insurance-type derivatives in the final sections. I introduced CDSs as a form of protection against credit events and noted that while CDSs are labeled as swaps, their mechanics and intent resemble those of an option contract. I also described swaptions (i.e., options on interest rate swaps) and explained how these instruments give parties the right to enter into a swap at future dates. I concluded with a discussion of options on futures contracts, describing and illustrating their mechanics and explaining why they are preferred over options on physical assets in many institutional contexts.

Throughout the chapter, I focused on providing a conceptual understanding of how these derivatives reallocate risk, rather than share it, and how market participants use them to cap losses, lock in returns, or transfer specific forms of risk to willing counterparties. This chapter lays the groundwork for later discussions that examine these instruments in more detail within individual asset classes and frameworks.

Chapter 6

Exchange-Traded Derivatives

In this chapter, I examine the structure, mechanics, and applications of exchange-traded derivatives (ETDs) across major asset classes, including equities, interest rates, currencies, commodities, and environmental markets. ETDs operate on standardized contracts supported by centralized exchanges and clearinghouses. This framework provides transparent pricing, uniform margining, daily mark-to-market settlement, and multilateral netting, which reduce counterparty risk and enhance market liquidity.

While the focus here is on the design and strategic use of ETDs, operational details such as margin calculations, collateral management, and liquidity considerations are covered more fully in the chapter on margin and rolling mechanics (Chapter 10). Similarly, the following chapter on OTC derivatives contrasts ETDs with the flexible but more complex structure of bilateral contracts.

I begin by highlighting the key features of ETDs that distinguish them from OTC derivatives. Then, I explore their applications across asset classes, emphasizing how institutional investors, asset managers, and corporate hedgers use these instruments in practice.

6.1 Key Features of Exchange-Traded Derivatives

ETDs share several defining characteristics that make them liquid, transparent, and operationally efficient. These features shape who uses these instruments, how they are applied, and how they interact with the broader financial markets. In this section, I focus on five core elements: contract standardization, centralized trading and execution, central counterparty clearing, margining and daily settlement, and regulatory oversight.

6.1.1 *Standardization of contract terms*

ETDs are built around strict standardization. The terms of each contract, such as contract size, tick size, and tick value, expiration schedule, delivery method, and strike intervals (for options), are set by the exchange and apply uniformly to all participants. This standardization ensures that contracts are fungible and can be traded anonymously on centralized exchanges.

Tick size and tick value are significant for managing risk and trading costs. A tick represents the smallest price movement allowed for a given contract, and the tick value is the monetary gain or loss from a one-tick move. For example, an E-mini S&P 500 futures contract has a tick size of 0.25 index points and a $50 multiplier, so each tick is worth $12.50. A crude oil futures contract, with a tick size of $0.01 per barrel and a 1,000-barrel contract size, has a tick value of $10.00. For Treasury note futures, the tick is 1/32 of a point, and with a $1,000 multiplier, the tick value is $31.25.

Tick values influence market behavior and trading strategies. Larger tick values may discourage high-frequency strategies by reducing price granularity, while smaller tick values tighten spreads but generate more frequent price updates. Exchanges carefully calibrate tick sizes to balance liquidity, volatility, and execution efficiency.

In contrast, over-the-counter (OTC) derivatives are typically customized contracts with bespoke notional amounts, dates, reference assets, or cash flow contingencies. While this flexibility allows precise tailoring for hedging or risk transfer needs, it sacrifices the liquidity and ease of standardization that define ETDs.

6.1.2 *Centralized trading and execution*

ETDs are executed on organized exchanges such as the Chicago Mercantile Exchange (CME), the Chicago Board Options Exchange (CBOE), Eurex, the Intercontinental Exchange (ICE), and the Singapore Exchange (SGX). These venues maintain continuous electronic order books, publish real-time trade prices, and support deep liquidity pools.

Orders are matched using price-time priority, and all participants benefit from transparent pricing and uniform access to market depth.

Conversely, OTC derivatives are negotiated bilaterally via dealer networks or messaging platforms. Market depth, execution speed, and pricing transparency in OTC markets depend heavily on counterparty relationships, and trading can become less efficient during times of stress.

6.1.3 *Margining and daily mark-to-market*

ETDs require participants to post initial and variation margins; all positions are marked to the market daily. This process ensures that gains and losses are settled continuously, preventing the accumulation of large, unsecured exposures.

If the market moves in favor of a position, the gain is credited to the trader's margin account; if it moves against the position, a margin call ensures that losses are promptly covered. This daily settlement cycle preserves the financial integrity of the market and provides confidence that the clearinghouse can absorb a member default.

Chapter 10, which describes margin and rolling mechanics, comprehensively addresses the operational details of margin calculation, collateral types, thresholds, and liquidity management.

6.1.4 *Transparency, liquidity, and regulatory oversight*

Because ETDs trade on centralized exchanges, they offer complete price transparency. Market participants can observe real-time quotes, trading volumes, and order book depth, and exchanges publish historical trade and settlement data. This transparency fosters strong liquidity, allowing large positions to be opened or closed efficiently, even in volatile markets.

ETDs are not only liquid in their own right but also function as benchmarks for pricing and hedging in related cash and OTC markets. For example, U.S. Treasury futures provide reference yields for dealers structuring interest rate swaps, while crude oil futures serve as the pricing basis for customized OTC forwards. Because the exchange environment produce publicly visible order books and continuous settlement prices, market participants can align their valuations and manage exposures against an accepted standard. This benchmark role distinguishes ETDs from customized OTC instruments, where price discovery is often opaque and bilateral.

ETDs also operate under robust regulatory oversight. The Commodity Futures Trading Commission (CFTC) supervises derivatives exchanges and clearinghouses in the U.S. Equity options fall under the jurisdiction of the Securities and Exchange Commission (SEC). The European Securities and Markets Authority (ESMA) and national regulators oversee listed derivatives markets in Europe. Clearinghouses supporting ETDs are considered systemically important and must comply with strict capital, governance, and risk management standards.

Because ETDs concentrate trading in standardized contracts, they mitigate counterparty risk through central clearing. Clearinghouses interpose between buyers and sellers, requiring daily variation margin and maintaining guaranty funds. This system significantly reduces the likelihood of default compared with bilateral OTC arrangements, where exposure depends on the counterparty's creditworthiness.

6.2 Exchange-Traded Equity Options and Futures

Equity exchange-traded derivatives are standardized contracts whose value is tied to the performance of individual stocks or stock market indices.[1] These instruments include stock options, stock index futures, stock index options, and stock index futures options.

6.2.1 *Stock options*

A key feature of stock options is their standardized contract size, which typically represents 100 shares of the underlying stock in most major markets, particularly in the U.S. Strike prices are established at regular intervals relative to the current trading price of the underlying stock, providing investors with a range of choices.

Expiration dates are also critical to contract structure, with available maturities ranging from short-term weekly options to longer-dated contracts. Among these, Long-Term Equity Anticipation Securities

---

[1]In addition to standard monthly expirations, many exchanges now offer *weekly options*, often referred to simply as "weeklies." These are short-dated options that typically expire on Fridays, providing traders with greater precision in managing short-term exposures. Weeklies are available on a wide range of underlying assets, including equity indices and individual stocks.

(LEAPS) are a unique tool for investors seeking extended exposure. LEAPS can have expirations stretching up to three years, making them particularly attractive for strategic positioning, long-term hedging, or building low-capital-cost synthetic equity exposures.

Stock options on individual equities in the U.S. are primarily American-style, meaning they can be exercised at any point up to and including the expiration date. This feature provides greater flexibility than European-style options, which limit exercise to the expiration date. Stock options are generally physically settled, meaning that the actual underlying shares are transferred if the option is exercised rather than being settled in cash. This direct link to the underlying equity enhances the appeal of stock options for investors seeking to manage or adjust their exposure to specific securities.

6.2.2 *Broad-based stock index options*

Stock index options provide portfolio managers with a powerful tool for obtaining exposure to the overall performance of a stock market, specific sectors, or targeted investment factors without the need to hold the individual securities that make up an index. These options are written on broad-based equity indices. They are *cash-settled*, meaning the payoff is determined by the difference between the final index level and the option's strike price at expiration. No shares are exchanged; a cash payment is made to the option holder.

For example, consider a call option on the S&P 500 index with a strike price of 4,900 and a contract multiple of $100. If the index closes at 5,000 on the expiration date, the option finishes in the money by 100 index points (5,000 – 4,900). The cash settlement amount is 100 points × $100 = $10,000. The seller of the option must pay the buyer $10,000 at settlement. If the index finishes at or below the strike price, the option expires worthless, and no cash changes hands.

A defining characteristic of stock index options is the *contract multiple*, which determines the notional exposure of the option contract. The notional value is calculated by multiplying the index level by the contract multiple, using the formula

$$\text{Dollar value of index} = \text{Index level} \times \text{Contract multiple}$$

Among the most actively traded and widely followed index options is the S&P 500 index option, listed on the CBOE. The standard contract has a \$100 multiple, so if the index level is 5,000, the contract represents a notional value of \$500,000 (5,000 × \$100). This high notional value makes standard S&P 500 options essential for institutional investors managing large portfolios, particularly for hedging broad market risk or expressing macro-level views.

To improve market accessibility, especially for smaller institutions and individual investors, exchanges have introduced scaled-down contracts such as the E-mini and micro E-mini index options. For instance, E-mini S&P 500 options have a \$50 contract multiple, cutting the notional value in half to \$250,000 when the index is at 5,000. This version maintains many of the strategic benefits of the standard contract but requires less capital and allows for more flexible position sizing.

Micro E-mini S&P 500 options offer a \$5 contract multiple for even smaller exposure, resulting in a notional value of just \$25,000 at the same index level. These contracts are suitable for retail traders and financial advisors managing smaller portfolios who wish to implement hedging, tactical allocation, or volatility strategies.

Similar sizing structures are available for other major indices. For example, Nasdaq-100 index options are offered in standard, E-mini, and micro E-mini versions, with contract multiples of \$100, \$20, and \$2, respectively. These contracts expose the tech-heavy Nasdaq-100 index and are popular among traders targeting growth-oriented sectors. Russell 2000 index options, which grant access to the small-cap segment of the U.S. equity market, are also available in multiple sizes, with a \$100 contract multiple for the standard version and with \$50 and \$5 for the E-mini and micro E-mini versions, respectively.

6.2.3 *Broad-based stock index futures*

Broad-based stock index futures provide exposure to the performance of major equity indices and are settled in cash based on the difference between the agreed-upon contract price and the actual index level at expiration. There is no delivery of the underlying securities. Instead, the contract is marked to market daily, and final settlement is made in cash at expiration. Each contract has a contract multiple that determines its notional value by multiplying the index level by a fixed dollar amount.

The S&P 500 futures contract uses a \$250 contract multiple. For example, if a trader enters a long position in the S&P 500 futures for

4,950 and the index settles at 5,000 on the expiration date, the gain is 50 index points. The final cash settlement amount would be 50 points × \$250 = \$12,500. The long position holder receives \$12,500, while the short holder pays the same amount. Conversely, if the index settles below 4,950, the long would incur a loss.

Due to its high notional exposure, this contract is widely used by institutional investors managing large portfolios. When the S&P 500 is at 5,000, a single standard contract represents \$1,250,000 in notional value (5,000 × \$250).

The CME introduced the E-mini S&P 500 futures with a \$50 contract multiple to accommodate a broader spectrum of market participants. At the same index level of 5,000, the notional value is \$250,000 per contract. These contracts retain deep liquidity and near-continuous trading access and have become the most widely traded equity index futures globally.

For even greater accessibility and position granularity, Micro E-mini S&P 500 futures were introduced with a \$5 contract multiple, yielding a notional value of \$25,000 when the index is at 5,000. These contracts allow retail investors and financial advisors to manage equity index exposure with smaller capital commitments and finer risk control while benefiting from exchange-traded futures' clearing, transparency, and margin efficiency.

Other major U.S. equity indices also offer broad-based futures contracts with similar tiered structures. The Nasdaq-100 futures track the technology-heavy index and are available in standard, E-mini, and micro E-mini versions, with contract multiples of \$100, \$20, and \$2, respectively. The DJIA futures, which follow a 30-stock blue-chip index, use a multiple of \$10 times the index level for the standard contract and \$5 times the index level for the E-mini. For small-cap equity exposure, Russell 2000 futures are offered with multiples of \$50 and \$5 for the E-mini and micro E-mini contracts, respectively.

6.2.4 *Stock index options and futures in U.S. sectors*

Stock index options and futures tied to U.S. sector indices allow investors to target specific areas of the economy. These instruments offer portfolio managers a flexible and efficient way to manage risk or gain exposure to sectors such as technology, healthcare, financials, energy, utilities, and industrials. Each sector contract tracks a corresponding S&P 500 sector index, enabling investors to tailor their strategies to the performance of a particular industry group.

On the futures side, sector exposure is available through E-mini S&P 500 sector futures contracts, each tied to a different sector index. These contracts include the E-mini S&P 500 Technology, Healthcare, Energy, Financials, Utilities, and Industrials futures. They all use a $50 contract multiplier and are cash-settled, allowing for leveraged exposure to their respective sectors without requiring ownership of the underlying equities.

Options on the corresponding S&P 500 sector indices are also available. These contracts include S&P 500 sector index options on the Technology, Healthcare, Energy, Financials, Utilities, and Industrials indices. They each use a $100 contract multiplier and follow European-style exercise, meaning they can only be exercised at expiration. This exercise structure supports a more strategic use of options for risk management and macro-sector positioning, rather than short-term trading.

For example, a portfolio manager looking to hedge against potential weakness in the technology sector might purchase put options on the S&P 500 Technology Sector Index. If the index falls below the strike price at expiration, the cash settlement reflects the difference. Suppose the strike price is 2,500 and the index settles at 2,400. The put option holder would receive (2,500 – 2,400) × $100 = $10,000 in cash. Alternatively, a trader who expects the healthcare sector to outperform might purchase call options on the S&P 500 Healthcare Sector Index. If the index closes above the strike at expiration, the trader will receive the corresponding cash difference, scaled by the $100 multiplier.

Sector-specific derivatives offer several advantages. They allow for targeted exposure without assembling a basket of individual stocks. For example, rather than buying and maintaining a portfolio of S&P 500 financial stocks, a portfolio manager can take a single position in the financials futures contract or the corresponding index option. These derivatives also enable capital efficiency through leverage, requiring only a fraction of the capital needed to replicate the same exposure via cash equities. Moreover, sector contracts in actively traded segments such as technology and financial services offer high liquidity, facilitating efficient trade execution with narrow bid-ask spreads.

Sector-specific derivatives also pose challenges. Liquidity is not uniform across sectors, and some less prominent sectors may trade infrequently or with wider spreads, making it difficult to execute large orders efficiently. There is also correlation risk: Although sector derivatives aim to isolate sector-level movements, broader market forces often influence multiple sectors simultaneously, which can reduce the precision of hedging or performance targeting strategies.

6.2.5 *Stock index futures and options based on investment factors*

Stock index futures and options tied to investment factors such as value and growth form a specialized subset of equity derivatives that enable precise exposure to distinct investment styles or risk premia. These instruments are linked to indices that classify stocks based on fundamental characteristics, allowing investors to access factor-based strategies efficiently without the need to assemble and manage individual security portfolios. As factor-based investing has gained traction among institutional and retail investors alike, the availability and importance of these contracts have grown significantly.

Several of this category's most widely used futures contracts are based on value and growth indices constructed from the S&P 500, Russell 1000, and Russell 2000 universes. For example, the E-mini S&P 500 Growth Futures and E-mini S&P 500 Value Futures provide leveraged exposure to the S&P 500's growth and value segments. Each contract carries a $50 contract multiplier and is cash-settled. These contracts are traded on the CME and offer quarterly expirations, making them suitable for managing strategic exposure to large-cap U.S. equity factors.

Investors seeking exposure to large-cap growth or value beyond the S&P 500 also turn to the Russell 1000 Growth Futures and Russell 1000 Value Futures, each using a $100 contract multiplier. These contracts provide efficient tools for implementing directional views or hedging portfolios tilted toward growth or value. For those focused on small-cap equities, the E-mini Russell 2000 Growth Futures and E-mini Russell 2000 Value Futures, also traded on the CME with $50 multipliers, offer tactical exposure to growth and value within the small-cap segment of the U.S. market.

In parallel, options on these factor indices are available with European-style exercise and are also cash-settled, making them particularly well-suited for institutional use. For instance, options on the S&P 500 Growth Index and S&P 500 Value Index use a $100 contract multiplier, allowing investors to hedge or speculate on the performance of either style. Similar contracts exist for the Russell 1000 Growth and Value Indices and MSCI USA Growth and Value Indices, giving investors access to various methodologies and market segments. These options are commonly used for relative value trades, hedging factor exposure, or implementing volatility-based strategies tied to market sentiment surrounding growth versus value.

The appeal of factor-based derivatives lies in their precision and efficiency. Instead of constructing a basket of value or growth stocks, portfolio managers can achieve targeted exposure with a single contract. This reduces transaction costs and implementation complexity, enhancing portfolio flexibility. For example, an investor expecting value stocks to outperform growth might take a long futures position in the S&P 500 Value Index and a short position in the S&P 500 Growth Index, or execute a similar strategy using call options on the value index and call options on the growth index in opposing directions. These pair trades are increasingly used to express macroeconomic views or to take advantage of mean-reversion dynamics between factors.

Futures on factor-based indices function similarly to traditional stock index futures, with notional exposure determined by multiplying the index level by the contract multiplier. For instance, if the S&P 500 Value Index is trading at 1,800, the notional value of a corresponding E-mini futures contract would be $90,000 (1,800 × $50). At expiration, these futures are settled in cash, with the gain or loss based on the difference between the contract price and the final index level. This makes them an efficient tool for both directional exposure and hedging.

6.2.6 *Non-U.S. stock index futures and options*

Non-U.S. stock index futures and options are essential tools for portfolio managers and traders who seek to gain exposure to global equity markets. These instruments offer a flexible, efficient, and cost-effective way to manage international risk, implement macro views, or diversify equity allocations across regions such as Europe, Asia, Australia, and emerging markets. By using these derivatives, investors can gain broad or targeted international exposure without directly purchasing the underlying foreign securities.

One of the most widely used international equity derivatives is the Euro STOXX 50 futures contract, which tracks the performance of 50 blue-chip companies across 11 eurozone countries. This contract is traded on Eurex and uses a €10 contract multiplier, offering a liquid and efficient way to hedge or gain exposure to European large-cap equities. The corresponding Euro STOXX 50 index options, also traded on Eurex and using the same €10 multiplier, are commonly used by institutions to manage risk or capitalize on volatility within the European equity market.

Another key European product is the FTSE 100 Index futures contract, traded on ICE Futures Europe, which provides exposure to the U.K.'s 100 largest publicly traded companies. The FTSE 100 futures, which also use a €10 multiplier, is frequently used for both hedging and speculative purposes related to the U.K. equity market. Meanwhile, for those focused on Germany specifically, DAX futures contracts, also offered on Eurex, track the DAX Index and use a larger €25 contract multiplier, making them a central tool for investors managing exposure to Germany's leading stocks.

In Asia, regional markets are represented by several essential contracts. The Nikkei 225 futures, traded on the Osaka Stock Exchange (OSE), offer exposure to Japan's largest and most prominent companies. These contracts are denominated in Japanese yen and use a ¥1,000 multiplier, making them particularly popular among investors who need access to Japan's equity market with scale and precision. Investors targeting Hong Kong can use the Hang Seng Index futures, traded on the Hong Kong Futures Exchange (HKFE), which use a HK$50 multiplier and track the performance of Hong Kong's key listed companies.

India is represented through the Nifty 50 Index futures, traded on the National Stock Exchange of India (NSE). These contracts use a ₹50 multiplier and provide broad-based exposure to India's top 50 companies across various industries.

For Australian equity exposure, investors can trade SPI 200 futures based on the S&P/ASX 200 Index and traded on the Australian Securities Exchange (ASX). These contracts use an A$25 multiplier and offer efficient access to Australia's top 200 listed companies.

In emerging markets, investors can access broad regional exposure through the MSCI Emerging Markets Index futures, traded on the CME. These contracts use a $50 multiplier, representing a basket of large- and mid-cap companies across more than two dozen developing economies. They are especially popular for hedging or tactical positioning related to macroeconomic developments in emerging regions. For more focused exposure to China, the FTSE China A50 Index futures, traded on the

Singapore Exchange (SGX), track the 50 largest A-share companies listed in mainland China. These contracts use a $1 multiplier and provide highly targeted access to a critical segment of China's domestic equity market.

Structurally, non-U.S. stock index futures and options are similar to their U.S. counterparts. They feature standardized contract terms, initial and maintenance margin requirements, and are typically cash-settled. Most contracts are listed on well-regulated exchanges, ensuring transparency and reducing counterparty risk. However, global investors must also account for differences in regulatory environments, contract specifications, currency denominations, and trading hours, which may impact liquidity and strategy execution. For example, while U.S. contracts are dollar-denominated and follow U.S. market hours, European and Asian contracts are priced in euros, yen, or local currencies and trade in alignment with their respective regional market hours.

6.2.7 *Options on stock index futures*

Options on stock index futures are exchange-traded contracts that grant the holder the right, but not the obligation, to enter into a long or short position in a stock index futures contract at a specified strike price. These options do not settle into the underlying stock index but the associated futures contract. The futures position, in turn, is cash-settled at expiration based on the underlying index level. This layered structure (i.e., an option that settles into a futures contract that is itself cash-settled) adds complexity to the instrument's mechanics and distinguishes it from standard stock index options.

Each option corresponds to a specific broad-based stock index futures contract, such as those on the S&P 500, Nasdaq-100, Russell 2000, or DJIA. The most traded versions are listed on the CME and are available in standard, E-mini, and micro E-mini formats, depending on the size and liquidity preferences of the investor.

Like the futures contracts on which they are written, these options are structured around a contract multiple. For instance, the standard S&P 500 futures option has a $250 contract multiple. If the strike price of a call option is 4,900 and the futures price at expiration is 5,000, the resulting futures position is 100 index points in the money. The futures contract would be cash-settled at a gain of 100 index points × $250 = $25,000.

This is the value of the underlying futures contract at settlement, assuming the option is exercised and the position is held through expiration. Note that the option itself is not directly cash-settled based on the index; it first creates a futures position at the strike price, which is then marked to market and ultimately cash-settled.

Stock index futures options are typically American-style, meaning they can be exercised at any point up to expiration. Upon exercise, a futures position is established at the option's strike price, subject to daily variation margin. If this position is not offset before the futures contract expires, it is cash-settled based on the final value of the index on the expiration date.

Contract sizing mirrors that of the underlying futures. For example, the E-mini S&P 500 futures option has a $50 contract multiple, while the micro E-mini version uses a $5 multiple. These scaled options allow for more precise exposure. A micro E-mini call option on the S&P 500 futures with a strike of 4,900, exercised when the futures price is 5,000, would lead to a futures gain of 100 index points × $5 = $500.

The same scaling structure is available for other major equity index futures. Nasdaq-100 futures options use $20 for the E-mini and $2 for the micro E-mini version. Russell 2000 futures options follow a $50 multiple for E-mini contracts and $5 for micro E-minis. These variations allow institutional and retail investors to fine-tune their exposure to broad-based equity index movements via the futures market.

In contrast to standard stock index options, where exercise leads to a cash payout based on the difference between the strike price and the final index level, options on stock index futures result in a futures position that itself follows the cash-settlement procedure. As a result, understanding the mechanics of both the option and the underlying futures contract is essential when working with these instruments.

Because index option prices embed the market's implied volatility, exchanges also list volatility index futures and options derived from those option prices; I turn to those next.

6.2.8 *Volatility index futures and options*

Volatility is the day-to-day variability of market prices. It sets expectations for how widely returns can swing over a month or a quarter and feeds two basic controls: (1) a risk budget, which is the amount of loss or volatility a portfolio is allowed to take; and (2) position sizing, which is how large each trade is set to ensure its potential loss stays within that budget. Because volatility also affects the cost of protection and how close a portfolio may come to risk limits, it is useful to observe and, when needed, trade the market's view of near-term volatility.

6.2.8.1 *Volatility indexes*

The best-known volatility measure for U.S. equities is the Chicago Board Option Exchange's volatility index, abbreviated VIX and often called the market's "fear gauge." In strict terms, the nickname applies to the index, which is built from S&P 500 option prices and summarizes the market's forward-looking view of volatility over roughly the next 30 days. The listed derivatives tied to it are the VIX futures and VIX options (which are options on VIX futures rather than on the spot index). Other families of stock index volatility indices exist as well, including the Nasdaq-100 volatility index (VXN), the Russell 2000 volatility index (RVX), and the Dow Jones volatility index (VXD). There are "VIX-style" measures for other asset classes, such as crude oil (OVX), gold (GVZ), and euro FX (EVZ).

Volatility derivatives directly expose implied volatility, not index price levels. Implied volatility is the market's forward-looking assessment of uncertainty embedded in option prices at a point in time; unlike realized volatility (computed from past returns), it is inferred from current option premiums and reflects prevailing expectations (see Chapter 11 for background on implied volatility). Exchanges summarize this option-implied uncertainty in volatility indices that represent a constant-maturity, 30-day measure of annualized volatility, calculated from a broad strip of index options (i.e., a wide set of calls and puts across many strike prices and the two nearest expirations around 30 days) combined into a single 30-day figure. The index is not a tradable asset or a price level but a statistic.

The index is quoted in percentage points. Thus, a reading of 16 means 16% annualized implied volatility over roughly the next 30 days. To translate an annualized figure into a one-month standard deviation, use the square-root-of-time rule:

$$\text{Volatility over } t \text{ years} \approx \text{Annual volatility} \times \sqrt{t}$$

For a month, take $t \approx 1/12$. Thus, $16\% \times \sqrt{1/12} \approx 4.6\%$.

Treat this as what today's option prices imply, not as a promise about what will actually occur.

6.2.8.2 *Volatility futures*

A volatility futures contract is a cash-settled agreement on the volatility index's special settlement value for a specific expiration date.[2] That is, there is no delivery of an asset at the contract's settlement date; instead, the contract pays the difference between the party's entry price and the final settlement value, multiplied by the exchange's contract size. For example, if a front-month volatility futures contract is traded at 17.50 today and the exchange's special settlement value on expiration morning is 18.20, a long position earns 0.70 points times the contract multiplier; a short position loses the same amount.

Like other listed futures in this chapter, volatility futures are margined and mark-to-market daily. That means gains or losses are credited or debited to the party's margin account each day as the futures price moves, not just at expiry. For example, buy one contract at 17.50; if the exchange settlement price at day-end is 18.00, the day's profit is 0.50 points times the contract multiplier and is added to the investor's margin balance. If the next day the price closes at 17.20, 0.80 points are debited. These daily cash flows continue until the investor closes the position or reach expiration, when the final cash settlement occurs.

6.2.8.3 *Options on volatility futures*

Exchange-traded options on volatility are almost always European-style (exercised only at expiration) and cash-settled (no assets change hands; the exchange pays or collects cash). Importantly, these options are written on the volatility futures contract, not on the spot volatility index. As a result, the payoff is determined by where the relevant futures contract settles at expiration, compared with the option's strike price.[3]

---

[2]To settle the futures contract cleanly, the exchange defines a special settlement value: a one-time, official index reading computed by a fixed method at a fixed time on the contract's expiration morning (often called the "special opening quotation," or SOQ). It's built from opening prices of the relevant index options on that morning and follows a published formula.

[3]Options on futures come in two settlement styles. In many markets, when it is worthwhile for the option buyer to exercise, that part gets a futures position at the strike price, gains/losses thereafter occur through daily variation margin on that futures contract. Other contracts are cash-settled at expiration, paying the difference between the futures' final

Suppose the nearest-expiring volatility futures are trading at 17.5 today and an option has a 20 strike. For a call option, the payout occurs at expiration only if the futures settlement value ends above 20. If the futures settle at 23.0, for example, the call pays the difference. In our example, 23.0 – 20.0 = 3.0 points in cash (scaled by the exchange's contract size). If the futures settle at 20.0 or lower, the call pays nothing. A put option works the same way in the opposite direction: It pays at expiration when the futures settle below the strike by the amount of the strike minus settlement.

6.3 Exchange-Traded Interest Rate Derivatives

Interest rate derivatives are financial instruments whose value is linked to movements in interest rates. They are widely used by institutional investors, banks, asset managers, and corporations to control interest rate risk, speculate on changes in interest rates, or arbitrage price differences across the yield curve. The most active exchange-traded interest-rate derivatives in the U.S. are listed on the CME.

Among the most historically important and widely traded interest-rate derivatives were Eurodollar futures and options, which allow participants to take positions on three-month U.S. dollar London Interbank Offered Rate (LIBOR) interest rates over a series of quarterly maturities. For decades, these contracts formed the backbone of short-term interest rate trading. However, Eurodollar futures have been phased out as part of the global transition away from LIBOR, which was found vulnerable to manipulation and lacking a sufficient volume of underlying transactions to support its integrity as a benchmark rate. In its place, regulators and markets have adopted the Secured Overnight Financing Rate (SOFR) as the preferred U.S. dollar risk-free benchmark rate, prompting a migration of short-term interest rate trading to SOFR-based instruments.[4]

---

settlement price and the strike (no futures position is created). The volatility options described in this section are European-style and cash-settled; they do not leave a futures position at expiry.

[4]The federal funds futures contract will also not be discussed here. That contract, formerly one of the key instruments for trading and hedging expectations about the U.S. Federal Reserve's target rate, has been largely phased out in favor of the SOFR futures.

This section focuses on the key exchange-traded interest rate derivatives that continue to serve as essential tools for managing interest rate risk in today's markets. Each instrument discussed below represents a different point on the yield curve or a distinct method of gaining exposure to short-term and long-term interest rates, and each has its own unique structure, trading characteristics, and market applications.

6.3.1 *Three-month SOFR futures*

Three-month SOFR futures are cash-settled futures contracts based on SOFR, the benchmark replacement for U.S. dollar LIBOR. SOFR is a broad measure of the cost of borrowing cash overnight, collateralized by U.S. Treasury securities in the repurchase agreement (repo) market. Published daily by the Federal Reserve Bank of New York, SOFR is fully transaction-based, reflecting actual trades rather than estimates, and is considered a robust and transparent benchmark for short-term interest rates.

These futures are listed on the CME and are designed to represent the market's expectations for average daily SOFR over three months. The contracts are similar in structure to the now-phased-out Eurodollar futures, but instead of being based on LIBOR, they are tied to SOFR, compounded daily over the contract term.

The price of a three-month SOFR futures contract is quoted as 100 minus the expected compounded average of SOFR for the contract's three-month period. For example, if the expected average SOFR over the term is 5.00%, the contract would trade for 95.00.

Each contract represents a $25 million notional value over three months. The minimum price fluctuation is 0.0025 points, which equates to $6.25 per tick. These contracts are cash-settled, with final settlement based on the compounded average SOFR, calculated daily by the CME for the specified contract period.

To illustrate how settlement works, suppose a trader buys a December three-month SOFR futures contract for 94.95, implying an expected average SOFR of 5.05% over the contract period. If the actual compounded average SOFR turns out to be 4.90% by the end of the three-month term, then the contract settles at 95.10%. The change in value is 0.15 points (95.10 – 94.95), resulting in a gain of $375 (0.15 ÷ 0.0025 = 60 ticks; 60 × $6.25 = $375) per contract.

6.3.2 *U.S. Treasury futures*

U.S. Treasury futures are among the world's most actively traded and widely used interest-rate derivatives. These standardized contracts offer investors an efficient and liquid means of gaining exposure to U.S. government debt and managing interest rate risk across various points along the yield curve. Traded on the CBOT, Treasury futures allow market participants to hedge fixed-income portfolios, implement yield curve strategies, or take directional views on changes in interest rates.

Each contract is tied to a particular segment of the yield curve, with futures available on 2-year, 5-year, 10-year, and 30-year maturities, along with "ultra" versions that provide tighter duration targeting. Treasury futures are physically settled, meaning the short position delivers a U.S. Treasury security to the long position at expiration. However, rather than being tied to a single security, each contract allows for the delivery of a range of qualifying Treasury securities that meet specific maturity criteria. This flexibility helps maintain liquidity and market depth while enabling alignment with the structure of the underlying cash Treasury market.

6.3.2.1 *Overview of Treasury futures contracts*

Each U.S. Treasury futures contract is based on a standard notional value of \$100,000 and is physically settled by delivering an eligible U.S. Treasury note or bond. The deliverable securities vary by contract type and are defined based on their remaining time to maturity at the start of the delivery month. Table 6.1 outlines the deliverable criteria for each major contract.

Because each futures contract allows delivery of multiple eligible Treasury securities, which can vary in coupon rate and maturity, the actual market value of each bond will differ. The exchange uses a conversion factor system to ensure fair and standardized settlement regardless of which bond is delivered. The conversion factor adjusts the invoice price to reflect the theoretical value of each deliverable bond, assuming a constant yield of 6% per year, compounded semiannually. This adjustment ensures that no deliverable bond is unfairly advantaged or disadvantaged during the delivery process. The CME publishes the official conversion factors for each eligible security associated with a contract for a given future.

Table 6.1. Deliverable Criteria for Each Treasury Futures

Contract Name	Eligible Deliverable Issues
2-Year Treasury Note Futures	Treasury notes with 1 year to 2 years 3 months remaining maturity
5-Year Treasury Note Futures	Treasury notes with 4 years 2 months to 5 years 3 months remaining maturity
10-Year Treasury Note Futures	Treasury notes with 6.5 to 10 years remaining maturity
Ultra 10-Year Note Futures	Treasury notes with 9 years 5 months to 10 years remaining maturity
30-Year Treasury Bond Futures	Treasury bonds with original and remaining maturity of at least 15 years
Ultra Treasury Bond Futures	Treasury bonds with original and remaining maturity of at least 25 years

6.3.2.2 *Mechanics of U.S. Treasury futures*

While U.S. Treasury futures are among the most liquid and widely used interest-rate derivatives, their structure is more complex than that of typical exchange-traded contracts. This added complexity stems primarily from their physical delivery requirements, which introduce elements beyond simply forecasting interest rate movements. Unlike cash-settled contracts, where final settlement is based on a single reference rate or index value, Treasury futures are settled through the delivery of actual U.S. Treasury securities selected from a defined basket of eligible bonds or notes.

This framework gives rise to several important mechanics that influence how these contracts trade, particularly as they approach expiration. Chief among these is the set of delivery options granted to short positions. Understanding these delivery rights is essential to appreciating how Treasury futures function in practice.

Beyond the delivery options themselves, market participants must also consider which bond the short will deliver, referred to as the cheapest-to-deliver (CTD). This designation can shift over time due to changing yield curve conditions and relative pricing in the cash market. Identifying the CTD security is central to accurately pricing futures contracts and managing associated risks.

Finally, the delivery value is settled through a standardized invoice price that adjusts for differences across deliverable securities. This calculation incorporates both a conversion factor, set by the exchange, and any accrued interest owed on the delivered bond.

Each component—the delivery option, the determination of the CTD security, and the invoice price—plays a critical role in the behavior and valuation of U.S. Treasury futures. Below, we explain each.

Delivery Options: A unique feature of U.S. Treasury futures is the set of delivery options granted exclusively to the short position—the party obligated to deliver a Treasury security at contract expiration. These options provide meaningful flexibility and economic value to the short while introducing delivery uncertainty for the long, who must accept whatever security is chosen for delivery, whenever the short elects to make it, within the rules of the contract.

The first delivery option concerns the choice of which Treasury security to deliver. Each futures contract permits delivery from various U.S. Treasury issues that meet specific eligibility criteria. For example, the 10-year Treasury note futures contract allows delivery of any Treasury note with a remaining maturity between 6.5 and 10 years as of the first day of the delivery month. The bonds eligible for delivery vary in coupon rate, price, and accrued interest. The short, aiming to minimize the cost of fulfilling the delivery obligation, naturally selects the most economically advantageous bond. This flexibility is commonly referred to as the quality option and allows the short to deliver the bond that results in the most favorable economic outcome under prevailing market conditions.

In addition to selecting the security, the short also determines the timing of delivery. Treasury futures contracts specify a delivery month—typically March, June, September, or December—during which the short may deliver on any business day. This timing option allows the short to observe interest rate movements and bond price fluctuations throughout the month and choose to deliver on the most beneficial date. Suppose market conditions become less favorable as the delivery month progresses. In that case, the short may accelerate delivery to mitigate loss or delay delivery if there is an expectation that conditions will improve.

A third, less widely known delivery right is the "wildcard" option. This option arises from the structure of the Treasury futures market, where the daily settlement price is established at 2:00 p.m. Eastern Time, when the futures market closes. However, the cash Treasury market remains open for trading until 5:00 p.m. During this window, the short knows the fixed settlement price of the futures contract but can still observe changes in the market prices of deliverable securities. Suppose the cash market price of the deliverable bond declines relative to the settlement price. In that case, the short may find it advantageous to issue a delivery notice and lock in a favorable transaction. If the market moves unfavorably, the short can wait and reevaluate the next day. This timing flexibility gives the short an additional source of option value and is particularly significant during periods of heightened interest rate volatility or unusual market movements.

Together, these three delivery options (i.e., the choice of which bond to deliver, the timing of delivery within the month, and the ability to act after the futures close but before the cash market closes) give the short a strategic advantage and must be taken into account when evaluating the cost and risk associated with holding a long or short position in Treasury futures. These embedded options add a layer of complexity to the contracts and are a key reason U.S. Treasury futures behave differently from simple cash-settled futures contracts. Understanding these mechanics is essential for interpreting price behavior, managing basis risk, and designing effective interest rate strategies using Treasury futures.

Determination of the Cheapest to Deliver: When a U.S. Treasury futures contract approaches expiration, one of the most important decisions faced by the short position is determining which eligible security is the cheapest to deliver. Although the contract permits delivery of any Treasury issue that meets the maturity requirements, the short will always aim to deliver the bond that minimizes the cost of satisfying the delivery obligation. This concept, referred to as the CTD, is central to the economics of Treasury futures and has important implications for how the contracts are priced and used in practice.

In simple terms, the CTD is the one that provides the short the most favorable financial outcome when the futures position is settled. Because each eligible bond differs in its coupon rate, market price, and accrued interest, some deliverable securities will be more costly to acquire and deliver than others. The short evaluates all eligible bonds and selects the one for which the market price, after adjusting for the futures invoice price and any accrued interest, results in the smallest net cost. From the short's perspective, this decision is analogous to choosing the least expensive tool from a toolbox that all perform the same function of fulfilling the delivery requirement.

The identity of the CTD is not fixed throughout the contract's life. It can shift as market interest rates, bond prices, and yield spreads change. For instance, if yields rise, longer-duration bonds may decline in value more sharply than shorter-duration ones, potentially making them cheaper to deliver. Alternatively, if high-coupon bonds become relatively undervalued due to market dislocations, they might become the cheapest option. As a result, traders continuously monitor relative value relationships among deliverable securities, particularly in the weeks leading up to the delivery month, to anticipate which bond is likely to be delivered.

Calculation of the Invoice Price: The final payment in a U.S. Treasury futures contract is determined by the invoice price, which is the amount the long must pay the short upon delivery of the underlying Treasury security. Because each futures contract allows for delivery of multiple eligible bonds or notes (each with different coupon rates, maturities, and market prices), the invoice price must adjust for these differences to ensure a fair and standardized settlement process. This adjustment is accomplished through a conversion factor which normalizes the value of all deliverable securities.

The conversion factor is a standardized value assigned to each eligible bond by the exchange. It represents the hypothetical price of that bond if it were to yield exactly 6% annually, with semiannual compounding. In essence, the conversion factor scales the futures price to reflect differences in the characteristics of the bond delivered. The conversion factor ensures that a high-coupon bond is not unfairly favored over a low-coupon bond simply because it pays more interest. Instead, it creates a level playing field so that any deliverable security can be fairly used to settle the contract.

To determine the invoice price, the futures settlement price, quoted as a percentage of the \$100,000 notional contract size, is multiplied by the conversion factor corresponding to the Treasury issue being delivered. Any accrued interest on the bond then increases the resulting amount since its last coupon payment date. This ensures that the short is compensated for interest earned while holding the bond and that the long receives a bond that is economically equivalent to its market value.

The general formula for calculating the invoice price is

$$\text{Invoice price} = (\text{Futures settlement price} \times \$100{,}000 \times \text{Conversion factor}) + \text{Accrued interest}$$

For example, suppose a trader is long one 10-year Treasury note futures contract, and the short chooses to deliver a bond with a conversion factor of 0.9525. On the day of delivery, the futures settlement price is 96-16, which translates to 96.5% of the notional contract value, or \$96,500. Additionally, suppose the accrued interest at delivery is \$1,350. The invoice price is calculated by multiplying the futures price by the conversion factor and adding the accrued interest. In this case, the calculation would be

$$\begin{aligned}\text{Invoice price} &= \$96{,}500 \times 0.9525 + \$1{,}350 = \$91{,}916 + \$1{,}350\\ &= \$93{,}266\end{aligned}$$

This is the total amount the long must pay the short to receive the delivered bond. The calculation ensures that regardless of which eligible bond is delivered, the financial exchange between the parties reflects a fair approximation of its value, adjusted for coupon, time to maturity, and accrued interest.

Options on Treasury Securities: Exchange-traded options on U.S. Treasury securities provide investors with the right, but not the obligation, to buy or sell a specific Treasury bond or note at a predetermined price. These options are written directly on Treasury securities. That is, the option's underlying asset is a specific U.S. Treasury bond or note.

These options are listed on exchanges such as NYSE American Options, allowing for either call or put positions on individual Treasury issues. If exercised, the transaction involves the physical delivery of the underlying Treasury security rather than cash settlement. The seller of the option must be prepared to deliver or receive the specific Treasury issue if assigned. The contract size typically corresponds to the \$100,000 face value of the Treasury security, matching the standard trading unit in institutional fixed-income markets.

Despite their standardized format and listing on regulated exchanges, options on Treasury securities are thinly traded and rarely used in practice. Their limited liquidity makes them less suitable for institutional hedging or speculative strategies. As a result, they play a relatively minor role in the broader interest rate derivatives market. Most market participants seeking options to U.S. interest rates prefer the more liquid and flexible options on Treasury futures, which allow for efficient exposure to specific points on the yield curve and are tied to contracts with active trading volumes, standardized durations, and streamlined delivery procedures.

Next, we describe options on Treasury futures, which are functionally similar but built on futures contracts and offer deeper liquidity, more flexible risk management, and broader institutional use.

Options on Treasury Futures: Options on Treasury futures are standardized derivative contracts that provide the holder with the right, but not the obligation, to enter a position in a corresponding U.S. Treasury futures contract at a predetermined price, known as the strike price. These options are traded on the CBOT. They are available for each major U.S. Treasury futures contract, including those based on 2-year, 5-year, 10-year, and 30-year Treasury securities and their ultra variants. While the options themselves do not involve the delivery of Treasury securities, they are physically linked to the Treasury futures market, meaning that if exercised and held to expiration, they can result in physical settlement through the delivery mechanism of the underlying futures contract.

Structure and Mechanics of Treasury Futures Options: Each option on a Treasury futures contract corresponds to a specific underlying futures contract with a notional value of $100,000. Treasury futures options are available as call or put contracts. A call option grants the holder the right to establish a long position in the underlying futures contract at the strike price, while a put option grants the right to establish a short position. These options are American style, meaning they can be exercised any time before expiration, and most contracts expire shortly before the first notice day of the underlying futures contract.

Options are quoted in points and fractions of 1/64th of a point. Since one full point equals $1,000 (representing 1% of the $100,000 notional amount), each tick (1/64th of a point) represents a value of $15.625. Upon exercise, the buyer of a call or put is assigned a position in the Treasury futures contract at the option's strike price. The counterparty to this transaction, the option writer, assumes the opposite futures position at the same price.

The key distinction between options on Treasury securities and options on Treasury futures is that, upon exercise, Treasury futures options create a futures position, not a claim to the underlying bond or note itself. However, if that futures position is held through to expiration, the party becomes subject to the physical delivery process of the futures contract. This includes the potential to deliver or receive an eligible

Treasury security, depending on whether the party is short or long in the futures market.

Delivery in the futures market involves the short selecting a deliverable Treasury issue, subject to eligibility criteria. The delivered security is invoiced using a price derived from the final futures settlement price, adjusted by a conversion factor published by the exchange and increased by accrued interest on the delivered bond. Thus, exercising a Treasury futures option can lead to an eventual physical delivery obligation or receipt of a Treasury security if not offset.

To illustrate how a Treasury futures option functions in practice, consider a call option on the 30-year Treasury bond futures contract. Suppose the option has a strike price of 120-00. If the holder exercises the option, they establish a long position in the Treasury bond futures contract at 120-00, equivalent to 120% of par, or $120,000.

Assume the futures settlement price on the delivery date is 122-16, corresponding to 122.5% of par, or $122,500. The short in the futures market selects an eligible Treasury bond with a conversion factor of 0.9500, and the accrued interest on that bond at the time of delivery is $1,500.

The invoice price is calculated using

$$\text{Invoice price} = \text{Futures settlement price} \times \text{Conversion factor} + \text{Accrued interest}$$

In this case:

Futures settlement price = $122,500
Conversion factor = 0.9500
Accrued interest = $1,500

Applying the formula:

$$\text{Invoice price} = \$122{,}500 \times 0.9500 + \$1{,}500 = \$117{,}875$$

This is the amount the long futures holder (who originally exercised the call option) must pay to the short futures position to receive the delivered Treasury bond. The delivered security is chosen by the short from among those eligible, according to the delivery terms of the Treasury futures contract. The conversion factor adjusts the invoice price to reflect differences in coupon and maturity, and the accrued interest ensures that the short is compensated for interest earned since the last coupon date.

It is important to recognize that this sequence—option exercise, futures position, and physical delivery—is governed entirely by the standardized procedures of the exchange and clearinghouse. The option does not directly involve any Treasury security but, through exercise and subsequent futures settlement, can lead to the actual delivery of a bond. This layered structure makes Treasury futures options unique in the exchange-traded derivatives market and requires a clear understanding of option and futures mechanics.

6.4 Exchange-Traded Currency Derivatives

Currency derivatives are exchange-traded instruments whose value is based on the exchange rate between two currencies. These instruments allow investors and institutions to obtain exposure to foreign exchange markets without directly buying or selling the underlying currencies. The most widely used exchange-traded currency derivatives are currency futures and currency options.

6.4.1 *Currency futures*

Currency futures are contracts that obligate the buyer to purchase—or the seller to deliver—a specified amount of one currency in exchange for another at a future date and at a predetermined exchange rate. These contracts are traded on exchanges such as the CME. The most traded contracts are quoted in U.S. dollars against major foreign currencies, such as the euro (EUR/USD), Japanese yen (JPY/USD), British pound (GBP/USD), Swiss franc (CHF/USD), Australian dollar (AUD/USD), and Canadian dollar (CAD/USD).

Each futures contract has a fixed notional size determined by the exchange. Contract sizes vary by currency. For example, the standard euro futures contract represents €125,000. The price is quoted in terms of U.S. dollars per euro, and the contract is settled in U.S. dollars. At expiration, most currency futures are physically settled, meaning that the notional amount of foreign currency must be exchanged for U.S. dollars based on the agreed futures price.

To illustrate, suppose a trader purchases one euro futures contract at a price of 1.1000. This implies an agreement to purchase €125,000 at a rate of \$1.10 per euro, for a total of \$137,500. If the contract is held to expiration and the spot exchange rate is 1.1200, the futures position settles at a profit of \$2,500. The gain is realized in U.S. dollars as part of the final settlement process.

6.4.2 *Currency options*

Currency options are listed on exchanges such as CME and Nasdaq PHLX, but the main listed contracts are not generally physically settled; they are typically structured either as options on FX futures (as on CME) or as U.S. dollar cash-settled options on currency values (as on Nasdaq PHLX), so exercise results in a futures position or a cash payment rather than an immediate spot exchange of currencies. Most exchange-traded currency options on these venues are European-style, meaning they can only be exercised at expiration. On the CME, exercising a Euro FX option typically converts into a position in one Euro FX futures contract with a notional of €125,000 at the option's strike price, rather than directly buying or selling the spot currency pair.

On U.S. exchanges, standardized foreign currency options are typically quoted in U.S. dollars per unit of the underlying foreign currency, and the option premium is paid in full upfront under traditional 'equity-style' margining conventions for options. Long option positions do not require additional initial margin beyond the premium, but short option positions are subject to daily valuation and margining by the clearinghouse, in a manner analogous to exchange-traded currency futures. In addition to standard-sized FX futures and options, exchanges such as CME Group offer smaller 'micro' FX futures and associated options, which provide the same contract design and risk characteristics as their full-sized counterparts but at a reduced notional value. These contracts are intended to accommodate smaller institutional trades and individual investors who need finer control over position sizing and margin exposure; for example, the Micro Euro FX futures contract represents €12,500, one-tenth the notional of the standard Euro FX futures contract, while maintaining the same underlying currency pair and quarterly expiration cycle. Micro FX futures and any options on them are cleared through the same central counterparty and follow the same basic consistency across the product suite while enhancing market accessibility.

6.5 Exchange-Traded Commodity Derivatives

Commodity derivatives are standardized, exchange-traded contracts that derive their value from the price of a physical commodity. These instruments are widely used to obtain or manage exposure to movements in commodity markets without engaging in direct physical transactions. The most commonly traded commodity derivatives include commodity futures, commodity options, and commodity index derivatives. Exchange-traded commodity derivatives span a broad range of underlying products. Table 6.2 shows the primary classes of commodities and typical examples within each group.

6.5.1 *Commodity futures options*

Commodity futures options, also referred to as options on commodity futures, give the holder the right, but not the obligation, to enter into a commodity futures contract at a specified strike price on or before a defined expiration date. These options are not based directly on the physical commodity but rather on the corresponding commodity futures contract. Each option is therefore linked to a specific futures contract and inherits its standardized terms, including the underlying commodity, contract size, delivery terms, and expiration schedule.

Most commodity futures options are American-style. Upon exercise, the holder assumes a futures position—long in the case of a call option and short in the case of a put option—at the strike price of the option. This position is then subject to the standard variation margin and daily mark-to-market procedures. If the resulting futures position is held to expiration and the underlying contract is physically settled, the long or short position may ultimately result in the delivery or receipt of the physical commodity.

Table 6.2. Primary Classes of Commodities and Typical Examples with Each Group

Commodity Class	Examples
Energy	Crude oil, natural gas, gasoline, heating oil
Metals	Gold, silver, copper, platinum, palladium
Agricultural	Corn, wheat, soybeans, coffee, cocoa, cotton, sugar
Livestock	Live cattle, feeder cattle, lean hogs
Softs	Orange juice, lumber, frozen concentrated orange juice, rubber

Mini and micro versions of commodity futures options are available for select contracts. These contracts mirror the structure and mechanics of their standard-sized counterparts but offer smaller notional values, making them accessible to a broader range of market participants who require more precise control over position size and capital commitment.

6.5.2 *Commodity index derivatives*

In addition to contracts on individual commodities, exchanges also list commodity index derivatives, which provide exposure to a diversified basket of commodities through a single instrument. These include futures and options on broad-based indices such as the S&P GSCI and the Bloomberg Commodity Index (BCOM).

Commodity index futures are cash-settled and reflect the weighted performance of multiple commodity sectors, including energy, metals, and agriculture. These contracts follow the same mechanics as other futures: They are standardized, marked to market daily, and subject to margin requirements. Index-based contracts do not involve physical delivery and are used to gain or manage exposure to the overall commodity market.

6.6 Exchange-Traded Weather Derivatives

Weather derivatives are contracts whose value is based on measurable weather outcomes rather than financial assets or physical commodities. These contracts enable the transfer of financial exposure to adverse or uncertain weather conditions. Unlike traditional commodity derivatives, they are not tied to the price or quantity of a deliverable good. Instead, the underlying is a weather index, calculated from temperature, precipitation, or snowfall data observed at specific geographic locations. Weather derivatives are listed on the CME and are typically used for monthly or seasonal exposures.

The most commonly traded weather derivatives are based on temperature, specifically Heating Degree Days (HDD), Cooling Degree Days (CDD), and Cumulative Average Temperature, with a contract period usually a calendar month. Table 6.3 lists these CME-traded derivatives and their underlying index.

Options on weather futures are also available for select cities and months. These are typically European-style, and exercise at expiration

Table 6.3. Weather Derivatives Traded on the CME

Contract	Abbreviation	Underlying Index	Typical Cities Listed	Contract Period
Heating Degree Day Futures	HDD Futures	Heating degree days (daily avg. temp 65°F)	Chicago, New York, Minneapolis	Monthly (winter: Nov–Mar)
Cooling Degree Day Futures	CDD Futures	Cooling degree days (daily avg. temp above 65°F)	Dallas, Atlanta, New Orleans	Monthly (summer: May–Sep)
Cumulative Average Temperature Futures	CAT Futures	Cumulative Average temp. (sum of daily averages)	Various U.S. cities (as designated)	Monthly
Precipitation Futures	Precipitation Futures	Monthly total rainfall (inches)	Portland, Seattle, Chicago (varies by listing)	Monthly
Snowfall Futures	Snowfall Futures	Monthly total snowfall (inches)	Minneapolis, Boston, Denver (varies by listing)	Monthly

Note: The settlement method is cash-settled based on the NOAA index value for the first three contracts and cash-settled based on NOAA measurements for the last two.

results in a futures position. The futures contract cash-settles based on the final published index value if held through to settlement.

6.6.1 *Contract mechanics and settlement*

All CME weather futures contracts are cash-settled, with no physical asset delivery. The underlying index value is calculated at the end of the contract period using publicly available data from the National Oceanic and Atmospheric Administration (NOAA) or other designated agencies. The final settlement value is based on the index result for the relevant location and month.

Each weather futures contract has a defined contract multiplier (e.g., $20 per index point), and tick sizes vary by contract type. Like other exchange-traded futures, positions are marked to market daily and subject to initial and maintenance margin requirements.

To illustrate, consider a CDD futures contract for Dallas in July, with a tick value of \$20 per index point. Suppose the cumulative CDD index for that month turns out to be 420. If a trader was long a contract priced at 400, the cash settlement would reflect a difference of 20 index points, resulting in a payment of \$400 (20 × \$20) to the long position.

6.7 Exchange-Traded Environmental Derivatives

Exchange-traded environmental derivatives are designed to facilitate trading in compliance instruments and environmental credits. These contracts are based on underlying assets such as greenhouse gas emission allowances, renewable energy certificates, and carbon offset credits, all of which are issued under regulatory or voluntary climate programs. The derivatives are used to manage exposures to regulatory risk and environmental compliance obligations, but the instruments themselves are traded on organized exchanges such as the Intercontinental Exchange (ICE) and the CME.

Unlike commodity derivatives, which are typically linked to deliverable physical goods, many environmental derivatives reference intangible instruments such as emissions allowances (rights to emit a specified amount of carbon dioxide) or certificates verifying renewable electricity generation. Settlement of these contracts often occurs through book-entry transfers in designated environmental registries, rather than through shipment of a physical good, although cash-settled structures are also widely used.

Table 6.4 summarizes the most widely traded exchange-traded environmental derivatives, including emissions allowance futures, renewable energy certificate (REC) futures, and standardized contracts on voluntary carbon credits. While a significant share of these contracts are designed for 'physical' delivery via electronic transfer of the underlying allowances or certificates within the relevant registry system at expiration, cash-settled contracts linked to benchmark prices or indices are also common, so it is more accurate to say that both physically settled and cash-settled structures are used extensively in practice.

Environmental derivatives are typically listed in monthly, quarterly, or annual formats, depending on the underlying program. For emissions contracts, the final settlement price reflects the market value

Table 6.4. Summary of Traded Exchange-Traded Environmental Derivatives

Contract Name	Underlying Instrument	Exchange	Contract Size	Settlement Method	Registry
EUA Futures	EU Allowance (under EU ETS)	ICE Futures Europe	1,000 metric tons CO_2	Physical (registry transfer)	EU ETS Registry
CCA Futures	California Carbon Allowance (under CA Cap-and-Trade)	ICE Futures U.S.	1,000 metric tons CO_2-e	Physical (registry transfer)	Western Climate Initiative (WCI)
RGGI Futures	Regional Greenhouse Gas Initiative Allowances	ICE Futures U.S.	1,000 short tons CO_2	Physical (registry transfer)	RGGI COATS
PJM-GATS REC Futures	Renewable Energy Certificate (1MWh) under PJM GATS	ICE Futures U.S.	1 REC (1 MWh)	Physical (registry transfer)	PJM GATS
NEPOOL Class I REC Futures	Class I REC under NEPOOL (New England)	ICE Futures U.S.	1 REC (1 MWh)	Physical (registry transfer)	NEPOOL-GIS
Nature-Based Carbon Offset (N-GEO)	Verified carbon offsets from nature-based projects	CME	1,000 metric tons CO_2	Physical or cash (depending on contract)	Verra and Gold Standard
CORSIA Offset Futures	Carbon offset credits aligned with ICAO aviation program	CME	1,000 metric tons CO_2	Physical (registry transfer)	Verra, ACR, or other eligible

of emission allowances near expiration, and delivery is conducted by registry entry. For REC futures, settlement involves transferring the required number of RECs to the buyer's account within the regional tracking system. For offset contracts traded on the CME, delivery takes place via recognized voluntary registries such as Verra or Gold Standard, with eligibility criteria and contract integrity governed by exchange rules.

6.8 Summary

In this chapter, I examine the structure, mechanics, and strategic applications of ETDs across a wide range of asset classes. I lay out the foundational features that distinguish ETDs from OTC derivatives, including their standardization, centralized trading and clearing, daily margining and mark-to-market, transparency, and regulatory oversight. These features make ETDs powerful tools for managing risk, enhancing liquidity, and supporting tactical and strategic investment decisions.

I then turn to specific asset classes, beginning with equity derivatives. I discuss options and futures on individual stocks and broad-based stock indices, including scaled E-mini and micro contracts, which broaden access and improve flexibility. I explain exchange-traded volatility derivatives—volatility index futures and options built from index option prices (e.g., VIX futures and VIX options)—to show how markets trade implied volatility directly. I also analyze contracts linked to U.S. equity sectors and factor-based indices, which allow investors to implement targeted views or hedging strategies with precision and efficiency, and I explore international stock index futures and options, highlighting the role of regional exchanges and the nuances of currency denomination, trading hours, and contract structure.

Next, I address exchange-traded interest rate derivatives. I review the transition from Eurodollar contracts to SOFR-based futures. I provided a detailed account of U.S. Treasury futures, including their physical delivery mechanics, conversion factors, and embedded delivery options. I explain how traders determine the cheapest-to-deliver bond and calculate invoice prices. I then present a discussion of options on Treasury securities and options on Treasury futures, clarifying the distinctions in their structure and use.

I also cover currency derivatives, including futures and options on major currency pairs, and describe how exchanges use contract sizing innovations—such as mini and micro formats—to broaden participation. I examine commodity derivatives, showing how futures, options, and commodity index contracts support price exposure across energy, metals, agricultural, and livestock markets. I conclude with discussions of weather and environmental derivatives, illustrating how exchange-traded formats have extended to contracts tied to temperature indices, precipitation, and environmental credits.

Throughout the chapter, I emphasize how ETDs have evolved into a highly regulated, scalable, and transparent system supporting a diverse ecosystem of users and strategies. These instruments offer essential capabilities for managing financial risk, executing strategies, and improving portfolio efficiency—capabilities that I explore further in the following chapter on OTC derivatives, where customization and structural complexity take center stage.

Chapter 7

Structure and Mechanics of Over-the-Counter Derivatives

In this chapter, I examine the structure and mechanics of over-the-counter (OTC) derivatives, which are customized contracts negotiated directly between counterparties. Unlike exchange-traded derivatives (ETDs) described in the previous chapter, which follow standardized terms and centralized clearing protocols, OTC derivatives provide flexibility and customization, allowing parties to tailor financial exposures precisely. This flexibility, however, comes with added complexity in documentation, valuation, collateralization, and risk management.[1]

My goal is to provide a clear and practical explanation of how OTC derivatives are structured and managed in institutional settings. I begin by explaining how counterparties negotiate and document these instruments, emphasizing the role of the International Swaps and Derivatives Association (ISDA) Master Agreement, trade confirmations, and credit support arrangements.[2] I then address how bilateral margining, collateral posting, and netting provisions work together to manage

[1]Descriptions of operational practices, such as collateral timelines, eligible assets, and rehypothecation, reflect publicly available materials from major custodians and clearing firms and insights from practitioner discussions.

[2]The discussion of the legal and operational framework for OTC derivatives—including ISDA documentation, collateralization, and clearing—draws in part on concepts presented in John C. Hull, adapted here for a practitioner-oriented perspective. More specifically, Hull provided a technical foundation for the sections on ISDA documentation, margining, and collateral practices, which have been reworked and expanded with current market

counterparty risk. But I leave detailed operational aspects such as collateral valuation, liquidity management, and margin optimization to the following chapter.

Throughout this chapter, I contrast the mechanics of OTC derivatives with ETDs covered in the previous chapter. I aim to show why OTC structure matters for market participants, regulators, and overall financial stability, as well as to highlight the legal and operational foundations supporting this critical segment of the global derivatives markets.

7.1 Negotiation and Documentation of OTC Derivatives

OTC derivatives are not traded on centralized exchanges. Each transaction arises from a negotiation between two counterparties, and the bespoke nature of these instruments makes careful documentation essential. Accurate and enforceable documentation records the economic terms of the trade and establishes the legal framework for credit protection, collateral posting, and dispute resolution. In this section, I describe the key documents that govern OTC derivatives, emphasizing the framework developed by the ISDA.

7.1.1 *The ISDA Master Agreement*

The ISDA Master Agreement is the foundation of most OTC derivatives trading relationships. This standardized legal contract sets the general terms and conditions for all transactions between two parties, covering close-out provisions, events of default, and netting arrangements. It does not define the economic terms of an individual trade but governs the overall legal relationship across all current and future transactions.

When two institutions enter OTC derivative trading, they typically sign a single ISDA Master Agreement. This approach streamlines the process by avoiding repeated negotiation of core legal provisions for every trade. The agreement includes:

- netting provisions, which allow offsetting payments to be combined into a single settlement;

---

practices, regulatory developments, and practitioner illustrations. John C. Hull, *Options, Futures, and Other Derivatives*, 11th ed. (Hoboken, NJ: Pearson, 2022).

- termination and close-out procedures, which define how to value and unwind positions if a counterparty defaults;
- events of default, such as bankruptcy or failure to meet margin requirements.

Two versions of the ISDA Master Agreement are widely used: the 1992 and 2002 editions. The 2002 version introduced more precise definitions of default events and broader credit event coverage, but many institutions still use the 1992 version for legacy portfolios. In practice, portfolio managers and risk teams often operate under both versions simultaneously, which has implications for netting and close-out analysis.

7.1.2 *Trade confirmations*

Each OTC derivative is finalized with a trade confirmation, which records the economic terms of the transaction and acts as an addendum to the Master Agreement. A confirmation specifies the notional amount, effective and maturity dates, reference asset or index, payment conventions, calculation agent, and key pricing details such as whether the contract is fixed-for-floating or based on a spread.

Confirmations typically follow standardized ISDA templates for widely traded products such as interest rate and credit default swaps. However, if both parties agree, they can be customized for more bespoke structures. In modern markets, most large institutions use electronic confirmation platforms such as MarkitSERV or Bloomberg VCON, accelerating the process and reducing operational risk.

7.1.3 *Credit Support Annex*

Most OTC derivatives agreements include a Credit Support Annex (CSA) to mitigate counterparty credit risk. The CSA is a schedule to the ISDA Master Agreement that governs collateral posting and receipt between the parties. It specifies:

- eligible collateral, such as cash, U.S. Treasuries, or high-quality sovereign bonds;
- thresholds, which define the unsecured exposure allowed before margin must be posted;

- minimum transfer amounts, which prevent nuisance collateral movements;
- haircuts, which apply discounts to collateral to reflect market or liquidity risk;
- valuation frequency, typically daily but negotiable for some products.

The CSA also defines how initial margin and variation margin are exchanged and what happens if collateral is not delivered in time. Recent regulatory changes have led to widespread adoption of two-way margining and the segregation of initial margin at third-party custodians for many uncleared derivatives.

Chapter 10 comprehensively covers operational details such as collateral valuation, daily mark-to-market flows, dispute resolution, and liquidity management.

7.2 Collateralization and Margining Practices

Collateralization is central to controlling counterparty risk in the OTC derivatives market. Unlike ETDs, where a central clearinghouse guarantees trades and enforces uniform margin rules, OTC derivatives require bilateral agreements on how collateral is posted, valued, and maintained. In this section, I explain how margining works conceptually in OTC markets, highlighting the roles of variation margin, initial margin, and the operational considerations of collateral management. I refer to Chapter 10 for step-by-step processes and calculations.

7.2.1 *Variation margin: Daily exposure management*

Variation margin is posted to reflect daily mark-to-market changes in the value of outstanding positions. When the market moves against a counterparty, that party must post collateral to offset the unrealized loss; when it moves in its favor, that party receives collateral. This mechanism keeps bilateral exposure neutral daily and is the primary tool for controlling day-to-day credit risk.

The CSA defines collateral types and valuation practices, including whether cash, government bonds, or other high-quality securities can be posted and how haircuts are applied to account for market risk.[3]

[3]Collateral valuation practices and haircut conventions follow CSA documentation.

Unlike ETDs, which rely on centralized clearinghouses for automatic variation margin settlement, OTC markets require bilateral reconciliation of exposures. Both parties must agree on the valuation before collateral moves, and discrepancies can lead to operational delays or disputes.

The operational details of daily margin flows, collateral posting, and reconciliation are discussed in depth in Chapter 10.

7.2.2 *Initial margin: Protecting against extreme events*

Initial margin protects against potential future exposure, the expected loss that could arise in the period required to close out positions after a counterparty default. This is particularly critical for uncleared OTC derivatives, where no central counterparty (CCP) intervenes during a failure.

Following the 2007–2008 Global Financial Crisis (GFC), regulators such as the Basel Committee on Banking Supervision and IOSCO mandated two-way initial margin for many uncleared derivatives. This margin is often held in segregated accounts at independent custodians to reduce the risk of rehypothecation and ensure recoverability in bankruptcy.[4]

Initial margin is conceptually calculated using historical value-at-risk (VaR) or expected shortfall over a defined margin period of risk (often 10 days).

The specific methodologies, model approvals, and recalculation practices are covered in Chapter 10.

7.2.3 *Margin disputes and operational risk*

Collateral management in OTC markets is operationally demanding. Each margin call must be calculated, agreed upon, and settled, sometimes across multiple asset types and time zones. Differences in pricing models or valuation inputs can trigger disputes, and even minor mismatches can lead to material discrepancies in required collateral for large portfolios.

---

[4]These requirements reflect the global framework established by the Basel Committee on Banking Supervision and the International Organization of Securities Commissions, which mandates two-way initial margin, collateral segregation, and standardized margin periods of risk for uncleared derivatives. See Basel Committee on Banking Supervision & International Organization of Securities Commissions. (2015). *Margin requirements for non-centrally cleared derivatives* (rev. Mar 2020). https://www.bis.org/bcbs/publ/d317.pdf.

Timely posting of margins is critical: Delays can trigger contractual defaults, forced close-outs, or reputational damage.

Operational protocols for dispute resolution, automated collateral management systems, and tools such as triResolve are covered in Chapter 10.

Collateralization transforms OTC derivatives into secured bilateral exposures, reducing systemic risk but introducing challenges related to liquidity, asset eligibility, and custodial arrangements. In the following section, I turn to how these exposures are further mitigated through netting and close-out protocols.

Many firms use automated collateral management systems that interface with market data providers, trade repositories, and legal documentation libraries to mitigate this risk. Industry-wide utilities such as the triResolve platform also help reconcile exposures and improve transparency across counterparties.

7.3 Netting and Close-Out

Netting and close-out provisions are essential for managing counterparty credit risk in OTC derivatives. These mechanisms allow market participants to reduce gross exposures, consolidate settlements, and ensure that defaults can be handled in a legally enforceable and operationally efficient manner. In this section, I explain payment netting, close-out netting, and the legal framework that makes them effective, while deferring detailed operational processes to Chapter 10.

Table 7.1 summarizes several high-profile legal and regulatory cases that illustrate counterparty risk management, netting enforcement, and collateral disputes in OTC derivatives.

7.3.1 *Payment netting: Reducing routine exposures*

Payment netting offsets reciprocal payment obligations due on the same day and in the same currency, allowing only the net amount to be settled. For example, if a firm owes $12 million on the fixed leg of an interest rate swap and is due $8 million on the floating leg, a single net payment of $4 million is made.

By consolidating cash flows, payment netting reduces operational complexity, limits settlement risk, and simplifies liquidity management.

Table 7.1. Selected Legal and Regulatory Cases in OTC Derivatives

Issue	Case	Brief Description
Counterparty Risk and Collateralization	*UBS AG v. Highland Capital Management, L.P.* (2010)	Dispute over a total return swap and inadequate margining, illustrating collateral requirements and termination rights in OTC swaps.
Central Clearing Mandates	*Lehman Brothers Holdings Inc.* Bankruptcy (2008)	Exposed massive systemic counterparty risk in uncleared OTC derivatives and prompted Dodd–Frank clearing and transparency reforms.
Documentation Standards and Disputes	*Citibank v. Brigade Capital Management, L.P.* (2020)	Mistaken syndicated loan payment highlighted documentation ambiguity and the importance of ISDA protocols and payment provisions.
Segregation of Client Collateral	*MF Global Inc.* Bankruptcy (2011)	Misuse of customer collateral—including margin for OTC derivatives—led to regulatory scrutiny and reforms to client asset segregation rules.
Market Conduct and Misrepresentation	*SEC v. Goldman Sachs (Abacus 2007–AC1)*	Goldman was charged with misleading investors about a hedge fund's role in selecting CDO assets, underscoring conflicts of interest in OTC product structuring.

Note: These cases highlight the legal, operational, and systemic issues in OTC derivatives markets, including margining practices, collateral segregation, documentation standards, and market conduct.

Daily operational workflows and system automation for netting calculations are covered in Chapter 10.

7.3.2 *Close-out netting: Managing default events*

Close-out netting is triggered by a termination event, such as a counterparty default, bankruptcy, or failure to meet margin obligations under the CSA. Once triggered:

1. All trades under the ISDA Master Agreement are terminated and valued at current market prices.
2. Gains and losses are combined into a single close-out amount.
3. Collateral posted under the CSA is applied to reduce the net payable amount, and any residual exposure becomes an unsecured claim in the counterparty's bankruptcy estate.

Close-out netting prevents a defaulting counterparty from selectively honoring favorable trades while rejecting losing positions. It is a cornerstone of modern derivatives credit-risk management.

Detailed collateral application and settlement flows during close-out are explained later in this section.

7.3.3 *Legal enforceability and systemic impact*

The enforceability of netting agreements is critical to institutional risk management and systemic stability. Recognized netting agreements allow institutions to report net rather than gross exposures, reducing regulatory capital requirements under Basel III. Without enforceable netting, the default of a single major counterparty could cascade into a chain of losses for its trading partners.

Regulators and market participants rely on legal opinions to confirm that netting and close-out provisions are enforceable across jurisdictions. This is particularly important for cross-border portfolios where insolvency laws may vary.

Netting and close-out and collateralization under the CSA transform OTC derivatives from significant gross exposures into manageable net exposures. This legal and operational framework underpins both firm-level risk management and the stability of the global derivatives market.

7.4 Valuation Practices and Model Risk

Because OTC derivatives are not traded on exchanges with transparent prices, their valuation depends on internal or third-party models that estimate fair value based on observable market data and assumptions. In this section, I describe how institutions value OTC derivatives, the sources of potential model risk, and the regulatory and operational practices used to mitigate it.

7.4.1 *Fair value estimation and mark-to-market*

Valuation typically involves applying a pricing formula using market-observed inputs for liquid OTC derivatives such as vanilla interest rate swaps or forward currency contracts. These inputs may include yield curves, spot rates, volatilities, or credit spreads. When these data are reliable, the derivative can be marked to market with relatively low uncertainty.

For more complex or less liquid contracts, such as long-dated exotic options, structured credit products, or path-dependent swaps, valuation relies on model-based estimates. These models incorporate assumptions about volatility surfaces, interest rate behavior, credit spreads, or other market dynamics. The resulting price is a theoretical estimate of the contract's current value, but not necessarily a level that could be realized in the market.

These practices follow the fair value measurement frameworks outlined in IFRS 13 and U.S. GAAP ASC 820, which establish the hierarchy of market inputs and the standards for model-based valuation disclosures.[5] Firms must regularly mark OTC positions to model-based fair value, adjusting for changes in underlying variables. These valuations feed directly into collateral calls, netting calculations, and counterparty exposure metrics.[6]

7.4.2 *Model risk and independent price verification*

Model risk arises because pricing models depend on assumptions, calibration choices, and subjective inputs. An incorrect assumption about volatility surfaces, yield curve dynamics, or credit correlations can produce misleading valuations.

---

[5] *International Accounting Standards Board* (2011). *IFRS 13: Fair Value Measurement. Financial Accounting Standards Board* (2011). *ASC 820: Fair Value Measurement.*

[6] See Chapter 10 for how mark-to-market valuations feed collateral calls, netting calculations, and exposure monitoring.

Institutions rely on independent price verification (IPV) to mitigate this risk, where model outputs are tested against market quotes, broker runs, or consensus pricing services. In addition, firms maintain a model validation function, staffed by quantitative analysts independent of the trading desk, to approve and periodically review models.

Some institutions apply fair value adjustments for uncertainty, illiquidity, or funding costs. These may include the following:

- *Credit Valuation Adjustment* (CVA): reflects counterparty risk.
- *Funding Valuation Adjustment* (FVA): reflects the cost of funding collateralized positions.
- *Model Valuation Adjustment* (MVA): accounts for residual model uncertainty.

These adjustments help ensure reported valuations reflect economic risk and meet regulatory and capital requirements, particularly under Basel III.

7.5 Regulatory Requirements and Best Practices

Valuation practices for OTC derivatives are subject to oversight by accounting standards, prudential regulators, and market conduct authorities. Accounting standards such as IFRS 13 and U.S. GAAP ASC 820 define the fair value hierarchy, requiring the use of the most observable market inputs and full disclosure of model assumptions and limitations. Prudential regulators, including the Federal Reserve, European Central Bank (ECB), and the Basel Committee on Banking Supervision expect institutions to maintain accurate valuations, independently verified, and consistent with internal and external reporting. Market conduct authorities and post-GFC frameworks such as Dodd–Frank in the U.S. and EMIR in the EU further emphasize transparency and robust risk control for OTC derivatives portfolios.[7]

Best practices include maintaining robust model governance policies, applying conservative assumptions when data are scarce, documenting pricing methodologies, and disclosing the sources and limits of model-based valuations. Institutions must align their internal valuations with

[7]See Basel Committee on Banking Supervision (2015), "Supervisory Guidance for Assessing Bank's Derivatives Valuation Practices," and IFRS 13/ASC 820 for accounting and fair value disclosure requirements.

financial reporting to prevent discrepancies between trading books and accounting statements.

Strong governance, model validation, and regulatory alignment are critical for maintaining investor confidence, capital adequacy, and systemic stability in the OTC derivatives market.

7.6 Collateral Terms and Liquidity Implications

Collateral plays a central role in managing credit risk for OTC derivatives. Because these derivatives expose each counterparty to risk default, collateral agreements are used to mitigate potential losses. In this section, I focus on how collateral frameworks operate and their impact on liquidity and funding. Detailed daily margin mechanics are covered earlier in Section 7.2 (*Collateralization and Margining Practices*) and further expanded in Chapter 9.

7.6.1 *Variation margin and initial margin*

Two types of margin are used in OTC derivatives:

- Variation margin offsets day-to-day mark-to-market changes, ensuring neither party accumulates large unsecured gains.
- Initial margin protects against potential future exposure between the last margin call and a default event.

Following the GFC, regulators imposed mandatory initial margin for many uncleared derivatives. This collateral must be segregated at independent custodians and cannot be rehypothecated (i.e., the receiving counterparty cannot reuse it for its own trading or financing activities), thereby reducing systemic risk.

7.6.2 *Dispute resolution*

Collateral calls may be contested due to differences in pricing models or valuation timings. Institutions follow formal dispute resolution protocols under the ISDA, which include:

- defined communication and escalation paths,
- tolerance thresholds to avoid disputes over immaterial differences,

- the use of automated collateral management and reconciliation tools to reduce manual errors.

7.6.3 *Impact on liquidity and funding*

Collateral requirements have a major effect on an institution's liquidity and capital management. Posting cash or high-quality liquid assets (HQLAs) reduces resources available for other uses, so firms often treat collateral as a scarce asset.

To optimize efficiency, institutions:

- centralize margin operations under a collateral management desk;
- monitor collateral velocity—how often collateral is posted, returned, or substituted;
- track rehypothecation rights and segregation requirements under uncleared margin rules.

Effective collateral management reduces credit exposure but introduces new liquidity and funding challenges, making it a core component of OTC derivatives risk management.

7.7 Legal Documentation and Operational Infrastructure

The proper functioning of the OTC derivatives market relies on a robust legal and operational foundation. This framework ensures that trades are executed, monitored, and enforced efficiently, reducing the risk of disputes and systemic disruption.

7.7.1 *ISDA Master Agreement*

As explained earlier in this chapter, the ISDA Master Agreement forms the legal core of most OTC derivative relationships. It governs all transactions between two counterparties and covers credit terms, netting provisions, and events of default.

The Master Agreement consolidates multiple trades under a single legal framework. This enables close-out netting if one party defaults, ensuring all contracts are terminated and a single net amount is calculated. (See Section 7.3, *Netting and Close-Out*, for a detailed discussion of its impact on risk reduction and regulatory capital.)

Each Master Agreement is supported by a schedule, which allows the parties to customize key terms such as governing law, cross-default provisions, and credit event definitions. These customizations align the contract with the counterparties' risk appetites and regulatory obligations.

7.7.2 *Confirmations and trade matching*

Every OTC transaction is finalized with a trade confirmation that specifies economic terms such as the notional amount, payment frequency, day-count convention, and reference index. Confirmations are typically exchanged electronically and must match exactly on both sides to be considered binding.

Trade confirmations are reconciled through matching platforms or messaging services. Rapid resolution of discrepancies is essential to avoid downstream errors in valuation, collateral calls, and margining (see Section 7.6, *Collateral Management and Margining*). Automation and straight-through processing have greatly improved both speed and accuracy.

Following the post-GFC reforms, central trade repositories now record most OTC derivative transactions, giving regulators visibility into market exposures and supporting systemic risk monitoring.

7.7.3 *Operational platforms and middleware*

Modern OTC derivatives portfolios depend on integrated operational platforms to manage their complexity. These systems support:

- trade capture and pricing,
- valuation and risk aggregation,
- collateral and margin management,
- regulatory reporting.

Middleware solutions link front-office trading activity with middle- and back-office functions, ensuring consistency in real-time pricing, counterparty exposure monitoring, and collateral workflows. Many systems connect to external services such as clearinghouses, custodians, and trade repositories.

Operational resilience is critical. Disruptions in messaging systems, pricing engines, or reconciliation tools can lead to missed margin calls or misreported exposures. As a result, institutions invest heavily in redundant systems, cybersecurity, and business continuity planning.

A robust legal and operational framework, anchored by the ISDA Master Agreement, reliable trade confirmation processes, and resilient operational platforms, ensures that OTC derivatives can function even under market stress, supporting both firm-level and systemic stability.

7.8 Summary

In this chapter, I examine the structure and mechanics of the OTC derivatives market, focusing on how these contracts are negotiated, documented, collateralized, and managed in institutional practice. My objective is to show how OTC derivatives differ from ETDs and to highlight the legal and operational frameworks that allow them to function safely in a bilateral market.

I began by describing the bilateral and customized nature of OTC derivatives, where trades are negotiated directly between counterparties rather than on a central exchange. This customization allows market participants to tailor exposures to highly specific hedging or investment needs; however, it also introduces greater complexity and counterparty risk.

I then explain how OTC derivatives are supported by documentation practices centered on the ISDA Master Agreement, trade confirmations, and the Credit Support Annex. These documents establish the rules for netting, close-out, and collateral posting, which are essential for managing credit exposure. I also highlight how enforceable netting and close-out provisions transform large gross exposures into manageable net exposures.

Next, I discuss margining and collateralization, distinguishing between variation margin, which neutralizes day-to-day market changes, and initial margin, which protects against potential future exposure in the event of default. I explain how collateral eligibility, haircut conventions, segregation and rehypothecation restrictions shape liquidity and funding needs for market participants.

I also address valuation practices and model risk, showing how OTC derivatives depend on models for fair value estimation when transparent market prices do not exist. Independent price verification, model governance, and fair value adjustments ensure that valuations are reliable and align with regulatory and capital requirements.

Finally, I examine the legal and operational infrastructure that underpins OTC derivatives. Reliable trade confirmations, trade repositories, integrated collateral platforms, and robust operational systems are essential for preventing disputes, maintaining transparency, and ensuring that margining and settlement occur without disruption.

At the end of the chapter, I provide a clear view of how OTC derivatives are structured and managed, how credit and liquidity risks are controlled, and why robust documentation, collateral practices, and operational resilience are essential to the stability of the OTC market.

With the legal, operational, and risk management framework for OTC derivatives now established, in the following chapter, I turn to instruments that extend beyond standard contracts. These include customized, structured, and exotic derivatives that address precise exposures, offer nonlinear payoffs, or embed multiple risk factors. While these products rely on the same foundations of documentation, collateral, and valuation discussed in this chapter, they introduce new dimensions of complexity ranging from path dependency to hybrid features that combine options, swaps, and forwards.

Chapter 8

Structured and Exotic Derivatives

In this chapter, I examine customized, structured, and exotic derivatives—financial instruments designed to achieve outcomes that standard contracts cannot fully address. Standard derivatives such as futures, swaps, and plain-vanilla options are highly effective for transferring linear or basic asymmetric risks, but real-world investment and hedging needs often require greater precision. Institutional investors, corporate treasurers, and wealth managers may need tailored risk-return profiles, multi-asset exposure, or structures that satisfy tax, accounting, or regulatory constraints.

Customized and exotic derivatives meet these needs by intentionally shaping payoff profiles. They embed features such as barriers, averaging, multi-asset linkages, or digital triggers to align risk and return with specific market views or operational requirements. Examples include structured notes that combine bonds with embedded options, barrier and lookback options that respond to price paths, and hybrids such as quanto options or correlation-linked payoffs. Most of these products trade in over-the-counter (OTC) markets or are developed on structured product desks for institutional strategies, where they can be engineered to match highly specific mandates.

I begin with structured notes and embedded derivatives, then explore path-dependent and structured payoff derivatives, including multi-asset and hybrid structures. Along the way, I highlight institutional applications, real-world examples, valuation challenges, and the risks and regulatory considerations accompanying these instruments. My goal is to explain how financial engineers design, price, and manage customized derivatives and show how complexity can serve a strategic purpose or conceal risk.[1]

8.1 Structured Notes and Embedded Derivatives

Structured notes are the most accessible form of customized derivatives, illustrating how financial engineering combines traditional debt instruments with embedded derivative features to create bespoke payoff profiles. Issued by banks and other financial institutions, these notes typically link a fixed-income base to options or other derivatives tied to equities, interest rates, currencies, commodities, or multi-asset baskets. This combination enables targeted outcomes such as enhanced yield, principal protection, or conditional equity exposure, results that standard bonds or stocks cannot achieve.

A *principal-protected note* demonstrates the basic logic. An investor pays $1,000 for a five-year note linked to the S&P 500. The issuer invests most of the proceeds in a zero-coupon bond maturing at $1,000 to secure principal repayment and uses the remainder to purchase S&P 500 call options. If the index rises, the options provide upside participation; if it falls, the investor still receives $1,000 at maturity. This structure allows for equity participation without capital loss, though it sacrifices dividends and often caps returns.

Structured notes vary widely in their design and embedded derivative components:

- *Reverse convertibles* offer high coupons but may repay in shares if the underlying asset falls below a barrier, embedding a short put.
- *Autocallable notes* provide fixed returns if the underlying remains above a barrier, automatically redeeming early if conditions are met.

[1]Hull's text provides the foundational definitions, pricing concepts, and classification frameworks for exotic options, including path-dependent and multi-asset derivatives. It is particularly useful for describing barrier options, lookbacks, and digitals, as well as illustrating valuation challenges that are briefly covered in this chapter. John C. Hull, *Options, Futures, and Other Derivatives*, 11th edition, Pearson Education, 2022. Das illustrates the wild world of derivatives through vivid, narrative-driven stories featuring real practitioners—traders, bankers, and clients. The book's humor comes largely from his satirical style. Satyajit Das, *Traders, Guns & Money: Knowns and Unknowns in the Dazzling World of Derivatives*, Revised Edition FT Press, 2010.

Table 8.1. Summary of Common Structured Notes and Embedded Derivatives

Structure Type	Embedded Derivative(s)	Typical Investor Objective	Key Risks and Considerations
Reverse Convertible	Short put on underlying asset	Generate high coupon income in exchange for equity risk	Potential repayment in depreciated shares; issuer credit risk
Autocallable Note	Barrier option(s) on underlying asset	Enhance yield with conditional early redemption	Market drop below barrier triggers principal loss; path dependency
Dual Currency Note	Currency option (short)	Earn higher interest by taking FX exposure	Adverse exchange rate moves reduce principal value; illiquidity
Convertible Bond	Equity call option	Participate in equity upside with bond downside protection	Equity volatility affects valuation; conversion terms may limit upside

- *Dual currency notes* pay interest in one currency and principal in another, combining bond-like income with a currency option.
- *Convertible bonds* allow holders to convert debt to equity if the stock rises, embedding an equity call for upside participation.

Table 8.1 summarizes the key characteristics of these instruments, highlighting the embedded derivative component, primary investor objectives, and major risk considerations for each structure type.

These instruments are generally not exchange-traded, carry issuer credit risk, and often have limited secondary liquidity, making them most suitable for buy-and-hold investors with specific market views.

Here are a few real-world examples:

- *Reverse Convertible* (*JPMorgan, 2022*): Linked to Tesla stock, this 12-month note offered a 14% annualized yield, with principal repaid in Tesla shares if the stock fell more than 30%.
- *Autocallable (BNP Paribas, 2023)*: Tied to the Euro Stoxx 50, this note paid an 8% coupon and automatically redeemed if the index

remained above a preset level. A 40% decline at maturity caused a corresponding principal loss.

- *Dual-Currency Note (Citibank, 2021)*: Sold to Taiwanese investors, this note paid 3.5% in USD but repaid principal in TWD at a fixed exchange rate, embedding a short USD/TWD option.
- *Convertible Senior Notes (AMD, 2020)*: $1 billion of convertible notes due in 2026 allowed conversion to AMD stock if its price rose, offering equity upside with bond-like downside protection.

These examples illustrate how structured notes and embedded derivatives meet precise investor objectives while introducing model risk, valuation complexity, and liquidity considerations that require careful governance.

8.2 Path-Dependent and Structured Payoff Derivatives

Path-dependent and structured payoff derivatives represent a more advanced form of customization than the structured notes and embedded derivatives introduced earlier. While structured notes typically combine a debt instrument with a single embedded option to produce a straightforward payoff profile, these derivatives add multiple layers of optionality, path dependence, and sometimes multi-asset linkages to create bespoke, nonlinear risk-return profiles. Together, they allow market participants, including institutional investors, corporate treasurers, and structured product desks, to express nuanced market views, enhance yield, and implement highly targeted risk-management strategies that standard derivatives cannot replicate.

8.2.1 *Path-dependent and exotic option structures*

Path-dependent options have payoffs that depend on both the terminal price of the underlying asset and the path taken to reach that price. These instruments allow precise risk and return customization beyond plain-vanilla European or American options and are commonly embedded in structured products to target specific volatility patterns, cost structures, or market conditions.

8.2.1.1 *Asian options*

Asian options calculate their payoff based on the average price of the underlying asset over a specified period, rather than solely on the price at expiration. Averaging reduces the impact of short-term volatility and makes these options less expensive than equivalent vanilla options.

Illustration of an Average Price Call: An airline buys a six-month Asian average-price call on jet fuel to hedge operating costs. The strike is $6.50 per gallon; the average is computed from monthly settlement prices. If the six-month average price is $7.00, the airline receives $0.50 per gallon on the contract, reducing fuel cost volatility caused by daily price spikes.

Illustration of an Average Strike Put: A metal fabricator uses an Asian average-strike put on aluminum. The strike price is determined by the average market price over the option's life, and the payoff is based on the difference between this average and the final spot price. If the average is $2,300 per ton but the final price is $2,100, the payoff is $200 per ton. This structure smooths hedging costs and reduces the effect of short-term rallies that might otherwise render a vanilla put worthless.

8.2.1.2 *Barrier options*

Barrier options are path-dependent derivatives whose payoff depends not only on the terminal price of the underlying asset but also on whether that price has crossed a predefined trigger (barrier) at any time during the option's life. Two main types exist:

- *Knock-In Options*: The option comes into existence only if the underlying price touches or breaches the barrier.
- *Knock-Out Options*: The option becomes void (ceases to exist) if the barrier is touched or breached.

Because the payoff is conditional, barrier options are generally cheaper than their equivalent vanilla counterparts. They allow investors to tailor exposures around specific market scenarios, reducing costs but adding event risk.

Illustration of a Down-and-Out Put (Knock-Out): A pension fund manager fears a moderate market decline but does not expect a crash. The portfolio manager buys a down-and-out put on an equity index with:

- strike: 6,000,
- barrier: 5,200 (knock-out level).

If the index finishes below 6,000 at the expiration date without ever touching 5,200, the fund receives the normal put payoff. However, if at any time during the option's life the index hits or falls below 5,200, the option is knocked out and expires worthless. The premium is cheaper than a standard put, but protection is lost if the market experiences a sharp drop that triggers the barrier.

Illustration of a Down-and-In Put (Knock-In): A hedge fund manager wants tail-risk protection but believes a market drop will be swift once it begins. The manager buys a down-and-in put with:

- strike: 6,000,
- barrier: 5,500 (knock-in level).

If the index never falls to 5,500, the option never activates, saving the fund the higher cost of a standard put. If it does breach 5,500, the option is triggered, and the fund can profit from further declines. The knock-in feature dramatically lowers the premium while protecting against severe downside moves.

Illustration of a Double Barrier Option: An investment banker structures a double knock-out range option on USD/JPY for a corporate client hedging currency exposure:

- strike: 130,
- lower barrier: 125,
- upper barrier: 135.

The option pays based on the difference between the strike and the final spot rate *only if* USD/JPY remains between 125 and 135 for the contract's life. If the rate touches either barrier, the option expires worthless.

The corporation enjoys a lower premium than for a simple vanilla option but sacrifices protection if the currency moves beyond expected bounds.

8.2.1.3 *Lookback options*

Lookback options allow the holder to "look back" over the option's life and determine the payoff using the optimal observed price of the underlying. They remove timing risk and provide the benefit of perfect hindsight in strike selection.

Illustration of a Floating-Strike Lookback Call: An investor buys a one-year floating-strike lookback call on a stock. The strike is set to the *lowest* price during the option's life, while the payoff is based on the final spot price. If the lowest observed price is $45 and the final price is $55, the payoff is $10 per share regardless of interim price fluctuations.

Illustration of a Fixed-Strike Lookback Put: A corporate procurement manager buys a fixed-strike lookback put with a strike of $100 on a key raw material used by the company. At expiry, the payoff is the difference between the strike and the *highest* price reached during the option's life. If the highest price is $120 and the final price is $95, the payoff is $25 per share, capturing the most advantageous protection point.

8.2.1.4 *Cliquet options*

Cliquet options (*ratchet options*) reset their strike periodically, such as monthly or annually, locking in gains and accumulating returns over the life of the contract. They are common in structured products aiming for steady upside participation with partial downside protection.

Illustration of an Annual Reset Cliquet: An investor buys a five-year cliquet option on an equity index with annual strike resets and a 10% annual cap. Each year, gains up to 10% are locked in and added to the total payoff at maturity. Even if the index falls in later years, prior locked-in gains remain part of the payout.

Illustration of a Monthly Reset Cliquet: A structured note linked to a monthly reset cliquet credits the investor with the sum of capped monthly returns (e.g., a maximum of 2% per month). If markets are volatile but frequently post modest monthly gains, the investor benefits from the accumulation of these capped returns, while the downside in any month is floored at zero.

8.2.2 *Structured payoff derivatives and custom hybrids*

Beyond path-dependent derivatives, another class of customized instruments involves structured payoffs—engineered combinations of standard derivatives that produce nonlinear, tailored return profiles. These structures allow financial engineers to construct payoff diagrams that meet highly specific investor objectives or hedging needs, often mimicking combinations of long and short options with embedded leverage, caps, or thresholds. They represent a creative extension of basic derivative building blocks, transforming familiar instruments into bespoke solutions for institutional, corporate, or high-net-worth investors.

A core building block in structured payoffs is the *digital option* (*binary option*), which pays a fixed amount if the underlying asset meets a specified condition and nothing otherwise. These options are frequently embedded in structured notes to define complex payoffs, such as "10% if the index rises above 4,000," regardless of how much it rises. While conceptually simple, binary payoffs create discontinuous risk profiles and can magnify losses under volatile market conditions, demanding careful risk management.

Structured products often embed these payoffs into more complex arrangements. Widely used examples include *reverse convertible notes* and the *autocallable structures*, discussed earlier in this chapter. These designs are prevalent in retail and private banking markets and institutional portfolios seeking enhanced yield with conditional downside exposure.

In commodity markets, structured payoffs are used to meet the needs of exporters and hedgers. Contracts such as *target redemption forwards* (TRFs) continue accruing until a cumulative profit target is reached. At the same time, *knock-in accumulators* obligate the buyer to accept increasing quantities of the underlying commodity at unfavorable prices if market conditions trigger. These instruments provide low-cost hedging with embedded leverage but introduce significant tail risk in adverse scenarios.

Structured hybrids can also link multiple risk factors to create multi-asset or cross-market exposures. A *quanto option*, for example, delivers returns on a foreign asset but pays in the domestic currency at a fixed rate, eliminating foreign exchange (FX) volatility. Such products are helpful in cross-border investments or in emerging markets where local liquidity is limited. At the institutional level, dealers frequently design *custom total return swaps* and *structured equity derivatives* to simulate hedge fund replication strategies, apply leveraged index overlays, or monetize restricted stock holdings. These products are often developed closely with portfolio managers and corporate treasurers to satisfy specific tax, accounting, or capital objectives.

Structured payoff derivatives thus represent the outer edge of derivative customization. They allow market participants to precisely shape exposures, reflecting the growing demand for bespoke yield solutions, risk-transfer structures, and regulatory arbitrage opportunities. Yet, this flexibility comes with heightened model risk, valuation opacity, and governance demands, reinforcing the need for robust oversight and expertise in their design and management.

Table 8.2 summarizes the key characteristics, payoff profiles, and common applications of major path-dependent and structured payoff derivatives described in the preceding sections. It provides a comparative view of their structural features and risk–return trade-offs.

8.2.3 *Real-world use cases for structured and exotic derivatives*

Exotic and customized derivatives are not abstract constructs; they are actively deployed across financial institutions, corporations, and government entities to solve problems standard instruments cannot address. These products respond to complex exposure profiles, market constraints, or regulatory considerations. Their practical relevance spans yield enhancement, corporate hedging, commodity risk management, insurance and reinsurance, hedge fund strategies, and regulatory capital optimization.

Table 8.2. Representative Path-Dependent and Structured Payoff Derivatives

Instrument	Key Features	Typical Use Cases
Asian Option	Payoff based on the average price of the underlying over a set period; reduces impact of short-term volatility spikes.	Airlines hedging jet fuel costs; commodity users smoothing input price volatility.
Barrier Option	Activates ("knock-in") or deactivates ("knock-out") if the underlying crosses a trigger level; can lower option premiums.	Equity hedges with conditional protection; structured notes with cost-reduction features.
Lookback Option	Payoff determined by the best or worst observed price during the option's life; offers hindsight advantage.	Tactical trading strategies; structured products seeking maximum gain capture.
Cliquet Option	Periodic strike resets with gains locked in; combines multiple forward-start options into one instrument.	Retail structured products targeting steady returns with partial downside protection.
Digital (Binary) Option	Fixed payout if a specified condition is met; otherwise zero; creates discontinuous payoff profiles.	Structured notes offering defined cash outcomes; yield enhancement trades.
Reverse Convertible Note	Bond combined with a short put; high coupon income, but principal may be repaid in shares if barrier breached.	Yield-seeking investors with conditional equity exposure.
Autocallable	Pays fixed returns if performance thresholds met; auto-redeems early if conditions satisfied.	Private banking products for clients seeking enhanced yield with capped risk.
Target Redemption Forward (TRF)	Continues until cumulative profit target reached; may terminate early on target achievement.	Exporter hedging with profit objectives; commodity traders locking in gains.
Knock-In Accumulator	Increases exposure if adverse market moves occur; low entry cost but high potential tail risk.	Commodity hedgers accepting conditional increased obligations.
Quanto Option	Returns linked to foreign asset but paid in domestic currency at fixed rate; removes FX volatility.	Cross-border equity or commodity investments without currency exposure.
Custom Total Return Swap	Transfers total economic return of an asset or index without ownership; can embed leverage or overlays.	Hedge fund replication; monetizing restricted stock; balance sheet optimization.

8.2.3.1 *Yield enhancement in low-rate environments*

Structured products such as autocallable notes and reverse convertibles have become central tools for private banks serving high-net-worth clients, particularly during low-interest-rate periods. For example, after the 2007–2008 Global Financial Crisis (GFC), banks such as BNP Paribas and UBS issued autocallable notes linked to the Euro Stoxx 50. These instruments offered yields far above government bonds by embedding short volatility exposure, typically selling downside puts and paying contingent coupons when the index remained above a barrier.

While effective for yield enhancement, these products exposed clients to significant losses if the underlying index fell below the trigger and remained depressed. This trade-off between income generation and tail risk remains central to their design.

8.2.3.2 *Corporate hedging with barrier options*

Multinational corporations use barrier options to hedge FX exposure while reducing upfront costs. For example, Caterpillar Inc. historically employed knock-in options to hedge JPY/USD exposure—a strategy that reduced premiums but left the company unhedged until activation, a trade-off often driven by budgetary and accounting considerations.

8.2.3.3 *Commodity producers and Asian options*

Energy and mining companies face price exposure over rolling periods. Rio Tinto, for example, has used average-price iron ore and copper options to align hedge payouts with the pricing conventions in its long-term supply contracts. This approach smooths earnings volatility while mitigating the impact of short-term price spikes.

8.2.3.4 *Insurance and reinsurance: Catastrophe bonds and derivatives*

Insurance-linked securities often feature exotic, non-market payoffs. Catastrophe (CAT) bonds and derivatives issued by Swiss Re and Munich Re are triggered by parametric events such as hurricane wind speeds or earthquake magnitudes. These structures allow insurers to transfer tail risk to capital markets.

A notable example occurred in 2017 after Hurricane Irma, when several CAT bond tranches were partially triggered, providing payouts based on model-derived damage assessments. Such instruments rely on actuarial modeling, often creating complexity that exceeds traditional financial risk modeling.[2]

8.2.3.5 *Hedge fund access via total return swaps*

Hedge funds and other leveraged investment vehicles frequently use total return swaps (TRSs) to gain synthetic exposure to equity indices and concentrated or less liquid stock baskets while avoiding direct ownership, which can be constrained by leverage limits, short-selling restrictions, or position-reporting requirements. A notable illustration is the 2021 collapse of Archegos Capital Management, a highly leveraged family office that built large, concentrated equity exposures through bespoke security-based total return swaps with multiple prime brokers; when the underlying stocks fell and margin calls could not be met, the unwinding of these opaque TRS positions amplified losses and exposed serious transparency and risk-management weaknesses across its dealer counterparts.

8.2.3.6 *Regulatory arbitrage and capital relief trades*

Banks have long used *customized credit derivatives* for regulatory capital management. A prominent example is *synthetic securitizations* executed by European banks such as UniCredit and Santander, which transferred the credit risk of loan portfolios to hedge funds and insurers via credit-default swaps (CDSs) or credit-linked notes.

These examples demonstrate that exotic derivatives are highly adaptable tools, capable of serving diverse institutional needs, ranging from yield generation and risk transfer to regulatory optimization and market access. However, their complexity introduces pricing opacity, model risk, counterparty exposure, and systemic vulnerabilities, demanding strong governance and oversight.

---

[2]René M. Stultz, "Risk Management Failures: What Are They and When Do They Happen?" *Journal of Applied Corporate Finance*, 20(4), 2008, pp. 39–48.

8.3 Design and Issuance: The Role of Dealers and Counterparties

The creation of customized or exotic derivatives is typically a collaborative process between the end-user, such as an institutional investor, hedge fund, or corporate treasurer, and a structuring team at a dealer or investment bank. These products are not purchased off the shelf. Instead, they emerge from a negotiated process of identifying the economic objective, assessing constraints, and engineering a solution that meets financial, regulatory, and operational requirements.

The design process begins with defining the desired exposure profile. This could include hedging a nonlinear risk (such as a cap on a rising commodity input), expressing a view on multiple market variables (such as relative equity index performance adjusted for currency), or generating yield within defined boundaries. Structurers then map these objectives into *replicable payoffs* using a combination of building blocks: vanilla options, swaps, forwards, and embedded barriers or triggers.

Pricing is performed using proprietary models, often extensions of Black–Scholes, binomial trees, or Monte Carlo simulations, as described in Part 5 of this book, with custom calibration to market volatility surfaces and correlation structures. Dealers quote a price or implied yield that embeds expected risk, hedging costs, liquidity, and capital utilization. The client may request multiple iterations to explore trade-offs between complexity and economics.

The documentation phase involves term sheets and, for more complex transactions, a confirmation governed by an ISDA Master Agreement, as described in the previous chapter. This governs credit events, netting, collateralization, and close-out provisions. In most cases, the instrument is not standardized, so it may carry limited secondary liquidity and is intended to be held to maturity or unwound through bilateral negotiation.

Dealers typically hedge their exposure dynamically using a combination of offsetting vanilla derivatives, cash instruments, and, in some cases, macro hedges. The complexity of the hedge, especially for path-dependent or discontinuous payoffs, adds to the product's cost and affects its quoted bid–ask spread. Exotic desks may warehouse some risk temporarily but are capital-constrained, meaning client demand must generally be matched by offsetting market flows or internal risk-sharing.

Leading derivatives dealers have a comparative advantage in their ability to structure and manage such positions. These products generate significant fees and relationship value, particularly with sophisticated clients seeking customized solutions. However, the lack of standardization, opacity in valuation, and bespoke nature of documentation also introduce concerns about transparency, valuation consistency, and model risk, particularly when used by institutions with limited internal risk capacity.

Asymmetries in information and capability thus define the dealer-client dynamic in custom derivatives issuance. While beneficial when well-governed, it can lead to mispricing, mis-selling, or complexity-induced errors without transparency, disclosure, and regulatory oversight.

8.4 Risk and Regulatory Challenges: Case Studies in Customized Derivatives

Customized and exotic derivatives can deliver highly tailored risk-return profiles, but their complexity, opacity, and illiquidity also introduce risks that extend well beyond those of standardized instruments. These include model risk, liquidity constraints, counterparty exposure, regulatory arbitrage, client suitability concerns, and legal and documentation vulnerabilities. Because such products often rely on internal pricing models, bespoke bilateral contracts, and limited secondary market activity, failures in governance can escalate into major financial and reputational damage.

The following real-world case studies illustrate how these risks materialize in practice: Société Générale's rogue trading losses, AIG's collapse in the credit default swap market, Archegos Capital's total return swap failures, Lehman Brothers' mis-sold minibonds, European banks' synthetic securitizations, and UBS's legal dispute with Highland Capital. Each example highlights a specific dimension of risk while collectively reinforcing the principle that complex derivatives demand rigorous oversight, model validation, and clear documentation.

8.4.1 *Model risk: Société Générale (2008 rogue trading scandal)*

In 2008, Société Générale incurred a €4.9 billion trading loss after a trader built massive unauthorized positions in equity index futures and swaps. Although the instruments were not highly exotic, weak internal controls, inadequate backtesting, and frequent overrides of internal risk models left the bank blind to its true exposure. This case demonstrates how model risk arises when governance fails, particularly for customized derivatives whose complexity and limited market transparency make mispricing hard to detect until losses are realized.

8.4.2 *Liquidity risk: Credit Suisse and the Archegos collapse (2021)*

The 2021 collapse of Archegos Capital Management exposed the acute liquidity risk of bespoke TRS. Archegos used multiple bilateral TRS agreements to build concentrated positions in volatile equities like ViacomCBS. When the stocks declined, Credit Suisse and other prime brokers could not quickly unwind their exposures due to the customized terms of the swaps and a lack of secondary liquidity. The resulting $5.5 billion loss at Credit Suisse highlights how illiquidity in exotic derivatives can amplify losses during market stress.

8.4.3 *Counterparty risk: AIG and credit default swaps on CDOs (2007–2008)*

During the GFC, American International Group's (AIG's) near-collapse stemmed from its issuance of highly customized credit default swaps (CDSs) on senior tranches of collateralized debt obligations (CDOs). These OTC CDSs were largely uncollateralized until AIG's credit rating was downgraded, triggering sudden collateral calls that the firm could not meet. The failure to properly manage counterparty risk in bespoke derivatives created systemic vulnerabilities that required over $180 billion in U.S. government support.

8.4.4 *Regulatory arbitrage: Synthetic securitizations in Europe*

European banks, including UniCredit and Santander, used synthetic securitizations to transfer the credit risk of loan portfolios to hedge funds and insurers via customized CDS or credit-linked notes. These structures reduced reported risk-weighted assets and freed up regulatory capital, despite offering limited genuine risk transfer. Regulators, including the European Banking Authority, later criticized such *regulatory arbitrage*, noting that opaque and highly tailored trades can undermine the spirit of prudential requirements and erode market confidence.

8.4.5 *Mis-selling and client suitability: Lehman Brothers minibonds in Asia (2008)*

Before its 2008 bankruptcy, Lehman Brothers sold structured notes branded as "minibonds" to Hong Kong and Singapore retail investors. These notes, which embedded digital options and credit-linked structures, became worthless after Lehman Brothers' failure. Many investors did not understand the embedded derivatives or the counterparty risk they carried. This case underscores the importance of client suitability reviews, clear disclosures, and the heightened mis-selling risk accompanying complex product distribution to retail markets.

8.4.6 *Legal and documentation risk: UBS v. Highland Capital (2010)*

The long-running litigation between UBS Securities LLC and Highland Capital Management, L.P. arose from a complex, restructured CDO/CLO warehousing and securitization transaction in which UBS agreed to finance and warehouse collateral and assume certain credit default swap and related risks, while Highland-managed funds were meant to bear the ultimate risk of losses. When the value of the warehoused collateral and CDS positions deteriorated during the financial crisis and the securitization failed to close, UBS alleged that Highland-related entities breached their contractual obligations, including by failing to provide agreed collateral support and by engaging in fraudulent transfers to shield assets; Highland disputed liability and advanced various defenses. New York courts ultimately entered substantial judgments in UBS's favor against Highland-related funds, underscoring how ambiguous allocation of risk, complex interlocking contracts, and insufficiently clear drafting in bespoke OTC and structured finance transactions—even when documented under standard ISDA and ancillary frameworks—can produce years of costly litigation and protracted uncertainty over rights and obligations.

Taken together with other case studies, this dispute illustrates that the danger in exotic and customized derivatives and structured deals often lies less in the instruments themselves and more in opaque valuation, weak internal controls, inadequate collateralization, poor counterparty governance, and misaligned incentives; when these are mismanaged, losses can escalate into regulatory scrutiny, reputational damage, and broader market spillovers.

This naturally leads to the next critical challenge: valuation and pricing. Unlike standardized instruments with observable market prices, customized derivatives often require complex modeling, scenario analysis, and careful calibration to market data. The following section examines how institutions approach pricing, the role of model governance, and the techniques used to navigate the inherent uncertainty of valuing bespoke derivatives.

8.5 Valuation and Pricing Considerations

Valuing customized and exotic derivatives presents challenges that are often absent in the pricing of standardized instruments. These products typically lack active secondary markets, which means there are no observable market prices to anchor valuation models. As a result, institutions rely heavily on internal models, assumptions about volatility and correlations, and scenario-based pricing techniques.

For simpler derivatives like European options, closed-form solutions such as the Black–Scholes model, described in Chapter 22, are sufficient. However, exotic derivatives often involve features such as path dependency, multiple underlying assets, early exercise conditions, or nonlinear payouts, which preclude closed-form solutions. Pricing these products may instead require numerical methods such as binomial trees, finite difference methods, or, most commonly, Monte Carlo simulations.[3]

Take, for example, a lookback option, where the payoff depends on the maximum or minimum value the underlying asset reaches during the option's life. Pricing this option requires modeling the full distribution of price paths over time rather than just the terminal price. Similarly, barrier options require tracking whether and when the underlying asset crosses a trigger level. These complexities increase the computational burden and sensitivity to input assumptions, especially volatility surfaces and jump risks.

Valuation is further complicated by illiquidity. Unlike exchange-traded options with market-implied volatilities, exotic options may require calibrating volatility assumptions using proxy data or extrapolations. Even small differences in model choice or input calibration can lead to substantial differences in price, raising the risk of model arbitrage or disputes between counterparties.

[3] These valuation methods are described in Chapter 20.

In institutional settings, this model risk is often addressed by using a "model approval" process, in which independent risk management or quantitative research teams validate the pricing engine and stress-test its assumptions. Traders may be required to mark their positions using both model values and observable proxy benchmarks, such as comparable vanilla options or CDS spreads. These practices help ensure that models do not systematically misstate the value of complex exposures.

Regulators have become increasingly focused on how these models are used and whether they are sufficiently robust. Under frameworks such as Basel III and Fundamental Review of the Trading Book (FRTB), banks must demonstrate the consistency and reliability of their pricing models, particularly for illiquid or hard-to-value products. In some cases, banks are required to add valuation adjustments—known as XVA metrics (such as CVA, DVA, and FVA, as described in the previous chapter)—to account for credit, funding, and liquidity risk embedded in customized derivatives.

Ultimately, the valuation of exotic and customized derivatives is less about finding a unique "correct" price and more about bounding a reasonable range of values under sound assumptions. The emphasis shifts from market discovery to model governance, scenario analysis, and the transparency of assumptions. This has implications for financial reporting, regulatory compliance, risk management, and client communications.

8.6 Summary

In this chapter, I describe how customized, structured, and exotic derivatives extend beyond the capabilities of standard instruments to meet specific investment objectives and risk profiles. These products, ranging from structured notes to path-dependent options and hybrid payoffs, allow market participants to intentionally design risk-return outcomes that align with yield, hedging, regulatory, or capital goals.

I describe structured notes and embedded derivatives, such as reverse convertibles, autocallables, dual-currency notes, and convertible bonds. I show how these instruments blend debt with derivative features to create tailored payoffs, using real-world examples to illustrate how financial engineers design products for enhanced yield, principal protection, or conditional equity exposure.

I then examine path-dependent and structured payoff derivatives, including Asian, barrier, lookback, digital, and cliquet options, and structured hybrids such as quanto options, TRFs, and custom total return swaps. I demonstrate how these products allow precise exposure management, multi-asset linkages, and bespoke risk transfer. I emphasize that their appeal lies in the ability to express nuanced market views and implement highly targeted strategies while introducing model and liquidity risks.

Next, I present real-world applications and institutional use cases, such as yield enhancement for private banking clients, corporate hedging with barrier options, commodity producers using Asian options, insurers issuing catastrophe bonds, hedge funds employing total return swaps, and banks structuring synthetic securitizations for capital relief. I highlight how these examples show customized derivatives' utility and complexity.

I also discuss the design and issuance process, detailing how dealers and clients collaborate to define objectives, engineer payoffs, and document trades under ISDA agreements.

I then examine risk and regulatory challenges through case studies, including Société Générale's rogue trading losses, the Archegos collapse, AIG's CDS exposure on CDOs, European synthetic securitizations, Lehman's minibond mis-selling, and the UBS v. Highland Capital dispute. I use these examples to illustrate model risk, liquidity risk, counterparty exposure, regulatory arbitrage, client suitability concerns, and legal and documentation vulnerabilities.

Finally, I focus on valuation and pricing considerations for exotic and customized derivatives. I explain that these products often lack observable market prices, requiring scenario-based models, Monte Carlo simulations, and careful input calibration. I show how institutions use model approval, independent validation, and valuation adjustments to manage pricing uncertainty and regulatory compliance.

Customized and exotic derivatives are potent tools for tailoring risk and return but require rigorous governance, transparent modeling, and strong oversight. By understanding their design logic, applications, and operational realities, one can identify when complexity serves a strategic purpose and conceals risk.

Chapter 9

Credit Derivatives

In this chapter, I focus on credit derivatives, financial instruments that allow market participants to transfer, manage, and trade credit risk separately from ownership of the underlying asset. Unlike interest rate or equity derivatives, which are primarily concerned with market risk, credit derivatives are specifically designed to isolate and redistribute the risk of default, credit deterioration, or rating migration. They provide a mechanism for institutions to hedge loan portfolios, protect against counterparty exposures, enhance yield, and optimize regulatory capital without selling the underlying loans or bonds.

I have chosen to dedicate an entire chapter to credit derivatives even though they are traded primarily in the over-the-counter (OTC) market and might, at first glance, appear to belong with other OTC derivatives. Credit derivatives merit their own treatment because they introduce unique structures, risks, and market practices that distinguish them from other OTC instruments. Their mechanics, especially the concepts of credit events, settlement procedures, and the separation of ownership from risk, are unlike those of swaps or options on traditional financial assets. Moreover, the regulatory, accounting, and systemic considerations surrounding credit derivatives have evolved in response to the lessons of the 2007–2008 Global Financial Crisis (GFC), making them a critical area of study in their own right.

In the sections that follow, I explain the principal instruments in the credit derivatives market, including single-name and index credit default swaps (CDSs), credit-linked notes (CLNs), total return swaps on credit assets (TRS-CA), and specialized products such as first-to-default baskets, credit spread options, and loan credit default swaps (LCDSs).[1] I also discuss the structure and trading of the OTC derivatives market, valuation and collateral practices, and the regulatory frameworks that govern margin, capital, and post-trade processes.

9.1 The Components of Credit Risk

Credit risk is the potential for financial loss arising from a borrower's, counterparty's, or reference entity's credit quality deterioration. While a complete failure to meet contractual obligations, known as *default risk*, is the most visible manifestation of credit risk, the concept is broader. It includes the effects of changes in market perceptions of creditworthiness, ratings migrations, and uncertainty about recovery after default. In practice, credit risk is best understood as the combination of default risk, credit spread risk, downgrade or migration risk, and recovery and settlement risk.

Default risk is the core of credit risk and represents the possibility that an issuer will fail to make scheduled interest or principal payments. A corporate bond issuer that misses a coupon payment or files for bankruptcy illustrates this risk. Default risk is the primary focus of CDSs, where protection buyers transfer the potential loss from a credit event to protection sellers in exchange for periodic premiums.

Credit spread risk arises even without a default. It reflects the sensitivity of a bond or loan's market value to changes in its credit spread (i.e., the extra yield investors demand over a risk-free benchmark to compensate for taking on credit exposure). When spreads widen due to market concerns about an issuer or its sector, the security's value declines, generating mark-to-market losses for the holder. Credit derivatives such as total return swaps transfer default and spread risk, making them essential tools for managing the market dimension of credit exposure.

---

[1] Collateralized debt obligations (CDOs) and synthetic CDOs were once a prominent category of credit derivatives, particularly in the 2000–2007 period, when they were widely used to repackage mortgage-backed securities and corporate bonds. Their issuance collapsed after the GFC due to catastrophic losses, investor withdrawal, and heightened regulatory scrutiny. Today, issuance is largely limited to collateralized loan obligations and private synthetic securitizations for regulatory capital relief, while the broad market for multi-name synthetic CDOs is virtually nonexistent.

Downgrade risk (also called *migration risk*) captures the impact of credit rating changes.[2] Even in the absence of default, a downgrade signals increased credit risk and typically leads to spread widening and lower asset prices. For example, a bond downgraded from A to BBB may trigger forced selling by institutional investors, reducing its price and increasing the cost of CDS protection. In derivative markets, downgrade risk affects valuations and can trigger additional collateral requirements, particularly in bilateral OTC agreements.

Recovery risk and *settlement risk* form the final component of credit risk. This risk reflects the uncertainty about how much value can be recouped after a default. In contrast, settlement risk concerns the timing and mechanics of fulfilling obligations in the event of a credit event. For instance, as will be explained later, a physically settled CDS requires the protection seller to deliver the notional value in exchange for the defaulted bond, whose recovery value may differ from model assumptions. Accurate recovery modeling and clear settlement procedures are critical for pricing and managing complex credit derivatives.

Credit risk can be explained through these components—default, spread, downgrade, and recovery/settlement and how credit derivatives redistribute exposures across market participants. This framework provides the foundation for understanding how instruments such as CDSs, CLNs, and structured credit products are designed to isolate, transfer, and manage specific aspects of credit risk.

9.2 Credit Derivative Instruments

The credit derivatives market encompasses a variety of instruments that allow participants to manage, transfer, or assume credit risk without directly trading the underlying loans or bonds. These instruments range from standardized contracts to highly structured products designed to meet specific risk management, yield enhancement, or capital

[2]Credit ratings provide an independent assessment of an issuer's creditworthiness or a specific debt instrument. They serve as a signal to investors about the likelihood that the borrower will meet its financial obligations on time and in full. The major credit rating agencies are Moody's Investors Service, Standard & Poor's (S&P) Global Ratings, and Fitch Ratings. For a more detailed discussion of credit ratings, including their methodology, uses, and historical development, see Chapter 16 in Frank J. Fabozzi and Francesco A. Fabozzi, *Bond Markets, Analysis, and Strategies*. Cambridge, MA: MIT Press, 2026.

optimization objectives. The most widely used products include CDSs, which protect against credit events such as defaults or bankruptcies. Other instruments extend the functionality of credit derivatives, including basket swaps such as first-to-default and *n*th-to-default structures, credit spread options, LCDSs, CLNs, and TRS-CA.[3]

In this section, I describe the principal instruments in the credit derivatives market, beginning with CDSs and then reviewing related products that enable more complex and tailored approaches to managing credit risk.

9.2.1 *Credit default swaps*

CDSs are the foundational instruments of the credit derivatives market. They allow credit risk transfer without transferring ownership of the underlying asset. A CDS is a bilateral contract between a *protection buyer* and a *protection seller* referencing a specific borrower (the *reference entity*) and often a designated bond or loan (the *reference obligation*).[4] In exchange for a periodic premium, the protection seller compensates the buyer if a credit event occurs. Credit events will be reviewed in a later section.

A CDS has two legs:

- The *premium leg*, where the protection buyer makes regular payments, typically quarterly, at a fixed *CDS spread*, is the annualized fee expressed in basis points that reflects the market's assessment of the reference entity's credit risk. This spread is applied to the notional amount, which represents the face value of credit risk being transferred.
- The *protection leg*, where the seller provides compensation upon a credit event via physical settlement (buyer delivers defaulted bonds for par value) or cash settlement (the seller pays the difference between par and market recovery value).

[3]For a more detailed discussion of credit derivatives, see Mark J. P. Anson, Frank J. Fabozzi, Moorad Choudhry, and Ren-Raw Chen, *Credit Derivatives: Instruments, Pricing, and Applications.* Hoboken, NJ: John Wiley & Sons, 2004.

[4]For a more detailed description of CDS, see Dominic O'Kane, "Credit Derivatives." Chapter 67 (pp. 1657–1684) in Frank J Fabozzi (editor), *The Handbook of Fixed Income Securities*. New York, NY: McGraw Hill, 2021.

ISDA's standardized documentation, described in Chapter 10, governs the definition of credit events, settlement procedures, and deliverable obligations, ensuring market consistency and enforceability.

9.2.1.1 *Single-name CDS*

A *single-name CDS* references one corporate, sovereign, municipal, or structured credit issuer. These instruments are used to hedge, speculate, or gain synthetic exposure to the credit quality of a single entity. The mechanics and cash flows of a single-name CDS are as follows:

- The protection buyer pays a quarterly premium on the notional amount.
- If no credit event occurs, the buyer continues making payments until the contract's maturity.
- If a credit event occurs, premium payments stop, and the protection seller must compensate the protection buyer for the loss associated with the defaulted obligation.

Compensation can occur through a physical settlement, in which the protection buyer delivers an eligible defaulted bond or loan to the protection seller in exchange for par value. In practice, the protection buyer typically offers the *cheapest-to-deliver* (CTD) obligation, an eligible bond or loan trading at the lowest market price. This allows the buyer to maximize the benefits of protection while the seller assumes the most adverse credit exposure permitted under the contract.

Pricing and Premium Calculation: The CDS spread reflects the market's default probability and expected loss assessment. Premiums are either:

- *running spread payments* (1% for investment-grade and 5% for high-yield reference names, per ISDA post-2009 convention), with an upfront adjustment when the market spread differs from the running spread, or
- full market spreads, used before standardization.

The premium leg of a CDS consists of the regular payments the protection buyer makes to the protection seller over the life of the contract. The CDS spread, the annualized fee expressed in basis points that reflects the market's assessment of the reference entity's credit risk, determines these payments. The spread is applied to the notional amount, representing the face value of transferred credit risk.

The general formula for a quarterly premium payment is

$$\text{Quarterly premium} = \text{Notional amount} \times \text{CDS spread (decimal)} \times \text{Days in accrual period}/360$$

where:

- Notional amount = face value of credit risk being hedged,
- CDS spread (decimal) = annualized spread ÷ 100 (e.g., 150 bps = 0.015),
- Days in accrual period ÷ 360 = day-count fraction for the quarter.

For example, consider a \$10 million notional CDS with a 150 bp annual spread and a 90-day accrual period. The quarterly premium is calculated as

$$\text{Quarterly premium} = \$10{,}000{,}000 \times 0.015 \times 90/360 = \$37{,}500$$

This means the protection buyer pays \$37,500 per quarter if no credit event occurs.

As another example, for a \$10 million notional single-name CDS with a 2% annual spread and 92 days in the quarter, the running spread:

$$\text{Quarterly premium} = \$10{,}000{,}000 \times 0.02 \times 92/360 = \$51{,}111$$

Under the running spread convention, an upfront payment is then added or received to reconcile the difference between the contractual spread and the prevailing market spread, using ISDA's standard CDS valuation model.

Economic Interpretation of a Single-Name CDS: The economic interpretation of a single-name *CDS* reflects how credit risk is transferred between the protection buyer and the seller. The protection seller occupies a position similar to being long the underlying bond. By selling protection, the seller receives a steady stream of premium payments, analogous to coupon income, but bears the risk of loss if the reference entity defaults or suffers a credit event. If the reference entity's credit quality remains stable or improves, the protection seller benefits from collecting premiums without paying.

Conversely, the protection buyer has an economic position analogous to being short the bond. The buyer pays the regular CDS premiums, which function similarly to the cost of carrying a short position but gains if the reference entity's credit quality deteriorates. A widening of credit spreads or the occurrence of a credit event increases the value of the protection because it entitles the buyer to compensation for the decline in the bond's market value.

Single-name CDS provides an efficient mechanism for accessing credit exposure in either direction. It allows investors to assume or hedge credit risk without fully funding a bond purchase, thereby creating leverage opportunities. In addition, CDS contracts facilitate short credit positions, which are often more difficult and costly to establish in the cash bond market. Single-name CDS enables precise credit risk management and flexible trading strategies by separating credit risk from funding and ownership.

9.2.1.2 *Index CDS*

An *index CDS* references a standardized basket of multiple reference entities, providing diversified credit exposure within a single contract. Prominent indices include the following:

- CDX.NA.IG: 125 investment-grade North American corporates.
- CDX.NA.HY: 100 high-yield North American corporates.
- iTraxx Europe: 125 European investment-grade corporates.
- SovX indices: baskets of sovereign issuers in CEEMEA or Asia-Pacific.

The key features of an index CDS are as follows:

- Index CDS premiums are paid quarterly, just like single-name CDSs.
- A credit event on a constituent reduces the notional amount for future premium calculations. Payments continue on the remaining notional, unlike a single-name CDSs, which terminates upon a credit event.
- New index series are issued semiannually (March and September), reflecting rating changes and defaults.

The economic function of the index CDS lies in its ability to provide efficient tools for hedging and macro credit positioning. A portfolio manager can adjust portfolio exposure to credit markets in either direction without trading the underlying bonds. Selling protection on an index CDS increases credit exposure and is economically similar to taking a long credit position, benefiting when credit conditions remain stable or improve. Conversely, buying protection reduces credit exposure, functioning like a short credit position, and increases in value when credit spreads widen or defaults become more likely.

Because index CDS contracts are highly standardized and trade with deep liquidity, they have become the preferred instruments for portfolio hedging and tactical credit strategies. Their liquidity and transparency also make them attractive for relative-value and basis trades, which exploit differences between the cash bond spread and the CDS spread. For example, a portfolio manager might purchase a bond while buying CDS protection or sell a bond while selling CDS protection, depending on where relative pricing offers an opportunity. This flexibility allows investors to implement directional, hedging, and arbitrage strategies efficiently across broad sectors or regions of the credit market.

9.2.2 *Credit-linked notes*

A *credit-linked note* (CLN) is a structured debt instrument that embeds credit risk transfer into a bond. Unlike a standalone CDS, which is a derivative contract, a CLN is an actual security issued by a bank or special purpose vehicle.[5] The noteholder receives regular interest payments, but part or all of the principal repayment is contingent on the performance of a specified reference entity or credit portfolio.

A CLN combines a traditional fixed-income investment with a short credit protection position. The issuer of the CLN sells credit protection, effectively entering into a CDS, and uses the proceeds from the note to collateralize that exposure. If no credit event occurs during the note's life, the investor receives full principal and interest. If a credit event occurs, the principal repayment is reduced by the loss amount defined in the note's terms. In this way, the investor earns a higher yield than a standard bond because the note compensates the buyer for taking on the embedded credit risk.

For example, a bank might issue a three-year CLN tied to a portfolio of investment-grade corporate bonds. The note could pay a 6% annual coupon, which is higher than the yield on comparable investment-grade

---

[5]For a more detailed description of CLNs, see Frank J. Fabozzi and Fred Hoffman, "Collateralized Loan Obligations." Chapter 30 (pp. 681–690) in *The Handbook of Fixed Income Securities.*

corporate bonds of similar maturity, but the principal repayment is contingent on the credit performance of the reference portfolio. If no defaults occur during the term, the investor earns the enhanced yield in full. If defaults arise, the investor bears the defined credit loss by reducing the principal returned at maturity.

CLNs serve several purposes in financial markets. Banks use CLNs to transfer credit risk from their loan portfolios to investors without selling the underlying loans, thereby achieving regulatory capital relief and freeing balance sheet capacity. Institutional investors, such as insurance companies and asset managers, use CLNs to gain targeted credit exposure and enhanced yields in a single, funded instrument rather than through separate bond and CDS positions.

While CLNs offer attractive income opportunities, they also carry risks. If the note is not fully collateralized, investors are exposed to the credit risk of the reference entity as well as the creditworthiness of the issuing bank. Illiquidity can also be a concern, as most CLNs trade in the OTC market with limited secondary activity. The valuation of a CLN depends on both the probability of default for the reference entity and the discounting of cash flows, making accurate modeling of credit spreads and recovery assumptions essential.

CLNs illustrate how credit derivatives can be embedded into investable securities. By integrating risk transfer into a funded note, they provide a mechanism for banks to offload credit risk and for investors to access higher yields in exchange for bearing this risk.

9.2.3 *Total return swaps on credit assets*

A TRS-CA is a credit derivative that transfers a reference asset's market and credit performance from one party to another without transferring actual ownership. In a TRS-CA, the *total return payer* agrees to pass through all cash flows and market value changes (coupons, principal repayments) and capital gains or losses of the reference asset to the *total return receiver*. In exchange, the receiver pays a floating interest rate plus a spread to the payer over the swap's life.

This credit derivative allows market participants to gain or shed exposure to credit assets synthetically. For the total return receiver, this contract provides the economic benefits and risks of owning the reference bond, loan, or structured credit portfolio without needing to fund the full purchase or hold the asset on the balance sheet. For the total return payer, this contract transfers the credit and market risk of the reference asset while retaining legal ownership, which can help manage regulatory capital and risk limits.

Consider a bank that holds a $100 million portfolio of corporate loans but wants to reduce its credit exposure without selling the loans and disrupting client relationships. By entering a total return swap on these loans, the bank agrees to pay the total return on the loan portfolio to a hedge fund in exchange for quarterly floating-rate payments. If the loans perform well, the hedge fund receives interest and any appreciation in value, while the bank earns the floating payments. If the loans suffer credit deterioration or default losses, the hedge fund absorbs those losses through reduced total returns, effectively protecting the bank.

Banks, hedge funds, and institutional investors widely use this credit derivative for three primary purposes. First, banks use them to achieve capital relief and risk transfer on loan portfolios while keeping the loans on their books. Second, hedge funds use them for leveraged credit exposure, as these credit derivatives require minimal upfront funding compared to direct purchases. Third, asset managers use them to gain exposure to otherwise illiquid or hard-to-access credit assets, such as syndicated loans or emerging-market bonds, without directly sourcing and custody the instruments.

Despite their flexibility, TRS-CA carries significant risks. The total return receiver bears the reference asset's full credit risk and market volatility and faces the possibility of substantial losses if defaults or spread widening occur. The total return payer, usually the asset owner, retains counterparty risk, as a default by the receiver could leave the payer exposed to adverse asset movements without full compensation. These credit derivatives are typically OTC instruments, making liquidity and collateral management essential for both parties.

TRS-CA illustrates how credit derivatives can unbundle economic exposure from ownership. They provide an efficient mechanism for transferring credit risk and leveraging balance sheets but require careful risk management to avoid magnifying counterparty and market vulnerabilities

9.2.4 *Other credit derivatives*

Beyond standard instruments such as CDS, CLNs, and TRS-CA, the credit derivatives market also includes several specialized products that serve niche purposes in credit risk management and trading. These instruments include first-to-default and *n*th-to-default baskets, credit spread options, and loan CDSs.

9.2.4.1 *First-to-default and nth-to-default swaps*

Basket credit default swaps allow market participants to gain exposure to the default risk of multiple reference entities in a single contract. A *first-to-default swap* protects a basket of credits but triggers a payout only upon the first default in the basket. This structure is cheaper than buying individual CDS on each reference entity because the probability of one default is higher than multiple defaults. Conversely, *n*th-to-default swaps protect after a specified number of defaults, such as the second or third default in a portfolio. These structures allow investors to take targeted views on portfolio credit risk and are frequently used for correlation trading or to transfer risk from concentrated loan portfolios.

9.2.4.2 *Credit spread options*

Credit spread options give the holder the right, but not the obligation, to benefit from changes in a bond or credit index spread relative to a benchmark. A call option on credit spreads pays off when spreads widen, making it a tool for hedging against credit deterioration or rising default risk. A *put option on spreads* benefits when spreads tighten, which is useful for investors speculating on improving credit conditions. Credit spread options are less common than CDS because they require liquid markets for implied volatility. Still, they provide a flexible alternative for managing spread risk without taking on the full default exposure.

9.2.4.3 *Loan credit default swaps*

LCDSs function in much the same way as standard single-name CDS but reference syndicated loans rather than bonds. *Syndicated loans* are large loans provided to a single borrower by a group of lenders, known as a syndicate, rather than by a single bank. This structure allows lenders to share both the funding and the credit risk when a company requires too large or risky financing for one institution to assume.

A syndicated loan is typically arranged by one or more lead banks, called lead arrangers or bookrunners, which negotiate the loan terms with the borrower and invite other banks or institutional lenders to participate. Each syndicate member contributes a portion of the total loan and earns interest and fees proportionately to its share. Syndicated loans are widely used in corporate finance, leveraged buyouts, project finance, and large infrastructure deals. They often carry floating interest rates (such as the Secured Overnight Financing Rate,[6] or SOFR, plus a spread) and may include covenants to protect lenders. Because they are actively traded in the secondary loan market, syndicated loans are suitable reference assets for derivatives such as LCDSs and securitized products such as CLOs.

In an LCDS contract, the protection buyer pays a premium to the protection seller, just as in a traditional CDS. Still, the reference obligation is a syndicated loan rather than a bond. If a credit event occurs, the protection seller compensates the buyer, and settlement is typically physical, requiring the delivery of the defaulted loan. Cash settlements are also possible, with payments based on the loan's market recovery value.

LCDS contracts allow banks and institutional investors to hedge credit risk on leveraged loan portfolios or to take synthetic credit exposure without holding the loans directly. By isolating credit risk from funding and ownership, LCDS provides an efficient tool for managing syndicated loan portfolios in primary and secondary markets.

9.3 Credit Events and Settlement in Credit Derivatives

This section explains what constitutes a credit event under credit derivative contracts and how settlement occurs once such an event is declared. Credit events are the contractual triggers that determine when protection under a CDS or related instrument is activated. Understanding how these events are defined, determined, and settled is fundamental to the operation of the credit derivatives market.

---

[6]SOFR is a benchmark interest rate for U.S. dollar-denominated derivatives and loans, based on the cost of borrowing cash overnight collateralized by U.S. Treasury securities in the repurchase agreement (repo) market. The Federal Reserve introduced it to replace the London Interbank Offered Rate (LIBOR) as a more robust, transaction-based benchmark. SOFR reflects actual market activity and is considered nearly risk-free because it is secured by Treasuries.

9.3.1 *Defining and determining credit events*

In the context of credit derivatives, a credit event is the contractually defined trigger that obligates the protection seller to compensate the protection buyer. The central concept determines when a CDS or related instrument will pay out. Unlike the market's casual notion of default, which can be broad and subjective, a credit event is precisely defined in the ISDA Credit Derivatives Definitions to ensure all parties agree on when protection is owed. This standardization has been critical to the growth and functioning of the credit derivatives market because it removes ambiguity and provides a clear framework for settlement.

A credit event reflects a material deterioration in the credit quality of the reference entity, which may be a corporation, sovereign, or other obligor named in the CDS contract. Corporate credit derivatives' most common credit events are bankruptcy, failure to pay, and restructuring. Bankruptcy occurs when the reference entity files for legal protection or is declared insolvent by a court. Failure to pay arises if the entity misses a required principal or interest payment on a qualifying debt obligation after any applicable grace period. Restructuring is more nuanced, occurring when debt terms are modified unfavorably to creditors, such as reducing interest or principal or extending the maturity, typically due to financial distress.

The precise definition of a credit event is essential because it determines when cash flows under a CDS stop and when the protection seller's obligation to compensate the buyer is activated. A company may face significant financial distress and see its bonds downgraded. Still, no credit event occurs unless it misses a payment, files for bankruptcy, or restructures its obligations in a manner that satisfies ISDA definitions. This distinction illustrates that market perceptions of risk and contractual triggers for risk transfer are not always aligned. CDS spreads can widen dramatically in anticipation of a problem without any actual credit event being triggered.

Credit event definitions are also tailored for different types of reference entities. For example, sovereign CDS include provisions for repudiation or moratorium, which apply if a government refuses to honor or delays debt payments without formally defaulting. LCDS adapts the credit event definitions to the syndicated loan market, focusing on missed loan payments or restructuring of loan terms. This tailoring ensures that credit derivatives align with the specific characteristics of the underlying debt market while maintaining consistency across ISDA-governed contracts.

Determining whether a credit event has occurred is handled through a formalized process to ensure fairness and consistency. Market participants can submit a question to the *ISDA Determinations Committee* (DC), which consists of major dealers and investor representatives, to vote on whether a credit event has occurred. This process, introduced after the GFC, has increased transparency and confidence by ensuring that CDS contracts are settled consistently across counterparties, reducing the risk of disputes or litigation.

9.3.2 *Settlement after a credit event*

Once a credit event has been formally declared, a CDS or other credit derivative transitions from the premium-payment phase to the settlement process, during which the protection buyer receives compensation, and the credit risk transfer is completed. The key objective of settlement is to provide a fair and predictable transfer of losses from the protection buyer to the protection seller while minimizing market disruption.

The process begins with notification and confirmation of the credit event, usually coordinated through ISDA's DC. After the event is declared, premium payments immediately stop, and the market prepares to settle the contracts. Standardized CDS positions are generally resolved through *ISDA-supervised auctions*, which establish a single market-based recovery price for the defaulted obligation and allow the large number of offsetting positions to be netted and settled efficiently. This ensures that all participants referencing the same entity settle on consistent terms.

The settlement process also involves position reconciliation and documentation. Market participants must confirm each trade's notional amounts, maturities, and deliverable obligations. Cleared trades, which are processed through a central counterparty (CCP), are coordinated by clearinghouses and settlement agents, including netting exposures and ensuring timely cash flows. Uncleared trades, by contrast, are bilateral agreements conducted directly between counterparties without central clearing. Their settlement relies on the ISDA Master Agreement and trade confirmations, requiring the parties to calculate the protection payment and exchange cash or deliver the defaulted obligations according to the agreed terms.

Timely settlement is essential. ISDA auctions and subsequent payments are typically completed within 30 days of the credit event to ensure rapid compensation and reduce uncertainty, particularly in volatile market conditions. Prompt and standardized settlements mitigate liquidity pressures that often arise during credit events, when market participants may already be managing other exposures.

Finally, the settlement process underscores the importance of standardization in credit derivatives. By clearly defining credit events, centralizing determinations, and coordinating settlement procedures, the market has created a framework that efficiently transfers credit risk from those seeking protection to those willing to bear it. This design has been a significant innovation, reinforcing the continued role of credit derivatives in hedging, risk management, and structured investment strategies.

9.4 Market Structure and Trading of Credit Derivatives

The credit derivatives market operates primarily OTC, where contracts are privately negotiated between counterparties rather than traded on formal exchanges. This structure allows for highly customized agreements, such as bespoke total return swaps or CLNs, but it also introduces counterparty and settlement risk. After the GFC, regulators implemented sweeping reforms to increase transparency and reduce systemic risk. Standardized single-name and index CDS are now cleared through CCPs, such as ICE Clear Credit in the U.S. and ICE Clear Europe, significantly lowering bilateral counterparty exposure. Central clearing also facilitates trade compression, which nets offsetting exposures and reduces the overall notional outstanding in the market.

The market's participants fall into two categories: dealers and end users. Global banks act as dealers, making markets in single-name CDS, CDS indices, and structured credit products. They act as intermediaries between end users, including hedge funds, asset managers, pension funds, insurance companies, and corporations. Hedge funds and proprietary trading desks use credit derivatives for directional and relative-value strategies. In contrast, asset managers and pension funds often focus on portfolio hedging or selective credit exposures. Insurance companies and banks also participate as sellers of credit protection, seeking to earn premium income in exchange for taking on credit risk. In some instances, sovereigns and supranational institutions enter the market for hedging or policy-related purposes, although their activity is relatively limited.

Liquidity in credit derivatives is concentrated in standardized products, especially CDS indices. The CDX family in North America and iTraxx in Europe and Asia provide efficient exposure to diversified corporate or sovereign credit risk baskets. CDS indices trade with tight bid–ask spreads and high volumes, making them the preferred instrument for hedging or expressing macro credit views. In contrast, single-name CDS liquidity varies widely and is deepest for large, frequently referenced issuers. CDS indices also roll on standardized dates, which helps align market activity and supports trade compression.

Standardization and documentation play a critical role in the credit derivatives market. The ISDA Master Agreement provides the legal framework for trading, while the ISDA Credit Derivatives Definitions specify key terms, including credit events such as failure to pay, bankruptcy, and restructuring. These definitions also cover settlement procedures and auction mechanisms, determining payouts after credit events. This uniform framework reduces legal uncertainty and facilitates the netting of exposures across counterparties.

Trading practices continue to evolve under regulatory oversight. Post-GFC reforms require most standardized CDSs to be cleared through central counterparties and reported to trade repositories to enhance transparency and reduce systemic risk. In the U.S., the Dodd–Frank Wall Street Reform and Consumer Protection Act of 2010 introduced mandatory central clearing, trade reporting, and margin requirements for standardized swaps, including CDSs. In Europe, the European Market Infrastructure Regulation (EMIR) established a parallel framework requiring central clearing for eligible derivatives, trade reporting to approved repositories, and stringent risk-mitigation standards for uncleared trades. Together, these regulations have transformed the credit derivatives market, reducing counterparty exposure and increasing regulatory transparency.

The current market structure balances the flexibility of bilateral agreements with the transparency and risk reduction benefits of central clearing and standardization. This framework underpins the efficient transfer of credit risk, supporting the broader role of credit derivatives in modern financial markets.

9.5 Valuation of Credit Derivatives

Valuing credit derivatives involves translating credit risk into monetary terms by combining market observations, modeled probabilities of default, and assumptions about recoveries in the event of default.[7] Unlike standardized interest rate or equity derivatives, most credit derivatives lack continuous, transparent market prices for every reference entity or

[7]For a more detailed description of CDS valuation, see Dominic O'Kane, "Credit Derivative Valuation and Risk." Chapter 69 (pp. 1685–1710) in *The Handbook of Fixed Income Securities.*

structure. As a result, valuation relies on models that estimate expected losses and incorporate market perceptions of credit quality. Valuation must capture the contract's predictable cash flows and the contingent payouts that depend on credit events.

9.5.1 *Valuing a credit default swap*

The CDS is the starting point for understanding credit derivative valuation. A CDS is valued on the principle that the premium leg (i.e., the series of payments made by the protection buyer) should equal the protection leg (i.e., the expected payout by the protection seller if a credit event occurs). The premium leg consists of regular quarterly or semiannual payments, applied to the notional amount, that continue until the contract matures or a credit event terminates the payments.

The protection leg represents the contingent compensation for the protection buyer. Its valuation requires estimating the probability of default over time, commonly expressed using hazard rates and survival probabilities. A *hazard rate* reflects the likelihood of default occurring in a small time interval. At the same time, the *survival probability* measures the chance that the reference entity remains solvent through a given date. This expected payout is then discounted to the present using market interest rates and adjusted for the assumed recovery rate, which reflects how much value creditors are likely to recoup after a default. A higher recovery assumption reduces the expected protection payment, and a lower recovery increases it.

Market participants quote CDS prices as spreads in basis points on the notional amount, reflecting the annualized cost of protection. A higher CDS spread signals higher perceived credit risk. For example, investment-grade corporates might trade at spreads of 50–150 basis points, while distressed or high-yield names can trade at spreads of hundreds or even thousands of basis points.

9.5.2 *Market models and computational methods*

The valuation of more bespoke or portfolio-based credit derivatives relies on market models that capture both the timing and magnitude of credit losses. Two conceptual approaches dominate:

1. *Reduced-form models* (*intensity-based models*) view default as a probabilistic event modeled by a hazard rate, without explicit reference to the firm's assets or balance sheet. These models are

valued for their flexibility and are widely used in CDSs and portfolio credit risk applications, as they can be calibrated directly to observed market spreads.

2. *Structural models*, which link default to the economics of the firm, often model the firm's asset value relative to its liabilities. These models provide economic intuition but are more data-intensive and less commonly used for active trading.[8]

For portfolios and structured products, Monte Carlo simulation and scenario-based pricing are common. These techniques allow the model to explore a range of potential default scenarios and market conditions, providing insights into expected cash flows and the distribution of potential losses.

9.5.3 *Mark-to-market and accounting considerations*

In addition to model pricing, institutions must mark credit derivatives to market to comply with accounting and regulatory standards. Market participants are expected to produce reasonable fair value estimates using market inputs and consistent modeling practices, even for instruments that trade infrequently. Under accounting rules, derivatives must be reported at fair value on the balance sheet, and changes in value are often reflected in profit or loss.

Illiquid positions, especially in bespoke credit derivatives or structured credit, require institutions to maintain model governance frameworks, document their assumptions, and apply adjustments where appropriate. These adjustments, often referred to collectively as XVA and discussed in Chapter 8, include credit valuation adjustment (CVA) for counterparty default risk, debit valuation adjustment (DVA) for the firm's own credit risk, and funding valuation adjustment (FVA) to account for the cost of funding collateralized trades.

Robust mark-to-market practices and transparent valuation methods are essential for regulatory compliance under Basel III and the Fundamental

---

[8] For a description of these two models, as well as, incomplete-information credit models, see Tim Backshall, Kay Giesecke, and Lisa Goldberg, "Credit-Risk Modeling." Chapter 42 (pp. 1051–1074) in *The Handbook of Fixed Income Securities.*

Review of the Trading Book (FRTB). Independent model validation, regular backtesting, and stress testing are now standard practices to ensure that reported valuations reflect the true economic risk of credit derivatives under both normal and stressed conditions.

9.5.4 *Summary of the valuation approach*

The valuation of credit derivatives is not about producing a single "correct" price. Instead, it defines a reasonable range of values supported by market data, model outputs, and documented assumptions. Accurate pricing underpins effective risk transfer, investor confidence, and regulatory compliance. In practice, combining market-based spreads, scenario analysis, and robust model governance enables institutions to manage credit derivative portfolios responsibly while maintaining transparency in financial reporting.

9.6 Applications of Credit Derivatives

Credit derivatives play a central role in modern financial markets because they allow institutions to separate and transfer credit risk without transferring ownership of the underlying asset. These instruments are used for four primary purposes: hedging credit exposure, enhancing yield, managing regulatory capital, and implementing speculative or relative-value strategies.

9.6.1 *Hedging credit exposure*

Banks and institutional investors use credit derivatives to protect against potential losses on loans, bonds, or portfolios of credit assets. A common approach is to purchase CDS protection on a specific borrower or a CDS index representing a sector or region. For example, a bank holding $100 million in corporate loans can hedge its default risk by buying CDS protection on the borrowers or on a corresponding credit index. If a credit event occurs, the CDS compensates the bank for its loss, allowing it to reduce portfolio volatility without liquidating the loans or jeopardizing client relationships.

9.6.2 *Enhancing yield*

Investors seeking higher returns can use credit derivatives to earn premiums in exchange for taking on credit risk. Selling CDS protection allows the investor to collect regular premium income if no credit event occurs. Similarly, buying CLNs or entering TRS-CA can provide enhanced yields compared with traditional bonds of similar maturity. These strategies are widely used by hedge funds, insurance companies, and pension funds that can manage default and mark-to-market risk.

9.6.3 *Regulatory capital and balance sheet management*

Credit derivatives also serve as tools for regulatory capital optimization. Under Basel III and FRTB rules, banks can reduce risk-weighted assets by transferring credit risk to other market participants. For example, a bank can enter synthetic risk transfer using CDSs or total return swaps on a loan portfolio, shifting credit risk to an institutional investor while retaining the loans on its books. This approach frees up capital for new lending or other strategic activities without triggering loan sales or client disruption.

9.6.4 *Speculation and relative-value strategies*

Credit derivatives allow investors to take positions on improving or deteriorating credit quality without buying or selling bonds. Hedge funds may buy CDS protection to express a negative credit view or sell protection to profit from tightening spreads. Traders also use credit derivatives in basis trades, which seek to exploit discrepancies between a bond's cash spread and the corresponding CDS spread, typically by buying the bond while simultaneously buying or selling CDS protection, or in correlation trades targeting relative value between different tranches or indices. These strategies can offer high returns but are highly sensitive to market volatility and liquidity conditions.

9.7 Summary

In this chapter, I examine the role of credit derivatives as tools for isolating, transferring, and managing credit risk without requiring the sale of the underlying loans or bonds. I explore the core instruments of the market—single-name and index CDSs, CLNs, total return swaps on credit assets, and other specialized structures—and show how each enables institutions to hedge, speculate, enhance yields, or optimize regulatory capital.

I also explain why credit derivatives warrant their own chapter, separate from discussing other OTC derivatives. Credit derivatives are unique because they depend on precisely defined credit events, formal settlement procedures, and a market infrastructure that balances flexibility with the need for standardization and regulatory oversight. Their use raises distinct issues of model risk, counterparty risk, liquidity risk, and systemic exposure, which have shaped both market practice and post-crisis regulatory reforms.

By understanding the structure, valuation, applications, and risk management of credit derivatives, one can appreciate how these instruments support financial institutions in managing credit exposure and capital efficiency. Used with discipline and strong governance, credit derivatives remain vital in global markets, offering powerful tools for hedging, risk transfer, and strategic portfolio management.

Part 3

Derivative Strategies and Portfolio Applications

Chapter 10

Executing Derivatives Strategies: Margin Practices and Rolling Mechanics

Effectively managing derivatives requires more than a well-designed trading or hedging strategy; it depends on a robust operational framework that supports execution, risk control, and liquidity management. Two of the most critical operational elements in derivatives markets are margin management and rolling strategies, which together form the backbone of day-to-day derivatives risk management.

In this chapter, I focus on the practical mechanics of margin and rolling, building on the foundational concepts of margining and collateralization introduced in the chapters on exchange-traded derivatives (ETDs; Chapter 6) and over-the-counter (OTC) derivatives (Chapter 8). Instead of redefining initial margin, variation margin, and close-out processes, I concentrate on how institutions monitor, fund, and optimize margin requirements in practice. Topics include collateral allocation, liquidity buffers, stress testing, dispute resolution, and the use of automation and integrated platforms to manage exposures efficiently.

The second part of the chapter examines rolling strategies, which allow traders and portfolio managers to maintain continuous exposure as derivative contracts approach expiration. Rolling is essential for long-term hedging, benchmark replication, and tactical positioning across futures, options, and swaps. I explain the mechanics of rolling, highlight key risks such as roll yield and basis risk, and present techniques to mitigate these effects across equity, fixed income, and commodity derivatives.

These operational processes enable institutions to maintain resilient derivatives portfolios, manage liquidity under stress, and meet regulatory and capital requirements. This perspective is essential for portfolio managers, traders, and risk officers seeking to implement robust, cost-efficient, and risk-aligned derivatives strategies within institutional risk governance frameworks.

10.1 Margin Requirements in Derivatives Markets

Margin is the operational foundation of derivatives risk management. It serves as a performance bond, ensuring that counterparties can meet their obligations and that losses are contained if a position moves against them. Unlike securities margin, which involves borrowing to increase exposure, derivatives margin is collateral posted to mitigate counterparty credit risk and support daily settlement.

Chapters 6 and 7 discuss the foundational concepts of margin (initial margin, variation margin, and close-out netting). Here, the focus is on the practical aspects of managing margins in institutional portfolios. Institutions track margin balances and exposure movements daily while projecting potential margin calls under various market scenarios to ensure liquidity is always available.

Funding and collateral allocation are central to this process. Institutions must determine which assets will be posted as collateral, considering eligibility rules and haircuts defined under the Credit Support Annex or clearinghouse regulations. Coordination with treasury functions is necessary to ensure that cash or high-quality liquid assets (HQLAs) can be deployed promptly to meet collateral calls. Because market conditions can change rapidly, stress testing is integral to the process. By modeling sudden market swings, firms can estimate the size of potential variation margin calls and maintain liquidity buffers to absorb these demands without disrupting normal operations.

Margin management also involves resolving disputes and ensuring smooth reconciliation with counterparties. Differences in valuation or margin calculations can arise due to timing, pricing models, or data inconsistencies. Modern institutions rely on automated reconciliation tools and structured dispute resolution protocols to prevent operational bottlenecks that could otherwise delay settlements.

Integrating margin management with institutional risk governance is critical. Daily margin processes feed into liquidity planning, capital allocation, and regulatory compliance. Collateral optimization systems help firms determine the most efficient assets to post, while risk aggregation platforms consolidate exposures across cleared and bilateral OTC portfolios. Automated alerts and workflow tools provide early warnings for large or unexpected calls, ensuring timely funding responses. By embedding margin management into the broader risk and liquidity framework, institutions can avoid forced asset sales, prevent regulatory breaches, and maintain trading capacity even during periods of market stress.

10.1.1 *Operational margin management*

Effective margin management is essential to maintaining institutional stability and market credibility in derivatives trading. Because margin represents collateral rather than borrowed funds, institutions must ensure sufficient liquidity is always available to meet their obligations. During heightened volatility, sudden market swings or spikes in implied volatility can cause margin requirements to increase sharply. Institutions that cannot respond quickly may face forced liquidations at unfavorable prices, compounding financial stress.

Maintaining a liquidity buffer is the first line of defense. Firms typically allocate HQLAs, such as cash, U.S. Treasury bills, or short-term repos, that can be mobilized immediately for collateral posting. The appropriate buffer size depends on portfolio leverage, historical volatility, and the margining practices of clearinghouses or prime brokers. A well-structured buffer allows firms to absorb unexpected margin calls without selling core portfolio holdings into a declining market.

Contingent liquidity facilities complement static buffers. These pre-arranged credit lines or repo agreements, often secured by government bonds or cash equivalents, provide same-day access to capital in the event of a margin spike. Institutions that integrate these facilities into their liquidity management frameworks are better prepared for sudden, systemic margin calls, such as those seen during the March 2020 COVID-19 market shock or the collapse of Archegos Capital Management in 2021. In both cases, institutions with planning and reliable liquidity access were able to maintain positions, while unprepared firms faced rapid deleveraging and, in some cases, default.

Automation is now a cornerstone of modern margin management. Real-time risk systems monitor margin balances, price movements, and key sensitivity measures (the "Greeks"), generating immediate alerts when exposures approach threshold levels. Advanced platforms can perform intraday recalculations, anticipate calls before they are issued, and link directly with treasury systems to enable rapid cash or eligible collateral transfers. These capabilities reduce the risk of missed or delayed postings, which can lead to penalties or forced trade restrictions. Institutions using predictive analytics can also model how new trades or market shocks will affect their liquidity and collateral requirements, improving decision-making under pressure.

Stress testing and scenario analysis provide the forward-looking perspective necessary for resilient margin planning. Institutions regularly simulate adverse events, such as sharp equity declines, volatility spikes, or widening collateral haircuts, to determine whether their buffers and contingent facilities can withstand extreme but plausible shocks. Historical and hypothetical scenarios, ranging from the GFC to COVID-era volatility, are tested alongside firm-specific risks such as concentrated positions or cross-margin exposures. Results are reviewed by senior risk committees and integrated into capital and liquidity planning, ensuring margin risk management is proactive rather than reactive.

Real-world examples highlight the consequences of inadequate preparation. Amaranth Advisors' collapse in 2006 and Archegos' failure in 2021 illustrate how insufficient liquidity and poor margin planning can rapidly liquidate concentrated positions, creating losses far greater than the initial margin shortfall. In contrast, institutions with disciplined monitoring, diversified collateral, pre-arranged liquidity, and automated systems could navigate the COVID-19 stress period without breaching margin requirements or triggering forced unwinds.

Institutions can create a resilient margin management framework even under severe market conditions by combining liquidity buffers, contingent funding, automation, and robust stress testing. These practices transform margin from a reactive obligation into a proactive risk control mechanism, allowing firms to effectively maintain market access, preserve capital, and manage derivative exposures.

10.2 Rolling Strategies

In derivatives markets, rolling refers to maintaining continuous exposure to an asset, index, or strategy by closing a contract nearing expiration and simultaneously entering a new one with a later maturity. Because derivative positions are inherently time-bound, portfolio managers seeking uninterrupted exposure must periodically roll expiring contracts. Rolling is a core operational function across asset classes, ensuring that investment strategies remain intact while minimizing gaps in risk coverage and avoiding unintended exposure lapses.

Rolling is essential to maintaining strategic continuity and managing operational and market risks. Liquidity in expiring contracts typically declines as the expiration approaches, and migrating to the next liquid contract helps improve execution quality and minimize transaction costs. Institutional investors, including pension funds and exchange-traded funds (ETFs), rely on timely and efficient rolling to maintain benchmark alignment and reduce tracking error.

10.2.1 *Mechanics of rolling*

Rolling is the operational process of replacing a derivative contract approaching expiration with a new contract with a later maturity, allowing a portfolio to maintain uninterrupted exposure. The process involves two coordinated steps: closing the expiring position and opening a replacement one.

For example, a portfolio manager holding a long futures position on an equity index, an interest rate instrument, or a commodity would sell the expiring contract and buy the next available contract month. In options markets, rolling involves closing the current option and opening a new one, often at the same strike price but with a later expiration date. However, strike adjustments may be made if market conditions or hedging objectives change. In the case of swaps such as interest rate or total return swaps, rolling may require unwinding the existing agreement and entering a new contract with comparable terms but an extended maturity.

The mechanics are broadly similar across asset classes. Equity, fixed-income, commodity, and currency traders rely on rolling to maintain duration exposure, hedge physical positions, or preserve synthetic portfolio overlays. Executing rolls efficiently minimizes exposure gaps, reduces tracking error, and helps align portfolios with benchmark requirements or hedging objectives.

10.2.2 *Importance of rolling*

Rolling is a core practice in derivative portfolio management because it ensures continuity of exposure. Allowing a contract to expire without rolling can create unintended gaps, leaving a portfolio temporarily unhedged or misaligned with its investment objectives. For instance, a fixed-income manager using Treasury futures to manage portfolio duration would lose that hedge if the futures were allowed to expire. Similarly, a commodities trader hedging energy prices would face unprotected exposure without a timely roll.

Rolling also plays a crucial role in market liquidity and execution efficiency. As a contract approaches expiration, trading activity naturally migrates to the next available maturity, and liquidity in the expiring contract declines. Executing the roll into the more active contract reduces bid–ask spreads, improves execution quality, and lowers slippage.

For institutional investors such as pension funds, ETFs, and mutual funds, rolling is critical for maintaining long-term exposure, minimizing tracking error, and meeting mandate requirements. Effective roll management allows these investors to preserve their intended market positions without disruption, ensuring that hedging strategies, benchmark replication, or tactical allocations remain intact through successive contract expirations.

10.2.3 *Challenges of rolling: Roll yield and basis risk*

While rolling is essential for maintaining continuous exposure, it introduces specific risks that can impact portfolio performance. Two of the most significant are roll yield and basis risk, which arise from how derivative contracts are priced relative to the underlying market.

Roll yield is the gain or loss incurred when replacing an expiring contract with a longer-dated contract. Its direction depends on the shape of the forward curve: when replacement contracts are more expensive than those being closed, the roll generates a negative yield; when they are cheaper, it generates a positive yield. This is common in stable or rising markets, especially for commodities with storage costs or equity indices with dividend expectations. In backwardation, where longer-dated contracts are cheaper, rolling produces a positive roll yield, effectively adding to returns.

For example, consider a trader long a June crude oil futures contract, rolling into a September contract. If the September contract trades at a higher price than the June contract, then the trader incurs a cost, a negative roll yield. If the September contract is lower, the roll generates a positive yield. This dynamic applies across asset classes, including interest rates, currencies, and equities. Over time, repeated negative roll yields can erode the performance of strategies such as index replication, while positive roll yields can enhance returns in favorable markets.

Basis risk arises when the expiring and replacement contracts do not align perfectly with the underlying exposure. Even a well-timed roll can leave a portfolio with slightly mismatched pricing or hedge effectiveness if the replacement contract responds differently to market conditions. Basis risk is particularly relevant in commodity and fixed-income markets, where seasonal factors, delivery schedules, or benchmark differences can cause price discrepancies between contract months.

Managing these challenges requires careful monitoring of the forward curve, liquidity conditions, and the pricing relationship between contract months. Sophisticated portfolio managers often schedule rolls strategically to minimize negative roll yield and reduce basis mismatches, using analytics to anticipate how market structure may affect execution costs and portfolio performance.

10.2.4 *Illustrating roll yield across asset classes*

Roll yield affects derivatives strategies across all major asset classes, including equities, fixed income, and commodities. The following examples demonstrate how the shape of the forward curve—contango or backwardation—directly impacts portfolio performance when rolling positions.

Equity Derivatives Example: A portfolio manager maintains a long position in E-mini S&P 500 futures. The expiring March contract is priced at 4,000, and the June contract is trading at 4,050. With a $50 contract multiplier, rolling into June costs $2,500 per contract: (4,000 – 4,050) × $50 = –$2,500.

This represents a negative roll yield in contango markets where longer-dated contracts are more expensive. If the June contract had instead been priced at 3,980, the roll would have produced a $1,000 gain per contract, reflecting positive roll yield in backwardation.

Fixed Income Derivatives Example: A bond portfolio manager uses 10-year Treasury futures to manage duration. As the March contract nears expiration, it trades at 112-16 (112.5 in decimal), while the June contract is priced at 112-00 (112.0). Rolling forward generates a positive roll yield because the longer-dated contract is cheaper: (112.5 – 112.0) × $1,000 = +$500 per contract.

Here, each basis point is worth approximately $1,000. If the June contract were priced higher than the March contract, the roll would result in a negative yield instead.

Commodity Derivatives Example: A trader rolls a long position in crude oil futures from April to July. April is priced at $78 per barrel, and July trades at $81. Since each contract covers 1,000 barrels, rolling forward costs $3,000 per contract: (78 – 81) × 1,000 = –$3,000.

This negative roll yield reflects contango, often caused by storage and insurance costs for physical commodities. If the market were in backwardation, such as during near-term supply shortages, the later-dated contract could be cheaper, generating a positive roll yield instead.

10.2.5 *Determinants of roll yield*

Roll yield is fundamentally driven by the price relationship between near-term and longer-dated derivatives contracts, reflecting the market's expectations, carrying costs, and structural dynamics. Several key factors determine whether the roll contributes positively or negatively to performance.

10.2.5.1 *Forward curve slope*

The primary determinant of roll yield is the shape of the forward curve, which plots contract prices across successive maturities. If the forward curve is sloping upward, longer-dated contracts are more expensive than those approaching expiration. Rolling up the curve results in a negative roll yield because the portfolio incurs a cost to maintain exposure. Conversely, the forward curve slopes downward in backwardation, meaning longer-dated contracts trade at lower prices than near-term ones. In this case, rolling produces a positive roll yield because the replacement contract is cheaper, effectively adding incremental return to the strategy. Forward curve slopes reflect underlying market expectations about supply, demand, interest rates, and storage costs.

10.2.5.2 *Cost of carry and interest rates*

The cost of carry (i.e., the expense associated with holding the underlying asset until the derivative contract matures) significantly affects roll yield. For financial derivatives such as equity index futures, the cost of carry includes the financing cost of capital used to hold the position, offset by any income from the underlying (e.g., dividends). If short-term interest rates are high relative to dividend yields, equity futures tend to trade at a premium, creating contango and potential negative roll yields for long positions. In fixed-income markets, the cost of carry reflects the opportunity cost of holding bonds versus rolling futures, and changing interest rate expectations can flip the forward curve from contango to backwardation, or vice versa.

10.2.5.3 *Storage and insurance costs in commodities*

Physical commodities introduce an additional determinant of roll yield: storage and insurance costs. Storing oil, natural gas, or agricultural commodities until future delivery incurs real costs, which are incorporated into the pricing of longer-dated contracts. These carrying costs naturally push the forward curve into contango, creating negative roll yields for long positions that must pay more to extend their exposure. Conversely, when inventories are low and market participants expect near-term shortages, backwardation can occur, offering positive roll yields to those rolling long positions. Commodity traders closely monitor storage spreads, inventory levels, and seasonal patterns to optimize rolling decisions.

10.2.5.4 *Market expectations and volatility*

Changes in market expectations for economic conditions, supply and demand, or policy developments can reshape the forward curve and alter roll yield outcomes. For example, rising interest rate expectations may flatten or invert the Treasury futures curve, shifting roll yield from negative to positive for bond managers. In commodities, sudden news about production cuts or weather-driven shortages can trigger backwardation, offering positive roll yield opportunities. High market volatility can amplify these effects, causing forward curve shapes to fluctuate more rapidly, making timing and strategy in rolling even more critical.

By understanding these determinants, portfolio managers can anticipate roll yield dynamics and design rolling strategies that align with their investment objectives. Proactive monitoring of these factors is essential to avoid performance erosion due to repeated negative roll yields and to capture potential gains when market conditions are favorable.

10.2.6 *Basis risk*

Basis risk arises when there is a difference between the price of the contract being rolled out of and the price of the new contract being rolled into. This discrepancy is inherent in all derivatives markets because contracts with different expirations reflect differing market expectations.

10.2.6.1 *What is basis*

The term "basis" refers to the difference between a derivative contract's price and the underlying asset's spot price. As a derivative approaches expiration, its price typically converges toward the spot price. However, the contract being rolled into reflects market expectations about interest rates, dividends, supply, or demand. This divergence between the maturing contract and the new one creates basis risk, which can lead to imperfect hedging or unintended exposures.

For example, a bond portfolio manager rolling a Treasury futures position might face basis risk if the new contract embeds expectations of falling interest rates that do not align with the fund's actual exposure. In equity derivatives, basis risk can emerge when dividend assumptions or implied volatility shift between the expiring and the replacement contract.

10.2.6.2 *Factors contributing to basis risk*

Several factors can affect the size and volatility of the basis when rolling derivative contracts:

- *Market expectations*: Changes in outlook for interest rates, dividend yields, commodity supply, or macroeconomic conditions can cause forward contracts to price differently from those expiring.

- *Market volatility*: Periods of heightened uncertainty can widen the price gap between contracts of different maturities, increasing the risk that the new contract does not replicate the exposure of the old one.
- *Liquidity dynamics*: As expiration approaches, trading activity often declines in the old contract and migrates to the next active contract. Limited liquidity in either contract can increase transaction costs and slippage.
- *Structural market events*: Contract specification changes, regulatory adjustments, market holidays, or shifts in margin requirements can all temporarily disrupt pricing relationships and magnify basis risk.

10.2.6.3 *Managing basis risk*

Effectively managing basis risk involves careful timing and execution of rolls to ensure that the new contract maintains the intended exposure of the expiring one. Traders often roll during periods of strong market liquidity to reduce execution costs and minimize slippage. Some institutions also spread the roll over several sessions to reduce market impact, closely monitoring open interest (i.e., the total number of outstanding contracts not yet closed or delivered) along with trading volumes to ensure that the new contract offers sufficient market depth and liquidity.

By understanding the drivers of basis risk and actively managing roll execution, portfolio managers can maintain more consistent exposures and avoid performance deviations caused by misaligned contracts.

10.3 Summary

In this chapter, I present the operational foundations necessary to execute and manage derivatives strategies effectively, focusing on two interdependent topics: margin practices and rolling mechanics. I show how mastering these elements strengthens liquidity management, mitigates counterparty risk, and ensures portfolios remain aligned with their strategic objectives.

I explain margin in derivatives markets, emphasizing its role as collateral rather than borrowed leverage. I describe how initial margin, variation margin, and maintenance margin operate within clearinghouse and bilateral frameworks, and I illustrate how margin protects market integrity by covering potential and realized losses. I demonstrate how institutions manage margin proactively through daily monitoring, liquidity buffers, contingent funding arrangements, and stress testing. Real-world failures such as Amaranth Advisors and Archegos Capital highlight the consequences of poor margin preparation.

I then turn to rolling strategies, which allow portfolio managers to maintain uninterrupted exposure by closing contracts approaching expiration and entering new ones with later maturities. I detail the mechanics of rolling across futures, options, and swaps, showing how timely execution avoids exposure gaps, reduces transaction costs, and aligns portfolios with benchmarks and hedges. I illustrate how roll yields—positive in backwardation and negative in contango—directly affect performance across equities, fixed income, and commodities. I examine basis risk arising from pricing differences between expiring and replacement contracts. I also explain how rolling interacts with liquidity, volatility, and benchmark alignment. These considerations help institutions manage transaction costs, reduce tracking error, and maintain consistent exposure when adjusting derivative positions.

By integrating disciplined margin management with efficient rolling strategies, institutions can maintain resilient derivative portfolios, meet liquidity and regulatory requirements, and preserve trading capacity even under stress. Mastery of these operational mechanics transforms derivatives from potential vulnerabilities into reliable instruments for hedging, benchmarking, and strategic positioning across asset classes.

Chapter 11

Foundations of Option Value: Understanding Options for Derivative Strategies

Up to this point in the book, I have introduced the basic characteristics of options: what they are, how they are structured, and the simplest ways they can be used. However, to move forward into the more detailed applications that I take up in this and the next part of the book, it is essential first to establish a stronger foundation for options. In this chapter, I turn to the fundamental factors determining an option's value. My goal is not to derive pricing models but to clarify the drivers of option value and to set out the key sensitivities that shape risk and reward when options are employed in practice. By focusing on concepts such as moneyness, time to expiration, volatility, and interest rates, I can show how the option value changes as market conditions evolve. This discussion strengthens the context for the strategies employed, introduced in the previous chapter. It also lays the groundwork for the formal valuation models I will describe in Part 5 of the book.

In this chapter, I also introduce the sensitivities of option prices, commonly referred to as the *Greeks*. Although the Greeks are mathematically defined as derivatives of option pricing models, they are first and foremost practical tools. Option traders and risk managers rely on them daily to monitor and adjust exposures, and a conceptual understanding of the Greeks greatly enhances intuition about how options respond to changes in the market. By presenting the Greeks in this practical light, I build familiarity with how they work before turning to the formal models from which they are derived.

Another concept that deserves early attention is implied volatility. In strict terms, implied volatility is extracted by inverting a pricing model; however, in practice, it is one of the most widely used measures in option markets. Implied volatility conveys the market's expectation of future uncertainty and is central to how options are quoted and compared. Introducing it here, alongside the Greeks, provides practical context for how options are discussed and traded daily in the markets.

This chapter, therefore, serves as a bridge: I focus on the qualitative components of an option's value, explore the economic factors that influence it, and develop a working understanding of how option prices respond to changes in these factors. To reinforce intuition, I include concrete illustrations and examples, but the emphasis remains on concepts rather than computations. With this groundwork in place, the stage will be set for the more formal derivation and application of option pricing models that appear in Part 5 of the book.

11.1 Decomposing the Option Price

An option's market price reflects the value investors are willing to pay for the rights and potential embedded within the contract. This price can be broken into two distinct components: intrinsic value and time value.[1] Understanding these two elements is crucial to comprehending how options are priced and why they behave as they do in fluctuating markets.

The *intrinsic value* of an option is its immediate, realizable value if exercised immediately. For a call option, intrinsic value is defined as the positive difference between the underlying asset's current price and the strike price. In contrast, for a put option, it is the amount by which the strike price is greater than the current price of the underlying asset. When this difference is negative or zero, the intrinsic value is zero; that is, options are never worth less than nothing in this framework.

[1] Do not confuse the "time value" of an option with the "time value of money," a foundational finance concept that relates to the discounted value of future cash flows. In the context of options, time value refers specifically to the portion of the option premium attributable to the possibility of favorable price movements before expiration.

The *time value* represents the portion of the option's price that cannot be realized through immediate exercise. It reflects the premium the market is willing to pay for the possibility that the option may become more valuable before expiration. Even when an option has no intrinsic value, it can still carry a significant time value if sufficient time remains and the underlying asset is volatile enough to make future movements likely.

We can represent this decomposition using a simple equation:

$$\text{Option price} = \text{Intrinsic value} + \text{Time value}$$

This relationship is best understood through a series of concrete examples. Consider a stock currently trading at $100. We examine several call and put options with different strike prices to see how their intrinsic and time values contribute to their market premiums (i.e., option prices) in Tables 11.1 and 11.2.

The breakdown of an option's market premium into intrinsic and time value provides a foundational lens through which to view option pricing. These two components help explain why an option may carry value even when it cannot be profitably exercised immediately, and why its price fluctuates with both the underlying asset and the passage of time. This framework also prepares us to take the next step: understanding how the relationship between the option's strike price and the price of the underlying asset—commonly referred to as "moneyness"—shapes both the

Table 11.1. Call Option Price Decomposition (Stock Price = $100)

Strike Price	Market Premium	Intrinsic Value	Time Value
$90	$12	$10	$2
$100	$5	$0	$5
$110	$2	$0	$2

Table 11.2. Put Option Price Decomposition (Stock Price = $100)

Strike Price	Market Premium	Intrinsic Value	Time Value
$90	$1	$0	$1
$100	$5	$0	$5
$110	$11	$10	$1

composition and behavior of option prices. We now turn to that concept in the following section.

11.2 Moneyness

A central concept in understanding option pricing is *moneyness*, which refers to the relationship between the price of the underlying asset and the option's strike price. Moneyness indicates whether an option would generate a positive payoff if exercised immediately, and it significantly influences the option's price behavior, particularly how intrinsic and time value interact.

There are three broad classifications of moneyness:

- An option is *in the money* (ITM) if exercising it would result in a positive payoff. For a call option, this occurs when the underlying asset's market price is above the strike price. For a put option, it occurs when the asset price is below the strike price.
- An option is *at the money* (ATM) when the asset price and the strike price are equal.
- An option is *out of the money* (OTM) if exercising it would result in no gain or loss. A call is OTM when the strike price is above the market price, and a put is OTM when the strike price is below the market price.

These distinctions matter because they determine whether an option has any intrinsic value. ITM options have positive intrinsic value; ATM and OTM options do not. However, all three can carry time value, especially if there is substantial time remaining to expiration or if the underlying asset is volatile.

In practice, moneyness is not just binary or categorical; it exists on a spectrum. This is why traders and analysts often refer to options as being *deep in the money* or *deep out of the money*.

An option is considered deep in the money when the difference between the underlying asset's market price and the strike price is substantial, making the likelihood of a profitable outcome at expiration very high. For example, a call option with a strike price of $60 when the underlying is trading at $100 is deep ITM. Such options behave increasingly like the underlying asset itself.

An option is considered deep out of the money when the strike price is far removed from the current market price, making it unlikely to become profitable before expiration. For example, a put option with a $60 strike price when the underlying trades at $100 is deep OTM. These options are inexpensive, often consisting entirely of time value, and are frequently used in speculative strategies with low costs and high leverage.

By expanding the basic moneyness framework in this manner, we can better understand how options behave across the entire range of price relationships. These distinctions will be referenced throughout the remainder of the chapter as we explore how moneyness affects sensitivity to market changes, the impact of time decay, and the design of option strategies.

Let us revisit the examples introduced in Tables 11.1 and 11.2 in the previous section, where the stock is trading at $100, and consider a range of call and put options with different strike prices. These are shown in Tables 11.3 and 11.4.

These examples reveal several important patterns in how moneyness affects the structure of an option's price:

- Deep in the money options, such as the $90 call and the $110 put, derive most of their value from intrinsic value. Since the payoff from immediate exercise is already substantial, the remaining time value is relatively small. The market assumes that these options are likely to expire in the money, so little additional premium is paid for the uncertainty.

Table 11.3. Moneyness for Call Options (Stock Price = $100)

Strike Price	Option Type	Moneyness	Intrinsic Value	Time Value (Premium)
$90	Call	In the Money	10	$3 (Premium = $13)
$100	Call	At the Money	$0	$5 (Premium = $5)
$110	Call	Out of the Money	$0	$2 (Premium = $2)

Table 11.4. Moneyness for Put Options (Stock Price = $100)

Strike Price	Option Type	Moneyness	Intrinsic Value	Time Value (Premium)
$90	Put	Out of the Money	$0	$2 (Premium = $2)
$100	Put	At the Money	$0	$5 (Premium = $5)
$110	Put	In the Money	$10	$3 (Premium = $13)

- At-the-money options, such as the \$100 call and put, have no intrinsic value, yet they carry the highest time value. This is because they are right on the edge—small changes in the underlying price could quickly push them into or out of the money. That uncertainty gives them a high responsiveness to price changes, which the market prices accordingly.
- Out-of-the-money options, such as the \$110 call and the \$90 put, also have no intrinsic value. However, they still carry non-negligible time value. This time value reflects the possibility, however remote, that the underlying asset may move far enough before expiration to make the option profitable.

Because moneyness is defined relative to the current price of the underlying asset, it is not static. It changes dynamically as the asset price fluctuates. A call option that is OTM today may become ITM tomorrow if the stock rallies. Similarly, an ITM put option can become an ATM or even OTM as the stock price rises. This shifting status directly affects how an option is valued over time.

Moneyness also helps explain why different options are used in other trading strategies. Deep ITM options behave much like the underlying asset but require less capital. ATM options, with their high time value, are often used for short-term directional bets, as they are susceptible to small changes in the underlying price. Though less expensive, OTM options offer asymmetric payoffs and are commonly used in speculative strategies or to build multi-leg spreads.

In summary, moneyness is not merely a descriptive label; it is a critical classification that governs an option's price composition, the likelihood of profitable exercise, and how the option behaves as market conditions change. It ties directly to the intuition established in the previous section and lays the foundation for understanding risk sensitivities, which we will explore next.

11.3 Key Determinants of Option Value

A range of economic and contractual variables drives an option's market value. Understanding these inputs is essential for analyzing option behavior and anticipating how prices respond to changes in market conditions. Each key variable affects either the intrinsic value or time value, and their influence can vary significantly depending on whether the option is a call or a put and whether it is American or European.

I now examine each primary input separately: the price of the underlying asset, volatility, time to expiration, interest rates, and dividends. I conclude the section with a comparative table that illustrates the directional impact of each input on the value of European options and highlights the differences with American-style options.

11.3.1 *Price of the underlying asset*

The most immediate driver of an option's value is the current price of the underlying asset. For call options, as the asset price increases, the option's value generally increases. Conversely, for put options, higher asset prices reduce the option's value.

This is intuitive when considering intrinsic value: A higher underlying price makes a call more likely to be in the money (and further so), whereas it makes a put less valuable. For example:

- A call option with a strike price of $100 becomes more valuable as the underlying price moves from $100 to $110.
- A put option with a strike price of $100 loses value in response to the same movement.

This relationship also affects delta, which we discuss in the following section on the Greeks. The closer an option is to being in the money, the more pronounced its sensitivity to changes in the underlying price.

11.3.2 *Volatility*

Volatility represents the expected degree of fluctuation in the price of the underlying asset over the life of the option. It is one of the most important inputs in determining the option's value, particularly its time value. In fact, in a hypothetical world with no volatility, options would have minimal value. If an asset's price were expected to remain fixed, the only options that would retain value are those already deeply in the money; the rest would likely never yield a profitable payoff.

The key reason volatility matters is that it increases the range of possible future outcomes for the underlying asset's price. With higher volatility, the likelihood that an option will finish ITM increases, even for options that are currently ATM or OTM. This effect applies to both calls and puts. For call options, higher volatility raises the chances that the asset's price will rise above the strike price. For puts, the chance of the asset falling below the strike increases. As a result, option value generally increases with volatility, regardless of the direction of the price movement.

The sensitivity of an option's value to volatility, however, varies by moneyness and time to expiration. Options that are ATM typically experience the most significant increase in value when volatility rises because their payoff is the most uncertain; that is, small movements in the underlying price could push them either into or out of the money. Similarly, options with longer times to expiration gain more value from increased volatility than those nearing maturity. The longer the time horizon, the greater the opportunity for the asset price to move sufficiently to make the option profitable.

In contrast, deep ITM or deep OTM options benefit less from an increase in volatility. Deep ITM options already have a high probability of finishing in the money, so more volatility adds little to their value. Deep OTM options, while they may gain some value, still have relatively low chances of becoming profitable, especially if the expiration is near.

To summarize, volatility expands the possible price paths for the underlying asset, thereby increasing the value of optionality. As such, it is a core driver of the time value component of the option price. The greater the uncertainty surrounding the future price of the asset, the more valuable the right, but not the obligation, to buy or sell it becomes.

Later in this chapter, we will return to the topic of volatility from a different angle: How traders infer the market's expectations of future volatility based on the prices of options themselves. That concept, known as implied volatility, builds directly on the understanding of how volatility affects option values, providing another lens through which to interpret pricing behavior in real-world markets.

11.3.3 *Time to expiration*

Time to expiration, or the remaining time until an option's maturity, is a fundamental determinant of an option's value. The longer the time remaining, the greater the possibility that the underlying asset's price may move in a favorable direction. This possibility creates time value, which is embedded in the market premium paid for the option. All else equal, options with more time to expiration are worth more than those with less because they provide more opportunities for profitable outcomes to emerge.

However, as the expiration date approaches, this time value steadily erodes. This phenomenon is *time decay*, reflecting the diminishing opportunity for the option to become valuable. Notably, the process of time decay is not linear. The rate of decline in time value accelerates as the option nears expiration. In the final days or weeks before maturity, even small reductions in time can cause noticeable drops in the option's price, particularly for certain types of options.

The pattern of time decay also depends heavily on moneyness, as described earlier in this chapter. ATM options experience the most rapid erosion of time value as expiration approaches. This is because ATM options derive their entire value from time value. There is no intrinsic value until the price breaks decisively above or below the strike price. Once time begins to run out and the chance of such a favorable move diminishes, the market reduces the price of the option accordingly. In contrast, deep ITM and deep OTM options tend to lose value more slowly because their likelihood of changing moneyness classification is relatively low. A deep ITM call, for example, already has significant intrinsic value and behaves more like the underlying asset; a deep OTM put, by contrast, has little likelihood of ever becoming ITM.

The influence of time to expiration also depends on whether the option is American or European in exercise style. European options can only be exercised at expiration. As a result, the time value of European options reflects only the probability that the option will expire ITM at maturity. For American options, however, the holder has the right to exercise at any point up to and including expiration. This early exercise feature can cause the time value to behave differently.

For instance, a deep ITM American call option on a dividend-paying stock might be exercised early to capture the dividend. Similarly, an American put option may be exercised early if the underlying price falls well below the strike price and the time value becomes negligible. This ability to realize value before expiration adds a layer of optionality, which can cause the time value of American options to decay more slowly or irregularly compared to European options.

However, this distinction cuts both ways. The impact of time to expiration on American-style options can sometimes be less predictable, especially when early exercise is not optimal. For example, an American call option on a non-dividend-paying stock should theoretically never be exercised early, making its behavior similar to that of a European call. In such cases, the pattern of time decay resembles that of its European counterpart. Thus, whether the time to expiration affects option value in the American context depends on the likelihood and timing of early exercise, a feature governed by factors such as dividends, interest rates, and volatility.

From a practical standpoint, understanding how time to expiration interacts with both moneyness and exercise style is crucial. Traders employing short-term option strategies, such as selling options with a few days to maturity, are susceptible to time decay. Likewise, portfolio managers evaluating long-dated options or embedded options in structured products must account for how slowly or quickly value erodes depending on where the option sits relative to the current market price and whether early exercise is a consideration.

Time to expiration is not merely a function of the calendar; it plays a central role in shaping optionality, risk exposure, and trading behavior. It influences both the magnitude and the pace of time value decay, and its impact must be understood in context, specifically by considering the option's moneyness, the level of volatility, and whether early exercise is permitted under the contract terms.

11.3.4 *Interest rates*

Interest rates play a meaningful role in determining option prices, particularly through their effect on the relative value of money over time. The interest rate referred to in this context is the risk-free rate, commonly represented by the yield on short- or medium-term government securities, such as U.S. Treasury bills or notes. This rate reflects the return available to investors in a riskless investment over the option's life and influences how future cash flows associated with the option are valued today.

To understand how this works, consider a basic financial concept called the "cost-of-carry framework." As explained in the previous chapter when discussing the pricing of futures and forward contracts, this term simply refers to how the value of holding (or "carrying") a position is affected by financing costs, interest rates, dividends, and other elements over time. Regarding options, the key idea is that the strike price, which is the price paid or received at expiration, represents a future cash flow. Higher interest rates reduce the present value of that future payment, and this adjustment impacts option prices.

For European options, which can only be exercised at expiration, the influence of interest rates follows a clear pattern:

- Call options become more valuable as interest rates rise. This is because the buyer of a call will pay the strike price in the future, and when interest rates are higher, the present value of that future payment is lower. The reduced cost of future payment increases the appeal of the call option today.

- Put options, in contrast, become less valuable when interest rates rise. A put allows the holder to sell the underlying asset at a fixed price in the future. If the present value of that future sale price decreases due to higher interest rates, the put becomes less attractive.

These effects are generally modest for short-dated options, where the time to maturity is brief and interest rates have limited time to exert influence. However, the impact becomes more pronounced for longer-dated options, where discounting plays a more significant role in valuation.

The analysis becomes more complex with American options, which allow early exercise at any time before expiration. The influence of interest rates is directionally similar—rising rates still tend to benefit calls and reduce the value of puts—but early exercise rights complicate the picture. For example, a deep ITM American put option may become more likely to be exercised early when interest rates rise, especially if the underlying asset price drops significantly and holding the option provides little remaining time value. Meanwhile, American call options on non-dividend-paying stocks are typically not exercised early, so their behavior with respect to interest rates closely resembles that of their European counterparts.

It's also important to note that the impact of interest rates does not exist in isolation. It interacts with other variables, such as time to expiration, volatility, and moneyness, to influence the overall value of an option. In low-rate environments, rate changes may have little practical effect. Still, in rising-rate environments or during periods of monetary tightening, the influence of interest rates can become more significant, especially for long-dated options and interest rate-sensitive underlyings.

Although the explanation here is conceptual, the formal role of interest rates in option valuation becomes much more apparent when we introduce pricing models in Part 5. There, interest rates will appear explicitly in the formulas that determine theoretical option values. Understanding how they affect call and put prices at a conceptual level now lays the groundwork for interpreting and applying those models in practice.

11.3.5 *Dividends*

Dividends directly and indirectly impact option prices because they affect the expected future price of the underlying asset. When a company pays a dividend, its stock price typically drops by approximately the dividend amount on the ex-dividend date (i.e., the first day the stock trades without the right to receive the declared payment. This anticipated price drop alters the attractiveness of both call and put options.

Expected dividends reduce the value of call options. A call gives the holder the right to buy the stock at a fixed strike price. If the stock price is likely to fall due to a dividend payment, the upside potential of holding the call decreases. As a result, the presence of dividends reduces the time value of the call and lowers its market price.

For put options, the opposite holds. A put gives the holder the right to sell the stock at a predetermined strike price. If the stock is expected to drop due to a dividend payment, the likelihood of the put finishing in the money increases, making the option more valuable. Therefore, all else being equal, expected dividends increase the value of put options.

These effects are already reflected in European option pricing models by reducing the expected future price of the underlying stock, typically by subtracting the present value of expected dividends over the option's life. However, American options are even more sensitive to dividends because they allow for early exercise.

In some cases, particularly when a call option is deep ITM, it may be optimal for the holder to exercise the call just before the ex-dividend date to acquire the stock and become eligible for the dividend. This decision hinges on the trade-off between forfeiting the option's remaining time value and gaining the dividend. If the value of the dividend exceeds the remaining time value, early exercise becomes optimal. As a result, dividend-paying stocks complicate early exercise decisions for American-style call options.

Put options, on the other hand, are rarely exercised early for dividend-related reasons. Instead, the anticipated price decline due to a dividend payment tends to increase their value without requiring early exercise.

It's also important to recognize that dividends affect not just individual equity options but also options written on stock indexes. Index options are usually cash-settled and European-style, and the indexes themselves are price-return indexes, meaning they do not reflect dividend reinvestments. Instead, the expected dividends of the constituent companies are implicitly factored into the pricing of index options by adjusting the projected forward value of the index. In this way, the collective dividend expectations for all companies in an index influence index option pricing, much like individual dividends affect single-stock options.

For example, consider an option on the S&P 500. If dividend expectations across the index increase—say, due to better-than-expected earnings or new dividend announcements—then the forward price of the index will be projected lower, which tends to reduce call option values and increase put values, in line with the logic described above.

Dividends affect option pricing by altering the expected path of the underlying asset's price. Their impact is especially significant for American options because of the potential for early exercise. A clear understanding of how dividends are treated across different options, whether individual equity or index-based and whether American or European in style, is essential for accurate valuation and informed decision-making around ex-dividend dates and dividend-sensitive strategies.

11.3.6 *Summary*

Table 11.5 provides a high-level guide to how option values change in response to key inputs. Notably, while European options can only be exercised at expiration, American options allow early exercise, which adds complexity. This distinction is particularly relevant for deep ITM puts and dividend-paying stocks, where the timing of exercise can affect valuation.

Table 11.5. Summary Table: Directional Impact of Key Inputs on European Option Values

Input Variable	Call Option Impact	Put Option Impact	Notes on American vs. European Options
Increase in Asset Price	Increases	Decreases	Same for both types
Increase in Volatility	Increases	Increases	Same in direction; magnitude may vary
Increase in Time	Increases	Increases	May reduce value for deep ITM American puts due to early exercise opportunity
Increase in Interest Rates	Increases	Decreases	Greater impact on European options; American puts are more sensitive to early exercise
Increase in Dividends	Decreases	Increases	Greater effect on American calls/puts due to early exercise potential

In the following section, we introduce the Greeks—tools that quantify the sensitivity of option prices to these very factors. Understanding the directional effects explored here is the first step toward effectively interpreting those measures.

11.4 The Greeks: Sensitivities in Option Pricing

A critical part of understanding options—and managing the risks they introduce—is developing familiarity with the *Greeks*. The Greeks are risk measures that describe how an option's value responds to changes in key input variables. Mathematically, each Greek letter corresponds to a partial derivative of the pricing equation concerning a specific input. These metrics are standard outputs of pricing models and are widely used in practice, generated by commercial trading platforms and risk systems. The Greeks are essential tools for both option valuation and risk management.

By quantifying how sensitive an option's price is to shifts in the underlying asset, volatility, time, or interest rates, the Greeks allow market participants to measure and control the exposures embedded in their positions. Whether holding a single option or managing a portfolio, these metrics provide actionable information to assess potential gains or losses under various scenarios.

Here, I introduce the five most common Greeks: delta, gamma, theta, vega, and rho. I describe each in its own section. While their mathematical definitions originate from pricing models, our focus here is on developing intuition and connecting them to practical applications.

11.4.1 *Delta: Sensitivity to the underlying asset price*

Delta measures the approximate change in the value of an option for a small change in the underlying asset's price. It is one of the most intuitive and widely used option Greeks. For call options, delta is positive because the option increases in value as the underlying asset price rises. For put options, delta is negative; the option gains value as the asset price falls.

For example, a call option with a delta of 0.60 implies that if the underlying asset increases by \$1, the option's value will increase by approximately \$0.60, assuming all other factors remain constant. Likewise, a put option with a delta of –0.40 would increase in value by \$0.40 if the underlying asset dropped by \$1.

Delta is closely tied to moneyness. An ATM call option typically has a delta close to 0.50, while a deep ITM call can have a delta approaching 1.00, meaning it moves almost point-for-point with the underlying asset. Conversely, a deep OTM call may have a delta near 0, reflecting the low probability that the option will finish in the money. For puts, the range of delta values is typically negative, between 0 and −1.00, depending on the moneyness.

Delta is not static. It evolves as the underlying price changes, time to expiration shortens, and implied volatility shifts. For example, the delta of an ATM option becomes more sensitive and shifts more rapidly as expiration nears, especially in low-volatility environments. This behavior underscores delta's importance as a sensitivity measure and a dynamic input for portfolio management.

Another key interpretation of delta is as a *hedge ratio*. If an option has a delta of 0.60, holding one option contract gives exposure equivalent to holding 0.60 shares of the underlying asset. Therefore, holding 100 call options (which typically control 100 shares each) with a delta of 0.60 provides exposure equivalent to being long 6,000 shares of the underlying.

This property allows traders and portfolio managers to build delta-neutral portfolios, where the overall exposure to small movements in the underlying asset is minimized. For instance, a trader who sells call options can buy shares in proportion to the delta of the short position to hedge directional risk. Delta-neutral strategies are central to options market making, risk management, and arbitrage.

In specific contexts, delta can also be loosely interpreted as the approximate probability that a European option will expire in the money, assuming no early exercise. For example, a delta of 0.25 suggests that, under the assumptions of the pricing model, there is roughly a 25% chance that the option will expire in the money. While this interpretation has limitations, especially for American-style options or under skewed volatility, it offers further insight into delta's role in option valuation.

Delta is not merely a measure of price sensitivity; it is a versatile tool for quantifying directional exposure, designing hedging strategies, and interpreting market expectations.

11.4.2 *Gamma: Sensitivity of delta to underlying price*

Gamma measures the rate of change of delta in response to movements in the underlying asset's price. While delta provides a linear approximation, indicating how much the option's value changes with a small change in the underlying price, gamma captures the curvature or convexity of the option's value profile.[2] It tells us how quickly delta will change as the asset price moves. This makes gamma essential for understanding the nonlinear behavior of options.

In practical terms, gamma is highest for ATM options with a short time to expiration, where the option's moneyness can swing easily due to even small price movements. These options are most sensitive to the underlying asset moving from one side of the strike to the other, resulting in significant changes in delta. Gamma tends to decline as an option moves deeper ITM or OTM, where delta becomes more stable and price movements have a less dramatic effect on the likelihood of expiring in the money.

For example, consider an ATM call option with a delta of 0.50 and high gamma. A small increase in the stock price might increase delta to 0.60, while a slight decrease might drop it to 0.40. That change in delta, captured by gamma, means that the trader's hedge ratio is shifting rapidly and must be continually adjusted to remain delta-neutral.

This property makes gamma especially important for hedgers and market makers. When gamma is high, a portfolio's delta is more unstable, requiring frequent hedge rebalancing to maintain a neutral position. This constant adjustment is referred to as gamma hedging, and it becomes more costly and difficult as the position gets closer to the option's expiration date or as the options approach the ATM level. The cost of gamma hedging is also linked to theta (time decay), as positions with high gamma also tend to lose time value quickly.

Gamma is also a key indicator of portfolio risk in volatile or rapidly changing markets. A portfolio with large positive gamma may benefit from sharp price swings, as it gains more when the market moves favorably than it loses when the market moves against it. This convexity can be desirable, but it also means the portfolio's risk profile is harder to predict. Conversely, a portfolio with negative gamma (standard for traders who sell options) can be exposed to sudden changes in direction, where delta moves against the position quickly, forcing aggressive and costly hedging adjustments.

---

[2]In calculus, gamma corresponds to the second derivative of the pricing function with respect to the underlying asset's price. Using a second derivative improves the accuracy of the linear approximation provided by delta.

Gamma is influenced not only by moneyness and time to expiration but also by implied volatility. In markets with elevated uncertainty, gamma can be more pronounced across a broader range of strikes, increasing the need for active risk management even for OTM positions.

Gamma measures how fast delta changes and reveals the instability of an option's directional sensitivity. While delta indicates how much an option's value moves with the market, gamma shows how quickly that exposure shifts in response to price changes. This distinction is critical for managing options portfolios, especially those structured to be delta-neutral. As expiration nears or market volatility rises, gamma risk becomes more pronounced, demanding more frequent and precise hedge adjustments. Traders and risk managers must stay attentive to gamma-driven shifts in exposure, as they can significantly affect both performance and risk control.

11.4.3 *Theta: Sensitivity to time*

Theta measures the rate at which an option's value declines purely due to the passage of time, assuming all other factors remain constant. As noted earlier in this chapter, theta is commonly called *time decay*, reflecting the diminishing potential for the option to finish in the money as expiration approaches. In other words, theta quantifies the value an option is expected to lose with each passing day, regardless of market movements.

For most long option positions, theta is negative. The option gradually loses value as time elapses. This is because the time value component of an option's price erodes daily. The longer an option has until expiration, the more time value it possesses. However, as expiration approaches, the probability of the option ending up in a profitable position decreases, especially if it is not already in the money.

The rate of this erosion is not constant. Theta accelerates as expiration nears, particularly for ATM options, which have the most to gain or lose from even small movements in the underlying. An ATM option may experience a rapid drop in time value in the final days before expiration, even if the underlying price remains unchanged. By contrast, deep ITM and deep OTM options tend to experience slower time decay because their payoff profiles are already fairly well-defined, either very likely or highly unlikely to be exercised profitably.

From the perspective of an option seller (writer), theta works in the opposite direction: It is a source of positive returns. If the option expires worthless, the seller retains the entire premium received. If the market does not move unfavorably, the seller benefits simply from the passage of time. This is why short options strategies are often described as "collecting theta." Sellers profit from the decay in time value, assuming other risks are managed.

For option buyers, theta represents a constant headwind. A long call purchased for speculative purposes must move into profitability quickly to overcome the daily loss from time decay. A sharp price move late in the option's life may not be enough to offset the loss of time value if the underlying hadn't moved sooner. Thus, timing is critical because buyers must be correct not only on their direction but also on when the move occurs.

Other factors also influence theta. Options on more volatile assets typically have higher premiums, which means greater time value to decay, but also faster decay as expiration nears. Moreover, long-dated options decay more slowly than shorter-term contracts, making them appealing to long-term investors who seek optionality with reduced theta risk.

In practice, theta is especially important for short-term strategies. Traders engaging in weekly or monthly option positions must closely monitor how rapidly their positions lose value, particularly around earnings announcements, economic reports, or other catalysts that concentrate volatility into narrow time windows.

Understanding theta helps explain why some strategies require quick, decisive price action while others benefit from sideways markets and uneventful time passing. Whether seeking to profit from price movement or from the mere passage of time, theta is a central consideration in any option position's construction and risk management.

11.4.4 *Vega: Sensitivity to volatility*

Vega measures the sensitivity of an option's value to changes in the underlying asset's volatility.[3] More specifically, it quantifies the change in the option price resulting from a one-percentage-point change in the implied volatility used in the pricing model. Implied volatility reflects the

---

[3] Vega is not a Greek letter, although it is customarily grouped with the Greeks.

market's expectations of future price fluctuations, rather than actual historical volatility, and it plays a central role in how options are priced.

A higher vega means the option's price is more sensitive to changes in volatility. For example, if an option has a vega of 0.10, a 1% increase in implied volatility will increase the option's value by approximately $0.10, with all else equal.

Both call and put options have positive vega. This is because an increase in expected volatility raises the probability that the underlying asset will experience large price movements, increasing the chances that the option will expire in the money, even if it is currently out of the money. Higher volatility increases the option's potential upside without changing the fixed nature of the downside (limited to the premium paid by the buyer), thereby increasing overall option value.

Vega is not constant over time. It varies based on several factors, particularly moneyness and time to expiration. Vega is typically highest for ATM options, where small changes in volatility have the most significant impact on the likelihood of exercising the option profitably. In contrast, deep ITM or deep OTM options tend to have low vega because increased volatility has little effect on their already high or low chances of finishing in the money.

Time to expiration also plays a significant role. Options with more time remaining are more sensitive to volatility because there is more opportunity for large price swings to occur. Therefore, long-dated options tend to have higher vega than near-term contracts. As expiration approaches, vega declines, just as the influence of volatility diminishes due to limited time for movement.

From a trading perspective, long vega positions (such as long calls or puts) benefit from rising volatility. This is especially useful in environments where uncertainty is expected to increase, such as before earnings announcements, economic data releases, or geopolitical events. On the other hand, short vega positions, such as selling options, lose value when volatility spikes, which is a common risk in quiet markets that experience sudden turmoil. This makes vega a critical consideration for traders who sell options to collect premium, as their strategies may appear profitable in stable environments but become vulnerable to unexpected volatility events.

Vega also plays a vital role in volatility trading strategies, where traders express views not on the direction of the underlying asset, but on expected changes in volatility. Strategies such as long straddles or strangles are designed to profit from increased volatility, while iron condors or short butterflies are typically structured to benefit from declining or stable volatility. In all cases, managing vega exposure is essential for risk control.

Finally, risk managers must understand a portfolio's overall vega to assess its exposure to changing market conditions. During periods of low implied volatility, vega risk can accumulate quietly in a portfolio of short options. If volatility rises sharply due to market shocks, earnings surprises, or macroeconomic uncertainty, the losses can be severe and abrupt.

Vega, therefore, is more than a sensitivity metric; it measures how much an option's value depends on market uncertainty. Whether trading options outright or managing risk in a larger portfolio, a strong understanding of vega is essential for navigating the dynamic nature of financial markets.

11.4.5 *Rho: Sensitivity to interest rates*

Rho measures the sensitivity of an option's value to changes in the risk-free interest rate used in option pricing models. It indicates that an option's price will change for a one-percentage-point change in the risk-free rate, assuming all other factors remain constant. Although often less prominent than other Greeks like delta, gamma, or vega, rho becomes important in specific contexts, particularly for long-dated options and instruments tied closely to interest rates.

For European-style options, the effect of interest rates on valuation is relatively straightforward:

- The value of a call option increases as interest rates rise.
- The value of a put option decreases as interest rates rise.

This behavior arises from how interest rates affect the present value of the strike price, which is paid or received at expiration. A higher interest rate reduces the present value of a future payment. For call options, this makes the obligation to pay for the strike in the future less costly in present-value terms, enhancing the call's appeal. For puts, the reduced present value of the amount the holder would receive if the option is exercised lowers its attractiveness.

While the logic behind rho is clear, its practical impact is often modest for most short-dated equity options, where the time horizon is too brief for small rate changes to affect valuation meaningfully. However, rho becomes much more significant for (1) long-term options, where the time horizon gives interest rate changes more time to accumulate and influence pricing; (2) fixed income options, such as options on Treasury futures or bond indices, where interest rates are a direct driver of the value of the underlying asset; (3) currency options, where interest rate differentials between two countries play a central role in determining forward exchange rates, which in turn directly influence option premiums; and (4) interest rate derivatives, such as swaptions or caps and floors, where rho sensitivity is often one of the dominant risk factors being hedged and managed.

The sign and magnitude of rho also vary depending on moneyness and time to expiration. ATM options with long maturities exhibit higher rho, while deep ITM or OTM options show lower sensitivity. Furthermore, in low-interest-rate environments, rho tends to be muted. Still, it can have a more pronounced effect in rising-rate regimes or periods of monetary tightening, especially for institutional portfolios exposed to both equity and fixed income derivatives.

From a portfolio management perspective, rho is rarely the primary target of Greek traders or risk managers. However, interest rate exposure can accumulate significantly in multi-asset portfolios, especially those holding foreign exchange options, convertible bonds, or structured products. A change in central bank policy or a shift in the yield curve can alter option valuations in ways not captured by delta, gamma, or vega, making rho a valuable component of holistic risk analysis.

In essence, rho connects option valuation to the broader macroeconomic environment, anchoring it in money pricing. While often overlooked, it becomes vital when rates are volatile, durations are long, or the underlying asset is directly sensitive to the level or direction of interest rates.

11.4.6 *Summary*

Table 11.6 provides an overview of the key Greeks, the variable each measures sensitivity to, and their practical interpretations. Each of these Greeks provides a different perspective for understanding the risks embedded in an option position. Together, they form a comprehensive

Table 11.6. The Greeks at a Glance

Greek	Sensitivity to	Description	Significance in Practice
Delta	Underlying asset price	Change in option value for \$1 change in asset price	Measures directional exposure; used for hedging and replication
Gamma	Underlying asset price	Change in delta for \$1 change in asset price	Measures delta instability; important for hedging adjustments
Theta	Time (passage of days)	Change in option value due to one day of time decay	Indicates time erosion; negative for buyers, positive for sellers
Vega	Volatility	Change in option value for 1 percentage point change in implied volatility	Captures volatility exposure; not a true Greek letter
Rho	Interest rate	Change in option value for 1 percentage point change in interest rate	Measures interest rate sensitivity; more relevant for longer maturities

framework for anticipating how option prices evolve as market conditions change. In practice, traders do not look at these sensitivities in isolation but in combination. For example, an option may have high delta and high theta, implying a trade-off between directional exposure and time decay.

In Part 5, we will explore how pricing models produce these Greeks as derivatives of their valuation formulas and how they are used in practice to structure, hedge, and monitor complex option strategies.

11.5 Implied Volatility

Implied volatility is one of the most widely used outputs from option pricing models and one of the most commonly misunderstood. While models such as the Black–Scholes–Merton model—which we cover in Chapter 22—treat volatility as an input, implied volatility flips the process: It is the value of volatility that, when plugged into the model, produces the observed market price of the option. In other words, implied volatility is not directly observed; it is inferred from market prices using a pricing model.

Implied volatility answers a simple question: Given the market price of this option, what level of volatility makes the model match the market price? Since option prices reflect expectations about future uncertainty, implied volatility is interpreted as a market-based forecast of future volatility. It reflects what market participants believe about the likelihood of large price movements in the underlying asset.

It is crucial to interpret implied volatility correctly. Unlike historical volatility, which is calculated from past price movements, implied volatility is forward-looking. It reflects the market's expectations regarding the underlying asset's volatility over the option's remaining life. A higher level of implied volatility does not necessarily mean the option is overpriced; it may reflect genuine uncertainty about upcoming events, such as earnings announcements, regulatory decisions, or central bank meetings. In this sense, implied volatility incorporates both objective risk and investor sentiment about future conditions. Furthermore, two options with the same implied volatility can still behave quite differently depending on where they sit relative to the underlying price. An ATM option, for example, is more sensitive to changes in implied volatility than a deep ITM or deep OTM option. This sensitivity is captured by the option's vega, which varies with moneyness and time to expiration. Therefore, understanding implied volatility requires context; it is not a standalone measure but rather one that must be interpreted considering the option's characteristics and the market environment.

It is crucial to know that implied volatility's limitations are only as good as the model used to infer them. If the model's assumptions (e.g., constant volatility, no jumps) are far from reality, the implied volatility may not represent true market expectations. Additionally, implied volatility does not predict direction but reflects uncertainty, not whether the market will go up or down.

As with the Greeks, implied volatility equips practitioners with tools to interpret, compare, and act on option prices without needing to first work through the details of the pricing model. It connects theory to observable prices, transforming option pricing models from abstract constructs into diagnostic instruments that reflect the market's evolving expectations. Understanding implied volatility before diving into formal pricing models lays the foundation for seeing how those models are applied, challenged, and recalibrated in real time.

11.5.1 *Calculating implied volatility and the volatility smile*

Suppose you are analyzing a European call option on a stock currently trading at $100. The option has a strike price of $100 and expires in three months. The market price of the option is $10. You input the known parameters—current stock price ($100), strike price ($100), time to expiration (0.25 years), and risk-free interest rate (say, 2%)—into the Black–Scholes–Merton option pricing model described in Chapter 22, but you don't yet know what volatility to use.

So, you try different values. When you enter a volatility of 20%, the model returns a price lower than $10. At 25%, the model outputs a price of exactly $10. This is your match. You conclude that the implied volatility of this option is 25%. The market is pricing this option as if it expects the stock to exhibit 25% annualized volatility over the next three months. The volatility is not observed directly. Instead, it's inferred (i.e., implied) from the price using the model.

Suppose you look at another European call option on the same stock with the same expiration date but a strike price of $110. This option is out of the money, but it's actively traded and quoted at $4. When you back out the implied volatility from the market price using the Black–Scholes model, it comes out to 35%, a full 10 percentage points higher than the ATM option. Why would that be? After all, as you see in our discussion of the Black–Scholes model in Chapter 22, it assumes that volatility is constant across all strikes, so shouldn't all options on the same stock with the same expiration have the same implied volatility?

This is where theory and practice diverge. In the real world, implied volatility is not constant across strike prices or maturities. Instead, suppose you plot implied volatility on the vertical axis and strike price on the horizontal axis for options with the same expiration. In that case, you often observe a U-shaped pattern, as shown in Figure 11.1. This shape, where implied volatility is higher for deep ITM and OTM options than ATM options, is referred to as the *volatility smile*.

However, the pattern is usually skewed rather than symmetrical in equity markets. Implied volatility often rises as strike prices fall, especially for stock index options or individual equities. This is known as the *volatility skew* or *volatility smirk*. In these cases, OTM put options (with lower strike prices) exhibit higher implied volatilities than OTM calls. This skew reflects the market's asymmetric expectations about potential downside risk.

Why does this happen? There are several real-world factors at play:

- *Market beliefs about non-constant volatility*: Unlike the Black–Scholes assumption of constant volatility, market participants recognize that volatility fluctuates over time and often spikes during market downturns. They price that expectation into the options.

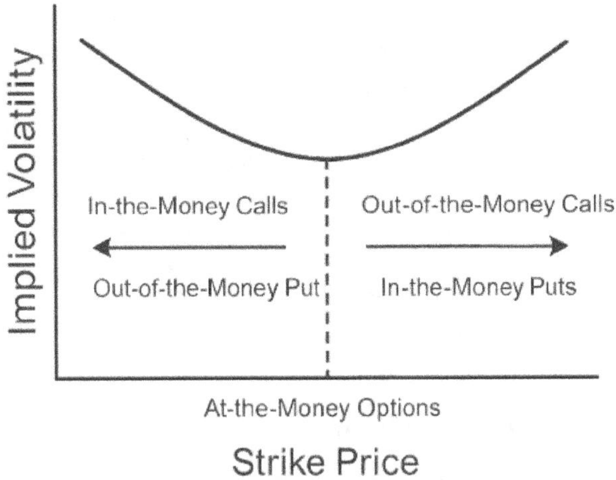

Figure 11.1. Volatility Smile

- *Crash protection demand*: Investors often buy OTM puts to hedge against large market declines. This demand drives up prices and thus the implied volatility of those options.
- *Jumps and fat tails*: The real-world return distribution of stocks is not perfectly lognormal. It exhibits fat tails, which means extreme movements are more common than the model assumes. Traders know this and price options accordingly.
- *Volatility risk premium*: Option sellers demand compensation for bearing volatility risk, especially for options sensitive to tail events. This premium can vary with moneyness and maturity.

As a result, the implied volatility surface (i.e., the three-dimensional shape that results from plotting implied volatilities by strike and maturity) is often far from flat. It may slope, curve, twist, or kink depending on investor expectations, current market stress, and structural factors such as supply and demand for certain option types.

Understanding the volatility smile and skew is critical for practitioners. It impacts everything from how options are priced and hedged to how strategies are constructed. For example:

- *Hedging portfolios*: Traders who rely on Black–Scholes Greeks must be aware that their hedge ratios may be less effective if they ignore volatility skew.

- *Spread construction*: When building vertical spreads, straddles, or butterflies, the difference in implied volatilities across strikes affects expected payoff and risk profile.
- *Volatility arbitrage*: Volatility traders may exploit anomalies in the smile—for instance, if implied volatility at one strike deviates materially from where it "should" be based on the rest of the curve.
- *Skew trades*: Traders can construct positions (such as risk reversals) that specifically target changes in the shape of the volatility surface rather than its overall level.

11.5.2 *Applying implied volatility*

Once implied volatility is extracted from market prices, it becomes a critical input in a wide range of trading, hedging, and risk management decisions. It serves as a market signal and a pricing tool for practitioners.

A typical application is comparing implied volatility across options with different strike prices and maturities to construct the volatility surface. Traders analyze the shape of this surface to understand how the market is pricing risk across different scenarios. For example, steep skews where implied volatility is higher for OTM puts than for calls may indicate demand for downside protection or a perception of asymmetric tail risk.

Implied volatility is also used to identify relative value opportunities. By comparing implied volatility to historical or forecasted realized volatility, practitioners can assess whether an option appears overpriced or underpriced. A strategy might involve selling options when implied volatility is substantially higher than historical norms on the expectation that the option premium overstates actual future price movement or buying when it appears unusually low ahead of a known catalyst, such as earnings or macroeconomic announcements.

In addition to pricing, implied volatility is critical for managing volatility exposure. A trader's portfolio may be long or short vega, that is, sensitive to changes in implied volatility. Managing this exposure is essential, particularly for volatility arbitrage strategies or when constructing delta-neutral hedges. For example, a delta-hedged position may still experience significant profit or loss swings if implied volatility rises or falls sharply, and understanding this sensitivity is crucial to risk control.

Implied volatility also plays a central role in calibrating and maintaining consistency across pricing models. Rather than using a fixed input for volatility, most trading systems dynamically feed in implied volatilities extracted from the market to price other options consistently. This is especially important for managing books that span multiple strike prices and maturities, where model coherence across the volatility surface is necessary to avoid arbitrage or mispricing.

Ultimately, implied volatility is widely regarded as a measure of market sentiment. A sudden rise in implied volatility often signals heightened uncertainty, fear, or the anticipation of significant price movements. During periods of market stress, implied volatility tends to spike across asset classes, reflecting investors' demand for protection. Conversely, declining implied volatility is often associated with calmer markets or rising confidence. In this way, implied volatility is not just a mathematical output but rather a window into how market participants collectively price risk.

11.6 Summary

In this chapter, I introduce the key building blocks of option pricing to help understand how options derive their value before diving into formal pricing models. I start by breaking down the market price of an option into two intuitive components: intrinsic value and time value. Using examples, I illustrate how each component behaves under various strike prices and market scenarios and explain why this decomposition is essential for anyone trading or analyzing options.

From there, I explain the concept of moneyness, a classification that tells us how the strike price compares to the underlying asset's current price. I explain what it means for an option to be in-the-money, at-the-money, or out-of-the-money, and I clarify terms such as "deep in-the-money" and "deep out-of-the-money," which frequently appear in professional discussions. I highlight how moneyness affects an option's intrinsic value, time value, and responsiveness to market changes.

I then examine the determinants of option value, focusing on how factors such as the underlying asset price, volatility, time to expiration, interest rates, and dividends influence an option's worth. I walk through each factor individually and explain how it influences calls and puts differently and how the impact can change depending on whether the option is European or American.

Next, I introduce the Greeks, which are tools used by practitioners to measure how sensitive an option is to changes in the market. Rather than relying on formulas, I provide intuitive explanations and examples that show how delta, gamma, theta, vega, and rho function in practice.

Finally, I turn to implied volatility, one of the most widely used and misunderstood concepts in options markets. I explain how implied volatility is derived from market prices and what it reveals about expected future uncertainty.

Chapter 12

Speculation with Derivatives: Concepts, Strategies, and Execution

Speculation is a primary motivation for participating in derivative markets. Unlike risk control, which seeks to reduce exposure, or arbitrage, which aims to exploit pricing inefficiencies, speculation embraces risk in pursuit of profit. Derivatives offer a powerful and flexible toolkit, enabling market participants to express views on the direction, volatility, or relative value of underlying assets with precision and leverage.

For speculators, derivatives are an attractive way to place leveraged bets on the direction, volatility, or timing of price changes. Unlike buying the underlying asset directly, these contracts offer both greater potential profits and increased risks. Speculators use derivatives to take positions on price movements, such as anticipating a stock or commodity's rise or fall. But speculation is not only limited to directional bets; it also includes trades focused on volatility. Strategies such as straddles or strangles, which we will describe, are designed to profit from large price swings, regardless of the direction. Additionally, derivatives offer leverage, enabling traders to manage large exposures with relatively small capital outlays. This magnifies both potential gains and potential losses. While all these instruments can be used for speculation, the choice of derivatives depends on the speculator's risk tolerance, view on volatility, and desired level of leverage.

With the growth of algorithmic trading, the rise of retail investors, and a rapidly evolving financial ecosystem, speculative use of derivatives has become more accessible than ever. What was once the domain of professionals operating on institutional trading desks is now within reach for a broader range of market participants. As a result, understanding the mechanics behind speculative strategies and how to structure them thoughtfully has become essential for anyone looking to actively engage in the markets.

Unlike long-term investing or risk control approaches that seek to manage underlying exposures, speculative strategies are typically designed to capitalize on short-term price movements, shifts in volatility, or perceived market mispricings. For many, the appeal lies not only in the potential for substantial returns but also in the intellectual challenge of interpreting market signals and positioning accordingly in a fast-moving environment.

While speculation naturally carries risk, it doesn't have to be reckless. With careful analysis, structured design, and sound risk management, speculation can become a disciplined and practical part of a broader trading approach. In this chapter, I explain the core ideas that shape speculative strategies, focusing on how they differ from other trading motives and why derivatives are particularly well-suited.

I begin with the foundational elements—key variables and decision points that shape speculative trades, including strike price, time to expiration, volatility, leverage, and market outlook. I also introduce tools such as payoff diagrams and scenario tables to help assess and visualize potential outcomes. These concepts set the stage for building strategies matching market expectations and individual risk tolerances. From there, I move into implementation. I walk through specific trading strategies—directional and non-directional—and show how they translate speculative views into structured positions. By combining principles with practice, I aim to provide a comprehensive understanding of how derivatives can be used as speculative instruments in dynamic market environments.

12.1 Foundations of Speculative Strategies Using Derivatives

Starting with a clear conceptual framework is essential to understanding how derivatives are used in speculative trading. Before exploring specific strategies or trade structures, I examine the underlying purpose of speculation, how it differs from other trading motives, and why derivatives offer a uniquely flexible platform for expressing speculative views.

12.1.1 *Conceptual foundations of speculation*

Speculation involves taking on financial risk to pursue profit, typically based on the belief that an asset's price will move in a specific direction or exhibit a particular pattern. Unlike risk control, which seeks to reduce or offset risk, and arbitrage, which seeks riskless profit by exploiting price discrepancies, speculation is inherently directional and opportunistic. It is driven by a view of future market behavior and a willingness to accept uncertainty in exchange for the possibility of substantial returns.

Speculators play a critical role in financial markets. By assuming risks others wish to avoid, they provide liquidity and support the price discovery process. Their willingness to trade based on expectations, whether informed by fundamentals, sentiment, or technical signals, adds depth to the market and helps set equilibrium prices. For example, a commodity producer may use futures to lock in prices, while a speculator takes the opposite side of the trade based on a belief that prices will move higher. In this way, speculation enables hedging and contributes to market efficiency. Historically, speculation has had a complex reputation. Yet, speculation has also driven innovation, such as the emergence of options markets in the 1970s and the growth of exchange-traded derivatives. When grounded in informed analysis and risk management, speculation is a legitimate and often essential market function.

Behavioral finance adds another layer to this understanding by highlighting the psychological and cognitive biases that influence speculative behavior. Overconfidence, i.e., the tendency to overestimate one's ability to predict market movements, is a common trait among speculators. Similarly, the gambler's fallacy is the belief that a change in fortune is "due" after a string of outcomes. Speculation is also tied to the pursuit of sensation or intellectual challenge, where the act of predicting markets becomes rewarding. These behavioral dimensions help explain why speculation persists despite frequent losses and why some traders are drawn to it, despite the associated risks.

In today's environment, speculation through derivatives is more accessible than ever. Retail platforms, algorithmic strategies, and real-time data have expanded the range of tools available to traders.

Whether executed by professionals using sophisticated models or by individuals with a market thesis and a trading app, speculation reflects a willingness to express a view and to take on risk in pursuit of reward.

12.1.2 *Developing a speculative mindset*

Speculating with derivatives is not simply picking a strategy and executing a trade. It requires an analytical, disciplined, and adaptive mindset. While the potential rewards of speculation can be substantial, so can the risks. The most successful speculators approach the market with a clear framework for decision-making and a willingness to learn from both outcomes and processes.

At the core of a sound speculative mindset is clarity of purpose. A well-designed speculative trade begins with a well-formed thesis, a view about the market, an anticipated event, or a structural imbalance. This thesis should not be based on vague intuition or untested assumptions. It should emerge from analyzing price patterns, volatility conditions, fundamental developments, or macroeconomic forces. The better the thesis is defined, the more effectively it can be translated into a strategy and evaluated for risk and reward.

Equally important is a commitment to objectivity. In speculative markets, the temptation to become emotionally invested in a position can be strong, particularly when the trade moves against expectations. An effective speculator can step back, reassess the trade on its merits, and act decisively, whether holding, adjusting, or exiting. Emotional detachment does not mean indifference; it means keeping speculation grounded in logic and probabilities, not hope or fear.

Speculators must also be prepared to accept losses. Even well-reasoned trades can fail due to randomness, misjudgment, or changing market dynamics. Losses are not necessarily signs of failure; they are part of the process. What matters is whether the trade was structured correctly, aligned with the initial view, and managed in accordance with the plan. A losing trade that followed a sound process can be more valuable in the long term than a winning trade that succeeded by chance.

This mindset also requires continuous learning. Markets evolve, instruments change, and new patterns emerge. Staying sharp means studying both successful and unsuccessful trades, seeking feedback, and refining methods. Experienced speculators often develop a personal playbook, strategies, setups, and risk parameters that match their strengths and market preferences. They do not try to trade everything; they specialize, observe, and adapt.

Finally, discipline ties everything together. This means executing trades consistently with pre-established rules, sizing positions appropriately, and focusing on long-term goals rather than short-term noise.[1] It also means knowing when not to trade when the edge is unclear, the setup is weak, or emotions are running high.

Speculation is as much about the process as it is about the outcome. Building a speculative mindset takes time, but the foundation allows strategies to be executed with consistency and confidence.

12.1.3 *Methodology for speculating with derivatives*

Speculating with derivatives involves more than simply guessing where prices will go. Successful speculation requires a structured approach integrating market analysis, strategy selection, and risk management. This section lays out the methodology for developing a speculative strategy using derivatives. The process includes determining your market thesis or "bet," evaluating potential outcomes, and managing risk in a way that maximizes the likelihood of success while keeping losses under control.

12.1.3.1 *Identifying the bet*

The first step in building any speculative strategy is to clearly define the nature of the bet being made. This foundational decision guides the choice of instruments, time horizon, and strategy type. Speculators must consider whether they expect the price of an asset to rise, fall, or remain within a particular range. This decision shapes whether the approach will be

[1] In financial markets, "noise" refers to short-term price movements or signals that lack meaningful information about an asset's fundamental value. These fluctuations are often driven by emotion, speculation, or random events rather than lasting changes in economic or financial conditions. Traders who respond to such signals without relying on fundamentals are known as "noise traders," and their activity can amplify volatility and obscure genuine market signals.

directional (based on a clear view about the price path) or non-directional (designed to profit from volatility or time decay regardless of price direction).

Equally important is defining the bet's timeframe. Some trades are short-term, reacting to expected price moves around specific catalysts such as earnings announcements or policy decisions. Others may be structured to benefit from broader, longer-term market trends or shifts in volatility. Identifying key market drivers is also crucial. These include upcoming events, macroeconomic trends, interest rate changes, or investor sentiment shifts that could influence the underlying asset's price.

A well-articulated market view will guide the selection of both the appropriate derivative instrument or instruments and the strategy structure. For instance, if the expectation is for a short-term price rise, a bullish strategy using a call option or a long futures contract may be appropriate. Suppose the expectation is for high volatility, but the direction is uncertain. In that case, strategies such as straddles or strangles that we discuss later in this chapter can be used to benefit from significant price movements in either direction.

12.1.3.2 *Evaluating the strategy*

After the initial bet is identified, the next step is to evaluate and refine the trade's structure to align with both the market outlook and personal risk tolerance. This involves selecting the type of derivative, defining the strategic objective, and analyzing the trade's risk/reward characteristics.

Instruments such as options are often preferred when the goal is to limit risk while retaining upside potential. A call option can be used to benefit from an expected price increase, while a put option may be used when a decline is expected. Futures contracts, by contrast, offer more direct exposure and leverage, but they carry more significant potential for both gains and losses. Swaps can also be used to speculate on variables such as interest rates or currency movements.

Defining the goal of the trade is critical. Directional strategies are appropriate when the speculator is confident about the direction of the price move, using instruments such as long calls or short futures. When the direction is unclear but volatility is expected to rise, non-directional strategies such as straddles or iron condors, explained later in this chapter, may be more effective, as they are designed to benefit from the magnitude of price movement rather than its direction.

12.1.3.3 *Assessing risk and reward*

Every speculative strategy involves trade-offs between potential returns and the risk of loss. A critical part of designing the trade is analyzing whether the expected payoff justifies the risk. The risk/reward ratio provides a basic framework for making this assessment. For instance, buying an out-of-the-money call option may offer significant profit potential; however, the likelihood of loss is also higher if the anticipated price movement does not materialize.

Position sizing is another key element of risk management. Even a sound strategy can expose a trader to excessive losses if the position is too large in relation to their available capital. Speculators should calibrate their trade size according to risk tolerance, capital availability, and the probability-weighted expectation of outcomes.

Ultimately, it is crucial to establish an *exit strategy* in advance. This includes establishing stop-loss levels to contain downside risk and take-profit points to lock in gains. Having a plan for when and how to exit—whether at expiration or earlier—helps reduce emotional decision-making and ensures that trades stay aligned with the original strategic intent.

12.1.3.4 *Evaluating the outcome at expiration*

For derivative contracts, the outcome at expiration is a key determinant of profitability. Speculators must understand how their positions will behave as expiration approaches and what conditions are required for the trade to be profitable.

In the case of options, profitability depends on how the asset's price compares to the strike price at expiration. A long call option becomes profitable if the underlying asset rises above the strike price, while a long put is profitable if the asset falls below the strike. Additionally, option values are affected by time decay and changes in implied volatility—two forces that can work for or against the position depending on the trade structure and market conditions.

Futures contracts do not involve time decay but require either offsetting the position or settling the contract at expiration. A long futures trade profits if the asset's price is higher than the entry price at expiration; a short futures trade profits if the price is lower. Understanding how expiration affects potential outcomes helps determine breakeven levels (i.e., the price at which the position results in neither a gain nor a loss) and assesses the likelihood of reaching those levels.

12.1.3.5 *Visualizing the outcome: Payoff tables and graphs*

Once a speculative trade is designed and evaluated, visual tools can help clarify potential results under different market scenarios. A payoff table shows the position's profit or loss at various prices of the underlying asset at expiration. This table highlights breakeven points, maximum gain, and maximum loss, allowing for a precise assessment of the trade's asymmetry and exposure.

A payoff graph presents the same information in a visual format. For example, the payoff for a long call option with a $50 strike price shows zero profit below $50, increasing gains as the asset price rises above that level. This type of graph enables traders to quickly visualize the relationship between asset price and trade outcomes, providing intuitive insights into the strategy's risk and reward characteristics.

With a clear understanding of the purpose, process, and mindset required for speculation, we now focus on the strategies themselves; that is, how derivative instruments are used in practice to express speculative views across various market conditions.

12.2 Strategic Applications of Speculation with Derivatives

Having established the conceptual, analytical, and behavioral foundations of speculative trading, we now turn to the practical side of implementation. This section examines how speculation is conducted using actual derivative strategies designed to express views on market direction, volatility, or price behavior over time. Each strategy builds on the principles introduced earlier (i.e., clarity of thesis, risk management, and disciplined execution) and translates them into actionable structures that traders across asset classes can use.

Whether the goal is to profit from a price increase, benefit from market indecision, or capitalize on a volatility event, the chosen strategy must align with the trader's outlook, time horizon, and risk tolerance. The following pages outline various directional, non-directional, and volatility-based strategies, explaining how they work, when they are most effective, and what trade-offs they involve.

These applications are not presented as rigid templates but as adaptable tools. The aim is to show how different instruments and configurations can be combined to reflect specific speculative views and market conditions. With this perspective, the section provides a practical extension of the framework developed earlier in the chapter.

12.2.1 *Directional strategies*

Directional strategies are designed to profit from a specific expectation about an asset's price movement, either upward or downward. These strategies reflect the most fundamental form of speculation: taking a position based on a belief that the market is mispriced relative to future developments. Directional trades are often straightforward in concept but can vary in complexity depending on the instruments used and the desired risk profiles.

The simplest directional strategies involve taking long or short positions in futures or options. A trader who expects the price of an asset to rise might go long on a futures contract or buy a call option. Conversely, a trader anticipating a decline may short a futures contract or buy a put option. Each strategy provides exposure to directional price changes but carries different implications regarding leverage, capital at risk, and payoff structures.

Going long on a futures contract gives direct exposure to price increases. If the asset's price rises, the position's value increases proportionally, and the gain can be realized by selling the contract or closing the position. The downside is that futures expose the trader to potentially unlimited losses if the price moves in the opposite direction. Margin requirements help control risk but also mean that gains and losses are amplified relative to the initial capital commitment.

Buying a call option is a more limited-risk way to express a bullish view. The maximum loss is limited to the premium paid, while the potential upside increases as the asset's price rises above the strike price. This strategy benefits from leverage and convexity (i.e., the characteristic that gains increase at an accelerating rate as the underlying price moves further in the trader's favor). The trade-off is that if the anticipated move does not materialize before the option expires, it may expire worthless.

Bearish views can be implemented through short futures positions or by purchasing put options. A short futures position profits when the asset's price declines, but it also comes with a theoretically unlimited risk if the market moves sharply higher. On the other hand, a long put option offers defined risk and the potential for substantial gains if the asset's price falls below the strike price. Like calls, puts benefit from sharp directional moves but suffer from time decay and declining volatility if the market remains quiet.

More sophisticated directional strategies involve vertical spreads, which combine long and short options at different strike prices to modify the payoff profile. For example, a bull call spread (long call + short call at a higher strike) limits both potential gains and losses, reducing the upfront premium while capping profits. Bear put spreads work similarly for bearish positions. These structures are often used when a trader has a strong directional view but wants to reduce costs or limit exposure.

Some speculators combine directional instruments to shape the payoff structure more precisely. For example, a trader might pair a long call option with a short futures contract to express a bullish outlook while partially hedging downside risk. This approach preserves upside exposure while reducing potential losses if the market turns sharply against the position.

Option spreads, such as bull put spreads or bear call spreads, are also frequently used to create directional positions with built-in risk controls. These strategies involve selling one option and buying another at a different strike within the same expiration period. The result is a trade that limits both potential gains and losses, often in exchange for a lower upfront cost or more favorable breakeven level. Combinations such as these allow traders to tailor their directional exposure more precisely. They are instrumental when the market view is strong but not absolute, or when capital constraints or volatility conditions make single-instrument trades less appealing.

The appeal of directional strategies lies in their simplicity and clarity. They reflect a clear market opinion and can be tailored to match a trader's risk appetite. However, directional strategies are also vulnerable to being wrong in direction, timing, or magnitude. Markets may drift sideways, move slowly, or react unpredictably to news. For this reason, effective directional trading requires more than conviction. It requires well-calibrated trade construction and disciplined risk management.

The following section turns to strategies designed for a different kind of speculation, where the trader is less focused on direction and more interested in profiting from price movement itself, regardless of whether the market is rising or falling.

12.2.2 *Non-directional strategies*

Non-directional speculative strategies are designed for traders who anticipate significant price movement in an asset but are uncertain about the direction of that movement. These strategies enable speculators to profit from volatility—whether the market rises or falls—by constructing trades sensitive to the magnitude, rather than the direction, of price changes.

These strategies are particularly effective when catalysts, such as earnings call reports, macroeconomic announcements, or political events, are expected to elicit sharp market reactions. Still, the directional outcome is difficult to predict. Non-directional strategies often utilize options, which can be structured to benefit from price swings, stability, or changes in implied volatility across different time horizons.

Non-directional strategies fall into three categories: (1) movement-based strategies, (2) range-bound strategies, and (3) volatility and time-based strategies. Here, I examine the most widely used non-directional strategies, including straddles, strangles, iron condors, butterfly spreads, and more advanced structures, such as calendar and double diagonal spreads. Each strategy will be explained with a description, a risk-reward profile, and a worked example.

12.2.2.1 *Movement-based strategies*

Movement-based, non-directional strategies are designed for traders who expect a large price movement in the underlying asset but are uncertain about its direction. These strategies do not rely on predicting whether prices will rise or fall; instead, they are designed to profit from any significant market movement, regardless of the direction the market takes. The key to success lies in the asset breaking out of a defined price range by enough to overcome the initial cost of the position. These strategies tend to perform best when implied volatility is low and expected to rise, such as before major events or announcements that could surprise the market. In what follows, I examine two of the most used movement-based strategies: the straddle and the strangle.

Straddle Strategy: The straddle is one of the most well-known non-directional strategies employed by speculators who anticipate a significant price movement in an asset but are uncertain about its direction. It is constructed by purchasing a call option and a put option on the same underlying asset, with the same strike price and expiration date. Because it includes both upside and downside exposure, the straddle is a pure volatility play; it performs best when the asset experiences a sharp move in either direction before expiration.

The appeal of the straddle lies in its simplicity and symmetry. If the asset's price rises significantly, the call option's value increases. If the price drops sharply, the put option becomes profitable. The strategy gains value when the underlying asset moves far enough away from the strike price to offset the combined premium paid for both options.

Despite its intuitive structure, the straddle requires careful consideration of costs. Because both options are purchased at the money, the total premium can be relatively expensive, especially when implied volatility is high. For the trade to succeed, the asset must move far enough before expiration to overcome the total cost of entry. If the asset remains near the strike price, both options may decay and expire worthless, resulting in a full loss of the premium paid.

The profit potential for a long straddle is theoretically unlimited to the upside and substantial to the downside, as an asset's price cannot fall below zero but can rise indefinitely. The maximum risk is capped at the total premium paid. This creates a convex payoff profile with two break-even points, one above and one below the strike price, beyond which the position begins to turn a profit.

For example, suppose a trader expects significant volatility in a stock ahead of its quarterly earnings announcement but has no firm conviction about the direction. The stock is currently trading at $50. The trader enters a straddle by purchasing a $50 call option for a premium of $4 and a $50 put option for a premium of $4, resulting in a total cost of $8.

To break even, the stock must move either above $58 (strike price plus total premium) or below $42 (strike price minus total premium) by expiration. If the stock rises to $63, the call option is worth $13, and the put expires worthless, yielding a net gain of $5 ($13 value minus $8 premium). If the stock drops to $35, the put is worth $15 and the call expires worthless, resulting in a net profit of $7. However, if the stock closes at exactly $50, both options expire worthless, and the trader loses the entire $8 premium.

This example illustrates both the convexity and the risk of the straddle. While it can generate large returns if the asset's price moves significantly, it suffers if the market fails to move or moves too slowly to overcome the cost of the options.

The straddle's payoff diagram forms a classic V-shape, with the point of maximum loss occurring at the strike price, where both options expire worthless. Profits grow as the asset price moves away from the strike price in either direction. Because this strategy relies on price movement, its value declines as time passes since the options lose part of their worth each day if the market does not move—an effect known as "time decay." The strategy is also sensitive to shifts in the market's expectations of future volatility: If investors suddenly anticipate greater price swings, the value of both options increases. In contrast, a drop in expected volatility reduces their value. These two effects (time decay and changes in implied volatility) are central to understanding option strategies and are examined in greater detail in Part 5. Straddles are typically most effective when entered before events expected to cause rapid, unpredictable market moves.

Table 12.1 and Figure 12.1 illustrate the payoff profile for a long straddle using the earlier example in which a trader buys a $50 call and a $50 put, paying $4 for each. The total premium paid is $8, making the breakeven points $58 and $42. The figure illustrates how the strategy yields increasing profits as the underlying asset's price deviates from the $50 strike price in either direction. This payoff curve shows the net profit and loss of the long straddle strategy at expiration. A maximum loss of $8 occurs at the $50 strike. Profits grow without limit as the asset moves above $58 or below $42.

Strangle Strategy: The strangle is a non-directional strategy designed for traders who expect significant price movement but prefer a lower-cost alternative to the straddle. Like the straddle, the strangle profits when the underlying asset moves sharply in either direction. However, instead of purchasing at-the-money options, the strangle uses out-of-the-money call and put options, reducing the total premium paid. The trade-off is that the underlying price must move farther for the strategy to become profitable.

Table 12.1. Payoff Table for a Long Straddle

Underlying Price at Expiration	Value of Call Option	Value of Put Option	Total Value	Net Profit/Loss
$35	$0	$15	$15	**+7**
$40	$0	$10	$10	**+2**
$45	$0	$5	$5	**–3**
$50	$0	$0	$0	**–8** (max loss)
$55	$5	$0	$5	**–3**
$60	$10	$0	$10	**+2**
$65	$15	$0	$15	**+7**

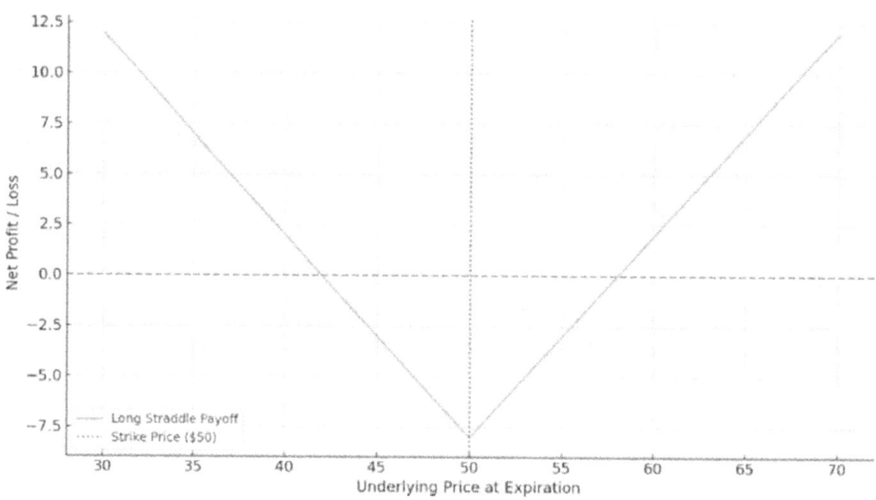

Figure 12.1. Payoff Diagram for a Long Straddle at Expiration

In a long strangle, a trader buys a call option with a strike price above the current market price and a put option with a strike price below the market price. This range exposes large price movements in both directions, reducing costs compared to a straddle. Because the options are out-of-the-money at initiation, they have no intrinsic value. However, if the underlying price moves sharply, one of the options becomes valuable while the other expires worthless.

Strangles are most effective in environments where implied volatility (i.e., the market's assessment of how much the underlying asset's price is likely to fluctuate in the future) is relatively low but expected to increase, such as before a major announcement. If volatility rises, the value of both options in the strangle tends to increase. However, like straddles, strangles are vulnerable to time decay, meaning the options lose value each day that the market fails to make a significant move. The position may therefore lose value if the expected price swing does not occur before expiration. A fuller discussion of implied volatility and time decay is provided in Chapter 11.

To illustrate a strangle, suppose a stock is trading at $50, and a trader anticipates sharp price movement but has no directional bias. They implement a strangle by purchasing a $55 call for $3 and a $45 put for $3, paying a total premium of $6.

For the position to be profitable, the stock must move above $61 (call strike + premium) or below $39 (put strike – premium). If the stock price rises to $65, the call option is worth $10, the put expires worthless, and the net gain is $4. If the stock falls to $35, the put is worth $10, the call expires worthless, and the profit is again $4. But if the stock remains between $45 and $55, both options expire worthless, and the $6 premium is lost.

The strangle's payoff diagram is similar in shape to the straddle's V-shape, but the center of the V is flatter and wider, reflecting that the position does not profit unless the underlying price moves farther away from the starting point. The strategy's risk is limited to the total premium paid, while its potential gain increases with the magnitude of the move. As shown in Table 12.2 and Figure 12.2, profits begin only when the asset moves sufficiently far beyond the strikes. The strategy results in a loss between the $45 and $55 range due to time decay and a lack of intrinsic value.

Table 12.2. Payoff Table for a Long Strangle

Underlying Price at Expiration	Value of Put Option	Value of Call Option	Total Option Value	Net Profit/Loss
$35	$10	$0	$10	**+4**
$40	$5	$0	$5	**–1**
$45	$0	$0	$0	**–6** (max loss)
$50	$0	$0	$0	**–6** (max loss)
$55	$0	$0	$0	**–6** (max loss)
$60	$0	$5	$5	**–1**
$65	$0	$10	$10	**+4**

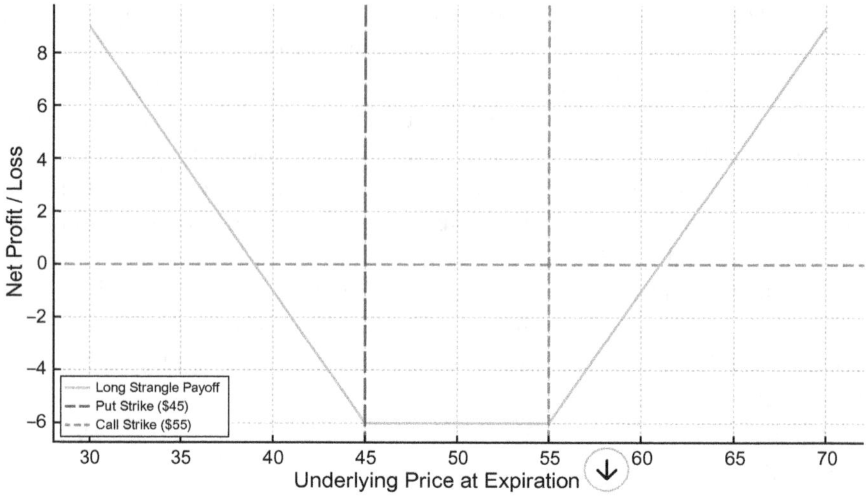

Figure 12.2. Payoff Diagram for a Long Strangle at Expiration

Let's compare the straddle and strangle strategies. A straddle involves buying a call and a put at the same strike price, usually at-the-money. This structure provides maximum sensitivity to price movement but comes at a higher cost, since both options have more intrinsic and time value. A strangle, by contrast, uses out-of-the-money options, with the call strike above the current market price and the put strike below it. This reduces the upfront cost of the trade, but the underlying asset must move further for the strategy to become profitable. In essence, straddles are better for modest but uncertain movements, while strangles are suited for more dramatic moves at a lower entry cost. The choice between them depends on the trader's volatility and price range outlook. Table 12.3 summarizes the differences between these two non-directional strategies.

12.2.2.2 *Range-bound strategies*

Range-bound, non-directional strategies are constructed to profit when the price of the underlying asset remains within a defined range over the life of the trade. Rather than seeking large moves, these strategies benefit from price stability, earning income through the slow erosion of option premiums, particularly when implied volatility is elevated and expected to decline. Traders employing these strategies typically believe the market

Table 12.3. Comparison of Staddle versus Strangle Strategy

Feature	Straddle	Strangle
Option Strikes	Same strike price	Different strike prices (wider range)
Cost (Premium Paid)	Higher	Lower
Breakeven Range	Narrower	Wider
Probability of Profit	Higher (if moderate move occurs)	Lower (needs larger move)
Maximum Loss	Total premium paid	Total premium paid
Best Used When	Expect strong move, uncertain direction	Expect very large move, but want to reduce cost

will remain anchored near a specific level, often due to technical resistance, mean reversion, or the absence of a strong catalyst. Because both profit and loss are limited, range-bound strategies offer a structured way to express a view on market stagnation while managing risk. In the following sections, I examine two widely used range-bound strategies: the iron condor and the butterfly spread.

Iron Condor Strategy: The iron condor is a non-directional strategy designed to profit from low volatility. Unlike straddles and strangles, which benefit from sharp price moves, the iron condor seeks to profit when the underlying asset remains within a well-defined range. It accomplishes this by combining two vertical spreads: a bear call spread and a bull put spread. The result is a position that earns premium income when the asset price trades between the two short strikes.

To construct an iron condor, a trader sells a call option at a higher strike and buys a further out-of-the-money call to limit risk. Simultaneously, the trader sells a put option at a lower strike and buys a further out-of-the-money put to create a risk-defined lower boundary. The premium collected from selling the call and put options represents the maximum potential profit, while the width between strike prices defines the maximum potential loss, less the premium received.

This strategy is ideal for range-bound markets, particularly when implied volatility is elevated and expected to decline. The iron condor also benefits from time decay, as the value of the short options diminishes over time if the price remains within range. However, it is vulnerable to significant price fluctuations in either direction and requires diligent risk management.

To illustrate the iron condor strategy, suppose a stock is trading at \$50. A trader expects the price to remain between \$45 and \$55 over the next month and initiates the following iron condor: (1) Sell a \$55 call for \$3, (2) buy a \$60 call for \$1, (3) sell a \$45 put for \$3, and (4) buy a \$40 put for \$1. The total premium received is \$4. This amount is the maximum profit earned if the stock remains between \$45 and \$55 until expiration. The maximum loss occurs if the stock finishes below \$40 or above \$60. In that case, the loss is the width of the spreads (\$5) minus the premium received (\$4), resulting in a net loss of \$1.

Breakeven points are calculated by adding and subtracting the net premium from the short strike prices:

$$\textit{Upside breakeven}: \$55 + \$4 = \$59$$

$$\textit{Downside breakeven}: \$45 - \$4 = \$41$$

The strategy is profitable as long as the stock closes between \$41 and \$59.

The iron condor's payoff diagram resembles a plateau, with the flat section in the middle representing the maximum profit zone. The position has two breakeven points—above and below the short strikes—and losses increase linearly as the asset moves outside this range but are capped by the long call and put options.

This strategy performs best in stable, low-volatility environments where the trader expects the underlying asset to remain within a tight range. Its defined risk and limited reward make it a popular choice for traders looking to generate income with a high probability of success, especially when volatility is elevated.

Table 12.4 and Figure 12.3 illustrate the iron condor constructed using a \$45/\$40 put spread and a \$55/\$60 call spread. The position earns the full \$4 premium if the asset remains between \$45 and \$55. Breakeven points occur at \$41 and \$59. Beyond those levels, losses are capped at \$1.

Butterfly Spread Strategy: The butterfly spread is a non-directional strategy designed to profit when an asset's price stays near a central strike price. It is a defined-risk, limited-reward trade that benefits from low volatility and time decay, making it a popular choice when the trader expects the market to remain stable. Unlike the iron condor, which profits from a wide range of prices, the butterfly spread targets a narrower range, offering a higher reward-to-risk ratio if the price remains close to the center.

Table 12.4. Payoff Table for a $45–$55 Iron Condor

Underlying Price at Expiration	Value of Call Option	Value of Put Option	Total Value	Net Profit/Loss
$35	$0	$15	$15	+7
$40	$0	$10	$10	+2
$45	$0	$5	$5	–3
$50	$0	$0	$0	–8 (max loss)
$55	$5	$0	$5	–3
$60	$10	$0	$10	+2
$65	$15	$0	$15	+7

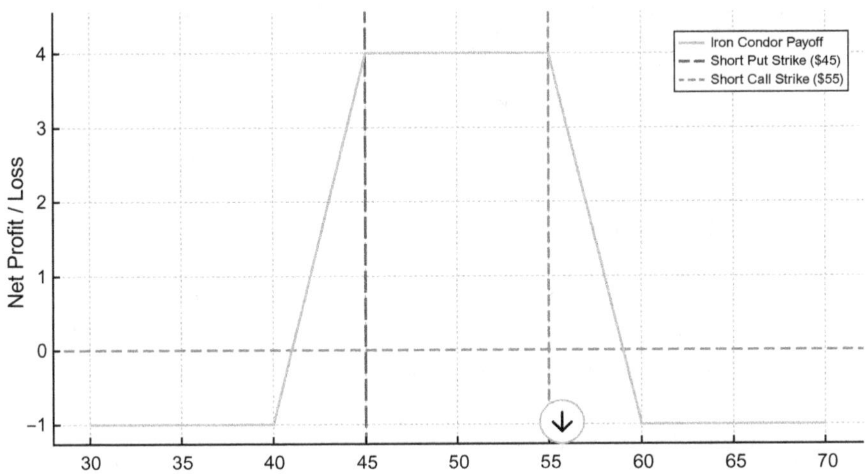

Figure 12.3. Payoff Diagram for Iron Condor at Expiration

A typical long call butterfly (though the same logic applies to puts) is constructed by (1) buying one lower-strike call, (2) selling two at-the-money calls, and (3) buying one higher-strike call. All options share the same expiration date. The structure creates a "tent-shaped" payoff profile, with the highest profit occurring if the asset closes at the middle strike price.

Because the outer options hedge the position, the maximum loss is limited to the net premium paid. The maximum gain occurs if the underlying asset closes exactly at the middle strike price, causing the short calls to expire in the money. In contrast, the long calls on either side offer minimal offsetting value.

To illustrate a long butterfly spread, suppose a stock is trading at $50, and a trader expects the price to remain near that level until expiration. They construct a butterfly spread using call options: (1) Buy one $45 call for $3, (2) sell two $50 calls for $5 each, and (3) buy one $55 call for $2. The total premium received is $10 (from the two $50 calls), and the total paid is $5 (for the $45 call) plus $2 (for the $55 call), resulting in a net credit of $3.

The maximum profit occurs if the stock closes at $50. At that point, the $45 call is worth $5, the $50 calls expire worthless (although they were sold for $10), and the $55 call also expires worthless. The total value is $5, and since the initial cost was negative (a $3 credit), the net profit is $5 – $2 = $3.

The maximum risk is the difference between the adjacent strike prices ($5) minus the net credit ($3), which equals $2. The breakeven points are:

Lower breakeven: $45 + $2 = $47

Upper breakeven: $55 – $2 = $53

The payoff structure of the butterfly spread is best understood through a visual illustration and a numerical breakdown. Table 12.5 and Figure 12.4 show the strategy's distinctive "tent-shaped" profile, with the peak at the middle strike price where maximum profit is realized. As the price moves away from this central point (up or down), the potential profit

Table 12.5. Payoff Table for a $45–$50–$55 Butterfly Spread

Underlying Price at Expiration	$45 Call Value	$50 Call Value (×2)	$55 Call Value	Net Option Value	Net Profit/Loss
$40	$0	$0	$0	$0	+3 (keep credit)
$45	$0	$0	$0	$0	+3 (keep credit)
$47	$2	$0	$0	$2	1
$50	$5	–$10	$0	–$5	+3 (max profit)
$53	$8	–$6	$0	$2	1
$55	$10	–$10	$0	$0	+3 (keep credit)
$60	$15	–$20	$5	$0	+3 (keep credit)

Note: All call values are calculated net of premiums, and the short call position is shown as a negative value (×2) to reflect the two sold contracts.

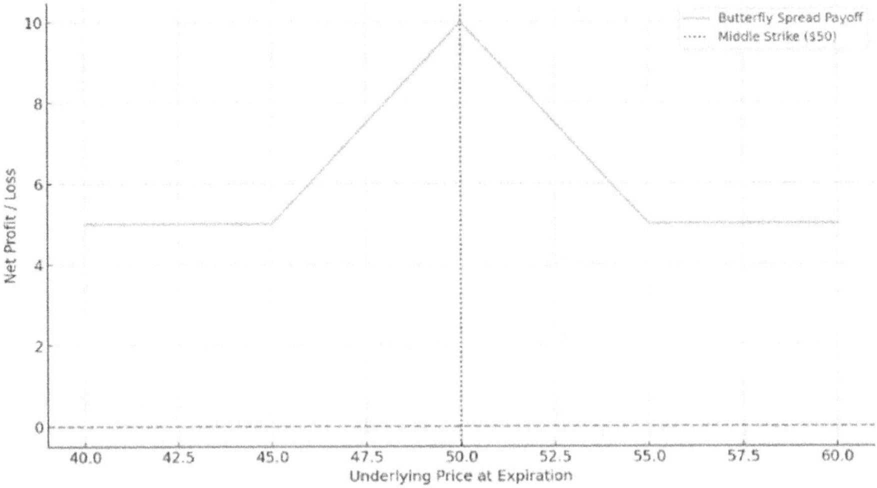

Figure 12.4. Payoff Diagram for Long Butterfly Spread at Expiration

declines, eventually reaching a capped loss equal to the net premium paid. The accompanying table provides specific examples of outcomes across a range of expiration prices, reinforcing how the strategy performs under different scenarios. The table and figure together clarify how this strategy balances risk and reward within a narrow price range.

12.2.2.3 *Volatility and time-based strategies*

Volatility and time-based non-directional strategies are designed to profit from the interplay between time decay and changes in implied volatility, rather than directional price movement. These strategies typically involve options with different expiration dates. They are structured to benefit when the underlying asset stays near a target price, allowing traders to capture value from the faster decay of shorter-term options relative to longer-term ones. While they may appear neutral regarding price direction, their success depends on how quickly the market moves, where it moves, and how implied volatility shifts over time. These strategies are beneficial when volatility is expected to rise or remain elevated around specific price levels. In the following sections, I examine two widely used approaches in this category: the calendar spread and the double diagonal spread.

Calendar Spread Strategy: The calendar spread, also known as a time spread, is a non-directional strategy designed to profit from differences in time decay and implied volatility between short- and long-dated options. It involves selling a short-term option and buying a longer-term option with the same strike price and underlying asset. Because the options share the same strike, the initial position is neutral regarding direction, but its profitability depends on the underlying asset remaining near that strike price over time.

The calendar spread generates profit when the short-dated option decays in value more quickly than the longer-dated one. This dynamic favors traders who expect little near-term movement but anticipate that volatility will rise or that the asset will hover near the strike price. If the underlying price remains near the strike as the front-month option expires, the short leg expires worthless or can be repurchased at a reduced cost, while the long leg retains time value.

The calendar spread is highly sensitive to changes in implied volatility. It typically benefits from increased volatility, particularly for the longer-dated option, which gains value relative to the near-term short option. However, significant moves away from the strike price, especially in the short term, can lead to losses if the short option moves in-the-money (i.e., when the option would generate an immediate profit if exercised). In such cases, the long leg may not have gained enough value to offset the loss on the short leg.

The following illustration demonstrates a calendar spread. Suppose a stock is trading at $50. A trader sells a 1-month $50 call for $2 and buys a 3-month $50 call for $4, resulting in a net debit of $2. This is the maximum amount the trader can lose.

The ideal scenario is for the stock to trade at or near $50 at the expiration of the front-month call. In that case, the short call expires worthless (or can be repurchased at a low price), while the long call still retains substantial time value. If the stock rises sharply or falls far from $50 during the front month, the short call may need to be repurchased at a higher cost or could expire in the money, potentially resulting in a net loss on the trade.

The payoff table and figure for a calendar spread are shown in Table 12.6 and Figure 12.5, respectively. The figure shows that the payoff diagram resembles a narrow, inverted "U" shape, peaking at the strike price. This figure shows the payoff for a calendar spread with both options struck at $50. The maximum profit occurs when the underlying asset closes near $50 at the expiration of the short-term option. The payoff

Table 12.6. Payoff Table for a Calendar Spread (1-Month Short Call, 3-Month Long Call)

Underlying Price at Short Expiration	Short Call Value	Long Call Value (Est.)	Net Position Value	Net Profit/Loss
$45	$0.00	$1	$1.00	–1
$48	$0.50	$2	$1.50	–0.5
$50	$2.00	$4	$2.00	0 (break-even)
$52	$4.00	$5	$1.00	–1
$55	$6.00	$6	$0.00	–2 (max loss)

Note: Values of the long option are approximated based on time remaining and volatility assumptions. Exact values depend on market conditions at the time.

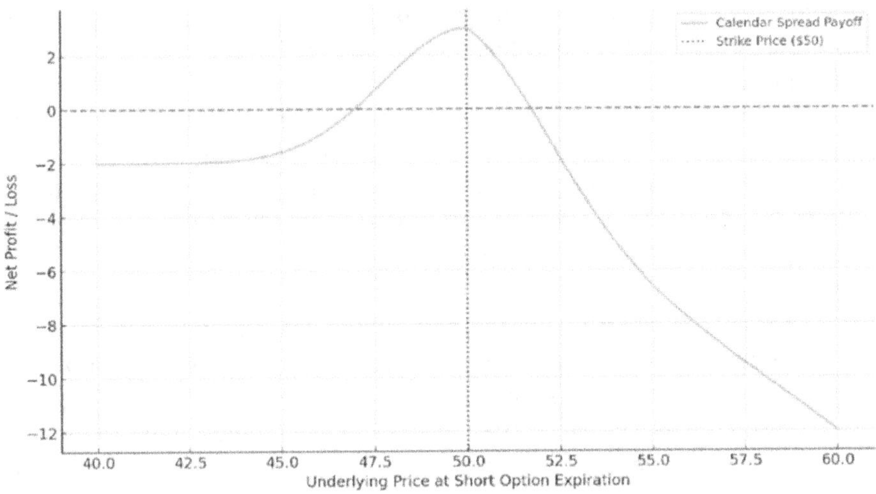

Figure 12.5. Payoff Diagram for Calendar Spread at Expiration of Short Option

declines on either side of this price as the position becomes less favorable.

The strategy performs best when the asset remains near the strike price through the expiration of the short-dated option. Losses occur when the underlying asset moves significantly in either direction, and the time value advantage of the long option is insufficient to offset losses on the short leg.

The calendar spread is most effective when implied volatility is low at initiation and expected to increase. It is also helpful when traders want to speculate on volatility without strong directional conviction, especially when the asset is expected to consolidate or pin to a specific level.

Double Diagonal Spread Strategy: The double diagonal spread is a more advanced, volatility- and time-based non-directional strategy. It combines elements of both the calendar spread and the strangle: Similar to a calendar spread, it involves selling short-term options and buying longer-term options; similar to a strangle, the options are placed at different strike prices, above and below the current market price. The result is a flexible structure designed to profit from time decay, stable prices, and potential changes in implied volatility.

The position is constructed by: (1) selling a near-term out-of-the-money call and a near-term out-of-the-money put, and (2) buying a longer-term out-of-the-money call at a higher strike and a longer-term out-of-the-money put at a lower strike. This creates a "diagonal" effect on both the call and put sides of the trade, with each leg using different expiration dates and different strike prices. The goal is for the underlying price to remain within a defined range through the expiration of the short-term options. In this scenario, the trader keeps most of the premium collected from the short options while retaining the longer-term legs, which still carry time value.

Because of its complexity, the double diagonal spread requires careful management and is best suited for traders with experience in options and volatility analysis. The strategy is ideal when implied volatility is low and expected to rise and when the trader expects the underlying to remain within a given range in the near term but wants some flexibility in the long term.

Consider the following as an example of a double diagonal spread. Suppose a stock is trading at $50. A trader constructs a double diagonal spread as follows: (1) Sell a 1-month $55 call for $2, (2) buy a 3-month $60 call for $3, (3) sell a 1-month $45 put for $2, and (4) buy a 3-month $40 put for $3. This results in a net debit of $2.

The maximum profit is achieved if the underlying price remains between the $45 and $55 strikes through the expiration of the front-month options. In that case, the trader retains the time value of the longer-dated $60 call and $40 put, while the short legs expire worthless. The maximum risk is limited to the initial $2 net debit plus any further loss that might occur if the underlying moves substantially and the longer-dated options increase in value or are exercised.

Table 12.7 and Figure 12.6 show the payoff table and diagram for our example, respectively. The double diagonal spread has a payoff diagram that resembles a soft-edged plateau, with profitability concentrated between the two short strikes. Unlike the sharp peak of a butterfly or the boxy shape of an iron condor, the double diagonal has a broader, smoother risk/reward profile. The structure allows for additional flexibility: the long-dated options may be held, adjusted, or closed after the short options expire.

The figure shows the ideal profit zone between the short strikes ($45 and $55), with declining profitability as the underlying moves

Table 12.7. Payoff Table for Double Diagonal Spread (1-Month/3-Month Legs)

Underlying Price at 1-Month Expiration	Short Put Value	Long Put Value	Short Call Value	Long Call Value	Net Position Value	Net Profit/Loss
$40	$5	$0	$0	$0	–$5	–$7
$45	$0	$1	$0	$0	$1	–$1
$50	$0	$2	$0	$2	$4	+$2 (best case)
$55	$0	$0	$0	$1	$1	–$1
$60	$0	$0	$5	$0	–$5	–$7

Note: Values of long options are estimated, and no early closeouts or adjustments are assumed after the short legs expire. Exact outcomes depend on market conditions and volatility.

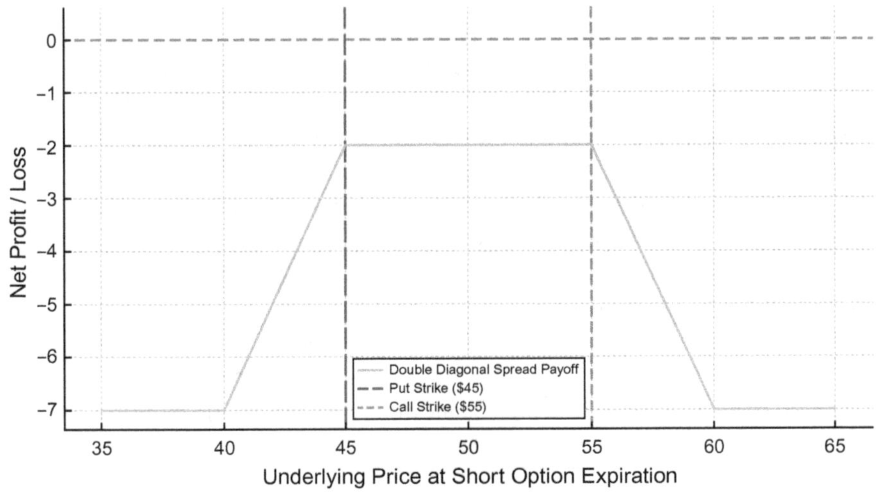

Figure 12.6. Payoff Diagram for Double Diagonal Spread at Expiration of Short Options

outside of that range. Losses are limited due to the protection offered by the longer-dated options.

The strategy is particularly useful during periods of low volatility preceding anticipated increases in market activity. It allows a trader to collect premium from short-term decay while still holding exposure to longer-term options that can benefit from directional or volatility shifts later on.

12.2.3 *Comparison: Directional vs. non-directional strategies*

While this section has focused on non-directional strategies, viewing them within the broader context of speculative approaches is important. Table 12.8 contrasts non-directional strategies with directional ones, highlighting the key differences in structure, risk profiles, and market assumptions. This side-by-side comparison helps clarify how a trader's view on price direction, volatility, and time horizon influences the choice of strategy.

Table 12.8. Comparison of Directional and Non-Directional Speculative Strategies

Aspect	**Directional Strategies**	**Non-Directional Strategies**
Market View	Strong conviction about price direction (up or down)	Expectation of volatility or range-bound movement, not direction
Objective	Profit from a rise or fall in the underlying asset's price	Profit from magnitude of movement (or lack of it), regardless of direction
Common Instruments	Long/short futures, calls, puts, vertical spreads	Straddles, strangles, iron condors, butterfly spreads
Risk Characteristics	Directional risk; can be asymmetric (limited loss or unlimited)	Typically defined risk but sensitive to volatility mispricing
Best Used When	Strong directional outlook or fundamental catalyst expected	Uncertainty about direction but clear view on volatility or tight price ranges
Primary Risk Factors	Incorrect direction, timing, or insufficient movement	Insufficient movement, delayed reaction, volatility compression

12.3 Evaluating and Managing Risk in Speculative Strategies

One of the most critical aspects of successful speculation is understanding and managing the risks involved. While speculative strategies can offer large rewards, they also come with the potential for significant losses. In this section, I'll discuss how to evaluate speculative strategies' risk/reward profile and explore risk management techniques that can help reduce the potential for large losses.

12.3.1 *Tracking profit and loss*

Evaluating a speculative trade begins with a clear understanding of how profits and losses develop over time. Unlike simply observing whether an asset's price has gone up or down, derivative positions require active monitoring of multiple variables, including market movement, time decay, and changes in implied volatility. As a result, mark-to-market accounting becomes essential. This means updating the value of the open position based on current market prices, even before the trade is closed or reaches expiration.

In the case of options, profit and loss are not linear and can change significantly without any movement in the underlying asset. For example, a position might lose value due to time decay, even if the trader's directional view remains intact. Alternatively, the position might increase if implied volatility rises, even when the price remains flat. Tracking profit and loss, therefore, means going beyond entry and exit prices. It involves understanding the evolving value of the trade based on all contributing inputs.

Many traders use real-time profit/loss dashboards provided by broker platforms or custom models built into spreadsheets. These tools update the theoretical price of the option or strategy based on live market data and recalculate unrealized gains or losses. This allows the trader to assess whether the position is progressing as expected or whether changing market conditions have altered the strategy's effectiveness.

It is also essential to distinguish between paper profits and realized gains. A trade may show a significant unrealized gain, but profit can erode without a disciplined exit or adjustment strategy. By consistently tracking the value of a position and comparing it to the original trade thesis, a speculator is better positioned to make informed decisions and protect gains before they evaporate.

12.3.2 *Exit planning and trade discipline*

One of the most overlooked elements of successful speculative trading is not what strategy to enter but when and how to exit. A well-conceived trade can quickly become a source of regret if it lacks a clearly defined exit plan. Without disciplined execution, speculators can fall prey to emotional decision-making, holding onto losing positions for too long or exiting profitable ones too soon.

Exit planning begins before the trade is placed. For each position, it is essential to define target profit levels, acceptable losses, and conditions for adjusting or exiting early. These decision points can be based on the underlying asset's price, changes in option value, or broader market conditions, such as shifts in volatility or approaching news events.

There are typically three types of exit triggers:

- *Profit Targets*: Predetermined points at which the position will be closed to lock in gains. For example, a trader might plan to close a straddle if the net value doubles, or to close a vertical spread once 75% of the maximum profit has been captured.
- *Stop Losses*: Limits on the amount of capital a trader is willing to risk. These can be absolute (e.g., a 50% loss on premium paid) or dynamic (e.g., based on changes in delta or a break of key technical levels in the underlying).
- *Time-Based Exits*: Some trades are designed around a specific event or time window, such as an earnings release or central bank announcement. If the anticipated catalyst passes without the expected move, the position may be exited early to avoid further time decay.

Discipline is critical not only in setting exit rules but also in following them. Traders often experience decision fatigue when faced with uncertain markets, and this can lead to hesitation, second-guessing, or chasing losses. A predefined exit plan reduces cognitive load and prevents emotions from distorting judgment.

It's also essential to review exit outcomes. Not all exits will be perfectly timed; some may leave money on the table, while others may cut off losses just before a reversal. But over time, disciplined exits that follow a consistent framework will help preserve capital, reinforce good habits, and reduce regret-driven trading.

In speculative trading, exit discipline is the final form of risk management. Entering a position may express a market view, but exiting well turns a good idea into a profitable outcome.

12.4 Summary

In this chapter, I examine speculation as a primary motivation for using derivatives, distinguishing it from risk management and arbitrage. I begin by defining speculation as a deliberate embrace of risk in pursuit of profit, emphasizing how derivatives provide a flexible and powerful means for expressing speculative views. I explain how speculators can profit from directional bets on price movements, volatility, timing, and relative value opportunities.

I develop the conceptual and behavioral foundations needed for successful speculation. This includes fostering an analytical, disciplined, and objective mindset. I emphasize the importance of developing a market thesis, evaluating outcomes under different scenarios, and managing risk using defined processes and tools such as payoff diagrams and scenario tables.

The heart of the chapter is devoted to strategic applications. I organize speculative strategies into directional, non-directional, and volatility/time-based. I present structured examples for each, explain risk/reward profiles, and illustrate outcomes with detailed tables and payoff diagrams. Non-directional strategies are further classified into movement-based, range-bound, and volatility/time-based approaches, with strategies such as straddles, strangles, iron condors, butterfly spreads, calendar spreads, and double diagonals examined in depth.

I conclude the chapter by addressing risk evaluation and trade management. I outline techniques for monitoring profit and loss, setting exit rules, and maintaining trade discipline. My goal is to show how speculation can be a structured and thoughtful activity when grounded in analysis and managed with care.

Chapter 13

Managing Risk with Derivatives: Principles, Practices, and Applications

Effective portfolio management requires more than identifying attractive investment opportunities; it also requires managing the risks accompanying those positions. In asset management, this process, often referred to as *risk management* or *risk control*, extends well beyond the traditional notion of hedging.

Hedging is technically a specific form of risk management in which offsetting positions are established to reduce or neutralize a particular exposure. Risk management more broadly involves identifying key risks in a portfolio, assessing their potential impact, and implementing strategies to align exposures with investment objectives and acceptable risk levels. In this chapter, however, the term "hedging" will be used more narrowly to mean taking positions using derivatives to achieve a targeted risk measure, such as a specific beta or duration, rather than simply eliminating an unwanted risk.

Although this chapter focuses on asset management applications, the risk management principles using derivatives apply across all domains, including corporate finance, banking, and insurance. In all these settings, effective risk management emphasizes controlling the type and magnitude of risk rather than attempting to eliminate all uncertainty. Eliminating risk entirely is rarely optimal; it can be costly, reduce upside potential, or introduce new unintended exposures.

Derivatives are central to risk management because they adjust portfolio exposures efficiently and flexibly without liquidating underlying asset positions. In practice, risk management often involves partial hedges that reduce volatility while leaving some exposure to market opportunities. Real-world risk management also recognizes that hedges are rarely perfect. Two common sources of residual exposure are basis risk and cross-hedging risk.

In this chapter, I set forth and illustrate the principles and techniques of risk management for asset managers while emphasizing that these methods apply in other areas of finance. It focuses on the strategic use of derivatives to manage portfolio risk, the trade-offs between risk reduction and cost, and the practical reality that hedges are often imperfect. Basis risk, cross-hedging, and dynamic, cost-aware risk control are central themes throughout the chapter.

13.1 Foundations of Hedging and Risk Control

Effective hedging is a cornerstone of modern portfolio risk management, enabling investors to reduce unwanted exposures while preserving the potential for desired returns. At its core, hedging with derivatives seeks to offset adverse price movements in a portfolio's assets by taking positions in derivatives that are expected to move inversely to those assets. However, in practice, the relationship between the hedge and the underlying exposure is rarely perfect. Market dynamics, instrument design, and the inherent complexity of financial markets mean that all hedges involve trade-offs. Understanding these trade-offs, particularly the sources and implications of residual risk, is essential for designing robust risk-control strategies.

The first step in this process is recognizing the most common sources of imperfection in hedging, basis risk and cross-hedging risk, which are explained as follows.

13.1.1 *Imperfect hedges and residual risk*

In practice, most risk management strategies result in *imperfect hedges* that leave residual risk. Two common sources of imperfection are basis risk and cross-hedging risk:

- *Basis risk* arises when the price of the derivative contract used for hedging does not move in perfect lockstep with the price of the asset or exposure being managed. Even when the derivative references the same underlying, differences in contract maturity, delivery terms, or market conditions can cause the hedge's gains or losses to differ from those of the underlying position. For instance, in futures markets, basis risk reflects changes in the difference between the futures price and the spot price, differences that can vary over time as supply-demand conditions, interest rates, or storage costs shift.

- *Cross-hedging risk* occurs when a derivative that is not a perfect match for the underlying exposure is used, such as hedging high-yield bonds with Treasury futures or hedging non-U.S. equities with S&P 500 index futures.

These risks illustrate that risk management is not about eliminating uncertainty but about making deliberate trade-offs to achieve more stable and predictable portfolio outcomes. That is, successful risk management requires balancing the desired level of risk reduction, the cost of implementing hedges, and the acceptance of some degree of tracking error or residual volatility.

13.1.2 *Strategic approach to risk management*

The foundation of risk management lies in understanding that complete hedging is rarely optimal. A strategic approach typically involves:

1. identifying key portfolio risks and quantifying their potential impact;
2. selecting appropriate derivative instruments that align with the exposure to be managed;
3. determining the hedge ratio or level of exposure adjustment to achieve the desired balance between risk reduction and residual opportunity;
4. monitoring hedge effectiveness over time, recognizing that market dynamics can alter the alignment between the portfolio and its risk controls.

By focusing on these principles, portfolio and risk managers can maintain resilient portfolios to adverse market movements while still participating in opportunities aligned with the investment mandate.

13.2 Risk Management Using Futures

Futures contracts are among the most widely used and cost-efficient instruments for implementing hedges, offering standardized terms, deep liquidity, and transparent pricing. Their versatility allows portfolio and risk managers to protect against adverse price movements in various assets, from agricultural commodities to equity indexes and interest-rate instruments. However, the effectiveness of a futures hedge depends on how closely the futures contract tracks the underlying exposure and how the relationship between cash and futures prices, known as the basis, evolves.

The discussion in this section first explains the core principles of hedging with futures, defining key concepts. Once these foundations are established, we turn to step-by-step numerical illustrations drawn from commodity markets. These examples clarify the mechanics of hedging and provide a framework that can be applied to more complex contexts, including equity and fixed-income portfolio management.

13.2.1 *Principles of hedging with futures*

The primary function of futures markets is to transfer price risk from those willing to pay to avoid it to those seeking to assume it for potential gain. In this context, hedging means employing a futures transaction as a temporary substitute for a transaction in the cash market. The hedge fixes a value for the cash position: if cash and futures prices move together, losses in one market are offset by gains in the other. When gains and losses offset exactly, the hedge is called a *perfect hedge* or a *textbook hedge*.

In practice, perfect hedges are rare. The realized profit or loss depends on the basis, the difference between the cash price and the futures price. That is,

$$\text{Basis} = \text{Cash price} - \text{Futures price}$$

As explained in Chapter 19, if a futures contract is priced according to its theoretical value, the difference between the cash price and the futures price should be equal to the cost of carry. The risk a hedger takes is that the basis will change because the futures will be mispriced relative to the cash price. This is called *basis risk*. Therefore, hedging involves substituting basis risk for price risk, that is, substituting the risk that the basis will change for the risk that the cash price will change.

Cross-hedging introduces not only the usual basis risk described earlier but also the additional risk that the futures contract's underlying instrument may not track the price movements of the asset or portfolio being hedged. A cross-hedge's effectiveness depends on the relationship between cash and futures prices and on how closely the hedged asset's value tracks the underlying of the futures contract.

Two basic hedge types apply across asset classes:

- A *short hedge* is used to protect against a decline in the future cash price of a financial instrument or portfolio. To execute a short hedge, the hedger sells a futures contract (agreeing to make delivery). Consequently, a short hedge is also known as a *sell hedge*. By establishing a short hedge, the hedger has fixed the future cash price and transferred the price risk of ownership to the buyer of the futures contract.
- A *long hedge* is undertaken to protect against an increase in the price of a financial instrument or portfolio to be purchased in the cash market at some future time. In a long hedge, the hedger buys a futures contract (agreeing to accept delivery). A long hedge is also known as a *buy hedge*.

13.2.2 *Commodity-based illustrations*

To make the mechanics of hedging with futures more concrete, we begin with examples from commodity markets. Commodities provide an intuitive setting because cash and futures prices are linked by physical supply, demand, and storage considerations, making the basis concept easier to visualize. These markets also offer straightforward real-asset examples of perfect and imperfect hedges and the influence of basis risk and cross-hedging risk. Once the principles are clear in this setting, the same logic can be applied to more complex financial instruments, such as equities and fixed-income securities, where the relationships between cash and futures prices are less direct but governed by the same underlying mechanics.

13.2.2.1 *Perfect hedge: No change in the basis*

Let's start with a perfect hedge. Suppose that a corn farmer expects to sell 30,000 bushels of corn three months from now. Assume further that the management of a food processing company plans to purchase 30,000 bushels of corn three months from now. Both the corn farmer and the management of the food processing company want to lock in a price today. Each wants to eliminate the price risk associated with corn three months from now. Suppose the corn's cash or spot price is currently $2.75 per bushel.

A corn futures contract is available with the following terms: (1) the settlement date for the contract is five months from now, and (2) 5,000 bushels of corn must be delivered. Notice that the settlement date is two months after the parties expect to lift their hedge. The futures price for this futures contract is currently $3.20 per bushel.

As the corn farmer seeks to lock in the price of corn to eliminate the risk of a price decline three months from now, the farmer will initiate a short hedge by selling futures contracts. That is, the farmer will promise to make delivery of corn at the current futures price. The farmer will sell six futures contracts because each contract calls for the delivery of 5,000 bushels of corn. Three months from now, the farmer will deliver corn at the prevailing price in the spot market and buy the corn futures contract, which will have two months to settle, to offset the short position in that contract. The price at which the farmer will buy the corn futures contract depends on the futures contract price three months from now.

The procurement manager of the food processing company seeks to lock in the cost of corn to eliminate the risk of a price increase in corn three months from now. Consequently, the procurement manager will place a buy or long hedge. That is, it will agree to accept delivery of corn at the futures price. Protection is sought against a price increase for 30,000 bushels of corn, so six contracts are bought. Three months from now, the food processing company will have to purchase corn in the spot market, paying the prevailing market price. The food processing company sells the contract at the then-prevailing futures price to offset the long corn futures position, which has two months remaining until settlement.

Let's look at what happens under various scenarios for the cash price and the futures price of corn three months from now when the hedge is lifted.

Suppose that when the hedge is lifted, the cash price declines to $2.00 and the futures contract price declines to $2.45. Note what has happened to the basis under this scenario. At the time the hedge was placed, the basis was –$0.45 ($2.75 – $3.20). When the hedge is lifted, the basis remains at –$0.45 ($2.00 – $2.45).

When the hedge was placed, the farmer wanted to lock in a price of $2.75 per bushel of corn, or $82,500 for 30,000 bushels. The farmer sold six futures contracts at a price of \$3.20 per bushel, or \$96,000 for 30,000 bushels. When the hedge is lifted, the value of the farmer's corn is \$60,000 (\$2.00 × 30,000). The farmer realizes a decline in the cash market value of his corn of \$22,500, but the futures price has declined to \$2.45, so the cost to the corn farmer to liquidate the futures position is only \$73,500 (\$2.45 × 30,000). The corn farmer realizes a gain in the futures market of \$22,500. The net result is that the gain in the futures market matches the loss in the cash market. Consequently, the corn farmer, by hedging, succeeds in ensuring a price per unit of \$2.75, precisely equal to the initial price the corn farmer intended to realize. This is an example of a perfect or textbook hedge.

Because the cash price declined, the food processing company would realize a gain of \$22,500 in the cash market but a loss of the same amount in the futures market. Therefore, this buy or long hedge is also a perfect or textbook hedge from the food processing company's perspective, ensuring a cost per unit equal to the initial price of \$2.75.

This scenario illustrates two critical points. First, for both participants, there was no overall gain or loss. This result is because we assume the basis did not change when the hedge was lifted. Thus, if the basis does not change, a perfect hedge will be achieved. Second, note that the procurement manager of the food processing company would have been better off by not hedging. The cost of corn would have been \$22,500 less in the cash market three months later. This should not be interpreted as a sign of poor planning by the procurement manager. The company is not in the business of speculating on the future price of corn. Hedging is a standard practice to ensure the price to be paid at the delivery date, thus eliminating future price uncertainty.

Suppose the cash price of corn when the hedge is lifted increases to \$3.55, and the futures price increases to \$4.00. Note that the basis remains unchanged at –\$0.45. As long as the basis remains unchanged, the cash and futures price we have assumed in this scenario will produce a perfect hedge.

The farmer will gain in the cash market because the value of 30,000 bushels of corn is \$106,500 (\$3.55 × 30,000). This represents a \$24,000 gain, compared to the cash value when the hedge was placed. However, the farmer must liquidate the position in the futures market by buying six futures contracts at a total cost of \$120,000, which is \$24,000 more than when the contracts were sold. The loss in the futures market offsets the gain in the cash market, and once again, there is a perfect hedge. The food processing company would realize a gain of

$24,000 in the futures market but would have to pay $24,000 more in the cash market to acquire 30,000 bushels of corn.

Note that the management of the food processing company under this scenario saved $24,000 in the cost of corn by employing a hedge. The farmer would have been better off not hedging and simply selling corn on the market three months later. Again, it must be emphasized that the farmer, just like the management of the food processing company, employed a hedge to protect against unforeseen adverse price changes in the cash market.

13.2.2.2 *Basis risk*

The scenarios described assume the basis does not change when the hedge is lifted. In the real world, the basis does, in fact, change between the time a hedge is placed and when it is lifted. Here is what happens when the basis changes, demonstrating what was referred to as basis risk.

Assume that the cash price of corn decreases to $2.00, as in the earlier scenario; also, assume that the futures price decreases to $2.70 rather than $2.45. The basis has widened from –$0.45 to –$0.70 ($2.00 – $2.70). For the short (sell) hedge, the loss in the cash market of $22,500 is offset only partially by a $15,000 gain realized in the futures market; consequently, the hedge results in an overall loss of $7,500.

There are two points to note here. First, if the farmer had not employed the hedge, the loss would have been $22,500 because the value of 30,000 bushels of corn is $60,000, compared to $82,500 three months earlier. Although the hedge is imperfect because the basis widened, the loss of $7,500 is less than that of $22,500 if no hedge had been placed. This is what we meant earlier when we said that hedging substitutes basis risk for price risk. Second, the procurement manager of the food processing company faces the same problem from an opposite perspective. An unexpected gain for either participant results in an unexpected loss of equal dollar value for the other. That is, the participants face a "zero-sum game." Consequently, the food processing company would realize an overall gain of $7,500 from its long (buy) hedge. This gain represents a gain of $22,500 in the cash market and a realized loss of $15,000 in the futures market.

13.2.2.3 *Cross-hedging risk*

Suppose that a zucchini farmer plans to sell 37,500 bushels of zucchini three months from now and that a food processing company plans to purchase the same amount of zucchini three months from now. Each party wants to hedge against price risk, but zucchini futures contracts are not traded. Both parties believe a close price relationship exists between zucchini and corn. Specifically, both parties believe that the cash price of zucchini will be 80% of the cash price of corn. The cash price of zucchini is currently \$2.20 per bushel, and the cash price of corn is currently \$2.75 per bushel. The futures price of corn is currently \$3.20 per bushel.

Let's examine various scenarios to see how effective the cross hedge will be. In each scenario, the difference between the cash price of corn and the futures price of corn at the time the cross hedge is placed and at the time it is lifted will be assumed to be unchanged at –\$0.45. We assume this so we may focus on the importance of the relationship between the two cash prices at the two times.

We must first determine how many corn futures contracts must be used in the cross hedge. The cash value of 37,500 bushels of zucchini at the cash price of \$2.20 per bushel is \$82,500. To protect a value of \$82,500 using corn futures with a current cash price of \$2.75, 30,000 bushels of corn (\$82,500/\$2.75) must be hedged. Each corn futures contract involves 5,000 bushels, so six corn futures contracts are used.

Suppose that the cash prices of zucchini and corn decrease to \$1.60 and \$2.00 per bushel, respectively, and the futures price of corn decreases to \$2.45 per bushel. The relationship between the cash price for zucchini and corn assumed when the cross hedge was placed holds at the time the cross hedge is lifted. That is, the cash price of zucchini is 80% of the cash price of corn. The basis for the cash price of corn and the futures price of corn is still –\$0.45 when the cross hedge is lifted.

The short cross hedge produces a gain of \$22,500 in the futures market and an exact loss in the cash market. The opposite occurs for the long cross hedge. In this case, there is neither an overall gain nor a loss from the cross hedge. That is, we have a perfect cross hedge. The same would occur if we assume that the cash price of both commodities increases by the same percentage and the basis remains unchanged.

Suppose that the cash prices of both commodities decrease, but the cash price of zucchini falls by a greater percentage than the cash price of corn. For example, suppose that the cash price of zucchini falls to \$1.30 per bushel while the cash price of corn falls to \$2.00 per bushel. The futures price of corn falls to \$2.45, so the basis is unchanged. The cash price of zucchini at the time the cross hedge is lifted is 65% of the cash price of corn, rather than 80% as assumed when the cross hedge was constructed.

For the short cross hedge, the loss in the cash market exceeds the realized loss in the futures market by $11,200. For the long cross hedge, the opposite is true. There is an overall gain of $11,200 from the cross hedge. Had the cash price of zucchini fallen by less than the decline in the cash price of corn, the short cross hedge would have produced an overall gain, while the long cross hedge would have generated an overall loss.

Although the zucchini–corn example illustrates cross-hedging risk using a fixed-price relationship between two cash commodities, financial cross-hedging typically requires a more rigorous statistical approach. In equity and fixed income applications, portfolio managers estimate the optimal hedge ratio (discussed later) using correlation and volatility measures between the asset being hedged and the available hedging instrument (e.g., equity index futures or Treasury futures). The finance illustrations will shift to this correlation-based method, which allows for more flexible and data-driven hedging strategies.

While commodity hedging provides clean, intuitive illustrations of hedge construction and risk, the same principles apply directly to financial assets. The following two sections extend these ideas to managing equity and interest rate risk using financial futures contracts.

13.3 Applications of Futures Hedging in Financial Asset Management

Futures contracts allow portfolio managers to adjust exposures quickly and efficiently without liquidating or restructuring the underlying holdings. In practice, futures are frequently used to control interest rate risk in fixed-income portfolios and market (beta) risk in equity portfolios, but the same principles apply across asset classes.

The appeal of futures for risk control lies in their liquidity, standardization, and low transaction costs. By taking offsetting positions in futures, a portfolio manager can reduce or increase exposure to market movements in a highly targeted way. For example, selling Treasury futures can reduce the duration of a bond portfolio, while buying equity index futures can temporarily increase the beta of an equity portfolio without purchasing additional stocks. These adjustments can be scaled to achieve either *full hedges* or *partial hedges* designed to reduce, but not eliminate, volatility.

In practice, effective risk management with futures requires quantifying the hedge position. The optimal hedge ratio (variance minimizing) and the number of futures contracts are commonly used formulas.

13.3.1 *Calculating the hedge ratio*

A *hedge ratio* is the proportion of a position's exposure covered or offset by a derivative hedge. In the context of futures, it quantifies how many contracts should be bought or sold to minimize the risk of adverse price movements in the underlying asset. The basic hedge ratio formula, when expressed in dollar terms, is

$$\text{Hedge ratio} = \frac{\text{Value of position to be hedged}}{\text{Value of one futures contract}}$$

This ensures that the notional value of the futures contracts matches the value of the position being hedged.

However, this naive hedge ratio does not account for imperfect correlations between the asset being hedged and the underlying asset of the futures contract. In practice, a more refined approach is needed when the asset being hedged differs from that underlying the futures contract, such as in cross-hedging, or when the hedge aims to minimize portfolio volatility rather than fully offsetting dollar exposure.

The optimal hedge ratio minimizes the variance of the hedged portfolio return. It is calculated as

$$h^* = \frac{\rho\, \sigma_S}{\sigma_F}$$

where:

- h^* = optimal hedge ratio,
- ρ = correlation between changes in the spot price and futures price,
- σ_S = standard deviation of the spot price changes,
- σ_F = standard deviation of the futures price changes.

This formula shows that the hedge ratio should be higher when the asset being hedged is more volatile or highly correlated with the futures contract. Conversely, it should be lower when correlation is weak or when the futures price is more volatile than the spot price.

The optimal hedge ratio is widely used in risk management to minimize the variance of returns rather than eliminate all exposure. It is crucial when the hedged asset is not identical to the derivative's underlying (e.g., through cross-hedging).[1]

13.3.2 *Calculating the number of contracts*

Once the hedge ratio is determined, the next step is to compute the number of futures contracts needed to implement the hedge. This translation from theoretical coverage to executable trades is critical in practice.

The general formula for determining the number of contracts is

$$N_f = \frac{V_p \times h}{F \times M}$$

where:

- N_f = number of futures contracts (rounded to the nearest whole number),
- V_o = value of the position to be hedged,
- h = hedge ratio,
- F = futures price,
- M = amount of the asset covered per futures contract.

This formula ensures that the value of the futures' position aligns proportionally with the intended amount of hedged exposure. If the hedge ratio is set to 1, the formula scales the futures position to match the portfolio's notional value. If an optimal hedge ratio is used, the hedge will typically be partial, reflecting an attempt to minimize variance rather than eliminate all directional exposure.

---

[1]Other methods for determining hedge ratios include regression-based approaches (using historical data to estimate the asset's beta relative to the futures contract), utility-based approaches (which incorporate risk aversion), and minimum variance hedge ratio techniques using generalized least squares estimators. These methods are particularly useful when the underlying price relationships are unstable. For a further discussion, see Frank J. Fabozzi and Francesco A. Fabozzi, "A Primer on Hedging with Stock Index Futures," *Journal of Derivatives*, 29(4), 39–60.

13.3.3 *Applications in equity portfolios*

Equity index futures are powerful tools for managing market (beta) risk in equity portfolios. A portfolio manager can reduce portfolio volatility by selling index futures, lowering exposure to market movements without selling the underlying stocks. Conversely, buying index futures increases beta when the goal is to participate more fully in market gains.

Risk management with equity index futures often involves *partial hedges* rather than full elimination of market exposure. Reducing beta toward zero, but not to zero, allows the portfolio manager to moderate risk while preserving stock selection potential.

13.3.3.1 *Calculating the number of futures contracts*

The number of equity index futures contracts needed for a hedge is determined by

$$N_f = \frac{V_P\left(\beta_t - \beta_p\right)}{F \times M}$$

where:

- V_p = value of the equity portfolio,
- β_p = current portfolio beta,
- β_t = target beta after hedging,
- F = futures price of the equity index,
- M = contract multiplier (e.g., \$250 for S&P 500 futures).

This formula allows the portfolio manager to calibrate the hedge to reduce market risk to the desired level while leaving residual exposure for alpha generation. Note that when the number of contracts is negative, it indicates the number of contracts to be sold. Conversely, when the number of contracts is positive, that indicates the number of contracts to buy.

13.3.3.2 *Portfolio beta reduction illustration*

Suppose a portfolio with a market value of \$200 million has a beta of 1.15, and the portfolio manager wants to reduce the beta to 0.95 using the S&P 500 futures contract. Suppose also that the S&P 500 futures contract is trading at 4,800. The multiple for the contract is 250. In this illustration, we have the following:

- V_p = 200,000,000 (portfolio value),
- β_p = 1.15 (current beta),
- β_t = 0.95 (target beta),
- F = 4,800 (futures price),
- M = 250 (contract multiplier).

Therefore, the number of futures contracts needed to reduce the portfolio beta from 1.15 to 0.95 is

$$N_f = \frac{200{,}000{,}000(0.95-1.15)}{4{,}800\times 250} \approx -33\,\text{contracts}$$

Since the sign is negative, it indicates the number of contracts to be sold. If, instead, the portfolio manager wanted to increase the beta from 1.15 to 1.35, the sign would be positive, indicating the number of contracts to be purchased. As seen, contracts must be sold to decrease the portfolio beta; futures contracts must be purchased to increase the portfolio beta.

When a portfolio manager adjusts portfolio beta with equity index futures, the hedge affects portfolio returns in both rising and falling markets. The futures' position generates offsetting gains or losses that moderate the portfolio's exposure to market movements. Using our beta-reduction illustration, let's walk through how to calculate the gain or loss on an S&P 500 futures hedge when the market moves +5% or –5%.

The portfolio return is

$$R_p = \beta_p \times R_m$$

where R_m is the market return.

First, consider the portfolio return without a position in the futures market. It is simply the portfolio return. Therefore,

- Market up +5% → 1.15 × 5% = 5.75%
- Market down –5% → 1.15 × (–5%) = –5.75%

When futures are sold, we can calculate the change in the futures price as follows, assuming that the futures price moves approximately with the market:

$$\Delta F = F \times R_m$$

Apply this formula,

- Market +5% → $\Delta F = 4{,}800 \times 0.05 = 240$
- Market −5% → $\Delta F = 4{,}800 \times (-0.05) = -240$

The dollar gain or loss on the short futures position is

$$\text{Futures gain or loss} = N_f \times M \times \Delta F$$

- Market +5% (short futures → loss)

$$\text{Futures loss} = 33 \times 250 \times (-240) = -1{,}980{,}000$$

As a percentage of portfolio,

$$\frac{-1{,}980{,}000}{200{,}000{,}000} \approx -0.99\% \approx -1.0\%$$

- Market −5% (short futures → gain)

$$\text{Futures gain} = 33 \times 250 \times 240 = +1{,}980{,}000$$

As a percentage of portfolio, it is approximately +1.0%.

Combining the portfolio and futures results,

- Market +5% → 5.75% − 1.0% = 4.75%
- Market −5% → −5.75% + 1.0% = −4.75%

Recall that the target beta was 0.95, which means that if the market moves up or down by 5%, the portfolio gain or loss will be 0.95 × 5%, or 4.75%, which was accomplished by shorting the futures contract.

13.3.4 *Applications for fixed-income portfolios*

Fixed-income portfolio managers frequently use Treasury futures to manage interest rate risk, particularly duration exposure. Dollar duration measures the price change in dollar terms for a 100-basis-point change in yield. Selling Treasury futures reduces the portfolio's effective duration, mitigating losses if interest rates rise. Conversely, buying futures increases duration, allowing the portfolio to benefit if interest rates fall.

13.3.4.1 *Calculating the number of futures contracts*

When using Treasury futures for duration management, the number of contracts required depends on the portfolio's dollar duration and the dollar duration of the futures contract:

$$N_f = \frac{\text{Target dollar duration} - \text{Dollar duration of portfolio}}{\text{Dollar duration per futures contract}}$$

where:

- Dollar duration of portfolio = Portfolio duration × Portfolio value
- Dollar duration per futures contract = Duration of the CTD bond × Futures price of the CTD

CTD is the cheapest-to-deliver bond, an important nuance in the mechanics of Treasury futures contracts. As explained in Chapter 6, a Treasury futures contract does not specify the exact bond that must be delivered at settlement; instead, it allows the short position to deliver any eligible bond from a predefined basket.

Illustration: Reducing Duration in a Bond Portfolio: Suppose a bond portfolio has the following characteristics:

- portfolio value = \$50,000,000,
- portfolio duration = 6.0,
- target portfolio duration = 4.0,
- Treasury CTD futures price = 112.5,
- duration of the CTD bond = 7.5.

The dollar value of the futures position is the product of the Treasury CTD futures price, adjusted for the conversion factor, and \$100,000. In our illustration,

$$112.5 \times \$100{,}000 \times 1 = \$11{,}250{,}000$$

The portfolio's dollar duration is computed as follows:

$$\text{Dollar duration of portfolio} = 0.06 \times \$50{,}000{,}000 = \$3{,}000{,}000$$

Since duration is the approximate change in the portfolio value per 100 basis points, the portfolio duration is shown as 0.06.

The target dollar duration is calculated by multiplying the portfolio value by the target duration. In our illustration, it is

$$\text{Target dollar duration} = 0.04 \times \$50{,}000{,}000 = \$2{,}000{,}000$$

The dollar duration of one futures contract is computed as follows:

$$\text{Duration of the CTD} \times \text{Dollar value of the futures position}$$

In our illustration, it is

$$0.075 \times 112{,}500 = \$8{,}437.50$$

Therefore, the number of futures contracts is

$$N_f = \frac{\$2{,}000{,}000 - \$3{,}000{,}000}{\$8{,}437.50} \approx -119$$

Note that 119 contracts should be sold since this will reduce portfolio duration.

When a fixed-income portfolio manager adjusts portfolio duration using Treasury futures, the hedge moderates how the portfolio responds to interest-rate movements. A short futures position generates gains if interest rates rise (bond prices fall) and losses if interest rates decline, reducing the portfolio's net interest-rate sensitivity.

Using the duration-reduction illustration, let's walk through how to calculate the portfolio outcomes with derivatives for interest-rate changes of ±100 basis points (1%).

From earlier calculations,

- dollar duration of portfolio: $3,000,000,
- target dollar duration: $2,000,000,
- dollar duration per futures contract: $8,437.50,
- number of contracts: 119 (short).

The dollar change in portfolio value is approximately

$$-\left(\frac{Duration}{100}\right) \times \text{Portfolio value} \times \text{Change in interest rates}$$

Interest rates up +100 bps (1%):

$$-\left(\frac{6}{100}\right) \times \$50{,}000{,}000 \times 0.01 = -\$3{,}000{,}000$$

Interest rates down −100 bps (1%):

$$-\left(\frac{6}{100}\right) \times \$50{,}000{,}000 \times (-0.01) = \$3{,}000{,}000$$

Treasury futures prices fall when yields rise and rise when yields fall.

The gain or loss for the Treasury futures contract is

Futures gain or loss = No. of futures contracts × Change in Treasury futures price:

- *Rates +1% (short → gain)*: Futures gain = 119 × \$8,437.5 ≈ +\$1,004,062
- *Rates −1% (short → loss)*: Futures loss = 119 × (−\$8,437.5) ≈ −\$1,004,062

Combining the portfolio and futures positions,

- *Rates +1%*: −\$3,000,000 + \$1,004,062 ≈ −\$1,995,938

As a percentage of the portfolio, the change is −4.0%, which is the interest rate risk exposure sought by the portfolio manager for a 100-basis-point increase in interest rates:

- *Rates −1%*: \$3,000,000 + \$1,004,062 ≈ \$1,995,938

As a percentage of the portfolio, the change is 4.0%, which is the interest rate risk exposure sought by the portfolio manager for a 100-basis-point incline in interest rates.

The duration-reduction strategy reduces the portfolio's sensitivity to interest-rate moves, achieving the target duration of 4.0.

13.3.5 *Strategic considerations*

Risk management using futures is most effective when guided by a systematic framework that integrates the following:

- *Exposure measurement*: quantifying duration, beta, or other key sensitivities in the portfolio.
- *Hedge calibration*: determining the number and size of futures contracts needed to reduce risk.

- *Monitoring and adjustment*: continuously assessing hedge effectiveness as market conditions evolve, with particular attention to basis movements and correlations.

Futures provide a flexible and cost-efficient foundation for risk control. Still, their effectiveness depends on understanding the potential for residual risk from imperfect alignment between the portfolio and the derivative instrument. Therefore, recognizing and managing basis and cross-hedging risks are central to successful futures-based risk management.

13.4 Risk Management with Options

Options are highly versatile instruments for risk management because they provide asymmetric exposure, allowing portfolio managers to limit downside risk while retaining some or all of the upside potential. In contrast to futures, which create linear changes in exposure, options can be structured to protect against adverse market movements without fully offsetting gains in favorable conditions. This characteristic makes options particularly valuable for risk control rather than simple hedging.

Options are widely used in asset management to shape the risk profile of both equity and fixed-income portfolios. Typical applications include protective puts and covered calls for managing market or interest rate risk. These strategies allow for targeted risk reduction, often through partial protection that balances cost with the desired level of downside mitigation.

13.4.1 *Protective puts and portfolio insurance*

A *protective put* is a classic risk-management tool that provides portfolio insurance. By purchasing a put option on an index or a key asset, a portfolio manager secures the right to sell it at a predetermined strike price. This limits losses if the market declines, leaving potential intact if the market rises.

Mathematically, the payoff from a put option is

$$\text{Put payoff} = \max\,(K - S_T, 0)$$

where K is the strike price and S_T is the underlying price at option expiration. The premium's cost reduces the net portfolio value but insulates it against deeper losses.

For example, an equity portfolio benchmarked to the S&P 500 can be partially protected by purchasing out-of-the-money index put options. This reduces exposure to large market drawdowns without forcing the sale of underlying holdings. In fixed-income portfolios, protective puts on Treasury futures can serve a similar purpose, insulating the portfolio from rising yields.

Option premiums represent an ongoing expense, and frequent use can materially impact performance. To manage this, many asset managers implement partial hedges or select strikes and maturities that balance protection and cost.

13.4.1.1 *Illustration: Protective put for an equity portfolio*

Assumptions:

- portfolio value: \$50 million,
- S&P 500 level: 4,800,
- put strike: 4,600 (slightly out of the money),
- put premium: 2% of notional,
- contract multiplier: 250.

Each S&P 500 option contract covers 4,800 × 250 = \$1,200,000.

$$N_f \approx \frac{\$50,000,000}{1,200,000} \approx 42 \text{ contracts}$$

The portfolio manager buys 42 puts to fully protect the portfolio.

Table 13.1 shows the outcome of this strategy for several assumed changes in the S&P 500. The protective put caps the portfolio's maximum loss near the premium cost, illustrating asymmetric risk control rather than linear hedging.

13.4.2 *Covered calls and risk reduction*

Another widely used portfolio overlay is the covered call strategy, in which a portfolio manager sells call options against existing long positions. By receiving option premiums upfront, the portfolio manager can offset small declines in portfolio value, modestly reducing net risk

Table 13.1. Outcomes of the Protective Put Strategies

S&P 500 Change	Unhedged Portfolio	Option Gain (Net of 2% Cost)	Hedged Portfolio
+5%	+5%	−2%	+3%
0%	0%	−2%	−2%
−5%	−5%	+3%	−2%
−10%	−10%	+8%	−2%

exposure. This income stream can smooth short-term returns, particularly in range-bound markets, and is often attractive for income-oriented mandates.

However, it is important to recognize that a covered call is not a true hedging strategy in the strict sense. While it can partially cushion minor price declines, it offers very limited downside protection in the event of a substantial market drop; the premium received will not offset significant losses in the underlying asset. The trade-off is that upside potential is also capped: If markets rise sharply, gains beyond the strike price of the sold calls are forfeited.

For this reason, covered calls are typically implemented in low-volatility environments or when the portfolio manager has a neutral-to-slightly bullish outlook, with the primary goal of enhancing yield rather than providing comprehensive risk protection. In some cases, combining protective puts with covered calls, forming a collar, creates a more balanced structure. A collar limits downside exposure through the put while financing part or all of its cost with call premiums, though it still constrains upside participation.

13.4.3 *Strategic considerations*

Options are best suited for risk-management objectives that require targeted or asymmetric protection. Effective implementation requires the following:

- *Cost management*: balancing option premiums against the level of protection desired.
- *Hedge ratio selection*: determining whether full or partial coverage best aligns with risk tolerance.

- *Timing and market conditions*: recognizing volatility, liquidity, and strike selection affects hedge effectiveness.

By incorporating options into the risk-management toolkit, portfolio managers can reshape the distribution of portfolio returns, mitigating downside risk while retaining upside participation. This approach aligns with the broader principle of risk control: managing exposures deliberately, cost-effectively, and in a manner consistent with portfolio objectives.

13.5 Risk Management with Swaps

Swaps are powerful tools for risk management because they allow portfolio managers to adjust interest-rate or credit exposure without selling underlying assets. In asset management, the most common swaps include interest rate swaps, credit default swaps (CDSs), and total return swaps (TRSs). These instruments are central to modern risk control because they offer flexibility, capital efficiency, and the ability to implement dynamic hedges.

Swaps enable portfolio managers to reshape the risk profile of a portfolio, aligning it with benchmark objectives or risk tolerance, often more efficiently than trading the cash market. For example:

- Interest rate swaps adjust portfolio duration without selling bonds.
- CDSs allow credit risk transfer without liquidating portfolios.
- TRSs allow exposure to be synthetically increased or decreased in equity or credit portfolios.

These instruments support tactical hedging and strategic risk-management programs and apply to fixed-income, multi-asset, and alternative strategies.

13.5.1 *Interest rate swaps for duration management*

A plain-vanilla interest-rate swap exchanges fixed and floating interest payments. From a duration-management perspective, the position taken in the swap determines whether portfolio interest-rate sensitivity is increased or reduced:

- *Pay fixed/receive floating* → reduces portfolio duration because the swap's value rises when rates increase and falls when rates decrease, offsetting part of the bond portfolio's price sensitivity. This position protects against rising interest rates.
- *Receive fixed/pay floating* → increases portfolio duration because the swap's value rises when rates fall, reinforcing the bond portfolio's gains in a declining-rate environment.

This duration effect can also be understood by viewing each swap position as equivalent to a combination of cash market instruments:

- A fixed-rate payer has the same interest-rate exposure as holding a floating-rate bond financed by issuing (shorting) a fixed-rate bond. A short fixed-rate bond position benefits from rising rates and loses when rates fall, which lowers the portfolio's overall duration.
- A fixed-rate receiver is equivalent to holding a fixed-rate bond financed by issuing a floating-rate bond. A long fixed-rate bond position gains value when rates fall, which increases the portfolio's duration.

Thinking in these terms links swaps directly to familiar bond exposures and makes it easier to anticipate a swap's effect on a portfolio's interest-rate sensitivity.

The desired change in dollar duration determines the size of the swap. Remember that dollar duration measures the price change in dollar terms for a 100-basis-point change in yield. The notional amount of the swap needed to achieve a target dollar duration is calculated as[2]

$$\text{Notional amount required} = \frac{\text{Target dollar duration} - \text{Current portfolio dollar duration}}{\text{Dollar duration per \$1 million of swap notional}}$$

[2] See Chapter 31 In Frank J., Fabozzi and Francesco A. Fabozzi, *Bond Markets, Analysis, and Strategies*. 10th ed., MIT Press, 2021.

13.5.1.1 *Illustration: Reducing duration with a pay-fixed swap*

A bond portfolio has the following:

- market value: $100 million,
- duration: 6.0,
- target duration: 4.0,
- dollar duration of swap per $1 million notional: 5.5.

Portfolio's current dollar duration is (6.0/100) × $100,000,000 = $6,000,000.

Target dollar duration is (4.0/100) × $100,000,000 = $4,000,000.

Dollar duration of swap per $1 million notional = (5.5/100) × $1,000,000 = $55,000.

The required swap notional amount is

$$\text{Notional amount required} = \frac{\$4,000,000 - \$6,000,000}{\$55,000} \approx -\$36.36 \text{ million}$$

The negative sign indicates entering a pay-fixed, receive-floating swap with a notional amount of $36 million. This reduces the portfolio's dollar duration from $6.0 million to $4.0 million, aligning interest-rate sensitivity with the target.

We can verify that this has reduced the current duration of 6 to the target duration of 4. For a notional of $36.36 million with a duration of 5.5, the dollar duration is

$$(5.5/100) \times \$36,360,000 = \$1,999,800$$

Since the swap position is paying fixed, this means that $1,999,800, or about $2 million, is the amount by which the dollar duration is reduced. Recall that the goal was to reduce the dollar duration by $2 million, resulting in a $4 million dollar duration relative to a market value of $100 million, thus yielding a duration of 4, representing the targeted duration.

13.5.1.2 *Increasing duration with a receive-fixed swap*

- Portfolio market value = $150 million.
- Portfolio modified duration = 5.0.

- Target modified duration = 6.5.
- Dollar duration of swap per $1 million notional: 4.8.

Portfolio's current dollar duration is (5.0/100) × $150,000,000 = $7,500,000.

Target dollar duration is (6.5/100) × $150,000,000 = $9,750,000.

Dollar duration of swap per $1 million notional: (4.8/100) × $1,000,000 = $48,000.

The required swap notional amount is

$$\text{Notional amount required} = \frac{\$9,750,000 - \$7,500,000}{\$48,000} \approx -\$46.88 \text{ million}$$

The positive sign indicates entering a receive-fixed, pay-floating swap with a notional amount of approximately $46.88 million. This increases the portfolio's dollar duration from $7.5 million to $9.75 million, positioning it to benefit more from a potential decline in interest rates.

Once again, we can verify that this has increased the current duration of 5 to the target duration of 6.5. For a notional of $46.88 million with a duration 4.8, the dollar duration is

$$(4.8/100) \times \$46,880,000 = \$2,250,240$$

Since the swap position is paying fixed, this means the dollar duration has increased by $2,250,240, or about $2,250,000. Recall that the goal was to increase the dollar duration by $2,250,000 million, which gives a $9,750,000 dollar duration relative to a market value of $150 million. Hence, the duration is 6.5, the targeted duration.

13.5.2 *Credit risk management using CDS*

CDSs allow managers to transfer credit risk without selling the underlying bonds.

- Buying protection reduces portfolio credit exposure.
- Selling protection increases exposure (and collects a premium).

For example, an investment-grade corporate bond portfolio can buy protection on a CDS index such as CDX IG to reduce spread volatility.

While this mitigates credit losses, cross-hedging risk remains because the portfolio may not perfectly match the reference index.

13.5.3 *Strategic considerations*

When integrating swaps and swaptions into a risk-management framework, portfolio managers must consider the following:

- *Exposure measurement*: Quantify interest-rate or credit sensitivities accurately.
- *Cost and collateral*: Swaps require margin or collateral posting and generate liquidity demands during market moves.
- *Basis and cross-hedging risk*: Swaps may not perfectly align with the cash portfolio's exposures.
- *Dynamic adjustment*: Reassess swap positions as market conditions and portfolio allocations evolve.

Swaps offer flexible, efficient, and dynamic risk control. They allow portfolios to be resilient to interest-rate or credit shocks without the disruption and transaction costs associated with restructuring cash holdings.

13.6 Cross-Hedging in Practice

Earlier in this chapter, I noted that cross-hedging is one of the two primary sources of residual risk in hedging, the other being basis risk. Cross-hedging occurs when the chosen derivative or hedging instrument is not an exact match for the underlying exposure but is used because a perfect match is unavailable. The discussion in this section begins with how to calculate the hedge ratio when cross-hedging. This includes both the simple dollar-for-dollar approach and the variance-minimizing hedge ratio, which incorporates the correlation between the returns on the underlying exposure and the hedge instrument and their relative volatilities.

Correlation is central to scaling the hedge appropriately, and its potential to change over time underscores the need for ongoing monitoring. The discussion in this section then turns to cross-hedging risk—the residual risk that remains when the hedge instrument and the underlying exposure move imperfectly together. Even with a well-calculated hedge ratio, correlations below one mean that gains and losses will not fully offset, and shifts in correlation can further reduce hedge effectiveness. This part of the discussion also considers measures of hedge performance, such as hedge effectiveness ratios. Finally, I present several illustrations that apply these concepts to real-world situations. These illustrations will cover asset classes and market contexts, demonstrating both cross-hedging strategies' versatility and limitations.

13.6.1 *Calculating the hedge ratio with cross-hedging and the role of correlation*

When the hedge instrument is not identical to the underlying exposure, calculating the appropriate hedge ratio requires adjusting for differences in price sensitivity and the degree to which the two instruments move together. A simple dollar-for-dollar or duration-matching approach, which assumes perfect correlation, can result in over- or under-hedging when the correlation between the two instruments is less than one.

The variance-minimizing hedge ratio adjusts for this by incorporating the correlation between changes in the value of the hedged asset and the hedge instrument, as well as their relative volatilities. In its general form, the hedge ratio h^* is given by

$$h^* = \frac{\rho \sigma_P}{\sigma_f}$$

where:

- ρ = correlation between portfolio and futures return (or price change),
- σ_P = standard deviation of the portfolio return (or price change),
- σ_f = standard deviation of the futures return (or price change).

This formula scales the hedge position by the degree of co-movement between the two instruments, with a correlation of one producing the same result as the simple ratio of volatilities described earlier in this chapter. Lower correlations proportionally reduce the hedge size, reflecting that the hedge instrument's price movements will not fully match those of the underlying exposure.

In interest rate applications such as cross-hedging a corporate bond portfolio with Treasury futures, the volatility terms can be expressed in dollar duration or price value of basis point (PVBP). The PVBP, also called the "dollar value of a 01" (DV01), measures the change in the dollar value of a security or portfolio for a one-basis-point (0.01%) change in yield. The hedge ratio then becomes

$$h^* = \rho \frac{\text{Dollar duration of bond or bond portfolio}}{\text{Dollar duration of the interest rate futures contract}}$$

Or, equivalently,

$$h^* = \rho \frac{\text{PVBP of portfolio}}{\text{PVBP of futures contract}}$$

This modification of the hedge ratio ensures that it accounts for differences in interest rate sensitivity and the imperfect correlation between the instruments. For example, suppose the dollar duration of a corporate bond portfolio is $1,200,000. In that case, the dollar duration of a Treasury futures contract is $85,000, and the correlation between their returns is 0.85, and the optimal hedge ratio would be

$$h^* = 0.85 \frac{\$1,200,000}{\$85,000} \approx 12$$

This means that 12 futures contracts would be used. Note that if it were naively assumed that the correlation is 1, then the number of futures contracts would be 14. By incorporating correlation, the variance-minimizing hedge ratio provides a more precise and risk-aware approach to cross-hedging, though it still requires active monitoring as market relationships evolve.

Note that the standard deviations and correlation are typically estimated from historical market data. The process begins by collecting price or return series for both the hedged asset and the hedge instrument over a relevant time horizon, typically daily or weekly observations for six months to two years, depending on data availability and the stability of the relationship. Returns are calculated as percentage changes in price (or value), from which the standard deviation for each series is computed. The correlation is then calculated as the Pearson correlation coefficient between the two return series. For interest rate applications, price changes may be expressed in terms of changes in yield, PVBP, or dollar duration to reflect interest rate sensitivity directly. The choice of historical period should balance the need for sufficient observations with the risk that older data may not represent current market dynamics.

13.6.2 *Cross-hedging risk*

As explained earlier, cross-hedging risk arises from imperfect correlation between the cash asset and the derivative used for risk management. Even when the hedge ratio is optimally calculated, less-than-perfect correlation means that some residual volatility remains in the hedged position.

The variance of the hedged portfolio incorporates the individual volatilities of the portfolio and the hedge instrument, the hedge ratio, and their correlation:

$$\sigma_H^2 = \sigma_p^2 + h^2\sigma_f^2 - 2h\rho\sigma_p\sigma_f$$

where:

- σ_H^2 = variance of the hedged portfolio,
- σ_p^2 = portfolio volatility,
- σ_f^2 = futures volatility,
- h = hedge ratio,
- ρ = correlation between portfolio and futures.

If $\rho = 1$, a perfect hedge is possible. When $\rho < 1$, residual volatility remains.

13.6.3 *Cross-hedging illustrations*

The following examples apply the concepts of hedge ratio calculation and cross-hedging risk to real-world situations. Each case shows how to select and size a hedge when the available instrument is correlated but not identical to the exposure, and how correlation affects hedge effectiveness.

13.6.3.1 *Cross-hedging an international equity portfolio with S&P 500 futures*

The first illustration examines cross-hedging an international equity portfolio using S&P 500 futures.

Consider a $100 million international equity portfolio composed primarily of European and Asian stocks. The portfolio manager wants to reduce market risk during a period of global uncertainty but only has access to liquid S&P 500 index futures for hedging. Historical data for the portfolio and the S&P 500 show:

- portfolio standard deviation $\sigma_p = 12\%$,
- S&P 500 futures standard deviation $\sigma_f = 15\%$,
- correlation $\rho = 0.65$.

Using the minimum-variance hedge ratio formula,

$$h^* = \frac{\rho\sigma_P}{\sigma_f} = \frac{0.65 \times 0.12}{0.15} \approx 0.52$$

This means the portfolio manager should hedge approximately 52% of the portfolio's notional value using S&P 500 futures.

The variance of the hedged portfolio is

$$\sigma_H^2 = 0.12^2 + 0.52^2 \times 0.15^2 - 2 \times 0.52 \times 0.65 \times 0.12 \times 0.15 \approx 0.0083$$

Therefore, $\sigma_H \approx \sqrt{0.0083} = 9.1\%$.

The strategy reduces volatility from 12% to approximately 9.1%, but residual risk remains due to the 0.65 correlation.

13.6.3.2 *Cross-hedging a corporate bond portfolio with U.S. Treasury futures*

Consider a $250 million investment-grade corporate bond portfolio with a duration of 7.2. The portfolio manager expects interest rates to rise but cannot access a liquid futures contract on corporate bonds. Instead, the portfolio manager uses U.S. Treasury bond futures as the hedging instrument. Historical data show:

- portfolio PVBP (dollar duration) = (7.2/100) × 250,000,000 = $18,000,000,
- PVBP of one Treasury futures contract = $85,000,
- correlation between daily portfolio value changes and Treasury futures price changes, $\rho = 0.88$.

First, compute the variance-minimizing hedge ratio in PVBP terms:

$$h^* = 0.88 \times \frac{\$18,000,000}{\$85,000} \approx 186 \text{ contracts}$$

This means the portfolio manager should short 186 Treasury futures contracts to reduce the portfolio's interest rate sensitivity.

If the correlation were 1, a simple PVBP match would require

$$h^* = \frac{\$18,000,000}{\$85,000} \approx 211 \text{ contracts}$$

The difference reflects the imperfect correlation and the adjustment to minimize residual variance. Even after implementing the hedge, cross-hedging risk remains because Treasury futures do not perfectly track corporate bond price changes—yield spreads between corporates and Treasuries can move independently of general interest rate shifts.

13.6.4 *Managing basis and cross-hedging risk*

Effective management of these risks involves:

- measuring historical correlations and basis behavior to estimate hedge effectiveness;
- using optimal hedge ratios to minimize variance rather than assuming a 1:1 hedge;
- monitoring for divergence during stress, as correlations often weaken in volatile markets;
- incorporating residual risk into the portfolio's overall risk budget and performance expectations.

By understanding and quantifying basis and cross-hedging risk, managers can set realistic expectations for hedge performance and make deliberate trade-offs between risk reduction and cost.

13.7 Practical Considerations in Risk Management

In practice, managing risk with derivatives extends beyond simply understanding their theoretical properties. It requires addressing real-world constraints and imperfections that can erode hedge effectiveness. Portfolio managers must weigh the trade-offs between reducing risk, controlling costs, maintaining liquidity, and managing residual exposures such as basis and cross-hedging risk.

13.7.1 *Measuring hedge effectiveness*

A hedge is effective only if it meaningfully reduces portfolio volatility or downside risk without introducing new unintended exposures. Hedge effectiveness is often evaluated in three ways:

- *Variance reduction*: measures the percentage decline in portfolio return variance after implementing the risk management strategy.
- *Tracking error*: for benchmarked portfolios, evaluates how well the hedge minimizes deviations from the benchmark after implementation.
- *Scenario or stress testing*: simulates outcomes under large market shocks to verify hedge performance in extreme conditions.

Partial hedges are common because they allow a portfolio to retain some upside potential while mitigating risk. For example, an equity manager might reduce beta from 1.2 to 0.9 rather than going market-neutral, or a fixed income manager might shorten duration without fully immunizing the portfolio. These approaches balance risk reduction with participation in favorable market moves, making them a flexible risk management tool.

Table 13.2 illustrates the potential outcomes of hedged and unhedged portfolios under different scenarios. The first two rows show how the hedge dampens the impact of U.S. market movements. However, the third row highlights a key basis or cross-hedging risk source. When foreign equity markets decline due to regional factors or currency devaluation, not U.S. market movements, the hedge provides no offsetting gain. This illustrates that cross-hedges mitigate but do not eliminate risk when underlying exposures differ.

13.7.2 *Partial hedges and dynamic adjustment*

Partial hedges are common because they allow the portfolio to retain some upside potential while mitigating risk. A fixed-income manager might shorten the duration partially rather than fully immunize the portfolio,

Table 13.2. Hedge Outcomes under Market and Basis Risk

Market Move	Portfolio Return	Futures P/L	Net Hedged Return
S&P 500 +5%	+6.0%	−2.6%	+3.4%
S&P 500 −5%	−6.0%	+2.6%	−3.4%
S&P 500 0%	−2.0%	0%	−2.0%

while an equity manager might reduce beta from 1.2 to 0.9 instead of going market-neutral.

Risk management is inherently dynamic. Market conditions, correlations, and portfolio exposures evolve, so hedge ratios require periodic recalibration. Dynamic adjustment ensures that hedges remain aligned with risk objectives and do not become stale or ineffective.

13.7.3 *Transaction costs, liquidity, and collateral*

The practical implementation requires careful consideration of transaction costs and liquidity. Futures and standardized options are generally liquid and inexpensive to trade, while swaps and swaptions may require collateral posting under Credit Support Annexes (CSAs).

Collateral and margin management are particularly critical for futures and swaps because adverse market moves can trigger variation margin calls, impacting portfolio liquidity. Even a theoretically perfect hedge can fail if operational errors occur or if a counterparty defaults.

13.7.4 *Comparative characteristics of selected derivative strategies*

The choice among derivative-based risk management tools depends on the trade-off between protection, cost, and opportunity foregone. Table 13.3 summarizes the key characteristics of five widely used approaches—futures hedges, swaps, protective puts, covered calls, and collars—highlighting differences in downside protection, upside potential, cost structure, and practical considerations.

This comparison illustrates that while strategies such as futures hedges and protective puts can provide substantial or complete downside protection, they do so at the cost of either foregone upside (in the case of futures) or explicit option premiums (in the case of puts). In contrast, as

Table 13.3. Comparative Characteristics of Common Derivative Risk Management Strategies

Strategy	Downside Protection	Upside Potential	Cost Profile	Typical Use Case
Futures Hedge	High (near-complete if perfectly matched)	None; gains in underlying fully offset	Low transaction cost; margin requirements	Beta reduction, duration hedging
Swaps	Moderate to high (depending on structure)	Preserved, unless swap terms offset gains	Low to moderate transaction cost; potential collateral posting	Interest rate, currency, or total return risk transfer
Protective Put	High (floor set by strike)	Full upside above strike	High; option premium required	Portfolio insurance, tail-risk protection
Covered Call	Low (offsets small declines only)	Capped above strike	Negative net cost (premium income)	Yield enhancement in flat/low-volatility markets
Collar	Moderate (put strike sets floor)	Capped above call strike	Low/zero net cost if premiums offset	Cost-effective risk banding

Notes: Swap effectiveness can vary widely based on the underlying exposure, the specific terms negotiated, and the credit quality of the counterparty. Unlike standardized futures or options, swaps are bespoke contracts, so their risk-mitigation profile depends heavily on the precision of the match between the swap terms and the portfolio's exposures.

discussed earlier in this chapter, covered calls and collars generally provide only partial downside mitigation, with call premiums offering some income offset. Swaps occupy a middle ground, allowing for targeted risk transfers such as converting floating-rate debt to fixed or altering duration without necessarily changing the underlying asset holdings.

The table underscores that there is no universally "best" strategy. The optimal choice depends on the portfolio's objectives, the investor's risk tolerance, and prevailing market conditions. Futures and swaps are generally favored for precise exposure adjustments, while option-based strategies such as puts, calls, and collars allow tailoring of risk/return trade-offs, albeit with more complex cost-benefit profiles.

13.7.5 *Integrating risk management into the portfolio process*

Successful risk management is a continuous process that includes:

- measuring and monitoring exposures in real time;
- evaluating hedge effectiveness using variance, tracking error, and stress tests;
- balancing costs and benefits of hedges relative to return objectives;
- dynamically adjusting hedges as market and portfolio conditions evolve.

When executed with discipline, risk management using derivatives improves the stability and predictability of portfolio outcomes. It supports the achievement of long-term investment goals without unnecessary exposure to adverse market movements.

13.8 Summary

Modern risk management in asset management is about strategically controlling exposures rather than eliminating all risk. Throughout this chapter, I provide several guiding principles that emerge for effective risk control with derivatives.

First, risk management differs from simple hedging. Hedging focuses on neutralizing a single exposure, while risk management involves monitoring and adjusting the entire risk profile of a portfolio in alignment with investment objectives. In practice, this often requires partial hedges and dynamic exposure management, enabling the portfolio to reduce downside risk while maintaining some upside potential.

Second, residual risk is inevitable, and effective management depends on understanding its sources. Basis risk occurs when the cash asset and derivative used for risk control do not align perfectly, and cross-hedging risk arises when no perfectly matching derivative exists, and a correlated instrument must be used instead. Acknowledging and incorporating these risks into the portfolio's risk budget allows for deliberate and informed trade-offs rather than unexpected outcomes.

Third, derivatives provide flexibility, efficiency, and precision for managing risk in both fixed-income and equity portfolios. Futures allow for rapid and cost-effective duration and beta adjustments. Options offer asymmetric protection, enabling portfolio managers to reduce downside exposure without fully surrendering upside opportunities. Swaps and swaptions allow for dynamic and capital-efficient risk control, including duration adjustments and credit risk management, without requiring major changes to the underlying portfolio.

Finally, best practices in risk management emphasize process and discipline. Effective risk control requires measurement and monitoring, cost-aware implementation, dynamic adjustment, and integration into the investment process. When executed thoughtfully, risk management using derivatives enhances the stability and predictability of portfolio outcomes while allowing investors to achieve long-term goals without unnecessary exposure to adverse market movements. As explained in Part 4 of this book, these same principles extend beyond asset management to corporate risk management, commercial banking, and investment banking, where managing interest-rate, credit, and market risks is equally essential.

Chapter 14

Derivatives in Asset Allocation and Multi-Asset Portfolios

Asset allocation decisions are the cornerstone of portfolio management, governing long-term investment outcomes, short-term performance, and risk exposures. Traditionally, these decisions were executed through cash instruments—directly buying or selling stocks, bonds, currencies, or real assets. However, derivatives have become indispensable tools in strategic and tactical asset allocation. From futures and options to swaps and forwards, derivatives provide the flexibility, cost efficiency, and precision necessary to manage multi-asset portfolios in a dynamic, global investment environment.

The integration of derivatives into asset allocation reflects the increasing need for capital-efficient implementation, precise exposure management, and rapid adjustability. Derivatives enable institutional investors to maintain target exposures even when faced with cash flow constraints, illiquid markets, or internal limitations. They also enable tactical shifts in response to macroeconomic developments without disrupting core asset holdings. Derivatives serve both defensive purposes, such as hedging risk, controlling volatility, or locking in portfolio duration, and offensive objectives, such as capturing short-term opportunities or expressing relative value views across asset classes.

Despite their growing prominence, using derivatives in asset allocation is complex. It requires a deep understanding of notional exposure versus economic exposure, embedded leverage, collateral mechanics, and counterparty risk. Moreover, successful implementation requires alignment with the institution's broader governance and risk framework. As the toolkit expands, from traditional exchange-traded contracts to customized over-the-counter (OTC) structures, investment professionals increasingly need to consider derivatives as essential building blocks in a portfolio's strategic and tactical design, not just optional add-ons.

In this chapter, I walk through how derivatives are used at different stages of the asset allocation process, from their role in strategic allocation to tactical positioning, multi-asset implementation, and the operational and risk considerations that influence how they are applied in practice. Along the way, I will include case studies and practical examples of how leading asset owners and multi-asset managers have integrated derivatives into their portfolios. I also address regulatory frameworks that shape derivative usage; for example, the UCITS directive in the European Union restricts the use of certain OTC derivatives and leverage, while the ERISA standards in the U.S. impose fiduciary constraints that limit derivatives considered speculative or insufficiently monitored.

14.1 Understanding Asset Allocation Approaches

This section provides background information about asset allocation approaches that are foundational to understanding the material covered in the rest of the chapter. While the primary focus of this chapter is on the role of derivatives in asset allocation, it is essential first to understand the strategic frameworks into which these instruments are integrated.

We review three core approaches to asset allocation—strategic, tactical, and dynamic—each offering a distinct perspective on how portfolio weights are determined and adjusted over time. These approaches differ in flexibility, reliance on forecasts, and sensitivity to market conditions, but all are widely used in institutional portfolio management. They also serve as the structural context in which derivatives are applied for exposure management, risk control, or tactical positioning.[1]

---

[1]For a more detailed discussion of the approaches, see Robert Arnott and Frank J. Fabozzi (eds.), *Asset Allocation: A Handbook of Portfolio Policies, Strategies & Tactics*, McGraw-Hill, 1988; William Kinlaw, Mark P. Kritzman, and David Turkington, *A Practitioner's Guide to Asset Allocation*. Wiley, 2017.

14.1.1 *Strategic and tactical asset allocation approaches*

Strategic and tactical asset allocation represent two distinct but complementary approaches to portfolio construction. *Strategic asset allocation* (SAA) is the long-term blueprint that defines how capital is distributed across major asset classes based on an institution's investment objectives, risk tolerance, and liabilities. This allocation is typically established by a fund's board or investment committee and is reviewed periodically.

In essence, SAA determines the overall market exposure of the portfolio, which refers to how much of the portfolio's performance aligns with broad market trends, such as stocks, bonds, or other major asset classes. For example, a pension plan might maintain a 60% equity and 40% fixed-income allocation to meet long-term liability needs. At the same time, an endowment might shift more toward illiquid alternatives to support perpetual spending. As Mark Anson emphasizes, this long-term allocation is designed to provide economic exposure, not to outperform the market; the returns are primarily driven by broad market performance rather than tactical shifts or security selection.[2]

By contrast, *tactical asset allocation* (TAA) involves shorter-term adjustments around the strategic baseline to exploit perceived market inefficiencies or shifts in relative valuation. Tactical moves are generally made by the internal investment staff or external asset managers rather than the board. They can include over- or underweighting asset classes, styles, or factors based on macroeconomic views, valuation anomalies, or momentum signals. These adjustments are often framed as alpha decision attempts to generate excess returns by deviating from the policy benchmark.

Anson provides a helpful framework for distinguishing SAA from TAA using the beta and alpha drivers' concepts. Strategic allocation is all about managing beta exposure, which involves setting target weights across asset classes and selecting appropriate benchmarks. Tactical allocation involves deploying alpha drivers, strategies expected to outperform benchmarks based on skill or informational edge. For example, adding a managed futures strategy to a traditional 60/40 portfolio could reduce downside risk while preserving upside, as shown through empirical analysis of historical distributions.

---

[2]Mark J.P. Anson, "Strategic Versus Tactical Asset Allocation." *The Journal of Portfolio Management*, 30(2) 2004, pp. 8–22.

The distinction is not just philosophical. SAA is often constrained by policy and governance rules; in contrast, tactical allocation demands skill and agility and, frequently, a willingness to incur higher transaction costs and tracking errors. In practice, the boundary between the two approaches can blur, especially when boards intervene during market stress or staff push for structural shifts. Nevertheless, maintaining a clear division of responsibilities—strategic policy set at the top, tactical decisions delegated to investment professionals—helps preserve institutional discipline and clarity of purpose.

14.1.2 *Dynamic asset allocation*

Dynamic asset allocation (DAA) is an adaptive investment approach that actively adjusts a portfolio's asset mix in response to evolving market conditions, economic shifts, or changes in investor objectives. Unlike SAA, which maintains fixed long-term target weights based on assumed capital market conditions and is periodically rebalanced, DAA allows for continuous re-evaluation and movement away from initial targets without reverting. The guiding principle is that portfolio construction should reflect the current environment rather than solely relying on historical averages.

Chen Sui highlights that while SAA is designed for stability and long-term discipline, it often assumes that markets revert to long-run equilibrium.[3] On the other hand, the DAA acknowledges that structural changes, such as shifts in monetary regimes, inflation surprises, or geopolitical realignments, can persist long enough to warrant significant adjustments to asset exposure. In this sense, dynamic strategies are less about short-term timing (as in TAA) and more about medium- to long-term positioning in response to regime changes.

DAA typically relies on models or macro frameworks incorporating forward-looking variables such as valuation spreads, volatility, yield curves, or growth signals. It is instrumental in volatile or structurally changing environments, where sticking to a fixed strategic mix could expose the portfolio to undue risk or missed opportunities.

[3]Chen Sui, "Stepping into Dynamic Asset Allocation." CAIA Association, 2024 https://caia.org/blog/2024/10/10/stepping-dynamic-asset-allocation.

While DAA offers greater responsiveness, it requires more sophisticated governance, forecasting capabilities, and risk monitoring. The strategy is best suited for institutions with the resources to assess macro signals and implement shifts in a disciplined and transparent manner.

14.2 Strategic Asset Allocation and the Role of Derivatives

SAA serves as the long-term blueprint for constructing a portfolio. It reflects an investor's objectives, risk tolerance, liabilities, and beliefs about market equilibrium. In institutional portfolios, SAA is typically formalized through a policy portfolio target mix of asset classes to deliver stable, risk-adjusted returns over time. While the underlying exposures are intended to be stable, the instruments used to maintain them can vary considerably. This is where derivatives play an essential role.

One of the most common uses of derivatives in SAA is to implement *overlay strategies*, where futures or swaps are used to synthetically adjust exposures without altering the underlying cash holdings. For example, a pension fund receiving a large cash inflow may not want to immediately purchase long-duration bonds due to market conditions, illiquidity, or operational lag. Instead, it can use Treasury futures to replicate the desired exposure until a cash-based investment is made. Similarly, equity index futures can be used to maintain target equity allocations during rebalancing windows or transitions between portfolio managers.

Derivatives also enable efficient beta exposure, particularly in asset classes where direct investment is costly or less liquid. Futures and total return swaps (TRSs) on equity indexes, fixed income benchmarks, or commodity baskets enable institutional investors to gain diversified exposure without the capital commitment or trading friction of physical assets. For instance, exposure to the MSCI Emerging Markets Index can be obtained via a swap, which typically offers lower transaction costs and greater efficiency than assembling a basket of individual securities.

Another key application is *duration management* in bond portfolios.[4] Interest rate swaps are widely used to align portfolio duration with the

---

[4]Duration is a measure of a bond's or fixed income portfolio's sensitivity to changes in interest rates. It estimates how much the price of a bond will change for a 1% (100 basis point) change in interest rates. Duration management is the practice of adjusting the

interest rate sensitivity of liabilities, especially for insurance companies and defined benefit pension plans. A portfolio manager can receive or pay fixed in a swap to lengthen or shorten portfolio duration without selling any bonds. This synthetic adjustment helps maintain consistency with long-term funding objectives while preserving the underlying asset mix.

Currency hedging is another critical derivative use at the strategic level. Global portfolios often face currency risk that can materially impact returns. Rather than adjusting foreign asset holdings, portfolio managers can use FX forwards or currency swaps to neutralize unwanted currency exposures. This preserves the international diversification benefits of the underlying assets while mitigating currency risk through policy.

What makes derivatives appealing for strategic allocation is that they allow portfolio managers to get exposure to an asset class without tying up all of the portfolio's funds. That means a portfolio manager can keep some of the fund's cash available for other investments. Derivatives also make it easier to stay on target when dealing with cash inflows or outflows, rebalancing, or policy shifts.

While derivatives expand the toolkit for asset allocation by enabling more precise risk and return management, Martin Haugh and Andrew Lo emphasize that their use introduces significant complexity.[5] They highlight the necessity for portfolio managers to monitor capital invested in cash assets and the portfolio's total economic exposure, including derivative positions, which often involve leverage. They discuss how effective risk management requires sophisticated systems to track exposures and ensure compliance with regulatory constraints and institutional policies, which may restrict derivative usage or impose additional oversight. Ultimately, Haugh and Lo argue that integrating derivatives into long-term investment strategies demands financial expertise, robust operational controls, and disciplined risk governance.

---

duration of a portfolio to manage interest rate risk and align it with a portfolio manager's interest rate outlook, liabilities, or risk tolerance.

[5] Martin B. Haugh and Andrew W. Lo, "Asset Allocation and Derivatives." *Quantitative Finance,* 1(1), 2001, pp. 45–72.

14.3 Tactical Asset Allocation with Derivatives

TAA involves temporary deviations from the strategic portfolio mix to exploit perceived market inefficiencies or macroeconomic signals. These positions, often short- to medium-term, aim to enhance returns or manage near-term risks. Derivatives are ideal for implementing these adjustments efficiently and flexibly, offering precision and speed without disrupting core holdings.

One of the defining advantages of using derivatives in tactical allocation is that they allow portfolio managers to express market views quickly, precisely, and with minimal disruption to the underlying portfolio. Whether using futures, swaps, options, or volatility products, these instruments provide a way to adjust exposures efficiently, often with lower transaction costs, greater capital efficiency, and fewer tax or operational hurdles than direct security trading. The following subsections illustrate how specific derivatives serve these purposes in different market contexts.

14.3.1 *Futures in tactical asset allocation*

Futures contracts are among the most widely used instruments for implementing TAA decisions. They allow managers to shift exposures across major asset classes quickly and cost-effectively. For instance, a portfolio manager expecting a short-term rally in equities can use equity index futures to temporarily increase exposure to the asset class, avoiding the transaction costs, tax consequences, and operational frictions of buying or selling individual securities. Similarly, a bearish view on interest rates can be expressed by shorting Treasury futures to reduce portfolio duration without liquidating long-term bond holdings. These characteristics make futures ideal for expressing high-conviction views while preserving the integrity of the broader portfolio structure.

Beyond discretionary applications, futures also play a central role in systematic tactical strategies. Sandy Sasha Rattray, David G. Maloney, and Otto Van Hemert examine a multi-asset trend-following approach that relies entirely on liquid futures markets to capture directional momentum across equities, bonds, commodities, and currencies. Their study shows that such strategies have generated persistent long-term returns and provided effective diversification during periods of equity market stress, including the 2007–2008 Global Financial Crisis and the early 2020 COVID-19 sell-off.[6] While trend-following is often classified as an independent strategy, it demonstrates the flexibility and responsiveness of futures in tactical allocation, allowing investors to dynamically tilt portfolios based on market conditions without altering strategic benchmarks.

14.3.2 *Options in tactical asset allocation*

Options provide portfolio managers with a means to shape the risk and reward of a trade, particularly when they aim to limit losses without sacrificing too much upside. For example, buying a call option on a stock index allows a portfolio manager to benefit if the market rises, but if it falls, the losses are limited to the cost of the option. That's what asymmetric payoffs mean: more potential upside than downside. Similarly, a protective put acts like insurance, helping guard against big drops in value.

These strategies are beneficial when a portfolio manager has a strong opinion about where the market might go but is not sure how bumpy the ride will be. And in markets that are not going anywhere—what traders call "sideways markets"—selling covered calls can be a smart way to earn extra income. The portfolio manager forgoes some upside if the stock rallies but retains the option premium if it remains relatively stable with minimal movement.

14.3.3 *Total return swaps in tactical asset allocation*

TRSs allow portfolio managers to express directional views across markets without buying or selling the underlying securities. For instance, a portfolio manager who prefers U.S. equities to European equities might enter a swap that receives the total return of the S&P 500 while paying the total return of the Euro Stoxx 50. This can be implemented efficiently and without market friction. As Small and Weisman highlight, TRSs help avoid issues like market access restrictions, custody complexity, or operational friction, especially when managing exposures across global

[6] Sandy Sasha Rattray, David G. Maloney, and Otto Van Hemert. "The Case for Trend-Following." *The Journal of Portfolio Management*, 46(4), 2020, pp. 17–33.

markets.[7] TRSs can also express broader macro views across asset classes. I will return to these broader applications in the later sections on multi-asset portfolios and cross-asset derivative strategies.

14.3.4 *Volatility derivatives in tactical asset allocation*

Volatility derivatives such as VIX futures, variance swaps, and option-based strategies enable portfolio managers to express views on market stress or calm by gaining direct exposure to volatility as a distinct asset class.

For example, a portfolio manager anticipating turbulence might "buy volatility" through long VIX futures or options to hedge against sharp equity drawdowns—sudden declines in stock prices that can rapidly erode portfolio value. Conversely, in stable markets with low fear, the portfolio manager may "sell volatility" through short positions or premium-collecting strategies to generate additional income.

These instruments act as a flexible overlay, allowing portfolio managers to adjust the portfolio's risk sensitivity in response to changing sentiment without altering core allocations. However, they must be used with strong risk oversight. Leverage and notional exposure can build quickly—especially in variance swaps or short-volatility trades—requiring robust controls on margin, liquidity, correlation effects, and compliance thresholds.

14.3.5 *Practitioner commentary: Designing coherent systematic tactical strategies*

Alexander Rudin, Global Head of Multi-Asset and Fixed Income Research at State Street Global Advisors, offers a practical perspective on tactical allocation using derivatives.[8] Alexander Rudin emphasizes that systematic multi-asset strategies should be seen as "coherent portfolios of ideas." This means diversifying signal inputs such as value, carry, and sentiment,

---

[7] Christopher Small and Andrew Weisman. "Exploring the Mechanics and Applications of Equity Swaps in Investment Portfolios." Chapter 21 (pp. 339–359) in Frank J. Fabozzi and Marielle de Jong (eds.), *Derivatives Applications in Asset Management.* Palgrave Macmillan, 2025.

[8] Adapted from an interview with Alexander Rudin, *The Journal of Portfolio Management*, Multi-Asset Special Issue, 51(5), 2025, pp. 1–7.

and ensuring that structural links across asset classes are embedded within the strategy. For example, sentiment indicators used to position equities may also inform positions in credit, given their shared sensitivity to risk appetite.

Rudin notes that signals used for TAA must be parsimonious and economically justified. "Each additional level of complexity must be justified by a measurable improvement in performance," he argues. Given the limited frequency of actionable data for multi-asset strategies, simplicity and economic grounding help avoid the common pitfall of overfitting.

He also outlines how strategies manage downside equity risk through active reallocation, diversification, and hedge overlays. Derivative overlays, such as volatility-managed equity exposures or protective option structures, are central to balancing trade-offs between cost and certainty. Importantly, liquidity and alignment with cash flow frequency are operational considerations that govern the viability of these tactical shifts.

14.4 Multi-Asset Portfolios and Cross-Asset Derivative Strategies

Multi-asset portfolios allocate capital across various asset classes to enhance diversification and deliver more resilient returns across market cycles. Managing such portfolios involves choosing the correct exposures and determining how and when to adjust them in response to macroeconomic conditions, volatility regimes, or valuation signals. Derivatives are central to these efforts. They serve as both building blocks and tactical levers, offering the flexibility to adjust exposures efficiently, hedge portfolio-level risks, and implement views without disrupting core holdings.

A prominent use case is the deployment of TRSs for expressing macro views across asset classes. In an asset allocation context, TRSs allow portfolio managers to implement high-conviction tilts, favoring U.S. equities over European equities or shifting from investment-grade to high-yield credit bonds without directly trading the underlying securities. For example, a portfolio manager expecting strong U.S. growth might enter a TRS to receive the return on the S&P 500 while paying the return on the Euro Stoxx 50. These synthetic positions preserve the integrity of the portfolio's long-term strategic allocation while providing an efficient vehicle for expressing shorter-term macro perspectives.[9]

---

[9]Christopher Small Andrew Weisman illustrate how institutional investors can use equity TRSs to express regional or asset class preferences without physically trading the

In multi-asset portfolios, derivatives are building blocks and integration tools across asset classes. These portfolios, spanning equities, fixed income, commodities, currencies, and alternatives, require sophisticated tools to manage exposures, correlations, and risk across disparate markets. Derivatives are uniquely suited to this task due to their flexibility, low capital intensity, and ability to deliver synthetic exposures.

A central benefit of derivatives in multi-asset management is the efficient expression of asset class exposures without disrupting portfolio structure. For example, a global macro fund might simultaneously hold S&P 500 futures, SOFR futures, and commodity index swaps to build a diversified market view without directly trading spot securities in each asset class. This reduces transaction costs and settlement complexity and supports the timely execution of cross-asset views.

Multi-asset managers also use volatility derivatives and cross-asset correlation trades to express views on systemic risk or portfolio diversification. For example, volatility index (VIX) futures or options might be used to hedge against equity drawdown risk, which is the risk of a sudden, significant decline in portfolio value from a recent peak, often triggered by market stress or volatility spikes. In contrast, correlation swaps can be used to speculate on the co-movement between asset classes. These instruments allow managers to fine-tune portfolio exposures in ways not feasible with physical assets.

Derivatives also facilitate overlay strategies, which are increasingly used in multi-asset settings. Currency overlays, which utilize forwards and options, enable the separation of currency risk from asset returns, particularly in portfolios with global allocations. Similarly, duration overlays using interest rate futures or swaps allow managers to target a specific interest rate sensitivity for the entire portfolio without modifying its underlying structure. Specialist teams or external overlay managers often manage these overlays.

Another innovative use in multi-asset portfolios is tail-risk hedging. Through strategies such as long out-of-the-money puts, variance swaps, or exotic option structures, portfolio managers can create asymmetric payoffs that protect portfolios in market crashes while preserving upside

---

underlying assets. They show that these instruments offer capital efficiency, reduce transaction costs, and facilitate implementation of active allocation views, such as overweighting U.S. equities relative to other market, within a broader portfolio structure. See Christopher Small Andrew Weisman, "Exploring the Mechanics and Applications of Equity Swaps in Investment Portfolios."

participation. Although expensive, these tail hedges can be calibrated and adjusted using derivatives in a dynamic and scalable way.

Finally, the ability to dynamically rebalance exposures using derivatives supports the implementation of strategic or tactical asset allocation in real time. Multi-asset strategies may adjust risk-on/risk-off exposures by adjusting derivative overlays rather than trading the underlying assets, especially in response to volatility-targeting mandates or macroeconomic triggers.

William Cazalet, Dimitri Curtil, and James Stavena discuss the details of implementing multi-asset overlay strategies.[10] They highlight real-world challenges, such as coordinating across currencies, sequencing trades, and ensuring the governance framework can support fast-moving tactical decisions.

14.4.1 *Tactical asset allocation using futures: A worked illustration*

Cazalet, Curtil, and Stavena provide an insightful illustration that serves as a framework for understanding how listed derivatives, particularly futures can implement TAA overlays efficiently and with minimal disruption to the core portfolio. The following illustration builds on their framework, using adjusted figures to demonstrate how derivatives enable capital-efficient exposure management in a real-world asset allocation setting.

14.4.1.1 *Core portfolio construction*

Let's start with a base portfolio of $20 million. The portfolio manager aims to maintain long-only exposure to the S&P 500 Index as a core holding, with a TAA overlay that reflects tactical tilts toward U.S. equities and long-duration U.S. Treasuries. Instead of deploying all capital into a passive S&P 500 ETF, the portfolio manager allocates $17 million to physical equities that replicate the index and uses equity futures to equitize the remaining $3 million, that is, to gain equity market exposure on idle cash through derivatives without actually purchasing additional stocks.

---

[10] William Cazalet, Dimitri Curtil, and James Stavena, "Use of Derivatives in Overlays/ Downside Protection and Upside Capture." Chapter 26 (391–406) in *Derivatives Applications in Asset Management.*

Assume the E-mini S&P 500 Index futures (3-month expiration) are trading at 5,200. Each contract has a multiplier of 50. The notional value of one futures contract is

$$5{,}200 \times 50 = \$260{,}000$$

To achieve $3 million in notional exposure using these contracts,

$$\$3{,}000{,}000/\$260{,}000 = 11.54 \Rightarrow \text{Round down to 11 contracts}$$

Thus, the portfolio manager uses 11 E-mini S&P 500 futures contracts, equitizing the cash component while retaining the liquidity for potential overlays. The initial margin required per contract is $13,000, totaling $143,000 and leaving capital for the tactical overlay.

14.4.1.2 *TAA overlay construction*

The portfolio manager's tactical view suggests overweighting equities by 10% and adding a 5% bond exposure to offset some equity volatility. To do this without altering the core holdings, they implement the TAA using futures:

- *Equity TAA Leg*: The portfolio manager wants an additional $2 million exposure to equities. Using the same E-mini futures,

$$\$2{,}000{,}000/\$260{,}000 = 7.69 \Rightarrow \text{Round up to 8 contracts}$$

- *Bond TAA Leg*: Assume 20-year Treasury bond futures are trading at $123.50 per $100 notional (each contract equals $123,500). The portfolio manager wants $1 million in exposure:

$$\$1{,}000{,}000/\$123{,}500 \approx 8.1 \Rightarrow \text{Round down to 8}$$

Now, the portfolio contains three sets of derivative positions: (1) 11 equity futures contracts used to equitize the $3 million cash reserve, maintaining full equity exposure for the core portfolio; (2) 8 additional equity futures contracts added as a tactical overweight to U.S. equities based on the portfolio manager's bullish short-term view; and (3) 8 Treasury futures contracts used to express a modest tactical allocation to long-duration bonds, aimed at diversifying risk and potentially benefiting from a flight-to-quality scenario if equities underperform.

The result is a tactical overlay that leaves the core portfolio intact but alters the exposure profile: Total equity exposure is now 130% of the original portfolio value (the original 85% from physical and equitized equity, plus eight contracts' worth of futures exposure). In comparison, bonds account for 5% of the notional exposure. These exposures are achieved synthetically—through futures—without shifting the actual asset allocation of the underlying holdings. This setup enables the portfolio manager to reflect their macro views in real time with minimal transaction costs, efficient capital utilization, and easy reversibility.

14.4.1.3 *Benefits and risk management*

The advantage is clear: The portfolio manager expresses a high-conviction macro view without disrupting the core S&P 500 allocation. Futures enable precise and quick exposure adjustments with low transaction costs and reduced capital outlay. The overlay allows responsiveness to market signals, instrumental in fast-moving macro environments.

This mirrors the implementation framework described by Cazalet, Curtil, and Stavena, who emphasize such overlays' operational clarity and efficiency. Moreover, their framework demonstrates how portfolio managers can manage margin requirements, minimize excessive turnover in core holdings, and mitigate basis risk through careful contract selection and rollover strategies.

14.4.2 *Tactical overlay using options: A convex payoff strategy in multi-asset portfolios*

In multi-asset portfolios, portfolio managers may hold a directional view on equities but prefer to express it through convex exposure. This structure participates in market upside while limiting downside risk. Rather than increasing equity exposure through futures or cash securities, they might express this view using call options, enabling them to participate in a potential rally without fully committing capital or exposing the portfolio to large losses.

The following illustration is based on an example provided by Cazalet, Curtil, and Stavena, who demonstrate how listed equity options can be used to implement tactical overlays in a capital-efficient and risk-controlled manner.[11] While the figures have been adapted for clarity and

[11] Cazalet, Curtil, and Stavena, "Use of Derivatives In Overlays / Downside Protection and Upside Capture."

simplicity, the trade's structure and purpose follow their original framework.

14.4.2.1 *Market context and objective*

Suppose a global balanced fund holds a 60/40 portfolio with $50 million in assets under management. The portfolio manager is tactically bullish on U.S. equities over the next three months but remains cautious about downside risk due to rising geopolitical tensions.

Rather than increasing equity beta, the manager decides to (1) maintain the existing 60% equity allocation and (2) allocate 0.5% of portfolio capital (i.e., $250,000) to a long call option strategy on the S&P 500 index, creating convex upside participation.

14.4.2.2 *Option strategy design*

Assume:

- S&P 500 index is at 5,200.
- 3-month call options with a strike of 5,300 cost 50 index points (i.e., $2,500 per contract since $50 × 50 = $2,500).
- Each option gives exposure to 50 units of the index (standard multiplier).
- $250,000/$2,500 = 100 call options purchased.

This options strategy adds a layer of upside participation without taking on full downside risk, a structure known as a *convex payoff.* Here's how it works:

- The most that the portfolio manager can lose is the cost of the options, which in this case is $250,000. The portfolio manager paid the total premium to set up the trade.
- If the market rises, the value of those call options increases. For every point the S&P 500 finishes above the 5,300 strike price at expiration, the portfolio earns $5,000 in profit. That's because the portfolio manager holds 100 call options, and each point is worth $50 per contract.
- The breakeven point is where the gain from the options offsets the initial cost. That happens if the index rises to 5,350, 50 points above the strike price. Any move beyond that adds to the portfolio's returns.

Let's say the S&P 500 finishes at 5,500 when the options expire in three months. That's 200 points above the strike price of 5,300. Here's how the payoff breaks down:

- The gross gain on the position is

$$(5{,}500 - 5{,}300) \times 100 \text{ contracts} \times \$50 = \$1{,}000{,}000$$

- After subtracting the $250,000 premium, the net gain is $750,000.

That's a 1.5% boost on a $50 million portfolio, all from a strategy that only put 0.5% of capital at risk. This kind of asymmetric return profile—a slight downside with a meaningful upside—is why portfolio managers use options tactically to express a bullish view without disrupting their strategic allocation.

14.4.2.3 *Portfolio impact and rationale*

This convex overlay lets the portfolio manager express tactical conviction in equities without increasing the portfolio's beta or downside risk. If the equity market stalls or declines, the loss is capped at the premium paid, preserving core capital. If markets rally, options can amplify the upside in a capital-efficient manner.

Cazalet, Curtil, and Stavena describe this option overlay as a tool for nonlinear asset allocation. This approach complements traditional rebalancing and beta tilts by embedding conditional exposure based on market outcomes. This technique is particularly valuable when the portfolio is constrained from increasing gross exposure (e.g., due to leverage limits or risk budgets) but still seeks to capitalize on asymmetrical return opportunities.

14.4.3 *Machine learning–driven allocation using derivatives*

As portfolio construction becomes increasingly data-intensive, machine learning (ML) techniques are playing a larger role in informing asset allocation decisions, particularly in multi-asset portfolios. When paired with the flexibility and speed of derivatives, ML-driven frameworks offer a powerful means of adapting to rapidly evolving market dynamics.

In practice, ML models detect patterns in historical and real-time data to forecast asset returns, volatility, and correlations. These models often process vast datasets that traditional quantitative models may overlook, including macroeconomic indicators, earnings revisions, sentiment signals, and high-frequency price movements. Based on these forecasts, derivatives serve as the implementation layer, enabling the portfolio manager to express views, adjust risk exposures, and rebalance positions in near real time.

For example, an ML model might predict rising cross-asset volatility and recommend reducing equity exposure while increasing hedges in interest rate markets. This recommendation could be executed using equity index futures and Treasury futures, or by adding VIX futures or variance swaps[12] as volatility protection. Derivatives allow for synthetic, capital-efficient trades, enabling the ML system to adjust positions dynamically without triggering large cash transactions or disrupting the strategic asset mix.

More advanced systems incorporate reinforcement learning algorithms[13] that adjust portfolio weights iteratively based on feedback from realized performance. These systems may alter exposures via index swaps,[14] FX forwards, or commodity futures as the portfolio seeks to optimize a risk-adjusted objective in changing environments. In such cases, derivatives act as adaptive tools for managing cross-asset exposures under tight tracking error or capital constraints.

Despite their promise, ML-driven allocation frameworks face challenges. Overfitting,[15] lack of interpretability, and regime instability can lead to unreliable signals. As such, institutions employing these models typically operate within well-defined governance frameworks that include position limits, human oversight, and scenario analysis. Importantly, using derivatives in these settings underscores the need for robust collateral management, real-time monitoring, and adherence to regulatory compliance.

Alexander Rudin shares this concern, warning that some strategies marketed as "AI-driven" are merely repackaged traditional quant models

---

[12] A variance swap is a derivative that allows investors to trade future realized volatility against current implied volatility, with payoffs based on the difference between the two.

[13] Reinforcement learning is a type of ML where algorithms learn to make sequential decisions by receiving feedback as rewards or penalties, much like trial-and-error learning.

[14] An index swap is a derivative contract in which one party agrees to pay the return on a specified index (such as an equity or bond index), while receiving a different return, such as a fixed or floating rate.

[15] Overfitting occurs when a model learns patterns specific to the training data, including noise, leading to poor generalization to new or unseen data.

or rely on opaque black-box architectures. He emphasizes that ML-derived signals must be grounded in clear economic logic and thoroughly tested for robustness. Overfitting and unreliable outputs may compromise strategy viability at scale without these safeguards.[16]

In summary, ML expands the information set used for allocation decisions, while derivatives provide the tools for implementation. The synergy between the two—data-driven insights and capital-efficient execution—makes this combination particularly attractive in multi-asset portfolios where adaptability and cross-market integration are essential.

14.5 Derivatives in Liability-Driven and Risk-Based Allocation Strategies

Institutional investors such as pension funds and insurance companies are increasingly incorporating liability-driven investment (LDI) and risk-based allocation frameworks, where the role of derivatives shifts from tactical exposure tools to essential instruments for aligning asset and liability sensitivities. In these contexts, derivatives are indispensable for controlling funding volatility, achieving capital efficiency, and tailoring risk exposures precisely.

In LDI strategies, the objective is not return maximization but stability in the funding surplus. Derivatives—especially interest rate swaps, inflation swaps, longevity swaps, FX forwards, and Treasury futures—enable plans to synthetically match the duration, inflation sensitivity, and other characteristics of long-dated pension liabilities without overcommitting capital to physical instruments. Kailan Shang and Zakir Hossen explain in the Society of Actuaries' Liability-Driven Benchmark Model that interest rate swaps allow for flexible duration extension. In contrast, inflation swaps and FX derivatives address cost-of-living adjustments and currency-denominated obligations in multinational plans. This integrated approach balances physical bonds with overlays constructed from derivatives, generating funding improvements through scenario analysis and risk capital projections.[17]

---

[16]"Interview with Alexander Rudin of State Street Global Advisors."

[17]Kailan Shang and Zakir Hossen. *Liability-Driven Investment: Benchmark Model.* Society of Actuaries, Apr. 2019, www.soa.org/globalassets/assets/files/resources/research-report/2019/liability-driven-investment.pdf.

Dynamic LDI expands on this by using derivatives, primarily Treasury futures and swaps, to manage real-time liability sensitivities. As NISA Investment Advisors notes, this approach enables plan sponsors to maintain a stable funded ratio[18] while rebalancing hedge ratios in response to evolving interest rate environments.[19] By not tying up capital in long-dated bonds, derivatives-based hedging supports agility and precision, especially when bond market liquidity is poor or valuations are unattractive.

Fiduciary management and overlay programs also rely heavily on OTC derivatives, such as inflation swaps, cross-currency swaps, and customized interest rate contracts, to build scalable and liability-aware investment solutions. Adam Dixon emphasizes that fiduciary managers use these instruments for passive hedging and dynamically adjusting exposures, rebalancing portfolios, and managing funding ratio triggers.[20] These overlays are governed by tight operational and legal frameworks, helping to mitigate the risk of collateral shortfall or counterparty failure.

Despite these benefits, derivatives introduce complex layers of risk that must be actively monitored and managed:

- Counterparty risk is a key concern, particularly with OTC contracts. While collateralization agreements (e.g., Credit Support Annexes) reduce this risk, they do not eliminate it, especially during times of stress when counterparties may delay or default.[21]
- Liquidity risk can materialize if large margin calls are triggered during volatile markets. In such cases, investors may be forced to

---

[18]NISA Investment Advisors, L.L.C. *An Overview of Dynamic Liability Driven Investing for Defined Benefit Pension Plans*. July 2011.

[19]In the pension context, a funded ratio measures a pension plan's financial health by comparing its assets and liabilities. Specifically, it is the ratio of the plan's actuarial assets (available to pay benefits) to its actuarial liabilities (the present value of promised future benefits). A funded ratio of 100% means the plan has exactly enough assets to meet its obligations; a ratio below 100% indicates an underfunded plan, while a ratio above 100% suggests a surplus.

[20]Adam J. Dixon. "The Application of OTC Derivatives to LDI and Fiduciary Management." *Investment & Pensions Europe*, January 2006. https://www.ipe.com/the-application-of-otc-derivatives-to-ldi-and-fidu/18538.article.

[21]Collateral thresholds, daily margining, and counterparty-specific credit risk metrics (e.g., CDS spreads) are key components of counterparty risk frameworks under ISDA documentation.

liquidate physical assets to meet cash demands, amplifying procyclicality.[22]

- Model risk and basis risk can also arise if the derivatives used for hedging are imperfect substitutes for the liability exposures they are meant to offset. For example, using nominal swaps to hedge real (inflation-adjusted) liabilities introduces tracking error that may widen over time.
- Operational risk becomes more pronounced in dynamic overlay programs where errors in execution, valuation, or collateral movements can disrupt portfolio alignment. Effective governance, robust IT systems, and experienced derivatives operations teams are critical for maintaining integrity under pressure.

Risk-based allocation strategies, such as risk parity, volatility targeting, or tail-risk budgeting derivatives, enable investors to scale exposures in proportion to risk rather than capital.[23] For example, a portfolio manager might use equity and Treasury futures to construct volatility-balanced portfolios or implement TRS to access assets without direct exposure to the balance sheet. While these strategies enhance capital efficiency, they too can become unstable in environments of non-linear correlation breakdown, such as during liquidity squeezes or central bank policy shocks.[24]

---

[22] The 2022 UK pension crisis exposed how small shifts in interest rates can trigger cascading collateral calls when leverage is layered via swaps and repo funding. See Ketan B. Patel, and Santiago I. Sordo Palacios, "UK Pension Market Stress in 2022—Why It Happened and Implications for the U.S." *Chicago Fed Letter*, No. 480, June 2023. https://login.morganstanleyclientserv.com/ux/

[23] Risk-based allocation strategies aim to distribute portfolio risk more evenly across assets or factors, rather than allocating based purely on capital. In risk parity, investors allocate capital such that each asset contributes equally to total portfolio volatility, often resulting in larger weights on lower-volatility holdings like bonds. Volatility targeting adjusts portfolio exposure based on changes in expected volatility, scaling up exposure when volatility is low and reducing it when volatility rises to maintain a consistent risk level over time. Tail-risk budgeting explicitly allocates resources to protect against extreme market events, often using derivatives such as options or credit default swaps to hedge against large drawdowns or systemic shocks. These approaches are designed to improve risk-adjusted returns by managing exposures dynamically and emphasizing diversification by risk contribution.

[24] In early 2020 and again in 2022, volatility-targeting strategies that relied on stable correlation structures faced unexpected drawdowns, primarily because traditional safe assets, such as government bonds and Treasuries, periodically behaved procyclically and lost

By incorporating derivatives not as tactical add-ons but as core instruments of liability and risk alignment, institutional investors can address complex challenges in capital allocation, duration targeting, and macro-resilience, provided they pair innovation with robust infrastructure and prudent oversight.

14.6 Portfolio Construction and Efficiency Considerations

Using derivatives to implement asset allocation strategies introduces unique challenges and opportunities in portfolio construction. Unlike traditional securities, derivatives allow for the decoupling of exposure and funding, meaning that investors can take on risk positions without committing full capital. This flexibility enhances capital efficiency but requires careful attention to leverage, liquidity, and operational risks.

One critical distinction is between notional exposure and economic exposure. The notional value of a derivative represents the reference amount on which cash flows are based, but it does not reflect the actual capital required to initiate the position. A futures contract, for example, may need only a fraction of its notional amount as margin. This embedded leverage can amplify gains and losses, so managing it is essential for maintaining intended risk levels across the portfolio.

Another consideration is margining and collateralization as discussed in Chapter 10. Derivatives typically require initial and variation margin, which ties up capital and must be forecasted accurately to avoid liquidity shortfalls. The cost of funding this collateral, particularly in portfolios using multiple derivatives across asset classes, can materially impact performance. Portfolio managers must balance the benefits of derivative use with the operational demands of maintaining sufficient liquid assets.

Liquidity is also a major factor. Exchange-traded derivatives such as equity or Treasury futures tend to be highly liquid, with tight bid-ask spreads and deep markets. In contrast, customized OTC derivatives may offer more precise exposure but are often less liquid and entail higher

---

their diversification benefits, breaking expected correlation patterns during market stress. See Tomasz Kaczmarek, Barbara Będowska-Sójka, Przemysław Grobelny, and Katarzyna Perez. "False Safe Haven Assets: Evidence From the Target Volatility Strategy Based on Recurrent Neural Network." *Research in International Business and Finance*, 60, April 2022, 101610.

transaction costs. In times of market stress, liquidity can deteriorate quickly, so prudent sizing and stress testing of positions are key components of derivative-based portfolio construction.

Another efficiency issue is the cost of rolling contracts as explained in Chapter 10. Because many derivatives have finite maturities, positions must be periodically rolled forward to maintain exposure. This introduces roll yield risk (positive or negative) depending on the shape of the futures curve. Asset allocators must incorporate the cost and timing of rolls into their rebalancing and implementation calendars.

A related challenge is basis risk, as explained in Chapter 13, the potential mismatch between the derivative used and the asset or exposure it is intended to replicate. For example, a portfolio manager might use a broad index futures contract to gain equity exposure. Still, tracking error can arise if the portfolio's underlying equities differ significantly in sector or region. Similarly, using interest rate swaps to hedge bond duration may not fully align with the duration or convexity of specific bond holdings.

Finally, the choice between synthetic and physical exposure must be weighed. Derivatives offer speed and capital efficiency, but in some cases, owning the physical asset provides benefits such as income, voting rights, or regulatory advantages. Applying synthetically or through cash instruments depends on the expected holding period, cost, liquidity, and portfolio context.

In sum, derivatives enable more flexible and efficient portfolio construction, but only when paired with strong risk controls, liquidity forecasting, and collateral management systems. The efficiency gains are substantial, but so are the operational demands. Success depends on investment knowledge, institutional readiness, and infrastructure.

14.7 Integrating Derivatives into Multi-Asset Portfolio Operations

Multi-asset portfolios combine a range of asset classes (i.e., equities, fixed income, currencies, commodities, and alternatives) within a unified investment framework. While these positions offer diversification and flexibility, they also introduce complexity in maintaining exposures, rebalancing positions, and managing correlated risks. Derivatives provide the essential infrastructure for navigating this complexity, enabling asset managers to construct and adjust exposures precisely and efficiently.

At the core of multi-asset implementation is the ability to manage broad exposures across asset classes using standardized contracts. Equity index futures, bond futures, interest rate swaps, FX forwards, and commodity futures are commonly used to build desired exposures or rebalance back to targets. These instruments allow portfolio managers to express macro views, manage risk budgets, or execute overlay strategies without disturbing underlying manager mandates or physical asset allocations.[2]

For example, a global balanced fund may use equity index futures to increase risk asset exposure following a sharp market correction, while holding cash to meet short-term redemptions. Alternatively, it may use interest rate swaps to reduce portfolio duration if anticipating a rise in rates, while avoiding the need to sell illiquid bonds. Derivatives allow these adjustments to occur efficiently and, importantly, across asset classes without waiting for capital movement or asset manager reallocation.

In currency management, derivatives are indispensable. Global portfolios are inherently exposed to foreign exchange fluctuations, which may or may not align with their risk budgets or return objectives. FX forwards, swaps, and options enable managers to adjust currency exposure independently of underlying asset positions for hedging or tactical purposes. Currency overlays are often parallel with asset class exposures to control currency risk at the portfolio level.

More advanced implementations may incorporate volatility, correlation, or carry as asset classes. Portfolio managers use options, variance swaps, and correlation swaps to express views on risk premia or to hedge tail events cost-effectively.

In risk parity or global macro portfolios, derivatives are used for exposure and scaling risk contributions. A risk parity manager may use leverage via futures or swaps to equalize risk across asset classes, ensuring that bonds, equities, and commodities contribute equally to portfolio volatility. Similarly, a macro manager may construct views across regions and sectors using long-short derivatives exposures without taking physical delivery.

Alexander Rudin further notes that portfolio construction in multi-asset strategies must translate signals of different frequencies and characteristics into consistent, scalable exposures.[25] This demands rigorous attention to liquidity constraints, mainly when derivatives are used across

[25] Interview with Alexander Rudin, *The Journal of Portfolio Management*, 2025.

public and private assets. Tactical overlays using futures, options, and swaps must account for the underlying cash flow patterns and strategy turnover. Without such alignment, derivative overlays risk becoming sources of liquidity stress in volatile markets.

Portable alpha strategies provide a compelling example of how derivatives enhance capital efficiency. In these strategies, investors gain market exposure (beta) synthetically using instruments like equity index futures or swaps, while allocating the underlying capital to separate alpha-generating strategies such as hedge funds, long-short credit, or private markets. This approach allows investors to pursue excess returns independently of the benchmark, made possible by derivatives' ability to separate market exposure from capital deployment.

While derivatives enable sophisticated multi-asset implementations, they also demand tight operational oversight. Exposure netting, margin calls, counterparty management, and real-time risk tracking are all required to ensure that derivatives continues to be consistent with portfolio objectives and regulatory constraints. As multi-asset portfolios grow more complex, the quality of derivative infrastructure increasingly determines implementation success.

14.8 Illustrative Applications and Case Studies

This section presents a series of illustrative cases drawn from institutional settings to clarify the practical use of derivatives in asset allocation. These applications demonstrate how derivatives can be used to efficiently manage exposures, hedge risks, or express tactical views, highlighting both their benefits and the associated operational considerations.

14.8.1 *Case 1: Implementing strategic exposure using futures*

A large U.S.-based pension fund undergoes its annual SAA review and determines that it is underweight global equities. However, the fund managers wish to avoid immediate disruption of the existing portfolio or triggering capital gains taxes. The solution is to use MSCI EAFE futures contracts to add the desired exposure to international developed markets. This overlay strategy allows the fund to gain the target exposure instantly, while a gradual transition to physical holdings is executed over the following months.

The key takeaway from this case is that futures can be used to gain broad market exposure quickly and cost-effectively. The notional exposure is adjusted via initial margin, making this capital efficient. Portfolio managers must monitor basis risk and maintain adequate margin liquidity.[26]

14.8.2 *Case 2: Risk parity via synthetic leverage*

A multi-asset risk parity fund seeks to equalize risk contributions from equities, bonds, and commodities. Because bond volatility is lower than equity volatility, the fund uses Treasury futures and commodity swaps to lever up the lower-volatility exposures. These derivatives allow the fund to scale up risk-adjusted weights without tying up large amounts of capital.

The key takeaway from this case is that derivatives enable synthetic leverage in a risk-controlled framework. This approach emphasizes the importance of daily monitoring and stress testing of derivative exposure, particularly under changing volatility regimes.

14.8.3 *Case 3: Currency overlay in a global equity portfolio*

An endowment fund with international equity holdings noted rising currency volatility and hedged its non-dollar exposures. It implements a currency overlay program using short-dated forward contracts on the euro, yen, and pound. These forward positions are rolled monthly and adjusted based on the tactical views of a dedicated overlay manager.

The key takeaway from this case is that currency forwards offer a clean way to manage currency risk without altering the underlying asset holdings. Operational coordination between investment teams and overlay managers is crucial to maintain alignment with asset exposures.

14.8.4 *Case 4: Tail risk hedge in a volatile environment*

A sovereign wealth fund is concerned about potential market dislocation due to geopolitical tensions. To mitigate downside risk, the fund purchases out-of-the-money put options on a global equity index. Though

[26]CME Group. *E-mini MSCI EAFE Futures Contract Specifications*, 2023.

these options are relatively expensive due to high implied volatility, the cost is justified as insurance against a high-impact event.

A key takeaway from this case is that options provide asymmetric payoffs, ideal for tail hedging. However, their use requires balancing cost and protective benefit, with clear objectives for when and how to use them.

14.9 Summary

In this chapter, I describe how derivatives can enhance asset allocation strategies. I explain how derivatives support SAA by enabling portfolio managers to maintain target exposures efficiently, particularly when limited liquidity or market conditions delay full capital deployment. Derivative instruments allow for notional exposure without requiring full investment in the underlying assets.

I then examine TAA, where derivatives provide flexibility and precision for adjusting exposures in response to short- to medium-term market views. I describe how equity and Treasury futures, total return swaps, options, and volatility-linked instruments can express directional views, manage drawdowns, and take advantage of market dislocations without altering long-term portfolio structure.

I also address how derivatives support DAA. By enabling real-time rebalancing and quick shifts in risk exposures, derivatives allow portfolio managers to respond rapidly to macroeconomic triggers, volatility regimes, or changes in market sentiment. These tools support more adaptive portfolio management across market cycles.

Finally, I show how derivatives play a central role in multi-asset portfolios. They serve as building blocks for cross-asset implementation, facilitate currency and duration overlays, and enable tail-risk hedging through instruments such as options and variance swaps. Derivatives enhance the ability to fine-tune exposures and maintain alignment with portfolio objectives while navigating diverse global markets.

Chapter 15

Evaluating Derivative Strategies Through Backtesting: Principles and Practices

Backtesting is a cornerstone of evaluating derivatives strategies, providing a framework to test their effectiveness and understand potential risks and returns before real-world implementation. Unlike traditional assets, derivatives pose unique challenges in backtesting due to their complexity, leverage, and sensitivity to market conditions. Derivative strategies often involve intricate variables, such as volatility, option Greeks, and implied forward rates, which require a distinct approach to modeling and data accuracy. Therefore, a rigorous backtesting process is essential to verify that a strategy performs as expected across various market conditions and to avoid costly real-world errors.

An article by Macrosynergy, a London-based macroeconomic research and technology company specializing in developing and implementing macro quantamental investment strategies,[1] explores the role of derivative returns and carry in strategy evaluation, particularly emphasizing how these factors can influence strategy viability and performance metrics.[2] The article details how derivative carry, or the expected return from holding a derivative position, can significantly impact strategy

[1] A quantamental strategy combines quantitative and fundamental investment. Quantitative models are used to analyze large datasets and identify patterns. At the same time, fundamental analysis provides context by examining a company's intrinsic qualities, such as its financial health, industry position, and macroeconomic factors.

[2] "Generic Derivative Returns and Carry (for Strategy Testing)." Macrosynergy, n.d. Available at https://macrosynergy.com/research/generic_return_carry/.

backtesting, as it interacts with various market conditions and anticipated influences outcomes. Additionally, it underscores the importance of incorporating realistic assumptions regarding derivative returns when assessing strategy performance, especially when derivatives are used for hedging or speculative purposes. These elements form essential considerations in any robust backtesting process, affecting risk and potential profitability.

Backtesting allows portfolio managers or the group responsible for backtesting to assess the historical performance of a strategy, helping them determine if it aligns with risk tolerance, return objectives, and market expectations. For derivative strategies, it is crucial to account for nuances such as margin requirements, liquidity constraints, and the impact of transaction costs, which can significantly affect performance. These elements must be incorporated into a robust backtesting framework to generate realistic insights into the strategy's potential viability. Furthermore, backtesting can highlight potential vulnerabilities or biases that might go unnoticed, especially in derivative strategies where leverage amplifies gains and losses.

In building this framework, practitioners should consider expert recommendations on creating robust and unbiased backtests. Marcos López de Prado advocates for practices that avoid common pitfalls, such as overfitting and look-ahead bias, emphasizing the importance of purging and embargoing data to prevent information leakage and ensuring that past data do not inadvertently influence future performance outcomes during testing.[3] These practices are particularly critical for derivatives, where data accuracy and integrity can significantly affect the reliability of backtest results.

In this chapter, I build on these foundational principles by outlining how to structure and execute a comprehensive backtest for derivative strategies. I begin by identifying the required data inputs, including market data and instrument-specific variables, and then describe how to incorporate transaction costs, margin requirements, and volatility surfaces into the simulation. I review several commonly used backtesting methodologies, such as historical simulation, walk-forward analysis, and Monte Carlo simulation, highlighting their strengths, limitations, and specific relevance to derivative strategies. I also explain how to evaluate backtest results using performance and risk metrics tailored to derivatives, including those that account for nonlinear payoffs and path dependency. Throughout the chapter, I emphasize how backtesting is not only a

[3]Marcos López de Prado, *Advances in Financial Machine Learning*. Hoboken, NJ: John Wiley & Sons, 2018.

technical exercise but also a critical risk management tool, helping practitioners avoid false confidence, uncover structural weaknesses, and validate strategic assumptions before real-world implementation.

15.1 Types of Backtests

Several methods have been used for backtesting derivative strategies. Each approach offers distinct perspectives on strategy performance, allowing portfolio managers to simulate and evaluate outcomes under varying conditions.

In evaluating the different types of backtesting methods, it is crucial to bear in mind the advice of Marcos López de Prado, who argues that backtesting should not serve as a means of refining or optimizing a proposed strategy; rather, it should be a distinct phase that validates the independent development of the strategy.[4] When optimization is introduced in backtesting, it risks overfitting, as the process may inadvertently adjust the strategy to fit historical data too closely. This practice can compromise the robustness of the results, as the backtest no longer accurately reflects how the strategy would perform in unseen market conditions. In line with this principle, a well-designed backtest should focus solely on the objective assessment of a completed strategy, thereby preserving the integrity and reliability of the results.

15.1.1 *Historical simulation method*

The *historical simulation method* is a backtesting approach that uses past returns or price changes to simulate potential future outcomes for a portfolio based on the assumption that historical price behavior can approximate future market conditions. In practice, historical simulation starts by collecting a dataset of historical returns or price changes over a specified period. These historical returns are then applied to the portfolio's current positions, effectively recalculating gains or losses as if the past market conditions were repeated in the future. However, this method has limitations. It inherently assumes that past price movements will recur similarly in the future, which can be problematic during market changes or crises, when historical patterns may not hold.

[4] López de Prado, *Advances in Financial Machine Learning.*

The method does not adjust for shifts in market volatility or correlations over time, leading to inaccuracies in risk estimation, especially if the historical data include only stable periods or omits high-volatility events. Moreover, this approach struggles to model extreme, rare events if they do not appear within the historical data window, which can result in underestimating tail risks. Another limitation is its inflexibility in generating synthetic scenarios, unlike methods such as Monte Carlo simulation, which can simulate a broader range of potential outcomes beyond historical observations.[5]

Although the historical simulation method generally aligns with Marcos López de Prado's principle that a backtest should objectively assess a completed strategy, there are nuances. Historical simulation involves applying a fixed approach to past data without refining or optimizing it during the backtesting process. This adheres to his principle of using backtesting as a purely evaluative tool. The method does not introduce optimization or adjust parameters based on backtest results, so it can maintain an objective stance, assessing how the strategy would have performed under historical market conditions. However, there is a potential caveat. Suppose historical simulation is used repeatedly with different parameter settings to identify a "best-fit" configuration. In that case, it can inadvertently lead to overfitting, which does violate his guidelines. This would occur if, for example, historical simulations are conducted in multiple trials to find a favorable outcome, essentially treating the backtest as an optimization tool. To adhere strictly to López de Prado's principle, practitioners should avoid iterative adjustments during the historical simulation and use a single set of predefined strategy parameters.

15.1.2 *Filtered historical simulation method*

The *filtered historical simulation* (FHS) method, developed by Giovani Barone Adesi, Kostas Giannopoulos, and Les Vosper,[6] is an enhancement

---

[5]For a more detailed discussion of the historical simulation method and its limitations, see Matthew Pritsker, "The Hidden Dangers of Historical Simulation." *Journal of Banking & Finance*, 30(2), 2006, 561–582.

[6]Giovani Barone Adesi, Kostas Giannopoulos, and Les Vosper, "Backtesting Derivative Portfolios with FHS." Chapter 3 in *Simulating Security Returns: A Filtered Historical Simulation Approach* (pp. 30–65), Palgrave Macmillan, 2014. For a discussion of the limitations of the FHS method, see Pritsker, "The Hidden Dangers of Historical Simulation."

of the traditional historical simulation method, particularly effective for backtesting derivative portfolios. Traditional historical simulation uses historical price changes directly to estimate potential portfolio losses if past returns can approximate future risks. However, it does not account for current market conditions, especially the time-varying nature of volatility, which is a significant limitation when backtesting portfolios sensitive to changes in market volatility, such as derivatives.

The FHS method addresses this limitation by applying a volatility model, typically a generalized autoregressive conditional heteroscedasticity (GARCH) model, to filter historical returns. This filtering process adjusts past returns to align with current market volatility, thus making the simulated outcomes more reflective of recent market dynamics. The FHS method rescales historical returns based on present volatility estimates for each backtest simulation. This adjustment allows FHS to create a distribution of potential portfolio losses that is dynamically informed by the current market environment, from which performance metrics such as Value at Risk (VaR) can be calculated more accurately.

One of the primary advantages of the FHS method over the traditional historical simulation method lies in its ability to incorporate time-varying volatility, which is particularly beneficial for derivative portfolios that are heavily influenced by shifts in volatility. Additionally, the FHS method implicitly maintains asset correlations within the simulation, preserving the relationships among assets without requiring further assumptions about correlation behavior. The incorporation of stochastic volatility also enhances the accuracy of VaR estimates by capturing a more realistic picture of potential losses under fluctuating market conditions.

However, FHS has its limitations. It assumes that correlations among assets remain constant over time, which may not always hold true, especially over longer historical periods. This assumption could lead to inaccuracies if the model does not adapt adequately to changing correlations. Adjusting the historical sample length can help mitigate this issue, but such adjustments also introduce a trade-off between estimator variability and the accuracy of risk metrics.

The FHS method conforms to López de Prado's principle when used to simulate the performance of a complete strategy without refining its rules or parameters based on the filtered data. However, if it is used to adjust the strategy based on FHS outcomes iteratively, that would breach the principle of independent strategy development before objective backtesting.

15.1.3 *Walk-forward method*

The *walk-forward method* is a robust approach to backtesting that strengthens the reliability of strategy assessments by dividing historical data into sequential segments. Developed to address the limitations of traditional historical simulation, the walk-forward method applies a rolling framework to evaluate strategy performance.[7] Unlike historical simulation, which keeps strategy parameters fixed across the entire dataset, walk-forward analysis divides data into multiple segments. Each segment contains an "in-sample" portion for optimizing strategy parameters and an "out-of-sample" portion to test them. This process is repeated across the entire dataset, simulating a dynamic trading environment where the strategy can adapt to changing market conditions.

Several key advantages make the walk-forward method preferable to traditional historical simulation. First, it reduces the risk of overfitting by optimizing strategy parameters on smaller, more relevant data samples instead of the entire historical period. This segmentation allows the method to gauge how strategies perform across varied market conditions, resulting in more resilient and adaptive strategy designs. Second, the method offers a more realistic performance assessment by testing each strategy segment on unseen data, simulating real-time application without "leakage" of future information. This iterative cycle of optimization and testing fosters consistency across time periods and supports the continued effectiveness of strategy parameters as market dynamics evolve.

Nevertheless, the walk-forward method is computationally demanding, requiring extensive data and processing power since each cycle involves optimizing and testing a new data segment. Additionally, the method's effectiveness can depend on the choices made for segment size and optimization techniques, necessitating careful planning to ensure reliable and meaningful outcomes.

It is important to note how this method's built-in optimization process may violate Marcos López de Prado's principle, which asserts that backtesting should focus solely on the objective assessment of a completed

---

[7]The walk-forward method was introduced in Robert E. Pardo, *The Evaluation and Optimization of Trading Strategies*. 2nd ed., Hoboken, NJ: John Wiley & Sons, 2008. For a comprehensive understanding of this methodology and its applications, see "How Can You Improve Your Backtesting With Walk-Forward Analysis?" at https://www.linkedin.com/advice/0/how-can-you-improve-your-backtesting-walk-forward.

strategy rather than on refining or adjusting it. In the walk-forward method, each "in-sample" segment is used to optimize strategy parameters before they are tested on the "out-of-sample" segment. This optimization step essentially adjusts the parameters to fit each data segment, tailoring the strategy incrementally to historical conditions, which is contrary to López de Prado's principle. According to López de Prado, backtesting should strictly serve as an evaluation phase for a fully formed strategy, where parameters are pre-determined and remain constant throughout the backtest. By contrast, the walk-forward method continually updates parameters, potentially leading to overfitting as the strategy adapts to each historical segment rather than being tested independently. This iterative adjustment process can compromise the robustness of the backtest by reducing the objectivity of performance results, as each parameter set is optimized specifically for each segment rather than being derived independently.

Therefore, while the walk-forward method enhances adaptability and offers a dynamic approach to changing market conditions, it conflicts with the principle of fixed, independent strategy development before backtesting. In light of López de Prado's principle, practitioners using the walk-forward method should exercise caution, balancing the benefits of segment-wise optimization with the risk of tailoring the strategy too closely to past data, potentially limiting its applicability to future, unseen conditions.

15.1.4 *Resampling method*

The *resampling method* is a backtesting technique designed to test a strategy's robustness by creating numerous hypothetical market scenarios from historical data.[8] Unlike the walk-forward method, which relies on a single sequence of historical events, resampling generates multiple synthetic datasets that simulate various potential market conditions. This approach is particularly useful in environments where strategies may need to withstand a wide range of economic cycles and interest rate environments.

In the resampling method, techniques such as bootstrap resampling are commonly applied. Bootstrap resampling involves randomly drawing

---

[8]For further reading and a detailed description of the resampling method, see Chapter 9 in David G. Luenberger, *Investment Science*. 2nd ed., Oxford University Press, 2013.

data points (often organized as quarterly or yearly blocks) from the original historical dataset, either with or without replacement. Each synthetic dataset constructed through resampling represents a possible market path that could have occurred based on historical data. By generating these multiple paths, resampling enables the backtest to evaluate a strategy's performance across varied scenarios. This diversity of simulated timelines reduces the likelihood of overfitting, as the strategy must prove resilient not just to one specific historical sequence but to a spectrum of potential market paths.

The resampling method enhances the objectivity of strategy evaluation. It challenges the strategy to perform consistently across different market environments without tailoring it to a specific historical period. Exposing the strategy to many economic conditions provides a more comprehensive assessment of its robustness and adaptability. This makes the resampling method particularly valuable for strategies that may need to perform reliably through high and low volatility cycles, differing interest rate trends, or other economic shifts.

The resampling method aligns with López de Prado's guideline that a backtest should focus on objectively assessing a completed strategy rather than refining it. Since resampling does not involve parameter optimization or iterative adjustment of the strategy itself, it adheres to the principle of evaluating a fixed, fully developed strategy. The hypothetical scenarios generated through resampling do not alter the strategy's parameters; instead, they create alternative market environments in which the predefined strategy is tested. This preserves the objectivity of the backtest by ensuring that the evaluation is based on a diverse range of economic conditions without adapting the strategy to fit any single scenario.

15.1.5 *Monte Carlo simulation method*

The *Monte Carlo simulation method* for backtesting is a versatile approach that evaluates the robustness of a trading strategy by simulating a wide variety of potential future market conditions through random sampling. Unlike traditional methods that rely solely on historical data, Monte Carlo simulations generate synthetic market scenarios using probability distributions for key variables, such as asset returns, volatility, interest rates, or exchange rates. By applying these distributions, Monte Carlo simulation creates a broad range of hypothetical outcomes that extend beyond those observed in past data. This allows for testing the strategy under diverse and hypothetical conditions, including rare or extreme events, which are crucial for assessing its stability in unlikely yet impactful scenarios.

The process begins by defining the probability distributions for the variables affecting the assets in a portfolio. These distributions are often based on historical observations but can be modified to reflect anticipated shifts or stress scenarios. Random sampling techniques generate numerous paths that simulate how these variables could evolve, producing thousands (or even millions) of possible future market trajectories. Each simulated scenario represents a unique sequence of economic and financial conditions, against which the strategy is tested to observe its performance under that specific set of assumptions. The Monte Carlo simulation provides a comprehensive view of potential risks and returns through this extensive sampling, capturing both expected and tail risks.

The flexibility of Monte Carlo simulation makes it particularly valuable for identifying tail risks, those rare but extreme events that can significantly impact portfolio performance. Including scenarios of extreme losses or highly volatile conditions reveals the variability in outcomes that may not be evident from historical-only methods. The method is commonly used in fixed-income and derivative portfolios, where returns are sensitive to interest rates or volatility. It allows portfolio managers to gauge how a strategy might respond to dramatic market changes or economic shocks.

The Monte Carlo simulation method adheres to López de Prado's guideline that backtesting should focus on evaluating a completed strategy, free from iterative adjustments. Since Monte Carlo simulation relies on predefined probability distributions and does not involve changing the strategy's parameters during the backtest, it avoids the risk of overfitting associated with parameter adjustments. Instead, the approach tests the strategy's robustness by subjecting it to a range of independent, probabilistically generated scenarios. This maintains the objectivity of the backtest, as the strategy is evaluated on a fixed rule set across varying simulated market conditions rather than being tailored to fit any particular scenario.

15.2 Data Requirements for Backtesting

Accurate and comprehensive data are the foundation of reliable backtesting for derivative strategies. Given the complexity of derivatives, data requirements go beyond simple price histories to include volatility measures, interest rates, transaction costs, and liquidity indicators. These data elements are essential for constructing backtests that realistically capture the dynamics of derivative instruments, which respond not only to underlying asset prices but also to market volatility, time decay, and other factors unique to derivatives.

15.2.1 *Historical pricing data for derivatives*

Unlike traditional assets, derivatives such as options and futures require granular historical data to assess their performance accurately. This includes the historical prices of the underlying assets and the prices of the derivatives, along with bid-ask spreads. Historical volatility data are critical in derivative backtesting, particularly for options, as they directly affect pricing. Additionally, implied volatility data, which reflect the market's expectations of future volatility, provide insight into how an option's price may respond to changing market conditions. As López de Prado emphasizes, high-quality data are non-negotiable in quantitative finance, especially when backtesting complex instruments such as derivatives, as poor data quality can lead to misleading or biased results.[9]

15.2.2 *Volatility and interest rate data*

Volatility is a key component in derivatives pricing, and backtests must account for its impact over time. Historical volatility, often calculated over various lookback periods, helps evaluate how past price fluctuations would have affected derivative performance. For options, implied volatility, available through options chains, is essential for backtesting, as it reflects the market's expectations of future volatility, impacting premium calculations. Furthermore, interest rates play a role in pricing derivatives, particularly futures and options, where the cost of carry and discount rates are fundamental inputs. Interest rate data should be collected over the relevant backtesting period to adjust for rate-sensitive strategies, especially those involving interest rate derivatives or swaps.

---

[9] López de Prado, *Advances in Financial Machine Learning.*

15.2.3 *Transaction costs and liquidity data*

Transaction costs and liquidity constraints are critical when backtesting derivative strategies, as derivatives often incur higher costs and can be less liquid than traditional assets. Transaction costs include brokerage fees, bid-ask spreads, and, for options, premiums. Failing to include these costs in backtests may overstate the strategy's potential returns. Liquidity data, such as trading volume and open interest, provide insight into how easily a derivative position could be opened or closed without significantly impacting its price. In thinly traded derivatives markets, price slippage and difficulty executing large trades can affect strategy performance, making liquidity data essential for backtesting accuracy.

15.2.4 *Incorporating data for margin and leverage considerations*

Many derivatives require a margin to cover potential losses, particularly in futures and options trading. Margin data and leverage ratios must be included in the backtest to reflect the strategy's capital requirements and risk exposure accurately. Leverage amplifies gains and losses, so simulating these effects in backtests is crucial to understanding the strategy's real-world implications. López de Prado highlights that failing to consider leverage in backtests can lead to unrealistic expectations, as it ignores the compounded effects of leveraged positions on portfolio risk and return.[10]

15.2.5 *Data quality and integrity*

Maintaining data quality and integrity is fundamental to effective backtesting. Data errors, such as missing values, incorrect timestamps, or inaccuracies in historical prices, can lead to biased results. To mitigate these risks, López de Prado recommends rigorous data validation processes, including cross-referencing with multiple data sources, to ensure consistency and accuracy throughout the backtest.[11] Additionally, employing data purging and embargoing techniques can help prevent the influence of

---

[10] *Ibid.*

[11] *Ibid.*

future data on past periods, a common issue in time-series data that can lead to look-ahead bias.

15.3 Key Metrics for Performance Evaluation

When backtesting derivative strategies, selecting appropriate performance metrics is crucial for accurately assessing potential profitability and risk. Derivatives exhibit unique characteristics, such as leverage, time decay, and sensitivity to volatility, requiring metrics that account for these factors. In backtesting, selecting the right mix of performance metrics is essential to accurately assess the viability of derivative strategies. By choosing appropriate metrics and adjusting them to account for the unique properties of derivatives, portfolio managers can develop a more nuanced understanding of potential risks and returns, enhancing the reliability of backtesting results. This section explores essential performance metrics to evaluate derivative strategies effectively, including profitability, risk-adjusted returns, and derivative-specific measures such as the Greeks.

15.3.1 *Profitability measures*

Profitability measures allow portfolio managers to determine if a strategy can achieve its return objectives over time. Simple measures, such as cumulative or average monthly returns, provide a quick snapshot of performance, but derivative strategies benefit from more nuanced metrics that account for risk.

Cumulative return and *annualized return* over the backtest period offer an overview of total profits, while annualized return normalizes performance, allowing comparisons across different time periods. *Risk-adjusted returns* (e.g., Sharpe and Sortino ratios) are vital for evaluating derivative strategies, considering both return and risk. The Sharpe ratio, which divides excess return by standard deviation, is widely used, but the Sortino ratio is often more appropriate for derivatives because it focuses on downside risk. This makes it particularly useful in options-based strategies, where protecting against downside risk is frequently a priority.

In addition to the standard Sharpe ratio, it is essential to account for the potential inflation of Sharpe ratios due to multiple testing biases. David Bailey and Marcos López de Prado introduce the concept of the

Deflated Sharpe Ratio (DSR), which corrects for selection bias and overfitting.[12] This adjustment is particularly relevant in backtesting frameworks where multiple strategies are tested, as it reduces the risk of data-mining bias by factoring in the probability of false positives. The DSR provides a more accurate reflection of strategy performance by adjusting the Sharpe ratio according to the number of tests conducted and the variance in Sharpe estimates across these trials. Incorporating DSR into backtesting practices ensures a more realistic evaluation of strategy risk and return, particularly when analyzing performance metrics derived from extensive simulations.

15.3.2 *Risk metrics*

Understanding a strategy's risk profile is critical, especially for derivatives where leverage and volatility exposure can magnify losses. Effective risk metrics include drawdown measures and volatility, which help gauge the risk associated with a strategy's returns.

The standard deviation of returns is a common measure of volatility, indicating the range of returns the strategy experienced over the backtest period. In the case of derivatives, the impact of volatility on strategy performance is particularly large, or "outsized"—meaning that it has a greater effect than usual, especially with options. This heightened sensitivity is due to the leverage and price dynamics inherent in derivatives. By monitoring both historical volatility (past fluctuations) and implied volatility (expected future fluctuations), investors can better assess the consistency of returns and gauge the risk posed by potential market movements. *Maximum drawdown measures* the peak-to-trough negative return decline in value over the backtest period, offering insights into potential losses during adverse market conditions. Average drawdown complements this by showing the typical decline in the strategy's value, providing a fuller view of downside risk. Derivative strategies, particularly those using leverage, can exhibit significant drawdowns, so these metrics are essential.

---

[12]David H. Bailey and Marcos López de Prado, "The Deflated Sharpe Ratio: Correcting for Selection Bias, Backtest Overfitting, and Non-Normality." *Journal of Portfolio Management*, 40(5), 2014, 94–107.

In addition to standard risk metrics, it is essential to account for the potential inflation of Sharpe ratios due to multiple testing biases. Campbell Harvey and Yan Liu emphasize that Sharpe ratios calculated in a setting where multiple strategies are tested can overstate a strategy's significance and profitability.[13] They recommend adjusting Sharpe ratios by applying a 'haircut' that varies with the initial Sharpe level and the number of tests conducted, providing a more accurate reflection of strategy performance. This adjustment helps reduce data mining biases and ensures that only genuinely significant Sharpe ratios are interpreted as such in performance evaluations.

15.3.3 *Derivative-specific metrics: The Greeks*

In options strategies, evaluating the Greeks (delta, gamma, vega, and theta) is essential, as these metrics reveal how sensitive an option's value is to changes in the underlying factors. The Greeks provide insight into both the performance potential and risks inherent in the strategy.

Delta measures the sensitivity of an option's price to changes in the underlying asset's price. A high delta means the option's value moves closely with the underlying asset, which is relevant in strategies replicating directional exposure. Monitoring delta in backtests helps assess whether a strategy achieves its intended market exposure.

Gamma represents the rate of change in delta in relation to price movements in the underlying asset. High gamma values indicate greater volatility in delta, which affects how sensitive the strategy is to shifts in the underlying asset's price. Backtesting gamma helps portfolio managers understand the stability of the strategy's exposure, especially in fast-moving markets.

Vega measures an option's sensitivity to changes in implied volatility, which is critical for strategies such as volatility arbitrage or those involving short options positions. High vega values mean the option is highly responsive to volatility changes, so tracking vega in backtests can help portfolio managers gauge how volatility shifts might impact strategy performance.

Theta, or *time decay*, quantifies the rate at which an option loses value as it approaches expiration. Theta is particularly relevant in income-oriented options strategies, such as covered calls, where portfolio

---

[13] Campbell R. Harvey and Yan Liu, "Backtesting." *Journal of Portfolio Management*, 42(1), 2015, 13–28.

managers seek to benefit from time decay. Monitoring theta in backtests ensures that the strategy's income expectations align with actual decay rates, providing a realistic assessment of potential profits.

15.3.4 *Other evaluation metrics*

In addition to standard profitability, risk, and derivative-specific metrics, some strategies may benefit from additional performance measures considering market conditions and leverage.

VaR estimates the maximum potential loss over a given time frame with a specified confidence level. VaR effectively measures tail risk for leveraged derivative strategies, providing a quantifiable assessment of the maximum expected loss during market stress. *Conditional Value-at-Risk* (CVaR), or expected shortfall, goes beyond VaR by estimating the average loss during extreme market events. CVaR is particularly relevant for tail-risk hedging strategies, where protecting against severe downturns is a primary objective.

15.4 Backtesting Process for Different Derivative Strategies

Backtesting derivative strategies involves testing them under realistic market scenarios to evaluate their effectiveness. Different derivative strategies have unique objectives for income, risk management, or tactical asset allocation. This section discusses specific backtesting processes for key categories of derivative strategies: income, risk management, and asset allocation/tactical overlay.

15.4.1 *Income strategies: Covered calls, cash-secured puts*

Income strategies with derivatives, such as covered calls and cash-secured puts, are popular in equity portfolios seeking enhanced yield. The backtesting process for these strategies should simulate the income generated from option premiums while accounting for market conditions, such as volatility and price trends, which influence option pricing.

In backtesting a covered call strategy, it is essential to establish parameters for strike prices, expiration dates, and the frequency of writing options. Portfolio managers typically select out-of-the-money calls to collect premiums while maintaining upside potential. For cash-secured puts, backtests should reflect how often options are exercised and the resulting acquisitions at lower prices.

The primary focus in backtesting income strategies is on premium income and downside risk. Metrics such as average monthly premium income, time decay (theta), and the frequency of option exercises provide insight into whether the strategy meets its income objectives. Additionally, the backtest should examine how well these strategies protect the portfolio during downturns.

15.4.2 *Risk management strategies: Tail hedging, credit risk management*

Risk management strategies, including tail hedging and credit risk management with derivatives, aim to limit downside risk during extreme market conditions. The backtesting process for these strategies requires scenario testing, stress testing, and examining the effectiveness of hedges over different market phases.

Tail risk hedging with derivatives, such as put options, protects portfolios from sharp declines. Backtesting these strategies involves simulating significant market downturns and testing the impact of premiums paid on overall returns. Stress testing scenarios, such as the 2007–2008 Global Financial Crisis (GFC) or the 2020 COVID-19 pandemic, can assess whether the hedge effectively mitigates losses. Key metrics include the strategy's drawdown reduction and its impact on the portfolio's overall return.

Credit default swaps (CDSs) hedge against default risk in bond portfolios. The backtesting process for CDS strategies should simulate a large number of scenarios with default occurrences in coherence with the bonds' credit ratings. Credit rating agencies' default probability tables are a helpful reference for doing so, as are the agencies' recovery rates, which give informed estimates of the loss given default. By taking averages across the scenarios, one can get an idea of the return and risk perspectives of bond investments subject to default risk. Introducing contagion effects between bonds in the backtest is possible by assuming a non-zero correlation between default events. In that case, scenarios are generated using a multivariate probability distribution rather than by a set of independent univariate distribution functions.

Going beyond the business-as-usual setting, one can simulate periods of widening credit spreads and higher default rates, focusing on the hedge's efficacy in mitigating stressed credit risk. Metrics such as spread changes, default probabilities, and the cost of CDS premiums are essential for evaluating this strategy.

15.4.3 *Asset allocation and tactical overlay strategies*

Derivatives are widely used in asset allocation strategies to adjust exposures dynamically and implement tactical overlays. Backtesting these strategies requires simulating how futures, options, or swaps impact asset allocation shifts and tactical exposures in response to market conditions.

Futures contracts allow portfolio managers to adjust exposure to asset classes, such as equities or fixed income, without reallocating the underlying assets. Backtesting these strategies involves examining the timing of futures positions, the costs associated with rolling contracts, and the effect on overall portfolio performance. Metrics such as return volatility, tracking error, and Sharpe ratio provide insight into the success of these futures-based shifts.

Tactical overlays using derivatives involve temporary exposure adjustments to capture short-term market trends. Backtesting these overlays requires simulating shifts in market sentiment and macroeconomic factors that may affect short-term performance. For example, using FX derivatives for tactical currency exposure in international portfolios can be backtested by modeling currency movements based on interest rate differentials and geopolitical events.

15.4.4 *Practical backtesting considerations*

When backtesting derivative strategies, it is essential to account for realistic market constraints, such as transaction costs, slippage, and margin requirements. These factors can materially impact performance, particularly for strategies involving high-frequency trading or complex derivative positions. Incorporating these costs in backtests provides a more accurate view of net returns and helps assess the feasibility of implementing the strategy in real-world markets.

Marcos López de Prado also suggests that strategies should be tested on both in-sample and out-of-sample data to avoid overfitting. López de Prado advises embarking and purging data to ensure that a backtest reflects a realistic trading environment without leakage from future information.[14] These techniques are particularly relevant in derivatives backtesting, where predictive accuracy and avoiding hindsight bias are crucial to reliable performance evaluation.

Out-of-sample (OOS) testing is a widely used method for strategy validation, but it has certain limitations. Harvey and Liu caution that repeated adjustments based on OOS tests can lead to biases, as researchers may unintentionally fit the strategy to past data rather than future conditions.[15] They suggest using OOS testing in conjunction with multiple-testing adjustments to address these limitations to balance type I and type II errors. By combining these methods, practitioners can achieve a more accurate assessment of a strategy's true viability, ensuring that performance metrics are not merely the result of favorable data splits.

15.5 Challenges and Pitfalls in Backtesting Derivative Strategies

Backtesting derivative strategies is complex and presents several unique challenges, as derivatives are sensitive to volatility, time decay, and leverage. Without careful attention to potential pitfalls, backtests can produce misleading or overly optimistic results. This section addresses common challenges and pitfalls in backtesting derivative strategies, including overfitting, data biases, transaction costs, and the modeling of derivative-specific risks.

15.5.1 *Overfitting and data-snooping bias*

Overfitting occurs when a backtested model is excessively optimized for historical data, resulting in a strategy that may perform well in-sample but fails to generalize to new data. This problem is widespread in derivative strategies, where numerous parameters (such as strike prices, expiration dates, and notional amounts) can be adjusted to maximize historical returns. *Data-snooping*, meaning repeatedly testing a strategy on the same dataset until favorable results are found, exacerbates this issue and can lead to spurious findings.

---

[14] López de Prado, *Advances in Financial Machine Learning.*

[15] Harvey and Liu "Backtesting."

López de Prado emphasizes the importance of purging and embargoing data to mitigate data-snooping bias, recommending that researchers split their data into training and testing sets to ensure that future information does not inadvertently influence the backtest results.[16] Using OOS testing or cross-validation can further validate that a strategy will perform in real-world scenarios, enhancing the robustness of derivative backtests.

In addition to data purging and embargoing techniques, cross-validation offers an effective approach to mitigating backtest overfitting. Harvey and Liu propose that using cross-validation techniques can help reduce the likelihood of overfitting by comparing the relative performance of a particular strategy among a pool of alternative strategies.[17] This method provides an extra layer of validation by testing the strategy across multiple data samples, enhancing the reliability of backtest results and supporting a more robust evaluation.

15.5.2 *Ethical reporting and multiple testing bias*

In backtesting, ethical transparency is critical to ensure that performance results accurately reflect a strategy's viability. A key challenge in this area is the risk of selection bias under multiple testing (SBuMT), a phenomenon where conducting multiple tests on a strategy can inflate apparent performance due to the increased likelihood of false positives. In backtesting, this bias can arise when researchers perform numerous trials on strategy variations but report only the most favorable results, potentially misrepresenting a strategy's true effectiveness.

Marcos López de Prado and I emphasize the importance of transparent reporting to mitigate the risks associated with SBuMT.[18] We propose a framework that encourages practitioners to disclose the full extent of all tests conducted, including any unsuccessful trials. This level of transparency ensures that the backtest results are not merely a product of repeated testing but a genuine assessment of the strategy's robustness. By adopting such ethical reporting practices, asset managers and researchers can

---

[16] López de Prado, *Advances in Financial Machine Learning.*

[17] Harvey and Liu, "Backtesting."

[18] Frank J. Fabozzi and Marcos López de Prado, "Being Honest in Backtest Reporting: A Template for Disclosing Multiple Tests." *Journal of Portfolio Management*, 45(1), 2018, 141–147.

enhance the credibility of performance claims and align with rigorous scientific standards.

15.5.3 *Look-ahead bias and survivorship bias*

Look-ahead bias, where information from the future unintentionally influences backtesting results, is a major concern in derivatives because of the unique time sensitivity of options, futures, and swaps. Look-ahead bias can lead to inflated returns by incorporating information not available at the time of decision-making. Ensuring that the backtest framework only uses data available up to each decision point is essential to avoid this bias.

Survivorship bias is another common issue, especially when working with historical data that may exclude derivatives or issuers that are no longer active. Excluding failed or delisted instruments can result in a skewed view of historical performance. Including all available instruments, even those that eventually expire worthless or fail, gives a more accurate picture of the risks and rewards associated with the strategy.

15.5.4 *Transaction costs and slippage*

Transaction costs and slippage are particularly relevant to derivative strategies, as they can significantly impact net returns. Derivatives often involve higher bid–ask spreads, fees, and margin requirements than those for traditional assets. For high-frequency or complex strategies, these costs can quickly erode potential profits. Additionally, *slippage*—the difference between the expected price of a trade and the actual execution price—can affect derivatives more than other asset classes, especially in less liquid markets or during times of high volatility.

Backtests should incorporate realistic transaction costs and account for potential slippage, particularly in frequent trading strategies. Estimating these costs accurately can prevent overly optimistic projections and provide a more realistic assessment of the strategy's viability. López de Prado underscores the importance of including transaction costs in backtesting, as omitting them can lead to inflated expectations and unrealistic performance results.[19]

---

[19]López de Prado, *Advances in Financial Machine Learning.*

15.5.5 *Modeling derivative-specific risks*

Derivatives introduce unique risks, including sensitivity to changes in volatility, time decay, and counterparty risk, that must be carefully modeled in backtests. For options, the Greeks (delta, gamma, theta, and vega) affect how the option's value changes over time and in response to the underlying asset's price movements. Neglecting these factors can lead to inaccurate backtesting results, particularly in options strategies where changes in volatility and time decay significantly impact outcomes.

For instance, theta, which represents the rate of time decay, is critical in income-generating strategies like covered calls. As options approach expiration, time decay accelerates, which must be reflected in the backtest to represent income accurately. Similarly, for volatility-based strategies, backtests should model shifts in implied volatility, as volatility tends to fluctuate significantly over time and can materially affect option premiums.

15.5.6 *Margin requirements and leverage constraints*

Leverage is inherent to many derivatives, amplifying both potential gains and losses. However, margin requirements can change unexpectedly, especially in volatile markets, impacting the strategy's risk and return profile. For instance, futures and options strategies often require collateral or margin deposits that increase as volatility rises, forcing portfolio managers to post additional capital or reduce positions.

Incorporating margin requirements and the effects of leverage into backtests ensures that the strategy's capital needs are accurately represented. Failing to account for leverage constraints can lead to unrealistic results, as it overlooks the potential for margin calls during adverse market movements. Additionally, López de Prado suggests stress-testing leveraged strategies to assess how they might perform under extreme conditions, as this helps reveal potential weaknesses that could emerge during volatile periods.[20]

---

[20] *Ibid.*

15.6 Challenges with Data Quality and Integrity

High-quality data are crucial for derivative backtesting, but obtaining clean, consistent, and comprehensive data for complex instruments can be challenging. Missing data, incorrect timestamps, errors in historical option prices, and implied volatility values can lead to inaccurate backtesting results. Ensuring data quality through rigorous validation and cross-referencing multiple sources can help minimize errors and improve the reliability of the backtest.

As López de Prado emphasizes, data quality is paramount in quantitative finance, particularly in derivative backtesting, where errors in historical pricing, volatility measures, or interest rates can distort results. Routine data validation and purging and embargoing techniques can mitigate the risk of data inaccuracies, ensuring that the backtest produces realistic and actionable insights.[21]

By understanding and addressing these common pitfalls in derivative backtesting, portfolio managers can improve the robustness of their analyses and reduce the risk of implementing untested or overly optimistic strategies. Addressing overfitting, transaction costs, margin requirements, data quality, and derivative-specific risks provides a more accurate view of a strategy's potential, enhancing confidence in backtesting results.

15.7 Interpreting and Applying Backtesting Results

Backtesting provides valuable insights, but interpreting and applying these results requires a careful understanding of both the limitations of backtesting and the context of the strategy being evaluated. This section outlines best practices for analyzing backtesting outcomes, identifying potential adjustments, and communicating findings effectively. It also discusses the importance of transparency, stress-testing, and accounting for real-world constraints to ensure that strategies are actionable and adaptable.

15.7.1 *Understanding limitations in backtesting outcomes*

Although backtesting can give a detailed view of how a strategy might perform under historical conditions, it does not guarantee future success.

[21] *Ibid.*

A backtest's validity is often limited by data quality, model assumptions, and market dynamics that may not replicate in the future. Therefore, interpreting backtest results requires a critical assessment of the underlying assumptions and an understanding that even robust backtests cannot account for all potential market scenarios.

One common misinterpretation of backtesting results is assuming that strong historical performance will lead to similar future outcomes. Market conditions, liquidity, and volatility change over time, affecting derivatives due to their sensitivity to these factors. When interpreting backtesting results, it is essential to consider how recent or extreme market conditions may differ from historical data used in the backtest.

Strategies that depend on specific assumptions, such as stable volatility levels or consistent transaction costs, may underperform if those assumptions prove inaccurate in real-world conditions. Sensitivity analysis, or testing how results vary when assumptions change, can provide insights into a strategy's robustness under different conditions. As López de Prado suggests, incorporating sensitivity analysis and avoiding overoptimization can prevent the backtest from being overly dependent on a narrow set of assumptions.[22]

15.7.2 *Adjusting strategies based on backtesting insights*

Backtesting should confirm the viability of a strategy and highlight areas for improvement. A well-designed backtest will identify weaknesses, such as excessive drawdowns or high sensitivity to certain market conditions, allowing portfolio managers to make informed adjustments before implementing the strategy.

Backtesting results can reveal how parameters affect performance, such as strike prices in options strategies or leverage levels in futures overlays. Adjusting these parameters based on backtesting insights can improve strategy resilience and reduce risk. However, balancing parameter adjustments with the risk of overfitting is important, ensuring that the strategy remains robust across various scenarios.

Running the strategy through hypothetical or extreme scenarios—such as sudden market crashes, interest rate spikes, or currency devaluations—can highlight additional vulnerabilities. These scenarios enable portfolio managers to adjust hedging levels, leverage, or other

[22] *Ibid.*

parameters to strengthen the strategy against unexpected events. Stress-testing derivatives is especially crucial given their potential for leverage and amplified losses during market stress.

15.7.3 *Communicating backtesting results and assumptions*

Transparency in reporting backtesting results is essential, mainly when strategies are presented to clients or investment committees. Effective communication should outline the strategy's objectives, assumptions, performance metrics, and any limitations affecting real-world outcomes. It is also important to disclose all costs, potential biases, and the frequency and rebalancing method.

Outlining the assumptions behind the backtest (e.g., static volatility, constant transaction costs, or margin requirements) provides context to help stakeholders interpret the results accurately. By disclosing these assumptions, portfolio managers can set realistic expectations and prevent misinterpretation of the backtest.

Presenting key metrics, such as Sharpe ratios, maximum drawdowns, and cumulative returns, in an accessible format (e.g., charts and graphs) allows stakeholders to understand the strategy's risk-return profile quickly. Graphs comparing the strategy's performance under various market conditions can highlight its strengths and weaknesses, enhancing the transparency of backtesting results.

15.7.4 *Accounting for real-world constraints*

Backtesting results often assume perfect execution, full liquidity, and consistent market conditions, which are rarely achievable in real-world trading. When applying backtesting results, portfolio managers should consider practical limitations, such as slippage, counterparty risk, and regulatory constraints, which may affect strategy implementation.

Real-world trading includes transaction costs, liquidity constraints, and slippage, especially for derivative strategies involving high trading frequency or large position sizes. Estimating these additional costs and potential execution issues can provide a more realistic view of net returns. For instance, a backtest of a high-frequency options strategy should adjust for bid-ask spreads, potential market impact, and slippage.

Derivative strategies may be subject to regulatory constraints, particularly regarding leverage limits, margin requirements, and reporting obligations. Integrating compliance-related factors into the backtest helps ensure the strategy is implementable within regulatory guidelines, avoiding potential risks associated with non-compliance.

15.7.5 *Enhancing reliability with purging and embargoing*

As López de Prado emphasizes, purging and embargoing are essential practices in backtesting to avoid data leakage and look-ahead bias.[23] Purging removes any data that could unintentionally reveal future outcomes, while embargoing restricts the reuse of the same data across multiple testing iterations. Applying these practices enhances the reliability of backtesting results by ensuring that past information does not improperly influence future outcomes, particularly for time-sensitive instruments like options and futures.

15.8 Enhancing Robustness in Backtesting

Ensuring the robustness of backtesting results is critical in creating reliable, actionable derivative strategies. Without robust testing, backtests may produce overly optimistic outcomes that fail under real market conditions. This section focuses on strengthening the robustness of backtesting processes, including using rigorous data-handling techniques, implementing realistic scenarios, and incorporating advice from industry experts such as Marcos López de Prado on avoiding biases and overfitting.

15.8.1 *Implementing rigorous data handling and validation*

Data accuracy is foundational to a robust backtest. Historical pricing, volatility data, and transaction costs are essential inputs that must be validated to prevent biases or errors. Additionally, derivatives often require more granular data than traditional assets, such as time-stamped prices for high-frequency trading or historical implied volatility for options.

---

[23] *Ibid.*

Ensuring data integrity through cross-verification with multiple sources is essential for producing valid results.

Data quality is improved by regularly cleaning data to remove outliers, address missing values, and ensure consistency across time frames. For example, inconsistent timestamps or erroneous price spikes can distort derivative backtesting results, so conducting thorough consistency checks minimizes these risks.

As recommended by López de Prado, purging and embargoing data are effective ways to mitigate look-ahead bias and data leakage. Purging involves removing any information from the dataset that could inadvertently reveal future market behavior while embargoing restricts the reuse of the same data across multiple testing iterations.[24] These practices help avoid scenarios where knowledge of future outcomes affects the model, which is particularly important in derivatives backtesting where market conditions can shift rapidly.

15.8.2 *Using out-of-sample testing and cross-validation*

Backtests should include both in-sample and out-of-sample data to verify a strategy's robustness. In-sample testing evaluates the strategy on historical data used to develop it, while out-of-sample testing assesses performance on unseen data, simulating real-world conditions. Cross-validation, or dividing data into multiple training and testing sets, allows for repeated testing across different segments of historical data.

Out-of-sample testing ensures that a strategy does not rely solely on patterns in the backtest data, providing a more realistic gauge of future performance. For instance, a volatility-based options strategy could be tested out-of-sample during different market conditions, such as high-volatility periods and stable markets, to verify its resilience across scenarios.

Cross-validation further strengthens backtest reliability by splitting data into subsets and rotating them between training and testing sets. This approach identifies if the strategy is overfitted to specific data segments, improving generalization and robustness for real-world applications.

---

[24] *Ibid.*

15.8.3 *Stress testing and scenario analysis*

Stress testing and scenario analysis are essential for understanding how derivative strategies may perform during extreme market conditions. Derivatives, particularly leveraged instruments, are sensitive to market shocks, making stress testing critical in assessing risk.

Simulating extreme events, such as the GFC or the 2020 COVID-19 pandemic, enables managers to examine how strategies withstand significant volatility. For example, testing a tail-risk hedging strategy during these periods shows if it can effectively protect against sudden downturns.

Creating scenarios based on hypothetical events, such as an interest rate spike or currency devaluation, can enhance robustness. These custom scenarios are valuable for assessing the limits of a derivative strategy's effectiveness in responding to specific risks, such as interest rate derivatives during rapid rate increases.

15.8.4 *Using synthetic data for extended analysis*

Synthetic data generation can provide additional testing scenarios for derivative strategies that require more extensive testing data, especially in rare market conditions. Synthetic data are artificially generated to mimic actual market behavior, allowing for scenario testing that might not be available in historical data alone.

López de Prado highlights the potential of using machine learning to generate synthetic data that mirror the behavior of real markets.[25] This approach allows for the creation of unique datasets, such as high-volatility environments or specific economic conditions, to test the resilience of a derivative strategy further. Synthetic data are handy for tail-risk or volatility-based strategies, as it simulates extreme events without reliance on limited historical data.

While synthetic data enhance robustness by introducing more scenarios, they should be used carefully to avoid overreliance on artificial patterns. Testing a strategy with synthetic data complements, but should not replace, historical testing, as real-world market behavior may differ from generated data.

---

[25] *Ibid.*

15.8.5 *Avoiding overfitting and optimizing realistic parameters*

Overfitting, or excessive strategy optimization to historical data, is a common pitfall in backtesting. Derivative strategies are particularly prone to overfitting due to the variety of parameters that can be fine-tuned, such as option strike prices, expiration dates, and leverage levels. Portfolio managers should aim for simplicity and avoid excessive parameter adjustments to ensure robustness.

Placing realistic constraints on parameters—such as setting limits on strike price ranges or leverage ratios—helps prevent overfitting. By keeping the strategy straightforward and limiting the number of adjustable parameters, portfolio managers reduce the likelihood of tailoring the backtest to historical quirks that may not repeat.

Regularization techniques, common in machine learning, can prevent a model from becoming too complex. López de Prado recommends penalizing overly complex models to maintain generalizability, which can be applied to backtesting by limiting model complexity and ensuring the strategy remains adaptable.[26]

15.8.6 *Documenting assumptions and reporting results transparently*

Transparency in reporting backtesting assumptions and results enhances a strategy's credibility and allows others to validate the findings. Documenting assumptions such as transaction costs, margin requirements, and rebalancing frequency ensures that stakeholders understand the context of the results.

Explaining assumptions, parameter selections, and data sources help prevent misinterpretations. By documenting each aspect of the backtest, portfolio managers create a reference point for replicating or modifying the strategy, facilitating continuous improvement. Consistent reporting of key metrics, such as cumulative returns, Sharpe ratios, and maximum drawdowns, across different backtesting scenarios enables comparison and supports informed decision-making. Transparent reporting allows stakeholders to assess whether a strategy meets its intended objectives and aligns with portfolio goals.

---

[26] *Ibid.*

15.9 Summary

In this chapter, I present a detailed framework for backtesting derivative strategies, focusing on the distinct complexities that derivatives introduce, such as embedded leverage, nonlinear payoffs, path dependency, and sensitivity to changing market conditions. I show why backtesting is foundational in evaluating these strategies, enabling practitioners to measure potential risk and return characteristics before actual capital is committed. By relying on a properly constructed backtest, I aim to help those involved in backtesting avoid costly implementation errors and false confidence that often stem from oversimplified assumptions or incomplete modeling.

I walk through the core components necessary to build a robust backtesting system, starting with the required data types. These include historical prices, implied and realized volatility, margin requirements, and estimates of transaction costs and slippage. I also explain why capturing contract-level details such as exercise style, cash versus physical settlement, and liquidity constraints is crucial when evaluating derivative-based strategies. These considerations allow the backtest to reflect more realistic trading conditions and improve the credibility of its output.

To demonstrate how different testing approaches can shape one's strategy interpretation, I explore five distinct methodologies: historical simulation, filtered historical simulation, walk-forward analysis, Monte Carlo simulation, and resampling. I describe each method's mechanics and assumptions, outlining when and why it may be appropriate. For example, I show how walk-forward analysis helps identify strategy degradation over time, while Monte Carlo simulation can test performance under extreme but plausible market scenarios. I emphasize that no method is inherently superior because each has trade-offs, and choosing the right tool depends on the type of derivative strategy being tested.

Throughout the chapter, I emphasize the critical importance of following sound principles to preserve the integrity of the backtest. Drawing on the work of Marcos López de Prado, I explain how to avoid data leakage and overfitting by using techniques such as purging and embargoing. I highlight the ethical responsibility to report results transparently, to disclose all versions of tested strategies, and to refrain from using backtests as a tool for *post hoc* optimization. These practices are essential for backtesting to remain a credible foundation for research and implementation in derivatives trading.

I also address operational and risk considerations in real-world testing and strategy deployment. I explain how margin requirements, liquidity constraints, and position sizing rules can materially affect performance outcomes and may render a seemingly successful strategy unworkable in practice. By incorporating these constraints into the testing process, I ensure that the results reflect feasible trading behavior and risk management protocols.

Finally, I tie these components together to present a coherent and practical guide for evaluating derivative strategies. By adhering to a rigorous backtesting discipline and integrating statistical techniques and domain-specific expertise, I show how practitioners can identify which strategies are robust, scalable, and aligned with institutional objectives. In short, I provide a roadmap for building trust in strategy performance, one grounded in realism, transparency, and analytical rigor.

Part 4

Institutional and Corporate Applications of Derivatives

Chapter 16

Derivatives in Corporate Treasury Management

Corporate treasurers safeguard the firm's financial health by managing liquidity, funding, interest rate exposure, currency risk, and, where applicable, commodity price volatility. Within this mandate, derivatives are deployed not for speculation but as tools to reduce earnings volatility, stabilize cash flows, and protect against adverse financial outcomes. Their application is driven by the need to align financial outcomes with the firm's business strategy, satisfy board-mandated risk policies, and meet investor expectations for financial predictability.

16.1 Strategic Framework and Applications of Derivatives in Treasury Management

To understand how corporate treasurers use derivatives in practice, it is essential to examine both the strategic intent behind their use and the specific instruments employed across different risk categories. This section outlines the internal frameworks that govern derivative usage, the primary types of exposures addressed, and the evolving practices shaping treasury operations today. From board-approved risk policies to real-world applications in interest rate, currency, and commodity markets, the following discussion highlights how derivatives are integrated into the day-to-day responsibilities of treasury teams seeking to manage risk and support broader financial objectives.

16.1.1 *Strategic purpose and governance*

Internal risk management frameworks guide the use of derivatives by corporate treasury functions, typically set out in board-approved hedging policies. These policies define the types of risk exposures that may be hedged, the permitted instruments, and the operational limits for hedging activities. In most cases, the objective is risk reduction, not profit generation. For example, a manufacturing firm with global operations may hedge foreign currency receivables to protect forecasted cash flows, or a company issuing floating-rate debt may use an interest rate swap to lock in its funding cost for debt. Unlike asset managers, corporate treasurers typically do not take open derivative positions or directional views on market movements.

16.1.2 *Core applications and instruments*

Corporate treasurers use derivatives across three primary risk domains: foreign exchange (FX), interest rates, and commodities. These instruments are critical for managing exposures that arise from global operations, financing structures, and supply chain dynamics.

FX exposure typically arises when firms engage in cross-border trade, operate foreign subsidiaries, or consolidate earnings in a single reporting currency. FX forwards and options are the most commonly used instruments for hedging forecasted revenues or expenses, intercompany dividends, or anticipated currency conversions associated with capital expenditures. For instance, a U.S.-based company expecting to receive €10 million in 90 days may use a forward contract to lock in the exchange rate, ensuring predictability in dollar-denominated revenues.

Interest rate derivatives, including swaps, caps, and collars, allow corporate treasurers to manage exposure to floating-rate debt or changes in funding costs. For example, a company with debt indexed to the Secured Overnight Financing Rate (SOFR) might enter a pay-fixed interest rate swap, effectively converting floating-rate obligations into synthetic fixed-rate loans. Conversely, firms anticipating rate declines may use swaps to move from fixed to floating exposures, reducing interest expenses over time.

Organizations are increasingly integrating derivatives into treasury operations to enhance their ability to manage financial risk. Swaps, forwards, and options have become essential tools for treasurers, enabling them to hedge against interest rate fluctuations, currency volatility, and commodity price changes. The strategic use of these instruments helps stabilize cash flows, improve the predictability of interest expenses, and shield profitability from adverse market movements. For example, interest rate swaps can convert variable-rate debt into fixed-rate obligations, while FX forwards and options help firms lock in exchange rates to protect future international revenues.[1]

These practical applications are broadly reflected in global treasury behaviors. A major international survey by Erasmo Giambona, John Graham, Campbell Harvey, and Desare Bodnar of over 1,100 risk managers found that nonfinancial firms primarily use derivatives to increase expected cash flows, cited by 87% of respondents.[2] Other key motivations include reducing earnings volatility (80%) and meeting shareholder expectations for risk mitigation (70%). Regarding instrument usage, 67% of firms use interest rate swaps, primarily in the over-the-counter (OTC) market, while 64% rely on FX forwards to manage currency risk. In contrast, commodity risk is more often managed through operational strategies, such as supplier diversification, with only 39% of firms using financial derivatives.

This preference for operational hedging is not limited to commodities. The study showed that 88% of firms manage credit risk operationally, compared to 40% using derivatives. Key deterrents to broader derivatives usage include regulatory burdens, accounting complexity, and risk aversion. In fact, 30% of firms indicated a reduction in hedging activity if forced to use only standardized derivatives under mandates such as Dodd–Frank. Collateral requirements and counterparty risk are significant concerns, cited by 70% and 68% of firms, respectively.

The 2022 Deloitte Global Treasury Survey reinforces these patterns, particularly in FX risk management.[3] Among 245 global treasury professionals, 76% reported using derivatives (primarily forwards, swaps, and futures) to hedge FX exposures, often complemented by operational methods such as internal netting. However, treasury teams face

[1] Deloitte. "Deloitte Global Treasury Survey 2022." *Deloitte Development LLC*, 8 Nov. 2022, www2.deloitte.com/content/dam/Deloitte/us/Documents/risk/us-deloitte-global-treasury-survey-2022.pdf.

[2] Erasmo Giambona, John R. Graham, Campbell R. Harvey, and Cesare Bodnar. "The Theory and Practice of Corporate Risk Management." *Journal of Financial Economics*, 149(3), 2023, 812–836.

[3] Deloitte. "Deloitte Global Treasury Survey 2022."

significant implementation challenges: 82% struggle with timely exposure identification, while 71% cite accurately forecasting cash flows as a hurdle.

Recent industry studies show that the use of derivatives is expanding in both scope and sophistication.[4] Treasury teams are hedging traditional exposures and adopting tools that integrate real-time data and visualization capabilities to better understand and manage their derivatives positions proactively. This shift from manual and fragmented processes to integrated treasury platforms enables faster, more informed decision-making, particularly in volatile macroeconomic environments.

Treasurers are also using derivatives to support broader strategic goals. A 2023 FEI Daily survey, sponsored by Northern Trust, found that 26% of corporate treasurers plan to increase allocations to ultra-short and short-term bond funds, often in combination with derivatives overlays.[5] In addition, 42% expect to use ESG-linked derivatives, such as green deposits or sustainability-linked swaps, reflecting a shift toward aligning financial risk tools with corporate responsibility initiatives.[5]

At the same time, caution remains warranted. A 2019 Kellogg Insight study of 87 oil and gas companies revealed that 62% of firms used derivatives for non-hedging purposes, such as earnings smoothing or meeting analyst expectations.

Finally, risk infrastructure is critical. A Capital Advisors Group white paper emphasized that concentrated counterparty exposure remains one of the most serious post-2008 risks in corporate derivative usage. The report advocates for diversified counterparties, limits tied to credit ratings, and outsourcing risk oversight in resource-constrained treasury departments.

Together, these studies reveal a treasury environment where derivatives are central to managing interest rate and FX exposures but are also increasingly used in liquidity management, portfolio optimization, and sustainability integration. As product use grows more sophisticated, governance frameworks, technology infrastructure, and internal expertise must also adapt to it.

---

[4] *Ibid.*

[5] "Survey: How Treasurers Are Positioning Cash With Possible 2024 Rate Volatility." FEI Daily, 18 Dec. 2023, www.financialexecutives.org/FEI-Daily/December-2023/Survey-How-Treasurers-Are-Positioning-Cash-With-Po.aspx.

16.2 Real-World Illustrations

Corporate treasurers use derivatives widely among large, globally integrated firms. Here are four examples. These cases illustrate the diversity of instruments used and the alignment of hedging strategies with each company's underlying business model.

16.2.1 *Delta Air Lines (fuel hedging)*

Delta Air Lines has a long history of using derivatives, including futures, swaps, options, and collars, to manage its exposure to jet fuel price volatility, especially during rising oil prices. These instruments have been deployed to lock in fuel costs, stabilize operating budgets, and support long-term financial planning. For example, *Forbes* reports that Delta's hedging strategy has involved buying futures contracts and call options and even acquiring the Monroe Energy refinery to provide a physical hedge against volatile market prices.[6] Industry coverage affirms that output from this refinery acts as a partial hedge, while short-term derivative contracts remain central to Delta's inventory hedging operations.[7]

However, Delta's hedging programs' effectiveness has been mixed, and a growing body of empirical research highlights both the strengths and limitations of such strategies. For example, a 2015 study by Peter Turner and Siew Hoon Lim found that derivatives, such as heating oil futures, can reduce jet fuel price volatility, but the reduction is only partial and inconsistent. No single cross-hedge instrument (not even heating oil) fully eliminates risk, and the choice of instrument and time horizon significantly affects the results.[8]

Case studies and simulations show that Delta has used various combinations of swaps, collars, and futures to hedge fuel costs over time, often with modest success. Compared to peers such as Southwest Airlines,

---

[6]"Delta Buys Oil Refinery in Fuel Hedging Bet." *Forbes*, April 30, 2012, www.forbes.com/sites/christopherhelman/2012/04/30/delta-buys-oil-refinery-in-fuel-hedging-bet.

[7]"Delta Refines Its Fuel Hedging with Monroe Energy." *Reuters*, August 18, 2015, www.reuters.com/article/us-delta-fuel-idUSKCN0QN1ZC20150818.

[8]Peter A. Turner and Siew Hoon Lim. "Hedging Jet Fuel Price Risk: The Case of U.S. Passenger Airlines." *Journal of Air Transport Management*, 42, 2015, 220–227. *PMC*, https://pmc.ncbi.nlm.nih.gov/articles/PMC7147842/.

Delta's approach has been less aggressive and more variable in outcomes. Southwest's long-term contracts have historically led to greater stability, while Delta's hedging results have fluctuated depending on market timing and strategy execution.[9]

From a performance perspective, Delta historically hedged a significant portion of its fuel consumption, typically more than American Airlines but less than Southwest. According to a 2009 study by Robert Trempski, about 16% of the variation in Delta's stock price returns from 1996 to 2005 was explained by changes in jet fuel prices and the broader market.[10] Still, the study did not find significant direct evidence that Delta's hedging activities dominated stock price variability. Hedging practices may have helped reduce fuel costs as a share of operating expenses; however, outcomes were also heavily influenced by macroeconomic events, such as Delta's 2005 bankruptcy.

Hedging gains and losses also varies widely with market conditions. For example, in years with sharp oil price drops (such as 2009), hedging positions often generated losses, reducing firm value. Yet, when such outlier periods are excluded, studies find that effective hedging correlates positively with firm value due to better cash flow stability and financial control.[11]

Recent analyses reinforce that airlines, including Delta, are increasingly divided over the benefits of fuel hedging. As oil price volatility increases, some carriers report hedging gains that soften the blow of market spikes, while others experience limited protection or outright losses.[12] These divergent outcomes highlight the importance of hedge design, timing, and adaptability.

---

[9] Wenqing Zou. "Research on Airline Fuel Hedging Strategies—Case Analysis and Literature Review." *Highlights in Business, Economics and Management*, 2024, https://pdfs.semanticscholar.org/86bc/334009d9a37cf6e5b1098f6fce707d64247c.pdf.

[10] Robert Trempski. "Does Fuel Hedging Add Value? Quantitative Analysis but Qualitative Insight." *Undergraduate Economic Review*, 5(1), 2009, Article 9. https://digitalcommons.iwu.edu/cgi/viewcontent.cgi?article=1065&context=uer.

[11] Brian Hornung. "Does Hedging Success Matter? An Empirical Study of Jet Fuel Risk Management." *University of South Florida Theses and Dissertations*, 2020, https://digitalcommons.usf.edu/cgi/viewcontent.cgi?article=9422&context=etd.

[12] Nicholas Dunbar. "Airlines Divided on Hedge Benefits as Oil Volatility Surges." *EuroFinance*, 28 Nov. 2018, www.eurofinance.com/news/airlines-divided-on-hedge-benefits-as-oil-volatility-surges/.

In summary, Delta Air Lines' use of derivatives reflects a well-established commitment to fuel cost management through financial engineering. The company's experience demonstrates that hedging can reduce risk, but it is not a guaranteed source of cost savings or value creation. Success depends on market conditions, strategic design, and disciplined execution. In the broader industry context, Delta's case underscores the view that hedging is a valuable tool but not a fail-safe solution.

16.2.2 *Cargill (commodities hedging)*

Cargill, as one of the world's largest agricultural commodities traders, routinely uses derivatives, including futures, options, swaps, and structured products, to hedge exposures to grains, oilseeds, freight rates, and currency volatility. Regulatory filings and legal documents from the Commodity Futures Trading Commission (CFTC) confirm that Cargill structures contracts with embedded price options and actively manages associated risks through positions in related futures and options markets.[13] For example, CFTC records reveal that Cargill's hedging strategies for grain producers often involve price optionality contracts (POCs). These contracts combine forward contracts with embedded options to allow producers to lock in floor prices while retaining upside potential. Cargill dynamically hedges these contracts using exchange-traded futures and options to neutralize risk.

Beyond agriculture, Cargill's risk management arm (Cargill Risk Management, or CRM) offers derivatives in energy, metals, and currencies to institutional clients. Industry analyses highlight CRM's use of barrier options, calendar averaging swaps, and accumulator swaps to tailor solutions for clients in volatile markets such as Brazilian sugar (hedged against real-dollar forex risk) and dairy commodities.[14] For instance, during the Brazilian real's 30% depreciation in 2015, CRM executed non-USD hedges for sugar producers, enabling them to lock in floor prices in local currency while mitigating forex exposure.

---

[13] *In the Matter of Cargill, Inc.* Commodity Futures Trading Commission, www.cftc.gov/sites/default/files/idc/groups/public/@lrdispositions/documents/legalpleading/idcargill112200.pdf.

[14] "Agricultural Commodities House of the Year: Cargill." *Risk.net*, 3 June 2016, www.risk.net/commodities/2458389/agricultural-commodities-house-of-the-year-cargill.

CFTC enforcement actions further illustrate the scale and complexity of Cargill's derivatives activity. In 2021, the CFTC fined Cargill $750,000 for swap reporting failures, including omissions in extensive trader reports and inaccurate commodity reference price data, a lapse attributed to internal system errors during a swap data repository transition.[15]

Cargill's derivatives framework is supported by its unique regulatory status as a limited-purpose swap dealer, a designation granted in 2013 that allows it to act as a derivatives dealer for agricultural and energy commodities while maintaining physical trading operations.[16] This structure enables CRM to offer OTC derivatives alongside physical commodity contracts, leveraging Cargill's global supply chain expertise to design hedges that align with clients' operational risks.

16.2.3 *ExxonMobil (foreign exchange and commodity hedging)*

ExxonMobil selectively uses derivatives to hedge FX risk related to its international operations. Analyses of ExxonMobil's financial risk management practices indicate that the company uses derivatives such as futures, swaps, and options to manage exposures to commodity price risk, interest rate fluctuations, and, when material, foreign exchange risk. While the impact of FX fluctuations is often immaterial to ExxonMobil's overall results, the company's use of derivatives for risk mitigation is well established in financial reporting and industry analysis.[17]

With respect to ExxonMobil's specific hedging strategies for commodity risk exposure, it specifies the following: "The following

---

[15] "CFTC Orders Cargill to Pay $750,000 for Swap Reporting Failures." *Commodity Futures Trading Commission*, 30 Sept. 2021, www.cftc.gov/PressRoom/PressReleases/8442-21. Earlier actions, such as a 2017 $10 million penalty for misrepresenting mid-market marks on swaps, underscore the operational challenges of managing derivatives transparency while balancing profitability. (See, *In the Matter of Cargill, Inc.*, CFTC Docket No. 18-03 (2017). Quimbee, www.quimbee.com/cases/in-the-matter-of-cargill-inc.)

[16] "CFTC Approves Limited Purpose Swap Dealer Designations for Cargill." *Commodity Futures Trading Commission*, 2, 2013, www.cftc.gov/PressRoom/PressReleases/6756-13.

[17] "Financial Risk Management: Exxon Mobil Hedging Strategies." *Desklib*, 14 March 2023, desklib.com/document/finance-assignment-hedging-strategies-assignment/.

particulars are demonstrative of the recommended derivative, the CME Crude Oil call options contract." It then provided the following:

Exposures to be hedged	Cost of purchasing the crude oil, USD1.04 B
Percentage proportion to be hedged	Fifty percent (50%)
Derivative to be used	CME crude oil options contract
No. of derivative contract each hedged	10400000000/27 = 385185185 contracts
Delivery months for each derivative	December 2017
Prices at the time of recommendations	USD27

It was accompanied by the following text:

> The company's engagement in the call option will allow Exxon Mobil to hedge the firm's position changes in the crude oil prices. Via the purchase of the call option, in case the strikeprice are beneath the market prices, Exxon Mobil will be able to exercise the option at the expiry date (December 2017) and take the advantage of the low prices. On the other hand, in case the strike price of the contract is above the market price, then Exxon Mobil can opt for no exercising the firm's option. Exxon Mobil, therefore, shall confine its downside of the premium paid to the writer of the option, nevertheless, the advantage benefits can go as higher as the surge in the crude oil prices in the market.

16.2.4 *Barrick Gold (gold forwards and collars)*

Barrick Gold has long been recognized as a pioneer and innovator in using gold derivatives to manage earnings volatility and optimize financial outcomes. Its hedging program, which became a case study at Harvard Business School,[18] was foundational to the company's strategy and capital structure. In the early years, Barrick primarily relied on simple forward

---

[18] The Harvard Business School Case Study by Peter Tufano is a foundational teaching and analytical resource on Barrick's risk management. It contrasts Barrick's hedging policies with those of its competitors, explains the mechanics of gold loans, forwards, options, and spot deferred contracts, and analyzes the strategic and operational implications of Barrick's approach. Peter Tufano, "American Barrick Resources Corporation: Managing Gold Price Risk." *Harvard Business School Case*, 293–128, April 1993. (Revised October 1995).

sales contracts; however, over time, the company developed a more sophisticated suite of instruments, including gold forwards, collars, and spot deferred contracts. These contracts allowed Barrick to lock in future revenues, reduce exposure to adverse spot price swings, and, crucially, often realize prices above the prevailing spot market.

A hallmark of Barrick's approach was its ability to negotiate highly flexible contract terms. For example, the company could roll contracts forward for up to around 10 years, an advantage made possible by the scale of its reserves and the strength of its balance sheet. This flexibility enabled Barrick to manage its hedge book actively, maximizing interest income and adapting to changing market conditions. Over a decade, industry estimates suggest that Barrick's hedging program contributed several hundred million dollars in additional revenue and earnings, corresponding to a meaningful premium over average spot prices, rather than attempting to time the market, helped the company secure favorable terms and maintain financial flexibility.

Academic and industry studies confirm that gold producers made extensive use of derivatives to hedge price risk, with Barrick among the most active and systematic users in the sector. For instance, a 2016 study by Tufano and others document the prevalence of gold price hedging among major producers, with Barrick's program often cited as a benchmark for best practice. Analysts have also noted that Barrick's consistent and disciplined approach to hedging, adding to its positions regularly rather than attempting to time the market, helped the company secure favorable terms and maintain financial flexibility.

However, Barrick's hedging strategy was not without controversy. As gold prices began to climb in the 2000s, the company's large hedge book, which had previously provided stability, became a liability. Mark-to-market losses mounted as the fixed prices in its contracts lagged the rising spot market, prompting Barrick to accelerate the elimination of its gold hedge book by 2009. By unwinding these contracts, Barrick regained full exposure to the upside of the gold price, reflecting a strategic shift in response to changing market dynamics.

In summary, Barrick Gold's use of derivatives, spanning forwards, collars, and innovative spot deferred contracts, set an influential standard for risk management in the mining sector and illustrates both the potential benefits and the evolving challenges of large-scale commodity price hedging.

16.3 Regulatory and Accounting Considerations

Without hedge accounting, derivative gains and losses must be recorded in current earnings, which can increase reported earnings volatility even when the underlying economic risk is mitigated.[19] As a result, many corporate treasurers limit the use of derivatives to situations where hedge accounting treatment is available or where the financial benefits of hedging outweigh the potential accounting costs. This regulatory environment reinforces the conservative orientation of treasury operations, highlighting the importance of robust internal controls and compliance procedures.[20]

Research and professional practice affirm that qualifying for hedge accounting treatment under U.S. (SFAS 133/ASC 815) and international (IFRS/IAS 39/IFRS 9) standards helps align the timing of derivative gains and losses with the hedged risk, thereby reducing volatility in reported earnings. While hedge accounting generally results in lower reported earnings and cash flow volatility, evidence from academic studies is mixed: Some find that the mere use of derivatives or access to hedge accounting does not uniformly lower earnings volatility across all firms and periods.[21] Nevertheless, hedge accounting is a key consideration for treasurers, and many avoid using derivatives for risk management unless the resulting accounting treatment reflects the economic rationale for hedging, supporting stakeholder understanding and investor perceptions.[22]

---

[19] "Beginner's Guide to Hedge Accounting." Chatham Financial. https://www.chathamfinancial.com/insights/intro-to-hedge-accounting.

[20] To qualify for hedge accounting under SFAS 133, an entity must document the hedging relationship at inception—including the hedged item, the derivative, the risk management strategy, and a reasonable expectation of high effectiveness using statistical or other methods. Ongoing prospective and retrospective effectiveness testing, typically performed at least quarterly, is required to ensure the hedge meets the 80–125% effectiveness threshold.

[21] Johannes Rammala and Franz Eduard Toerien. "The Relationship Between Earnings Volatility and Corporate Risk Disclosures." *South African Journal of Economic and Management Sciences,* 27(1), 2024.

[22] See Veliota Drakopoulou. "Are the Recent Restatements of Financial Institutions 10K's due to the Perceived Earning Volatility Caused by SFAS 161?" *Accounting and Finance Research*, 7(4), 2018, 122–137.

Under U.S. and international accounting rules, derivatives must be recorded at fair value on the balance sheet. Hedge accounting—available for fair value and cash flow hedges—can be applied if the firm documents the hedging relationship at inception, proves its effectiveness, and maintains ongoing compliance. Studies also indicate that hedge accounting under IFRS enhances earnings transparency by reducing information asymmetry between firms and outsiders.[23]

16.4 Summary

In this chapter, I explain how corporate treasurers use derivatives to manage financial risks, support business strategy, and meet stakeholder expectations. I focus on how treasurers apply derivatives—not for speculation, but to reduce earnings volatility, stabilize cash flows, and ensure predictability in funding and currency exposures. The risks I address include interest rate movements, foreign exchange fluctuations, and, in some cases, commodity price volatility.

I describe the strategic framework that guides the use of derivatives in treasury operations. I show how board-approved risk policies define what exposures may be hedged, which instruments are permitted, and how activities are monitored. I then discuss the primary tools (i.e., interest rate swaps, FX forwards, options, and commodity contracts) and describe how treasurers use these to address specific exposures tied to global operations, capital expenditures, and financing structures.

Drawing from major surveys and empirical studies, I highlight how most nonfinancial firms use derivatives to increase expected cash flow and reduce earnings volatility. At the same time, I point out that many firms still prefer operational approaches, especially for commodity and credit risk, due to concerns about regulation, accounting complexity, and counterparty risk. I also describe how treasury teams increasingly adopt ESG-linked derivatives, use derivatives overlays in short-duration portfolios, and turn to real-time platforms to better monitor and manage exposures.

I include several real-world examples to illustrate how firms apply these strategies. I show how Delta Air Lines uses a mix of derivatives to

---

[23] Argyro Panaretou, Mark B. Shackleton, and Paul A. Taylor. "Corporate Risk Management and Hedge Accounting." EFMA Annual Meeting Papers, Milan, 2009.

hedge jet fuel costs, though with mixed success. I describe how Cargill tailors commodity and currency hedging using structured products and price optionality contracts. I explain ExxonMobil's selective approach to FX and crude oil hedging, including its use of call options. Finally, I examine Barrick Gold's extensive use of gold forwards and collars, which offered long-term benefits but eventually required unwinding as market conditions changed.

I close the chapter by addressing the regulatory and accounting environment. I explain how hedge accounting under U.S. and international standards affects the timing and recognition of derivative gains and losses. Many treasurers avoid using derivatives unless hedge accounting treatment is available, given the risk of increased reported earnings volatility. I also emphasize that qualifying for hedge accounting requires rigorous documentation, effectiveness testing, and ongoing compliance, reinforcing the need for strong internal controls.

Chapter 17

Derivatives in Commercial Banking

The use of derivatives in commercial banking differs significantly from their application in corporate treasury functions. While corporate treasurers typically use derivatives to hedge identifiable exposures such as future interest payments or currency conversions, commercial banks deploy derivatives as part of a portfolio-level strategy that encompasses the institution's entire balance sheet and income statement risks.

This distinction reflects the unique role of commercial banks as financial intermediaries and liquidity providers, whose business models depend on maturity transformation, interest rate spreads, and credit intermediation. As a result, banks face multidimensional risks, including interest rate, currency, credit, and liquidity risks, that cannot be effectively managed on a transaction-by-transaction basis. Instead, banks use derivatives to optimize their net interest margin, manage their economic value of equity (EVE), and meet regulatory capital and liquidity requirements across a broad portfolio of loans, securities, and funding instruments.

Structural changes in banking and regulatory expectations partly drove the shift to portfolio-based risk management. Since the 1990s, banking institutions have moved from a model focused primarily on credit quality to integrating market, liquidity, and operational risks in a consolidated risk framework. Derivatives, especially interest rate swaps, caps, floors, swaptions, and currency forwards, have become key instruments in executing this shift.

As Franklin Allen and Anthony Santomero argued, the modern financial intermediary is not just a lender of funds but an active transformer and manager of risks.[1] This perspective explains why derivatives are central to this role, enabling banks to hedge, restructure, or transfer risk exposures more efficiently than through traditional asset-liability tactics alone. This conceptual framework underpins much of the derivative activity in commercial banking today.

As this chapter will show, commercial banks use derivatives to hedge individual trades and align balance sheet dynamics with strategic objectives, improve capital efficiency, and meet regulatory expectations for robust risk management. These uses require strong governance, modeling capability, and an understanding of how derivative exposures integrate with broader bank risk positions.

17.1 Evolution of Risk Intermediation in Banking

The evolution of derivatives used in commercial banking reflects a broader transformation in how banks manage risk. Originally, derivatives were used primarily for sensitivity exposures, such as mismatches in interest rate sensitivity or foreign currency obligations. Over time, banks developed more sophisticated risk management frameworks and built dedicated derivatives desks to support hedging and trading functions.

The distinction between hedging and trading is critical. Hedging involves using derivatives to offset pre-existing risk exposures and reduce volatility in income or capital. These activities are typically aligned with asset-liability management (ALM), where banks aim to maintain a stable net interest margin and protect EVE. In contrast, trading with derivatives involves intentionally taking on market risk to profit from price movements, meet client demand, or manage warehouse risk in preparation for securitization or asset sales.

The growth of trading operations has expanded the scope of derivatives use far beyond traditional balance sheet hedging. Banks increasingly maintain centralized derivatives trading desks, often co-located

---

[1]Franklin Allen and Anthony M. Santomero. "The Theory of Financial Intermediation." *Journal of Banking & Finance*, 21(11–12), 1997, 1461–1485.

with their capital markets functions. These desks execute hedging strategies for ALM and business units and act as profit centers, engaging in market-making, client facilitation, and, in some cases, proprietary trading. However, proprietary trading is now tightly restricted under the Volcker Rule, a provision of the Dodd–Frank Act that prohibits banks from making speculative investments with their capital, except in limited circumstances such as market-making or risk-mitigating hedging activities.

As Allen and Santomero point out, commercial banks don't simply lend money but actively manage a spectrum of risks using financial instruments.[2] What started as credit transformation has evolved into a much broader role, thanks partly to the rise of over-the-counter (OTC) derivatives. These contracts allow banks to fine-tune their risk exposures and shift risk across different markets as needed.

Tools such as interest rate swaps, currency swaps, caps, floors, and credit derivatives enable banks to shape their overall risk profile, not only at the loan level but also across entire portfolios. For instance, if a bank is concerned that falling interest rates will hurt returns on its loan book, it might use a receive-fixed, pay-floating swap to lock in earnings. Similarly, credit default swaps (CDSs) can help hedge against concentrated credit exposure or protect loans temporarily held before being bundled and sold through securitization.[3] These instruments are no longer only about managing risk in ALM but are also used in product pricing, deal structuring, and liquidity strategy.

Over time, banks have built out specialized derivatives desks to manage this complexity. These teams work closely with front-office units, treasury, capital markets, and risk departments to help align the bank's balance sheet with its broader goals. As emphasized in regulatory guidance such as the OCC's *Comptroller's Handbook on Risk Management of Financial Derivatives*, measuring and managing risk-adjusted performance across different business lines now depends heavily on the models, data, and discipline that these centralized desks bring.

---

[2] *Ibid.*

[3] Securitization refers to the process of pooling financial assets such as loans or mortgages and packaging them into securities that can be sold to investors. This allows banks to transfer credit risk off their balance sheets and free up capital for new lending.

17.2 Asset-Liability Management Integration

One of the primary ways commercial banks utilize derivatives is to support their ALM strategies. ALM is all about ensuring the structure of a bank's assets (such as loans and securities) aligns with its liabilities (such as deposits and borrowings) in a manner that protects profitability and manages risk. In this context, derivatives play a key role in stabilizing the bank's net interest margin (i.e., the difference between interest earned on assets and interest paid on liabilities), especially when interest rates move unexpectedly.

Interest rate swaps are among the most commonly used derivatives in ALM. A bank that lends primarily at fixed rates but funds itself with short-term, floating-rate deposits may be exposed to rising rates, which increase its funding costs without a corresponding rise in income. To address this mismatch, the bank may enter a pay-fixed, receive-floating swap, which offsets some interest rate risk by generating floating-rate income that moves in line with its liabilities. Conversely, banks with floating-rate loans and fixed-rate funding might use receive-fixed, pay-floating swaps to create a more stable earnings profile.

Caps and floors are also used to shape interest rate exposure, particularly in uncertain environments. A bank may enter an interest rate cap to protect against rates rising above a certain level while still benefiting if rates fall. These derivatives offer flexibility without requiring banks to fully commit to a fixed or floating position.

Derivatives are also central to managing the bank's EVE, a long-term measure of how interest rate changes affect the value of assets and liabilities. While gap analysis and duration matching can help identify imbalances, they often don't offer real-time solutions. That's where derivatives come in. They allow banks to adjust exposures quickly, especially in response to shifts in the yield curve or market volatility.

Banks use derivatives not to simply manage risk but to do so efficiently as well. Rather than restructuring the balance sheet directly, such as by replacing loans or deposits, derivatives offer a capital-light and more flexible way to rebalance exposures. This is particularly useful in a regulatory environment where capital and liquidity requirements, such as those outlined in Basel III, the global banking framework developed after the 2007–2008 Global Financial Crisis (GFC), restrict how quickly and aggressively banks can adjust their balance sheets. Basel III imposes stricter capital ratios, leverage limits, and liquidity standards, making derivatives a more flexible tool for managing risk without triggering regulatory penalties or capital inefficiencies.

At the same time, effective derivatives use in ALM requires strong governance. This includes board-approved hedging policies, clear risk limits, regular performance monitoring, and independent risk oversight. Tools such as value-at-risk (VaR) models, stress testing, and scenario analysis enable banks to understand how derivatives perform under various interest rate and market conditions. As the OCC's guidance on derivatives use emphasizes, these controls are essential for ensuring that derivatives support, rather than undermine, the institution's overall risk strategy.[4]

In sum, derivatives allow banks to manage interest rate and liquidity risk without having to restructure the entire balance sheet. This gives them the flexibility to protect earnings, meet capital requirements, and remain competitive, even in the face of volatile markets. The following section will focus on how banks apply derivatives across broader risk categories and regulatory mandates.

17.3 Regulatory Oversight and Risk Controls

As the use of derivatives in commercial banking has grown more sophisticated, so too have expectations for how these instruments are managed and overseen. Regulators recognize the value of derivatives in hedging and managing risk. However, they also emphasize the need for strong governance, rigorous controls, and precise documentation to prevent misuse or unintended exposures.

In the U.S., the OCC has provided longstanding guidance on the prudent use of financial derivatives. According to OCC Bulletin 1997-43, banks must maintain board-approved policies, independent oversight, and comprehensive risk management frameworks to support their derivatives activities.[5] Institutions are expected to clearly distinguish between hedging, trading, and arbitrage purposes and ensure that derivative transactions

---

[4] *Office of the Comptroller of the Currency.* "Risk Management of Financial Derivatives." OCC Bulletin 1997-43, 26 Oct. 1997, https://www.occ.gov/publications-and-resources/publications/comptrollers-handbook/files/risk-mgmt-financial-derivatives/pub-ch-risk-mgmt-financial-derivatives.pdf.

[5] *Ibid.*

are appropriately measured, monitored, and reported. The OCC guidance stresses the importance of:

- defining the objectives and permissible uses of derivatives,
- establishing quantitative exposure limits,
- conducting regular stress testing and scenario analysis,
- maintaining internal audit and compliance review functions,
- ensuring transparency in valuation models and pricing assumptions.

Basel III, the global regulatory framework developed by the Basel Committee on Banking Supervision in response to the GFC, also introduced stricter capital adequacy, leverage, and liquidity standards.[6] Under Basel III, derivatives contribute to the calculation of a bank's risk-weighted assets and must be backed by sufficient capital to absorb potential losses.

The framework also requires banks to post variation and initial margin for many OTC derivatives and to account for counterparty credit risk through measures such as the Credit Valuation Adjustment (CVA). CVA is an adjustment to the fair value of a derivative that reflects the risk of counterparty default, based on the likelihood that the counterparty may fail to fulfill its obligations and the potential loss given default. Under Basel III, banks must hold capital against CVA risk, even without actual default, because changes in a counterparty's credit spread can cause mark-to-market losses.[7] This ensures that credit deterioration is captured proactively and factored into pricing and capital planning.

To comply with these requirements, banks must track exposures on a net basis and often utilize central counterparties (CCPs) for standardized derivatives to mitigate systemic risk. Derivative portfolios must be incorporated into Internal Capital Adequacy Assessment Processes (ICAAPs) and linked to economic capital and VaR models. This ensures that derivative risks are not treated in isolation but are integrated into the bank's overall capital planning.

---

[6]Basel Committee on Banking Supervision. "Basel III: A Global Regulatory Framework for More Resilient Banks and Banking Systems." *Bank for International Settlements*, revised June 2011, www.bis.org/publ/bcbs189.htm.

[7]Basel Committee on Banking Supervision. "Guidelines: Capital Requirements for Bank Exposures to Central Counterparties." *Bank for International Settlements*, Apr. 2014, www.bis.org/publ/bcbs282.htm.

Beyond quantitative measures, regulators expect qualitative rigor in governance and accountability. Derivative use must be documented, not only from a trade execution standpoint but also with purpose statements, hedge effectiveness testing, and accounting alignment under standards such as ASC 815 (formerly FAS 133). Banks must demonstrate that derivative contracts serve legitimate risk-mitigation or client-facilitation purposes, rather than speculative intent.

These regulatory frameworks underscore that derivatives are not "off-balance-sheet tricks" but core risk management instruments subject to the same standards of discipline, disclosure, and prudence as any other major banking activity. In fact, due to their complexity and potential for leverage, derivatives often require even greater scrutiny.

As the following section shows, commercial banks are also adapting to new demands, such as liquidity optimization, digital risk management, and ESG-aligned derivatives, that add further dimensions to the governance of these instruments.

17.4 Evolving Practices in Derivatives and Balance Sheet Strategy

The role of derivatives in commercial banking has expanded significantly, moving beyond traditional hedging to support broader balance sheet optimization, liquidity management, and operational agility. This evolution reflects both regulatory pressure and the increasing complexity of financial markets, which have prompted banks to utilize derivatives more strategically and dynamically.

One major area of innovation is liquidity and capital efficiency. Derivatives now play a central role in how banks manage regulatory liquidity and funding constraints under Basel III. In particular, interest rate swaps and foreign exchange (FX) derivatives are used alongside collateral management tools to shape funding profiles, mitigate the liquidity impact of margining, and improve access to high-quality liquid assets (HQLAs), especially when combined with collateral transformation and repo-based funding strategies.[8]

---

[8]Basel Committee on Banking Supervision. "Basel III: The Net Stable Funding Ratio." *Bank for International Settlements*, Oct. 2014, www.bis.org/bcbs/publ/d295.htm.

Banks are also turning to derivatives to improve flexibility in adjusting their balance sheets' risk profiles. This enables faster responses to yield curve shifts, central bank policy changes, or funding market dislocations, especially when rebalancing ALM positions or modifying the duration of fixed-income holdings.

Another area of growth is in digital and analytics-driven derivatives operations. Many banks are now consolidating risk, treasury, and trading functions onto integrated digital platforms, allowing for real-time valuation, automated collateral and margin calls, and dynamic optimization of collateral usage. These platforms support more responsive balance sheet management and improve coordination between derivatives desks and broader risk governance teams. Consistent with regulatory guidance on risk management of financial derivatives, institutions that adopt such integrated, data-driven systems are better positioned to manage market volatility and regulatory stress scenarios through disciplined, enterprise-wide risk measurement and control.[9]

In addition, stress testing and scenario analysis have become more sophisticated, integrating macroeconomic shocks, yield curve twists, and idiosyncratic counterparty events to evaluate how derivatives portfolios behave under extreme conditions. These tools go beyond traditional VaR models to assess tail risks that may arise during heightened market uncertainty. This expanded toolkit enhances the role of derivatives in defending against known exposures and preparing for more complex, regime-shifting market environments.

Overall, derivatives have moved from primarily hedging instruments to multi-purpose tools for navigating capital, liquidity, and market risk constraints. This shift requires banks to invest in stronger modeling, integrated systems, and cross-functional coordination, ensuring that the flexibility offered by derivatives is matched by a robust understanding of their risks and regulatory consequences.

17.5 Foundations of Derivatives Use in Banking Practice

Today's use of derivatives in commercial banking reflects decades of intellectual development and institutional learning. Although the modern applications are highly technical and embedded within complex digital

[9] *Office of the Comptroller of the Currency*. "Risk Management of Financial Derivatives."

systems, the foundational ideas that shaped how banks use derivatives can be traced to early academic work and major market events that redefined risk management standards.

As noted earlier, one of the most influential conceptual shifts came from the work of Allen and Santomero,[10] who argued that banks were evolving beyond their traditional role as credit intermediaries into broader risk intermediaries. Rather than simply lending and collecting interest, banks were becoming platforms that restructured, repackaged, and redistributed financial risk. This perspective highlighted the growing importance of derivatives as tools that enable financial institutions to align exposures with their strategic objectives while responding to market demands in real time.

Building on this idea, Santomero and Trester underscored that financial innovation, including the growth of derivative instruments, fundamentally alters banks' risk profiles and can amplify the complexity of managing those risks. In their analysis, the increasing sophistication of banking portfolios made traditional, narrowly siloed approaches to risk oversight inadequate, reinforcing the case for more systematic and coordinated risk management processes within banks.[11]

These academic insights anticipated many of the governance structures and regulatory frameworks that now define derivatives used in banking. Concepts such as risk-based capital, VaR, and economic capital modeling emerged alongside the proliferation of derivatives desks and portfolio-level risk strategies. The move toward internal risk modeling under Basel II and Basel III owes much to this foundational thinking.

Historical events further shaped the operational and regulatory landscape. The collapse of Barings Bank in 1995, caused by unchecked derivatives speculation, served as an early warning of the risks of poor oversight. The GFC reinforced this lesson on a global scale. It revealed how credit derivatives, particularly in opaque OTC markets, could amplify systemic risk when controls, transparency, and capital buffers were lacking. In the aftermath, regulators imposed stricter reporting, collateral, and capital requirements, notably through Basel III and national

---

[10]Allen and Santomero. "The Theory of Financial Intermediation."

[11]Anthony M. Santomero and Jeffrey Trester. "Financial Innovation and Bank Risk Taking." *Journal of Economic Behavior & Organization*, 35(1), 1998. 25–37.

supervisory guidance such as the OCC's derivatives oversight framework.

Ultimately, the foundation of modern derivatives used in commercial banking is built on a combination of theory, crisis response, and institutional adaptation. Academic research clarified the new role of banks as risk intermediaries. Market failures demonstrated the dangers of unmanaged complexity. Moreover, regulators developed the rules that now govern the use of these powerful instruments. Understanding this history is essential to appreciating why derivatives are not merely tactical tools but part of a strategic, regulated infrastructure within contemporary banking.

17.6 Managing Interest Rate Risk and Balance Sheet Duration

Interest rate risk is among the most fundamental exposures faced by commercial banks. Since most banks fund long-term loans with short-term deposits, they are vulnerable to changes in the interest rate environment. When interest rates rise, deposit costs can increase faster than the yield on long-term assets, compressing net interest margins. Conversely, falling rates may benefit funding costs but reduce asset yields.

Banks use interest rate swaps, caps, floors, and forward rate agreements (FRAs) to mitigate this risk. These instruments allow banks to synthetically adjust the duration of their liabilities or assets without altering the underlying portfolio. For instance, as noted earlier, a bank concerned about rising rates may enter a receive-fixed, pay-floating interest rate swap, effectively turning a portion of its fixed-rate loan portfolio into floating-rate exposure to reduce duration mismatch. Alternatively, banks may use pay-fixed swaps to lock in future interest revenue when holding a floating-rate loan book.

Interest rate derivatives are also critical in stress testing and the EVE frameworks banks use to assess long-term interest rate risk under different scenarios. These frameworks are integrated into regulatory reporting and internal risk management standards under Basel guidelines.[12]

---

[12] Basel Committee on Banking Supervision. *Interest Rate Risk In The Banking Book: Standards*. BIS, 2016.

17.7 Credit Risk Transfer and Credit Derivatives

While banks traditionally manage credit risk through loan underwriting and internal credit scoring, credit derivatives offer an additional tool for transferring or hedging specific credit exposures. The most widely used instrument is the CDS, which protects against default or credit deterioration of a particular reference entity or portfolio.

Banks may use CDSs in two ways: (1) to hedge loan exposure, particularly to large or concentrated borrowers, and (2) to gain synthetic credit exposure without holding the actual loan or bond. For example, a bank with substantial exposure to a specific sector, such as energy or commercial real estate, may purchase CDS protection on sector-representative issuers to offset systemic risk.

CDSs can also be used in loan syndications,[13] where the lead bank may retain economic interest but offload default risk through protection sellers. Moreover, credit-linked notes (CLNs), which embed CDS features, allow banks to transfer credit risk to investors in a bond-like format.

17.8 Managing Foreign Exchange and Cross-Border Risk

FX risk is a material concern for banks operating across multiple currencies or servicing multinational clients. Derivatives such as FX forwards, swaps, and options hedge currency mismatches in loan and deposit books, foreign-denominated funding exposures, and capital repatriation flows.

Consider a European bank issuing a loan in U.S. dollars while funding it in euros. Without hedging, the bank assumes risk on both principal and interest payments. A cross-currency basis swap allows the bank to lock in future currency exchanges and floating-rate payments in both currencies, eliminating the mismatch.

Banks may also manage structural FX risk through long-dated forwards or natural hedging strategies, such as foreign earnings

[13] Loan syndication is the process by which multiple lenders jointly fund a single loan, typically arranged by one or more lead banks. It allows risk sharing among lenders and provides large-scale financing to borrowers.

consolidation. These exposures are closely monitored within ALM and are often subject to policy limits set by board-level risk committees.[14]

17.9 Use of FRAs and Short-Term Rate Management

FRAs are widely used by commercial banks to hedge short-term rate movements, particularly in the context of managing floating-rate loan portfolios or anticipated funding costs. For example, if a bank expects to roll over funding in 90 days, it may enter a 3×6 FRA to lock in the borrowing cost between months three and six. This helps reduce uncertainty in net interest income forecasts.

FRAs are also used by banks with loan commitments indexed to short-term rates, allowing for proactive risk management before loan drawdown. FRAs are often replaced by short-term interest rate futures in liquid markets, but they remain valuable for tailor-made exposures.

17.10 Regulatory and Accounting Framework

Banks' use of derivatives is governed by the Basel III framework, which requires banks to hold capital against counterparty credit risk associated with derivative exposures. The Standardized Approach for Counterparty Credit Risk (SA-CCR) determines how these exposures are measured and is designed to provide a more accurate assessment of potential future exposure, especially for longer-dated or nonlinear instruments.

Banks must also comply with accounting standards that require derivatives to be marked to market and reported on the balance sheet. Where hedge accounting is applied, the effectiveness of the hedge must be rigorously documented and tested, which adds operational and compliance complexity. As a result, many banks operate centralized risk control units to oversee derivative usage and ensure compliance with accounting, regulatory, and internal risk limits.

---

[14] Gerhard Schroeck, *Risk Management and Value Creation In Financial Institutions*. Wiley, 2002.

17.11 Summary

In this chapter, I examine how commercial banks use derivatives as core tools for managing risk across their entire balance sheets. Unlike corporate treasurers who hedge individual exposures, I explain that banks use derivatives to address broad, portfolio-level risks (i.e., interest rate, credit, currency, and liquidity) that stem from their roles in maturity transformation and credit intermediation.

I trace how banks have evolved from using derivatives for simple hedging to relying on them for ALM, capital efficiency, liquidity planning, and regulatory compliance. Tools such as interest rate swaps, caps, floors, FX forwards, CDSs, and FRAs help banks stabilize earnings, reshape exposures, and meet regulatory standards without constantly restructuring their balance sheets.

I highlight how derivatives support ALM strategies. I also emphasize the importance of strong governance (e.g., stress testing, VaR models, hedge documentation, and board oversight) in strengthening derivatives rather than weakening a bank's financial position.

Regulatory expectations have grown alongside derivative usage. I explain how banks must follow Basel III, OCC guidelines, and accounting standards such as ASC 815, which shape capital, reporting, and risk measurement requirements. Measures such as the CVA and the SA-CCR are central to these rules.

Chapter 18

Derivatives in Investment Banking

Investment banks play a unique role in the financial ecosystem. Unlike corporate treasurers and commercial banks, which primarily use derivatives for hedging balance sheet or operational risk, investment banks use derivatives as core tools of financial engineering, deal execution, and client service.[1] Their derivatives activity is not limited to managing institutional exposure. It also extends to product innovation, underwriting support, and structuring complex financial solutions tailored to the needs of issuers and investors.

Derivatives are integral to investment banking services such as equity and debt underwriting, mergers and acquisitions, capital markets advisory, and structured finance. These applications frequently involve constructing synthetic exposures, managing embedded risks during syndication, and designing payoff profiles to meet specific client objectives. While market risk management remains essential, derivatives in this domain are typically used in a transactional, tactical, and highly customized manner.[2]

For example, Goldman Sachs uses equity options to hedge exposure from structured equity financing and pre-IPO placements. JPMorgan Chase has deployed interest rate swaps and swaptions in volatile bond

[1]For a detailed description of the role of investment bankers, see Chapter 8 in Frank J. Fabozzi, *Capital Markets: Institutions, Instruments, and Risk Management*. MIT Press, 2025.

[2]Rene M. Stulz. "Should We Fear Derivatives?" *Journal of Economic Perspectives*, 18(3), 2024, 173–192.

markets to stabilize underwriting risk. Citigroup and Deutsche Bank have applied credit default swap (CDS) indices to manage sovereign and emerging market exposures, while Barclays has structured foreign exchange (FX) overlays for clients issuing Eurobonds in currencies mismatched to their revenue base. These cases illustrate the diversity and creativity of investment banks applying derivatives to manage deal-specific and structural risks.

18.1 Transactional Hedging and Pre-Deal Risk Management

When underwriting equity or debt securities, investment banks assume temporary exposures to interest rates, FX, credit spreads, or equity prices; these exposures are hedged using derivatives to stabilize revenues and reduce capital-at-risk between deal launch and pricing. For instance, during a fixed-rate bond underwriting, the bank may enter interest rate swaps or Treasury futures to hedge against rising yields that could reduce investor demand or pressure pricing. In cross-border equity or debt offerings, FX forwards or cross-currency swaps may be used to lock in the value of proceeds or to hedge foreign-denominated issuance.[3]

The ability to hedge underwriting risk efficiently is a key factor in competitive deal pricing and internal capital allocation. These hedging strategies are typically executed by dedicated trading desks within the investment bank, often in close coordination with syndicate and origination teams.

18.2 Equity Derivatives and Client Structuring

Investment banks frequently use equity derivatives to construct structured equity solutions for clients with concentrated holdings, restricted shares, or share-based compensation packages. A typical application is the equity collar, in which a client simultaneously purchases a put option and sells a call option, effectively setting downside protection and upside participation limits. These transactions may be embedded in prepaid

[3] See Mark Deacon, Andrew Derry, and Darius Mirfendereski, *Inflation-Indexed Securities: Bonds, Swaps, and Other Derivatives*. Wiley, 2004.

forward contracts or total return swaps to provide liquidity, tax deferral, or leverage.

In IPO advisory and pre-IPO planning, banks may offer executives and early investors option overlays, lock-up hedges, or structured sales plans, using derivatives to balance liquidity, volatility, and insider restrictions.[4] Such custom solutions often rely on deep in-house derivatives expertise and require pricing models that account for path dependency, illiquidity, and counterparty risk.

18.3 Credit and Commodity Structuring

In debt capital markets, investment banks use CDSs to manage exposure to issuers during the underwriting window or to facilitate synthetic securitizations. For example, a bank underwriting a high-yield bond may purchase CDS protection to mitigate default risk until the bond is distributed. Similarly, CDS index tranches or total return swaps may transfer exposure to structured credit products.

In commodity-linked financing and project finance,[5] derivatives allow investment banks to create hedgeable cash flow structures. For instance, in energy infrastructure deals, commodity swaps can stabilize revenue streams from future output, enabling more favorable debt structuring. Investment banks may intermediate these swaps directly or arrange third-party hedging solutions for the issuer.

---

[4] Franklin Allen and Anthony M. Santomero. "The Theory of Financial Intermediation." *Journal of Banking & Finance*, 21(11–12), 1997, 1461–1485.

[5] Project finance is defined as the financing of a specific economic unit in which a lender is satisfied to look initially to the cash flows and earnings of that economic unit as the source of funds from which a loan will be repaid and equity serviced and to the assets of the economic unit as collateral for the loan within a specified risk framework. See Chapter 1 in Carmel de Nahlik and Frank J. Fabozzi, *Project Financing: Analyzing and Structuring Projects*. World Scientific Press, 2021. For a discussion on using derivatives in project financing, see Chapters 15–18 in Carmel de Nahlik and Frank J. Fabozzi, *Project Financing: Financial Instruments and Risk Management*. World Scientific Press, 2021.

18.4 Medium-Term Note Programs and Structured Notes

Investment banks frequently act as arrangers and dealers in medium-term note (MTN) programs,[6] where issuers offer bespoke securities linked to interest rates, currencies, equities, or credit indices. Derivatives such as interest rate swaps, cross-currency swaps, or equity options are used to (1) hedge issuer risk, converting back into the issuer's preferred currency or fixed/floating exposure, and (2) match investor preferences, such as providing leveraged participation, capital protection, or exposure to non-traditional indices. Investment banks play a central role in designing payoff structures, managing hedging positions, and distributing products to institutional investors.

18.5 Derivatives in Infrastructure and Project Finance

Infrastructure finance refers to financing large-scale, long-lived physical assets essential for economic productivity and public welfare. These include transportation systems (e.g., airports, rail, and highways), energy infrastructure (e.g., power plants, transmission lines, and renewables), water and waste systems, telecommunications, and social infrastructure (such as schools and hospitals). These projects are typically capital-intensive, have long economic lives, and generate stable, often regulated, cash flows.

Investment banks and financial intermediaries are central to structuring, arranging, and underwriting infrastructure transactions. Their functions include (1) designing capital structures that balance risk-sharing among sponsors, lenders, and public stakeholders; (2) underwriting and syndicating loans, issuing project bonds, and securing multilateral or

[6]An MTN is a debt instrument with the unique characteristic that such notes are offered continuously to investors by an agent of the issuer. Investors can select from several maturity ranges: nine months to one year, more than one year to 18 months, more than 18 months to two years, and so on up to 30 years. For an explanation of how MTNs are created using derivatives, see Chapter 25 in Fabozzi, *Capital Markets*.

development bank participation; (3) advising on and providing derivative contracts (e.g., interest rate swaps and currency swaps) to hedge long-term exposures; and (4) packaging mature infrastructure assets into investment-grade instruments to attract institutional investors.

18.5.1 *Specialized applications in infrastructure finance*

The use of derivatives in infrastructure finance extends beyond broad structuring roles into more targeted applications that address specific financial risks. These specialized applications, from interest rate and currency risk management to commodity price stabilization and embedded structuring, allow investment banks to tailor financing solutions that align project cash flows with investor requirements and market realities. The following sections outline how these tools enhance the financial viability and resilience of complex, long-dated infrastructure projects.

18.5.1.1 *Interest rate risk management*

Most infrastructure projects rely on floating-rate debt through syndicated loans, development bank financing, or project bonds indexed to reference rates such as the Secured Overnight Financing Rate (SOFR). Because revenues from infrastructure assets (e.g., airport gate leases and utility tariffs) are typically fixed or capped, project sponsors often enter into interest rate swaps to convert floating-rate obligations into fixed-rate liabilities. These swaps stabilize debt service requirements and improve the predictability of coverage ratios,[7] which are critical for maintaining credit ratings and ensuring debt sustainability.[8] For example, in developing airport terminals, such as the Terminal One redevelopment at JFK International Airport, interest rate swaps have been used to hedge the cost of tax-exempt bond financing issued through PPP

---

[7]Coverage ratios measure a project's or company's ability to meet debt obligations using operating income or cash flows. Lenders and credit rating agencies use coverage ratios to assess the financial stability and risk of default in long-term projects.

[8]E.R. Yescombe and Edward Farquharson. *Public-Private Partnerships for Infrastructure: Principles of Policy and Finance* (2nd ed.) Butterworth-Heinemann, 2018.

structures. By synthetically locking in long-term fixed rates, airport authorities and project special-purpose vehicles (SPVs) can align financing costs with the duration of lease agreements and passenger revenue streams.

18.5.1.2 *Currency risk mitigation in cross-border capital*

When infrastructure projects are financed with foreign capital or multilateral lending, currency risk becomes a primary concern. Project revenues are usually denominated in local currency, while financing may be in U.S. dollars, euros, or yen. This mismatch is often addressed through FX forwards, cross-currency swaps, or long-dated currency options that hedge the periodic principal and interest payments.

For instance, infrastructure projects in Latin America or Africa rely on dollar- or euro-denominated capital from international banks or development finance institutions. To ensure the stability of debt service relative to local-currency cash flows, project sponsors may enter cross-currency swaps that convert future payments into local currency equivalents at predetermined exchange rates. Institutions such as the World Bank's International Finance Corporation (IFC) and the Currency Exchange Fund (TCX) often act as intermediaries to provide these hedging instruments in emerging market transactions.[9]

18.5.1.3 *Commodity derivatives in energy and transport projects*

For infrastructure projects linked to energy prices, such as gas-fired power plants or fuel-based transport networks, derivatives hedge commodity input or output prices. For example, in public transport systems where diesel or natural gas is a significant cost component, commodity swaps or options are used to cap price exposure and ensure operating budget stability.

[9]IFC. Local Currency and Hedging Solutions. International Finance Corporation, World Bank Group, n.d.; and The Currency Exchange Fund (TCX), OECD Blended Finance Case Study, 2025.

In renewable energy projects, sponsors may use forward power purchase agreements (PPAs),[10] electricity futures, or basis swaps to hedge the spread between market and contract prices. This allows developers to lock in revenue expectations and support the structuring of non-recourse project debt.[11]

18.5.1.4 *Structuring and embedded derivatives in infrastructure bonds*

Investment banks structuring infrastructure bonds, including green bonds and revenue-backed securities, often incorporate embedded derivatives to enhance investor appeal or tailor cash flow profiles. Examples include inflation-linked bonds with Consumer Price Index (CPI) swaps, callable features hedged with swaptions, or dual-currency notes with embedded FX options. Banks act as hedging counterparties and structuring agents in these transactions, managing deal risk and optimizing payoff structures.

These instruments are particularly prevalent in European infrastructure markets, where long-dated inflation-linked cash flows are attractive to pension funds and insurers. For example, UK-based infrastructure projects have historically issued Retail Price Index (RPI)-linked bonds[12] hedged using inflation swaps, aligning debt service with inflation-adjusted revenue from long-term concessions.

---

[10] A PPA is a long-term contract where a buyer agrees to purchase electricity at a fixed price in the future. It is similar to a derivative because it locks in future pricing, helping both parties hedge against electricity price volatility. Some PPAs even settle financially, exchanging price differences rather than physical power.

[11] Claire Kreycik, Karlynn S. Cory, and Toby Couture, Cory, *Innovative Feed-In Tariff Designs That Limit Policy Costs*. National. Laboratory of the Rockies, 2011. https://research-hub.nrel.gov/en/publications/innovative-feed-in-tariff-designs-that-limit-policy-costs/.

[12] RPI bonds are inflation-linked bonds whose principal and interest payments adjust in line with the UK Retail Price Index (RPI). This structure protects investors from inflation by increasing both coupon payments and the redemption value as RPI rises. The UK government commonly issues them as index-linked gilts.

18.5.2 *Regulatory capital and risk management*

Derivatives held in trading and structuring books are subject to Basel III capital requirements, particularly under the Fundamental Review of the Trading Book (FRTB), which imposes stricter guidelines for risk measurement and model approval (Basel Committee on Banking Supervision, 2019). Investment banks must also adhere to central clearing mandates for standardized derivatives under Dodd–Frank and EMIR and must report positions to designated trade repositories.

From an accounting perspective, most derivatives in investment banking are marked to market, with gains and losses recorded in earnings. Derivative exposures and embedded features must be disclosed under IFRS 7 or FASB Topic 815, with additional reporting for counterparty risk, credit valuation adjustments, and hedge effectiveness where applicable.

Effective internal control systems are essential for monitoring risk limits, model assumptions, and exposure concentrations across derivative portfolios. These controls form part of the bank's broader risk governance framework, supporting trading desk supervision, risk management committees, and regulatory audit trails.[13]

18.6 Comparative Summary: Institutional Uses of Derivatives

In this chapter and the prior two, I examine how different types of financial institutions apply derivatives to meet their strategic and operational goals. Corporate treasurers, commercial banks, and investment banks use similar instruments, but their motivations, constraints, and implementation practices vary significantly. In this section, I compare these institutional users side by side, highlighting the core distinctions in how and why derivatives are deployed across each domain.

While corporate treasurers, commercial banks, and investment banks all use derivatives, their motivations, instruments, and applications

[13]Gerhard Schroeck. *Risk Management and Value Creation In Financial Institutions*. Wiley, 2002.

reflect each institution's unique economic functions. These differences arise not from the types of derivatives used—many of which overlap—but from how and why they are applied within each organizational context.

Corporate treasurers are primarily focused on risk mitigation and earnings stability. They employ derivatives to hedge exposures to interest rates, FX movements, and commodity prices, all of which can affect operating cash flows and financial results. Treasurers operate under strict governance policies, often requiring that each derivative position be tied to a specific exposure and eligible for hedge accounting. Their derivative use is generally defensive and policy-constrained.

Commercial banks, by contrast, manage risks at the portfolio level. Their exposure arises from transforming short-term liabilities into long-term assets and accumulating credit and market risks across their lending and investment activities. Derivatives manage interest rate and FX mismatches, protect loan portfolios, and optimize risk-weighted assets. Bank derivatives activity is integrated into asset-liability management (ALM) and governed by regulatory capital and disclosure requirements under Basel III and national accounting standards.

Investment banks use derivatives most tactically and creatively. Their derivative use is tied directly to capital markets activities: structuring deals, underwriting securities, building client solutions, and managing transactional risks. They design and price complex derivatives embedded in structured notes, cross-border offerings, and synthetic exposures. Investment banks' trading books are subject to market risk capital charges, fair value accounting, and clearing obligations. Their approach is driven by client demand, deal structure, and market innovation, often pushing the boundaries of financial engineering.

Understanding these differences is critical for evaluating the role of derivatives in the financial system and designing institutional policies, capital models, and governance frameworks tailored to each domain's risk profile.

Table 18.1 summarizes these distinctions across institutional types, highlighting differences in objectives, risk focus, instruments, and governance frameworks.

Table 18.1. Comparative Summary: Derivative Use by Institutional Type

Category	Corporate Treasury	Commercial Banking	Investment Banking
Primary Objective	Hedge operational and financial risk	Manage balance sheet and credit risk	Support transaction execution and structuring
Risk Focus	FX, interest rate, and commodity price risk	Interest rate risk, credit risk, FX exposure	Market risk, credit risk, and cross-asset structuring
Instrument Types	Forwards, swaps, options, FRAs	Interest rate swaps, FX swaps, FRAs, CDSs	Swaps, options, CDSs, structured notes, equity collars, synthetic TRSs
Typical Use Cases	Hedging forecasted cash flows or debt costs	Managing duration mismatch, hedging loan portfolios	Hedging underwriting exposure, designing structured products
Approach to Risk	Transaction-level hedging, policy-driven	Portfolio-level hedging, regulatory compliance	Tactical and transactional, client-centric structuring
Governance and Constraints	Board-approved hedging policy, hedge accounting eligibility	ALM committees, capital treatment under Basel III	Trading desk limits, risk desk oversight, FRTB compliance
Accounting Standards	FASB ASC 815/IFRS 9 hedge accounting	FASB ASC 815/IFRS 9, with rigorous effectiveness testing	Fair value accounting, derivative disclosure under IFRS 7/FASB
Regulatory Framework	SEC and internal controls	Basel III (SA-CCR), national prudential regulation	Basel III (FRTB), Dodd–Frank/EMIR, trade reporting requirements
Derivative Culture	Conservative, policy-bound	Strategic, balance sheet-integrated	Innovative, structuring-oriented, often client-driven

18.7 Summary

In this chapter, I describe how investment banks use derivatives to support client transactions and structure tailored solutions across capital markets activities. I begin by discussing how interest rate swaps and options manage exposure during underwriting, particularly in equity and debt issuance. These tools allow investment banks to reduce risk as they navigate the period between deal origination and final pricing.

I then examine how investment banks design structured equity solutions, including equity collars and prepaid forwards, to help clients manage concentrated positions. I also describe how credit derivatives such as CDSs and TRSs support credit structuring during underwriting. In addition, I discuss the role of commodity derivatives in creating hedgeable structures for energy- and infrastructure-related transactions.

Finally, I explain the use of derivatives in infrastructure finance, including interest rate and currency risk management, commodity-linked structuring, and the transfer of syndication risk through credit instruments. I conclude the chapter by comparing derivative use across corporate treasury, commercial banks, and investment banks, showing how institutional context shapes both the objectives and implementation of derivative strategies.

Part 5

Valuation Frameworks for Derivatives

Chapter 19

Futures and Forwards: Core Valuation Principles

In this chapter, I introduce the fundamental principles governing the valuation of two of the most widely used risk-sharing derivatives: forwards and futures contracts. These instruments play a central role in financial markets by enabling participants to transfer and manage various types of risk, including commodity price fluctuations, interest rate exposure, and currency volatility. Although the broader universe of risk-sharing derivatives includes swaps and other structured contracts, I focus here on the analytical tools and concepts specific to forwards and futures. This narrower scope allows me to establish a clear, self-contained valuation framework based on no-arbitrage logic and replication strategies, underpinning modern financial theory.

I develop the pricing framework using the concept of arbitrage and the law of one price. By assuming that identical cash flows must command identical prices in competitive markets, I derive conditions under which a derivative's price must align with a replicating portfolio of traded instruments. This approach enables valuation relationships for forward and futures contracts, beginning with simplified settings and extending to more general market environments. The principle of no arbitrage anchors the entire analysis and serves as the central pricing tool.

Later in the chapter, I examine how the basic pricing relationships for forwards and futures begin to break down when idealized assumptions are relaxed or contract-specific features are introduced. When the assumptions of the basic valuation model are violated, as often occurs in practice, the no-arbitrage pricing framework may require modification. I also consider how futures prices can diverge from forward prices due to the impact of daily mark-to-market. These deviations have real implications for hedging effectiveness and valuation accuracy. By highlighting these limitations and extensions, I emphasize that pricing must always be interpreted in the context of specific market conditions and contract designs.

19.1 Arbitrage

Arbitrage is a trading strategy that seeks to profit from price discrepancies by simultaneously buying and selling the same or equivalent asset in different markets. When an asset is priced lower in one market and higher in another, a trader can buy it at the lower price and sell it at the higher price, typically through a short sale in the market where the asset is overpriced. Many financial markets have mechanisms that facilitate short selling, allowing traders to implement this strategy. The result is a riskless profit, a hallmark of arbitrage. In practice, however, pure arbitrage opportunities are rare and fleeting. When they do arise, they are quickly exploited by market participants, whose actions rapidly eliminate the price difference and restore equilibrium.

Another form of arbitrage occurs when two packages of assets, portfolios, or combinations of securities trade at different prices even though they produce the same payoffs in all future states. According to the *law of one price*, a fundamental concept in finance, if two packages deliver identical future cash flows under all scenarios, they must have the same price today. An arbitrage opportunity exists when this principle is violated: The undervalued package can be bought while the overpriced package is sold short. The resulting profit, equal to the difference in their prices, is realized without risk exposure because both packages yield the same outcome regardless of which future state occurs.

To illustrate this, consider the example shown in Table 19.1. The table presents three assets, A, B, and C, available today. Each asset will have one of two possible payoffs one year from now, depending on whether state 1 or state 2 occurs. We assume these are the only two possible states over the investment horizon. This simple setup allows us to construct a package of assets A and B that replicates the payoffs of asset C and examine whether an arbitrage opportunity exists based on their prices.

Table 19.1. Price of Three Assets and Their Values in Two States

Asset	Price	Value in State 1	Value in State 2
A	\$70	\$50	\$100
B	\$60	\$30	\$120
C	\$80	\$38	\$112

Let's use the following notation:

W_A = the percentage of asset A in the package
W_B = the percentage of asset B in the package

Then, the value of a package consisting of asset A and asset B under the two states can be expressed mathematically as follows:

Package value if state 1 occurs: $\$50W_A + \$30W_B$
Package value if state 2 occurs: $\$100W_A + \$120W_B$

Can we create a package consisting of asset A and asset B that will reproduce the value of asset C regardless of the state that occurs one year from now? That is, we want to select W_A and W_B such that:

If state 1 occurs: $\$50W_A + \$30W_B = \$38$
If state 2 occurs: $\$100W_A + \$120W_B = \$112$

The value on the right-hand side of the above two equations is the value of C in each state. We can solve these two equations algebraically, obtaining a value of 0.4 for W_A and 0.6 for W_B. Thus, a package consisting of 0.4 of asset A and 0.6 of asset B will have the same payoff as asset C. How much will it cost us to construct this package consisting of asset A and asset B? As the prices of asset A and asset B are \$70 and \$60, respectively, the cost is

$$0.40(\$70) + 0.60(\$60) = \$64$$

Note that the price of asset C is \$80. Thus, for only \$64, an investor can obtain the same payoff regardless of whether state 1 or state 2 occurs as asset C. This arbitrage opportunity can be exploited by buying assets A and B in the proportions given above and shorting (selling) asset C. This action allows the investor to lock in a profit of \$16 (\$80 − \$64) today, regardless of what happens one year from now. By selling asset C, the investor must pay \$38 if state 1 occurs and \$112 if state 2 occurs. The investor will obtain the necessary amounts to make the payments in either state that result from the payoff of assets A and B. This is done without any cash outlay on the part of the investor.

The bottom line of an arbitrage strategy is that once an arbitrage opportunity is identified, to capture riskless profit, buy the cheaper package and sell (short) the more expensive one. That is, the arbitrage strategy involves the adage "buy low and sell high," a fundamental principle when investing and applicable to two packages of assets.

19.1.1 *Limits to arbitrage*

When attempting to implement an arbitrage strategy, investors may encounter practical obstacles that hinder their ability to execute the necessary trades. These impediments impose what are known as *limits to arbitrage*. Common barriers include market frictions, liquidity constraints, difficulty accessing financing, restrictions on short selling, and legal or regulatory limitations.

Arbitrage assumes a perfect capital market in which all assets can be traded freely and without cost. In such an idealized setting, trades by arbitrageurs do not affect asset prices, and exploiting mispricing does not introduce new distortions. However, in real-world markets, this assumption rarely holds. When a market is illiquid, large trades can significantly move prices. This phenomenon is known as *market impact cost,* an implicit transaction cost. The assumption of a frictionless market also ignores explicit transaction costs such as brokerage commissions, custodial fees, and bid–ask spreads. Market impact cost, by contrast, reflects the price slippage caused when executing sizable trades. It represents the difference between the execution and price that would have prevailed without the trade. A highly liquid market, by definition, minimizes market impact costs and makes arbitrage more feasible.

Another challenge arises from the need to borrow or lend funds as part of many arbitrage strategies, particularly those involving futures or forwards. The availability of capital at competitive rates is critical. If borrowing is restricted or comes at prohibitively high costs, it limits the investor's ability to carry out the trade. Similarly, many arbitrage opportunities require short selling—selling an asset not currently owned to repurchase it later—and any limitations on short selling, whether due to market infrastructure or regulatory rules, further constrain arbitrage.

Finally, legal and regulatory restrictions, such as bans on short sales during market stress or capital controls in cross-border transactions, can also prevent market participants from exploiting arbitrage opportunities, even when price discrepancies are evident.

19.2 Valuing a Futures/Forward Contracts

As discussed earlier in this book, the primary difference between futures and forward contracts lies in the timing of cash flows due to margin requirements. Although the underlying valuation principles are the same, the mark-to-market process differs between futures and forward contracts. Futures are standardized instruments that are marked to market daily through the clearinghouse, while forward contracts may incorporate negotiated mark-to-market provisions that differ in timing, frequency, and collateral requirements. As a result, valuation differences between forwards and futures arise from the distinct cash-flow and financing effects created by these settlement conventions.

In this section, we focus on deriving the value of a futures contract, recognizing that the valuation of a forward contract follows the same economic structure but adjusts for the negotiated nature of its mark-to-market and collateral terms. We begin with a numerical illustration to build intuition before presenting the formal economic model that yields the theoretical futures price.

19.2.1 *Illustrative pricing: Determining fair value through arbitrage*

To illustrate how arbitrage strategies can be used to determine the fair value of a futures contract, we begin with simplified numerical examples. These examples illustrate how discrepancies between futures prices and theoretical values create arbitrage opportunities. We examine two common scenarios: one in which the futures contract is priced above fair value, allowing for a *cash-and-carry arbitrage* strategy, and one in which the futures contract is priced below fair value, enabling a *reverse cash-and-carry arbitrage*. Each strategy demonstrates how investors can use a self-financing portfolio to lock in a riskless profit. After presenting these illustrations, we formalize the pricing logic by deriving an equation for a futures contract's theoretical (fair) value based on the relationship between the spot price, the cost of carry, and any income from the underlying asset.

19.2.1.1 *Cash-and-carry arbitrage when futures are overpriced*

Suppose there is a futures contract on an underlying asset, let's call it Asset Delta. To illustrate the determination of the fair value of this futures contract, we make the following assumptions:

1. In the spot (cash) market, Asset Delta is currently trading at $120.
2. Asset Delta pays a known cash flow of $16 per year, distributed in four quarterly payments of $4, with the next payment scheduled in exactly three months from now.
3. The futures contract expires and settles three months from today.
4. The three-month interest rate at which funds can be borrowed or lent is 6% per year.[1]

Now, suppose the futures contract is trading in the market at $126. Consider the following strategy:

- Sell the futures contract at $126.
- Buy Asset Delta in the spot market for $120.
- Borrow $120 for three months at 6% annual interest (1.5% for three months).

This strategy requires no initial capital outlay, as borrowed funds financed the purchase entirely.

At the end of the three months (the futures settlement date), the investor receives the $4 dividend (the annual dividend of $16/4) from holding Asset Delta. Asset Delta is then delivered to settle the short futures position, and the loan must be repaid. The profit from this strategy is as follows:

1. *From the futures contract*: Deliver Asset Delta and receive $126.
2. *From the loan*: Repay $121.80 (the amount borrowed plus interest for three months).[2]
3. *From dividends*: Collect $4 from Asset Delta's scheduled dividend.

Total proceeds: $126 (futures) + $4 (dividend) = $130
Total outlay: $121.80 (loan repayment)
Profit: $8.20

---

[1]To simplify the illustration, we assume simple interest is used for borrowing and lending. In later chapters on option pricing, we will adopt continuous compounding to align with the pricing models typically used in that context.

[2]Three-month interest on $120 at 6% annual rate (simple interest): 120 × 0.015 = 1.80. Total repayment = $121.80.

This profit is realized without any capital investment and regardless of the Asset Delta's market price at expiration. It is a classic example of an arbitrage profit.

In an efficient market, such an opportunity would not persist because arbitrageurs would sell the overpriced futures contract and simultaneously buy Asset Delta in the spot market, bidding up the spot price and driving down the futures price until no riskless profit remains.

This arbitrage-based approach to capturing mispricing, where the asset is purchased using borrowed funds and held until futures expiration, is known as a *cash-and-carry strategy*. The name reflects the structure: the investor borrows cash, buys the asset, and carries it until delivery under the futures contract.

19.2.1.2 *Reverse cash-and-carry arbitrage when futures are underpriced*

Now, suppose instead that the futures price for Asset Delta is \$112, rather than \$126. This pricing opens the door for a different arbitrage opportunity. In this case, the investor would employ a *reverse cash-and-carry strategy*. Consider the following steps:

- Buy the futures contract at \$112.
- Sell short Asset Delta in the spot market for \$120.
- Invest the \$120 proceeds at a 6% annual interest rate for three months.[3]

Again, the strategy requires no upfront investment since the sale of Asset Delta generates the funds needed to carry out the trade.

At the end of the three-month period:

- The short seller must repurchase Asset Delta to close the short position.
- The futures contract ensures that Asset Delta can be acquired at \$112.
- The proceeds invested from the initial short sale have earned interest during the period.

Since the asset was shorted, the seller must pay the lender of the asset the dividend that the lender would have received, \$4 in this case.

---

[3] Simple interest is assumed for clarity in this example. Continuous compounding will be introduced when we discuss option pricing models.

Let's summarize the results:

From the futures contract: Buy Asset Delta for \$112 and deliver it to close the short position.
From the investment: The \$120 invested for three months at 6% earns interest of \$1.80, for a total of \$121.80.[4]
Dividend payment: Pay \$4 to the lender of the borrowed asset.
Total proceeds: \$121.80 (from investment)
Total outlay: \$112 (purchase of asset via futures) + \$4 (dividend payment) = \$116
Profit: \$121.80 − \$116 = \$5.80

This is another riskless arbitrage profit, achieved without any capital investment. As before, such pricing inconsistencies are unlikely to persist in an efficient market. Arbitrageurs would rush to buy the underpriced futures contract and short the asset in the spot market, eventually pushing prices into alignment.

This approach is a reverse cash-and-carry strategy because it involves selling the asset first, investing the proceeds, and buying it through the futures contract. It is the mirror image of the cash-and-carry trade, serving the same purpose: eliminating pricing discrepancies between the spot and futures markets.

19.2.1.3 *Establishing the equilibrium: The fair futures price*

Is there a specific price at which neither arbitrage strategy yields a profit? Yes, the arbitrage opportunity disappears when the futures price aligns with the fair (theoretical) value. Based on the previous examples, suppose the futures contract for Asset Delta is priced at \$116. Using this price, let's examine the outcomes of both the cash-and-carry and reverse cash-and-carry strategies.

First, consider the cash-and-carry strategy:

- Sell the futures contract at \$116.
- Buy Asset Delta in the spot market for \$120.
- Borrow \$120 for three months at a 6% annual rate.

---

[4]Three-month interest on \$120 at 6% annual rate (simple interest): 120 × 0.015 = 1.80. Total return = \$121.80.

Three-month outcome:

1. *From the futures contract settlement*: Deliver Asset Delta and receive $116.
2. *From the loan*: Repay $121.80 (principal plus simple interest).
3. *From dividend*: Receive $4 from holding Asset Delta.

Total proceeds: $116 (futures) + $4 (dividend) = $120
Total outlay: $121.80 (loan repayment)
Net result: Loss of $1.80

This small loss implies that selling the futures at $116 is too low to create a true arbitrage opportunity. The strategy is not profitable.

Now, consider the reverse cash-and-carry strategy:

- Buy the futures contract at $116.
- Sell short Asset Delta for $120.
- Invest the $120 proceeds at 6% annual interest for three months.

Three-month outcome:

1. *From the settlement of the futures contract*: Buy Asset Delta for $116 to return to the lender.
2. *From the investment*: $120 earns $1.80 in interest, totaling $121.80.
3. *Dividend obligation*: Pay $4 to the lender of Asset Delta.

Total proceeds: $121.80
Total outlay: $116 (futures purchase) + $4 (dividend payment) = $120
Net result: Gain of $1.80

Now, suppose the futures contract is priced instead at $120, exactly matching the net cost of carry-adjusted spot value. Let's test both strategies again at this price.

Cash-and-carry strategy:

- Sell futures at $120.
- Buy spot at $120.
- Borrow $120.

Three-month results:

- Receive $120 at delivery.
- Receive $4 dividend.
- Repay $121.80 loan.

Proceeds: $120 + $4 = $124
Outlay: $121.80
Net profit: $2.20 → arbitrage still exists.

Now, try with futures price = $121.80:

Proceeds: $121.80 + $4 = $125.80
Outlay: $121.80
Net profit: $4

Clearly, something is inconsistent with the assumptions. To correctly align, let's match the previous parameters from earlier: The spot price was $120, the dividend was $4, and the loan repayment was $121.80.

The only price that will produce no arbitrage profit or loss under both strategies is as follows:

- Futures price = $117.80
- Spot = $120
- Dividend = $4
- Loan repayment = $121.80
- So, $117.80 (futures) + $4 (dividend) = $121.80 → no profit/loss

At this price,

- *Cash-and-carry*: $117.80 + $4 − $121.80 = $0
- *Reverse cash-and-carry*: $121.80 − ($117.80 + $4) = $0

Thus, $117.80 is the equilibrium futures price, the price at which neither arbitrage strategy is profitable. This is known as the futures contract's theoretical or fair value. Any deviation above or below this level invites arbitrage, which should quickly drive the price back to equilibrium in an efficient market.

19.2.2 *Deriving the theoretical value of a futures contract*

The arbitrage strategies discussed in the previous section—cash-and-carry and reverse cash-and-carry—form the basis for determining the theoretical value, or fair value, of a futures contract. This value reflects the price at which no arbitrage profit can be earned, assuming market participants can borrow, lend, and transact without constraints.

To calculate the theoretical futures price, we require the following inputs:

- the spot price of the asset in the cash market, denoted by P;
- the cash yield (such as dividends or interest) earned on the asset until the settlement date, denoted by y;
- the financing cost, or the interest rate at which funds can be borrowed or lent until the settlement date, denoted by r.

19.2.2.1 *Cash-and-carry arbitrage strategy*

To derive the theoretical futures price, consider a cash-and-carry strategy:

- Sell the futures contract at price F.
- Buy the asset in the spot market at price P.
- Borrow funds at rate r to finance the purchase of the asset.

On the settlement date:

1. The futures contract is settled by delivering the asset and receiving F.
2. The loan is repaid: $P + rP$.
3. The asset yields a cash flow: yP.

Total proceeds: $F + yP$
Total outlay: $P + rP$
Profit: $F + yP - (P + rP)$

To eliminate arbitrage, this profit must be zero. Setting the expression equal to zero and solving for F, we get

$$0 = F + yP - (P + rP)$$

Solving for F, we get

$$F = P + P\,(r - y) \qquad (19.1)$$

The theoretical future price is therefore given by equation (19.1).[5]

19.2.2.2 *Reverse cash-and-carry arbitrage strategy*

The same result can be derived using a reverse cash-and-carry strategy:

- Buy the futures contract at price F.
- Sell short the asset in the spot market, receiving P.
- Lend the proceeds at rate r.

On the settlement date:

1. The futures contract is settled by purchasing the asset at F.
2. The investment grows to $P + rP$.
3. A dividend of yP must be paid to the lender of the borrowed asset.

Total proceeds: $P + rP$
Total outlay: $F + yP$
Profit: $P + rP - (F + yP)$

Again, setting the profit to zero and solving for F, we would recover the same expression for the theoretical futures given by equation (19.1).

---

[5] With continuous compounding, the theoretical futures price is

$$F = Pe^{(r-y)T}$$

where P is the spot price, r is the continuously compounded financing rate, y is the continuously compounded cash yield, and T is the time to settlement. The constant e is the base of the natural logarithm, approximately equal to 2.71828.

19.2.2.3 *Numerical example*

Let's now apply the pricing formula to the Asset Delta example. The spot price of Asset Delta is $P = 120$. Asset Delta pays a quarterly cash flow of \$4. Since the next payment is three months from today (i.e., within the life of the futures contract), this \$4 payment should be included as a known cash yield from holding the asset. Let's express this as a percentage of the asset price. Since the annual dividend is \$16 and the price is \$120, the annual dividend yield is 13.1333%, Thus, the quarterly yield on Asset Delta is 3.3333% (13.1333%/4).

Next, we incorporate the quarterly financing cost, the interest rate at which funds can be borrowed or lent over the three-month horizon. Assuming a 6% annual interest rate and using simple interest, the quarterly financing rate is $r = 6\%/4 = 1.5\%$, or 0.015.

Now, we substitute these values into the theoretical pricing formula given by equation (19.1):

$$F = P + P(r - y) = 120 + 120(0.015 - 0.033333) = 117.80$$

So, the theoretical futures price is approximately \$117.80. This is the price at which neither a cash-and-carry nor a reverse cash-and-carry arbitrage strategy would yield a profit, assuming perfect markets with no transaction costs, symmetric borrowing and lending rates, and certainty in dividend payments. We confirmed this earlier in this section.

A cash-and-carry arbitrage would become profitable if the actual futures price were higher than \$117.80. A reverse cash-and-carry strategy would generate a riskless gain if it were lower. In an efficient market, such deviations should be short-lived, as arbitrage activity would push the price toward equilibrium.

19.2.2.4 *Understanding the cost of carry*

The difference between an asset's futures price and its spot price can be explained by the *cost of carry*. This concept plays a central role in determining whether a futures contract will trade at a premium, a discount, or parity relative to the current spot price.

The cost of carry is defined as the net financing cost of holding the underlying asset until the futures contract's expiration. It is the difference between the financing cost r and the asset's yield y and is denoted as

$$\text{Cost of carry} = \text{Financing cost} - \text{Cash yield} = r - y$$

Depending on the sign and magnitude of $r - y$, the futures price F can behave differently relative to the spot price P:

- *Positive carry* ($y > r$): The yield from holding the asset exceeds the financing cost. In this case, the futures price will be *below* the spot price, and the contract is said to trade at a *discount*.
- *Negative carry* ($r > y$): The financing cost exceeds the asset's yield. The futures contract will be priced *above* the spot price, which is said to trade at a *premium*.
- *Zero carry* ($r = y$): The financing cost and yield are offset. In this case, the futures price equals the spot price.

Understanding the cost of carry is critical for pricing futures and identifying arbitrage opportunities. Traders and portfolio managers use this framework to evaluate pricing deviations, form hedging strategies, and make asset allocation decisions involving futures contracts.

19.2.2.5 *Convergence on the delivery date*

As the futures contract approaches its expiration date, its price must *converge* to the underlying asset's price in the cash (spot) market. This principle of convergence ensures that the futures price F and the spot price P are equal on the delivery date.

This outcome follows directly from the theoretical pricing relationship. As time to maturity approaches zero, both components of the cost of carry (i.e., the financing cost r and the asset yield y) effectively shrink to zero. Since neither interest can be earned nor yield received instantaneously, the cost of carrying the asset disappears.

In other words, the futures price must equal the spot price at expiration because there is no remaining time over which financing costs or asset yields can accrue. Any deviation at that point would represent a riskless arbitrage opportunity, which market participants would immediately exploit and eliminate.

This convergence is critical to the logic of futures markets and is enforced by the delivery and settlement mechanisms. It also underlines the effectiveness of futures contracts as hedging tools, ensuring that the futures price reliably tracks the underlying asset as the contract matures.

19.2.3 *A closer look at the theoretical value of the futures contract*

The pricing of futures contracts using arbitrage arguments leads to a clean and elegant result: The futures price equals the spot price adjusted for the cost of carry. This relationship, given by equation (19.1), provides a theoretical benchmark around which actual futures prices are expected to trade. However, this formula is derived under idealized assumptions that are rarely held in practice. When these assumptions are violated (as often seen in real markets), the actual futures price may diverge from the theoretical value. These divergences are not necessarily mispricings; they reflect real-world constraints, costs, and complexities that inhibit the frictionless arbitrage process.

This section explains the key factors that lead to deviations from the theoretical futures price, offering a more nuanced understanding of how futures prices behave in practice. We group these factors into six categories.

19.2.3.1 *Interim cash flows and marking to market*

The theoretical model assumes that any income from the underlying asset, such as dividends or coupon payments, is either nonexistent or received upon delivery. Additionally, it assumes that futures contracts are not subject to interim cash flows resulting from the mark-to-market process.

Many underlying assets pay income before delivery. Stocks may pay dividends, and bonds may pay interest during the life of a futures contract. Moreover, futures contracts are marked to market daily, which creates a stream of interim cash flows based on the daily gain or loss in the contract's value.

These interim cash flows affect both the timing and reinvestment of profits and losses. For example, if the market moves in favor of an investor holding a long futures position, the mark-to-market process releases cash early, which can be reinvested. Conversely, a losing position may require additional margin funding.

To adjust for this in future pricing, models must account for the impact of daily settlement, which can be particularly significant in volatile markets or when interest rates are high.

19.2.3.2 *Asymmetric borrowing and lending rates*

The theoretical pricing formula assumes that an investor can borrow and lend at the same risk-free rate to exploit mispricing. This symmetry is essential to derive a unique fair value. In reality, borrowing and lending rates differ. Borrowing rates tend to be higher due to credit risk and collateral requirements. Lending rates are often lower, especially for short-term cash investments.

To account for this, we define two alternative expressions for the futures price depending on which arbitrage strategy is used:

- *Cash-and-carry strategy* (requires borrowing):

  $$F = P + P(r_B - y)$$

  where r_B is the borrowing rate.

- *Reverse cash-and-carry strategy* (involves lending):

  $$F = P + P(r_L - y)$$

These expressions define an *arbitrage-free range*, or *no-arbitrage bounds*, within which the actual futures price can fluctuate without violating market efficiency.

Let's use as our example Asset Delta. We have

- *Spot price*: $P = 120$
- *Asset yield for the quarter*: $y = 3.3333\%$
- *Lending rate*: r_L = annual 5.2% = 1.3% for the quarter
- *Borrowing rate*: r_B = 8% annual rate = 2% for quarter

Upper Bound on Futures Price: Assume an investor buys the asset and borrows funds at the annual borrowing rate of 8% (r_B = 2% for quarter). The theoretical futures price is

$$120 + 120(0.02 - 0.033333) = 118.40$$

Lower Bound on Futures Price: Assume an investor sells short the asset and lends proceeds at an annual rate of 5.2% (r_L = 1.3% for the quarter). The theoretical futures price is

$$120 + 120(0.013 - 0.0333333) = 117.56$$

The no-arbitrage bounds for the futures price are $117.56 \leq F \leq 118.40$. If the market futures price is equal to or above 117.56 or equal to or below 118.40, arbitrage opportunities arise, assuming no market frictions such as transaction costs or restrictions on short selling.

19.2.3.3 *Transaction costs and market frictions*

Another assumption underlying theoretical pricing is that there are no transaction costs. In practice, this is far from true. Market participants incur costs at several points in the arbitrage process, including:

- brokerage fees and commissions,
- bid–ask spreads,
- exchange and clearing fees,
- market impact when executing large trades.

These costs reduce or eliminate potential arbitrage profits. For instance, if an arbitrage strategy yields a theoretical profit of $0.80 but incurs a $0.75 implementation cost, the net gain may be too small to justify execution, particularly at an institutional scale. Consequently, transaction costs widen the no-arbitrage bounds, allowing the actual futures price to deviate further from the theoretical price without triggering corrective trades.

19.2.3.4 *Proceeds and constraints on short selling*

The reverse cash-and-carry strategy requires shorting the underlying asset. The theoretical model assumes that the asset can be borrowed without restriction and that the proceeds from the short sale can be fully reinvested at the market rate. However, in practice, there are frictions. First, short sales require margin and may involve stock borrowing fees. Second, for retail investors, proceeds from the sale are often held by the broker and are not available for reinvestment. Finally, even institutional investors may face collateral requirements or borrowing costs that reduce profitability.

These frictions mean the investor may earn less than the stated lending rate on short-sale proceeds, effectively raising the lower arbitrage boundary. The result is an upward bias in the observed futures price relative to the midpoint of the theoretical range.

19.2.4 *Delivery options: Uncertainty in deliverable asset and date*

Many futures contracts, particularly those based on government securities or commodities, permit multiple deliverables. The short party to the contract often has the right to choose among several eligible assets and select the specific delivery date within the delivery window.

These delivery options benefit the short and impose uncertainty on the long. For instance, if the short in a Treasury note or bond futures contract can deliver the cheapest-to-deliver bond, the futures contract buyer is exposed to an unknown final settlement value.

The presence of such embedded delivery options adds value to the short position and, correspondingly, causes the futures price to trade below what would be implied by a model that assumes a fixed deliverable. This adjustment must be factored into the market and can lead to persistent divergence from the basic arbitrage price given by equation (19.1).

19.2.5 *Basket delivery and imperfect tracking*

Finally, some futures contracts are written on indices or baskets of assets (e.g., equity index futures or commodity baskets). In these cases, it is impractical, if not impossible, to buy or short every index component in the exact weights. Instead, traders construct tracking portfolios that approximate the behavior of the index. However, such portfolios may exhibit basis risk, which arises when the returns of the portfolio deviate from those of the actual index it is intended to track. This is often due to differences in composition, weighting, or timing between the portfolio and the benchmark. As a result, arbitrage becomes imperfect and involves additional risks. Traders may require a greater price discrepancy to initiate trades, leading to wider deviations between the futures price and its theoretical value.

19.3 Summary

In this chapter, I present an introduction to the valuation of risk-sharing derivatives, focusing specifically on futures and forward contracts. I begin by laying the foundation with a discussion of arbitrage and the law of one price, which serve as the theoretical basis for derivative pricing. I then introduce the replication principle and explain how it allows for pricing derivative contracts in frictionless markets.

I derive the valuation of forward contracts by examining the arbitrage relationship between spot and forward prices under the assumption of risk-free borrowing and lending. I present both generalized and straightforward pricing formulas and highlight the distinction between cash-and-carry pricing and theoretical forward pricing.

I then turn to futures contracts, focusing on how the daily mark-to-market affects valuation. I show how futures prices can differ from forward prices due to the impact of daily settlement and differences between borrowing and lending rates. I use examples to illustrate how these differences influence pricing and emphasize how marking-to-market introduces an additional layer of complexity compared to forward contracts.

To close the chapter, I examine how the basic pricing model breaks down when the specifications of a futures contract violate the assumptions underlying the no-arbitrage framework. I consider cases where the borrowing and lending rates differ, marking-to-market affects cash flows, and other contractual features disrupt the ability to exactly replicate payoffs. I show how these violations alter the theoretical pricing relationship through examples and explain the conditions under which futures and forward prices may diverge.

Chapter 20

Quantitative Foundations for Option Pricing

This chapter provides the essential mathematical and conceptual foundations necessary to understand the range of option pricing models used in practice. While option pricing aims to determine a fair value for options, the methods used to achieve that value vary significantly in structure, assumptions, and applicability. This diversity arises because different types of options—European, American, exotic, or path-dependent—present different modeling challenges and because real-world financial markets rarely conform to idealized assumptions.

Rather than beginning with a single model, such as the well-known Black–Scholes–Merton framework, I introduce the standard intellectual and mathematical building blocks underpinning all major option pricing models in this chapter. The chapter is motivated by the recognition that these foundations not only justify these models but also help explain when a given model may fail or require modification. The goal is not to train someone to derive these models from scratch but to equip them with the tools to understand the assumptions, interpret the outputs, and choose the right model for the context.

To achieve this, I begin the chapter by explaining stochastic processes, focusing on geometric Brownian motion, which forms the backbone of many classical pricing models. I then explore how modeling asset returns, rather than prices, leads to the lognormal distribution assumption that underlies models such as Black–Scholes.

The cumulative normal distribution is introduced next, along with an explanation of how it is used in closed-form pricing models. A closed-form solution is a formula that directly expresses an option's value as a function of known variables, such as the underlying price, strike price, volatility, time to expiration, and interest rate, without requiring iterative calculations or numerical simulations. This is important because it enables fast, transparent, and consistent market valuation, especially for standard instruments such as European options. The cumulative normal distribution plays a central role in these models by translating assumptions about normally distributed returns into precise probability weights, determining the likelihood of an option expiring in the money and its expected payoff value. Here, these 'probability weights' reflect the model's mathematical weighting structure rather than real-world probabilities; the formal risk-neutral interpretation appears later in the chapter.

I then examine the crucial role of volatility (its interpretation, assumptions, and empirical challenges) and conclude with the core concept of risk-neutral valuation, which unifies nearly all pricing models through the principle of arbitrage-free pricing.

Finally, I set the stage for why we need multiple valuation frameworks. By examining the limits of standard assumptions—constant volatility, continuous price movement, and static interest rates—I motivate the inclusion of alternative methods such as numerical simulation, stochastic volatility modeling, and machine learning (ML) approaches later in the book.

These topics provide the foundation for understanding how and why different option pricing models work, when to use them, and how to interpret their results in modern financial markets.

20.1 Modeling Uncertainty: The Role of Stochastic Processes

All option pricing models begin with a fundamental question: How do asset prices evolve over time in the face of uncertainty? Since future prices are unknown and influenced by countless unpredictable factors, financial models rely on mathematical tools called *stochastic processes* to describe asset behavior in probabilistic terms.

A stochastic process is a mathematical model that describes how a variable, such as an asset price, evolves over time in a way that incorporates randomness. It defines a sequence of random variables, one for each point in time, representing the range of possible outcomes the variable might take and the associated probabilities. The most widely used stochastic process in finance is *geometric Brownian motion* (GBM), the foundation for the Black–Scholes–Merton model and many other analytical pricing frameworks. GBM assumes that asset prices move along a continuous and smooth path, with uncertainty introduced in a statistically defined and structured manner.

Under GBM, asset prices are modeled as changing continuously, meaning there are no sudden jumps or gaps in the price path. This reflects the idealization of a frictionless market (i.e., an idealized market with no transaction costs, taxes, bid–ask spreads, or delays), allowing assets to be traded instantly and costlessly, where trading can occur instantly. Furthermore, the model assumes that price changes are proportional to the current price level, so higher-priced assets experience larger absolute changes. This assumption leads to modeling *returns*, specifically, continuously compounded returns, as normally distributed. Consequently, asset prices follow a lognormal distribution: They cannot fall below zero and are positively skewed. This progression from GBM to normally distributed continuously compounded returns and then to lognormally distributed prices is shown formally in the derivation that follows.

One of GBM's main attractions is its tractability, that is, its mathematical simplicity and solvability. This tractability provides a convenient framework that supports the derivation of closed-form pricing formulas, most famously the Black–Scholes equation. Because GBM yields analytically manageable expressions, it enables faster and more transparent valuation of options, essential for implementation in trading systems, risk models, and financial reporting.

Moreover, GBM serves as a natural context for applying the principle of risk-neutral valuation, a method of pricing options that simplifies the modeling process by assuming that all assets grow at a risk-free interest rate, regardless of their actual risk. Under this approach, instead of trying to model how real-world investors perceive risk and demand compensation, the model adjusts probabilities so that the expected return of the underlying asset equals the risk-free interest rate. This allows options to be priced solely based on arbitrage logic by constructing replicating portfolios and ensuring consistency in pricing, without needing to incorporate subjective assumptions about investor preferences or risk tolerances. This simplification makes risk-neutral valuation powerful and widely applicable in financial modeling.

Despite the advantages of GBM, it is ultimately a simplification. It assumes that the drift (i.e., the expected rate of return) and volatility (i.e., the standard deviation of returns) remain constant over time. It also assumes that markets are frictionless and that asset prices evolve continuously with no sudden jumps. These assumptions are often violated. For instance, market prices can experience abrupt movements, or jumps, due to events such as earnings announcements, geopolitical developments, or macroeconomic shocks, which the smooth evolution implied by GBM captures.

Moreover, empirical studies of asset returns have documented a phenomenon known as "volatility clustering," where periods of high volatility tend to be followed by periods of low volatility, and vice versa. This contradicts the GBM assumption of constant volatility, indicating that risk levels change in a predictable pattern over time.

Another departure from GBM's assumptions lies in the shape of the return distribution. Rather than being symmetric and thin-tailed, as implied by the normal distribution of log returns, actual financial returns often exhibit asymmetry (or skewness) and heavy tails. Skewness reflects that large negative or positive returns are not equally likely; markets tend to exhibit more frequent sharp declines or, in some cases, extreme rallies. Heavy tails are significant because they signal a higher probability of extreme outcomes (i.e., substantial losses or gains) than a normal distribution would predict.[1] While infrequent, these tail events can disproportionately affect portfolio performance and financial stability. As a result, models that ignore fat tails tend to underestimate the likelihood and impact of market shocks. This limits the reliability of standard risk measures, such as variance or standard deviation, which treat all deviations from the mean equally and assume extreme events are exceedingly rare.

---

[1]For an educational overview of the implications of fat-tailed and heavy-tailed return distributions in portfolio construction, risk modeling, and performance evaluation, see Michele Leonardo Bianchi, Gian Luca Tassinari, and Frank J. Fabozzi, "Fat and Heavy Tails in Asset Management," *Journal of Portfolio Management*, 49(7), 2023, 236–263. A more comprehensive and technical treatment of heavy-tailed modeling and its applications can be found in Michele Leonardo Bianchi, Stoyan V. Stoyanov, Gian Luca Tassinari, Frank J. Fabozzi, and Sergio M. Focardi, *Handbook of Heavy-Tailed Distributions in Asset Management and Risk Management*, World Scientific Press, 2019.

Therefore, understanding and accounting for tail behavior is critical in option pricing and risk management.[2]

These empirical realities have motivated the development of more sophisticated models. Stochastic volatility models allow volatility to vary randomly over time, capturing the clustering behavior observed in practice. Jump-diffusion models incorporate sudden, discontinuous price movements and the continuous component of GBM, offering a better fit for markets that experience shocks. These enhancements introduce additional mathematical complexity but provide a more realistic description of financial markets' behavior.

Despite these limitations, GBM remains a cornerstone of financial modeling. It provides an intuitive and analytically tractable foundation from which other models are derived or compared. Understanding GBM is essential for practitioners because it underlies the structure and logic of many pricing tools in everyday use, even those that eventually depart from its assumptions.

20.2 The Cumulative Normal Distribution Function

The *cumulative normal distribution function* is a key component of analytical option pricing models, most notably the Black–Scholes formula. While this may appear to be a purely mathematical detail, it plays a central role in quantifying risk and probability within these models.

The cumulative normal distribution function, typically denoted as $N(d)$, gives the probability that a normally distributed random variable will be less than or equal to a specific value. In option pricing, this function expresses probability under the assumption that returns are normally distributed and allows the model to compute the likelihood of particular outcomes within the risk-neutral framework, where all assets are assumed to grow at the risk-free rate.

Because $N(d)$ is based on the standard normal distribution (a bell-shaped distribution with mean zero and standard deviation one), it represents the area under this curve to the left of the point d. Thus, $N(d)$

---

[2]These stylized facts are well documented. See Rama Cont, "Empirical Properties of Asset Returns: Stylized Facts and Statistical Issues." *Quantitative Finance*, 1(2), 2001, 223–236.

corresponds to the probability that a standardized normally distributed variable will take a value less than or equal to d.

Several benchmark values are especially useful. For example, $N(0) = 0.5$ because half of the standardized outcomes lie below the mean. Likewise, $N(1)$ is approximately 0.84 indicating that about 84% of the distribution is below one standard deviation above the mean, while $N(-1)$ is approximately 0.16, reflecting the proportion below one standard deviation below the mean. These values, obtained from statistical tables or numerical routines, play an essential role in the Black–Scholes option-pricing model described in Chapter 22.

In the Black–Scholes option pricing model described in the next chapter, two terms, $N(d_1)$ and $N(d_2)$, appear prominently. Each serves a distinct but related purpose. $N(d_2)$ is often interpreted as the risk-neutral probability that the option will finish in the money; that is, it gives the likelihood that the asset's price at expiration will exceed the strike price, making a call option exercisable. $N(d_1)$ is related to the option's *delta*, which measures the sensitivity of the option's price to changes in the underlying asset price. While not a literal probability, $N(d_1)$ incorporates both the chance of exercise and the degree of exposure to the underlying asset's price movement.

These functions transform the theoretical model into a probabilistic valuation tool. They allow us to interpret the value of an option not merely as a formulaic result but as a weighted combination of possible future outcomes. For example, the call option price in the Black–Scholes model is often described as the difference between the expected present value of acquiring the asset and the expected present value of paying the strike price, with both components weighted by the appropriate cumulative normal probabilities.

The cumulative normal distribution's mathematical properties also make it especially suitable for use in closed-form models. Its smooth, continuous shape and symmetry around the mean simplify integration and differentiation, enabling tractable solutions. In practical terms, these functions are evaluated using built-in algorithms in software platforms, trading terminals, and spreadsheet tools, eliminating manual computation. Yet, understanding what they represent conceptually helps practitioners interpret the output of models and make better-informed decisions.

While the cumulative normal distribution relies on the simplifying assumption of normally distributed returns, a feature often violated in real markets, it nonetheless provides a transparent, interpretable, and widely used mechanism for embedding probabilistic logic into option pricing models. It bridges the gap between statistical theory and financial intuition by assigning meaning to the values calculated by the model.

20.3 Risk-Neutral Valuation

At the heart of modern option pricing theory is a powerful and elegant idea: the *risk-neutral valuation principle*. It allows us to value uncertain future cash flows not by explicitly adjusting for risk preferences but by computing the expected payoff under a transformed probability measure and then discounting at the risk-free interest rate.

In a risk-neutral world, all assets are expected to grow at the risk-free interest rate, regardless of their actual risk characteristics. That sounds unrealistic, and it is. However, the brilliance of this idea lies in its use as a mathematical construct: We can transition from the real world (with risk preferences and variable expected returns) to a simplified, arbitrage-free world where pricing becomes more tractable. Crucially, we are not saying investors are risk-neutral, only that we can value derivatives *as if* they were, provided we apply the right probability adjustments.

This shift from real-world to risk-neutral probabilities enables options pricing without requiring knowledge of investors' utility functions or risk aversion levels.

20.3.1 *Why risk-neutral probabilities are used rather than real-world probabilities*

It may seem natural to use real-world probabilities when pricing derivatives since those represent beliefs about what will actually happen. However, real-world probabilities reflect the likelihood of outcomes and investor preferences and attitudes toward risk. Because investors demand compensation for bearing risk, real-world probabilities are distorted by subjective risk premiums and expectations.

Incorporating these preferences into pricing would require detailed knowledge of each investor's utility function, an impractical and challenging task. To avoid this complexity, option pricing models use risk-neutral probabilities, which are mathematically adjusted to remove the effects of risk aversion. These adjusted probabilities do not describe beliefs about the future but instead serve as tools for consistent, arbitrage-free pricing.

Under risk-neutral probabilities, all assets are assumed to grow at the risk-free interest rate, and differences in return expectations due to risk preferences are set aside. This simplification allows derivatives to be priced based purely on the structure of payoffs and the principle of no arbitrage.

Consider a simple numerical example. Suppose an asset is priced at \$100 and can move to \$120 or \$80 tomorrow. The real-world probability of the asset rising might be estimated at 60%, and the probability of it falling at 40%. These probabilities reflect market sentiment and risk premiums.

Now, assume an option pays \$10 if the asset rises to \$120 and nothing if it falls to \$80. Using real-world probabilities, the expected value of the payoff would be

$$(60\% \times 10) + (40\% \times 0) = 6$$

However, this \$6 includes compensation for risk and may not reflect the no-arbitrage price. Instead, risk-neutral valuation adjusts the probabilities so that the expected return of the underlying asset equals the risk-free interest rate. Suppose, under the risk-neutral measure, both outcomes are assigned a 50% probability. Then, the expected payoff becomes

$$(50\% \times 10) + (50\% \times 0) = 5$$

This expected payoff is discounted at the risk-free interest rate to determine the option's value. The discounting effect is minimal for a one-day period, so the option's value is approximately \$5 under the risk-neutral measure, lower than the \$6 expected payoff under real-world probabilities.

This difference illustrates the purpose of risk-neutral valuation: to provide a consistent, arbitrage-free method for pricing derivatives independent of subjective views about risk. Instead of attempting to reflect beliefs about the market, the model ensures that any derivative price is linked directly to replicable strategies and that there are no arbitrage profits.

20.3.2 *Role in linking replication and pricing*

Risk-neutral valuation is not a mere theoretical convenience. It serves as a bridge between two powerful and complementary concepts in option pricing: On one side is the idea of replication, where the value of a derivative is determined by constructing a portfolio of basic instruments, such as stocks and bonds, that mimics the derivative's payoff; on the other side is probabilistic valuation, which determines value by calculating the expected payoff under adjusted, risk-neutral probabilities and discounting it at the risk-free rate.

Although these approaches may seem different, they are fundamentally connected and, under no-arbitrage conditions, lead to the same result. The replication argument provides a constructive path to pricing, while the probabilistic approach offers a cleaner and, often, more flexible computational method.

20.4 Option Valuation Frameworks

There is no single method for valuing an option. Different valuation frameworks may be used depending on the option's characteristics, the structure of the underlying asset, and the practical need for flexibility or speed. Option valuation methods fall into four categories: (1) analytical framework, (2) numerical framework, (3) stochastic framework, and (4) ML framework. This section explains each approach at a conceptual level.

20.4.1 *Analytical framework*

The analytical framework refers to a class of option valuation models that yield closed-form solutions. As explained earlier, a closed-form solution is an explicit mathematical formula that provides the option's value as a direct function of known inputs. Once these values are specified, the formula can be applied directly to compute the option's value in a single step, eliminating the need for iterative procedures or simulations. The most famous and widely used example of this approach is the Black–Scholes model, which revolutionized option pricing by offering a tractable and elegant solution for European-style options on non-dividend-paying stocks.

Analytical models, including the Black–Scholes model, are built upon simplifying assumptions that make the underlying mathematics solvable. These include the assumption that the underlying asset can be traded continuously, meaning investors can adjust their positions at any time without delay or cost. This assumption supports the concept of continuous hedging, a cornerstone in the derivation of many option pricing models. Another key assumption is that market variables, such as volatility and interest rates, remain constant throughout the option's life, allowing for mathematical tractability but ignoring the reality of changing market conditions. Additionally, these models assume that asset prices evolve continuously and smoothly, typically modeled using a stochastic process that I describe later in this chapter. This excludes sudden price jumps, liquidity constraints, and transaction costs, which can be significant in financial markets.

Despite these limitations, analytical models have proven remarkably robust and helpful in practice, especially for standard, highly liquid options that do not exhibit complex features such as early exercise rights or path dependence. For instance, European-style calls and puts on large-cap equities often closely meet the assumptions of the Black–Scholes model, making the resulting price estimates both accurate and valuable. Analysts and traders favor these models because they are computationally efficient, intuitive to interpret, and easy to use in spreadsheets or automated systems. Even in settings where the assumptions are known to be imperfect, analytical models often serve as valuable benchmarks or starting points for further analysis using numerical methods or market calibration techniques.

20.4.2 *Numerical framework*

When an option's features are too complex for a closed-form solution or when model assumptions do not align with empirically observed market behavior, numerical methods are employed. These methods approximate an option's value by simulating or discretizing its behavior over time. They do not produce a formula but rather an estimate based on computational procedures. Three common numerical approaches are the (1) lattice model, (2) Monte Carlo simulation, and (3) finite difference methods.

20.4.2.1 *Lattice models*

A lattice model is a discrete-time numerical framework used to model the evolution of an asset's price and to value derivative securities, such as options. This model, the subject of Chapter 21, constructs a grid, often referred to as a lattice or a tree, that maps out a range of possible paths the asset price might follow over the option's life. Each point in the lattice, referred to as a *node*, represents a possible future price of the underlying asset at a specific point in time, and each movement from one point to the next represents a small advance in time accompanied by an upward, downward, or neutral shift in price. The model proceeds by dividing the time to expiration into a series of short intervals and calculating the asset's potential price movements at each step, resulting in a branching structure of price scenarios.

Once the entire lattice of asset prices has been generated, the option's value is computed by working backward through the tree, a method known as *backward induction* and illustrated in Chapter 21. This process starts at the final nodes of the tree, which correspond to the option's payoff at expiration. It successively moves backward to determine the option's value at each preceding node, ultimately arriving at its current value. This approach enables the model to incorporate features such as early exercise and path-dependent behavior flexibly and systematically.

The binomial model is the most basic form of a lattice model.[3] At each time step, the asset price can move to one of two values, up or down, by a certain percentage. Despite its simplicity, the binomial model captures many essential features of option pricing. More advanced versions, such as trinomial or multinomial lattices, allow for three or more possible price outcomes at each time step. These refinements yield a denser grid of price paths, more accurately approximating the continuous range of possibilities found in real markets and enhancing the model's accuracy, particularly for options with long maturities or complex features.

Lattice models are particularly well-suited for valuing American-style options, which can be exercised at any point up to expiration. The backward induction procedure easily accommodates early exercise decisions at each tree node. Lattice models are also helpful when pricing options on assets that pay discrete dividends or in settings where volatility is not constant and must be adjusted at different points in the tree. Their flexibility makes them a powerful tool for handling a wide variety of option structures that cannot be addressed with closed-form analytical solutions.

I provide a detailed illustration of how the lattice model operates in Chapter 21.

---

[3] In 1979, John Cox, Stephen Ross, and Mark Rubinstein introduced and formalized the lattice model (specifically, the binomial tree) as a practical tool for option valuation. John C. Cox, Stephen A. Ross, and Mark Rubinstein, "Option Pricing: A Simplified Approach." *Journal of Financial Economics*, 7(3), 1979, pp. 229–263.

20.4.2.2 *Monte Carlo simulation*

Monte Carlo simulation is a widely used numerical method for valuing options by modeling the evolution of the underlying asset's price across a large number of simulated scenarios.[4] Unlike analytical models, which rely on simplifying assumptions to derive closed-form solutions, Monte Carlo methods take a statistical approach, capturing the randomness and complexity inherent in real-world asset price movements.

To estimate an option's value, the simulation generates many possible future paths for the underlying asset's price from the present to the option's expiration. These paths reflect how the asset's price might evolve over time and are constructed using a stochastic process, typically geometric Brownian motion, as introduced earlier in this chapter. Each path incorporates the model's deterministic elements, such as the asset's expected return and volatility, and a random component that introduces market uncertainty.

This randomness is introduced using a random number generator, which produces sequences of values that imitate the statistical properties of true randomness. These values are calibrated and transformed to produce normally distributed variables that drive the asset's price fluctuations in the simulation.

For each simulated path, the option's payoff is calculated at expiration or intermediate points if early exercise or path dependency is involved. Once all payoffs have been determined, they are averaged and discounted to the present using the appropriate risk-free interest rate. This results in an estimate of the expected present value of the option, consistent with the principles of risk-neutral valuation.

Monte Carlo methods are particularly effective for path-dependent options, where the payoff depends on the entire asset price trajectory rather than the final value. These features are challenging to model using closed-form solutions or even lattice approaches, but Monte Carlo simulation naturally accommodates them by recording the full price path.

---

[4] In his seminal 1977 paper, Phelim Boyle introduced the Monte Carlo simulation technique as a method for valuing options, particularly advantageous for cases where analytical solutions such as the Black–Scholes formula are unavailable or intractable. Though the initial focus was on European options, his work laid the foundation for a vast literature on simulation-based derivative pricing methods, including extensions to complex and path-dependent options. Phelim Boyle, "Options: A Monte Carlo Approach," *Journal of Financial Economics*, 4(3), 1977, 323–338.

One of the key strengths of the Monte Carlo simulation is its flexibility. It can incorporate various market complexities, including stochastic volatility, price jumps, multiple underlying assets, and time-varying interest rates. This makes it the preferred tool for pricing exotic options and other complex derivatives. Furthermore, because the simulation produces a distribution of outcomes, it provides insight into the range and shape of possible payoffs, not just the expected value.

Despite its advantages, the method does have limitations. Monte Carlo simulation is computationally intensive, often requiring thousands or even millions of paths to produce accurate and stable estimates, particularly for options with early exercise features. Monte Carlo methods are less efficient than other techniques for American-style options, which allow exercise before expiration. Nevertheless, enhancements have been developed to address this shortcoming by approximating the optimal exercise strategy.

20.4.2.3 *Finite difference methods*

Finite difference methods estimate the value of an option by solving a simplified, step-by-step version of the mathematical equation that describes how the option's price changes over time. Instead of relying on a single formula or simulating random price paths, this approach builds a grid representing different points in time and levels of the underlying asset's price. The option's value is then calculated at each point on the grid, typically by moving backward from expiration to the present.

Although this step-by-step process might resemble a lattice model, the foundation differs. Lattice models track possible paths the asset price might take, while finite difference methods solve an equation that captures the option's changing value over time and across price. This makes finite difference methods particularly well-suited to options with more complex features, such as the ability to exercise early (as in American options), barriers, or features tied to interest rates or credit conditions.

The method's strength lies in its structure and flexibility. It enables the precise modeling of how an option behaves under various market conditions, even as they evolve over time. While the method may seem abstract, it is based on the same financial principles as other models, simply employing a more mathematical approach to capturing how option prices evolve.

20.4.3 *Stochastic framework*

The stochastic framework takes option modeling a step further by recognizing that key inputs to pricing models (e.g., volatility, interest rates, or even the behavior of asset prices themselves) are not fixed but rather random variables that evolve unpredictably over time. While the basic Black–Scholes model assumes constant volatility and interest rates for mathematical simplicity, these assumptions often fall short in real-world markets, where such parameters vary significantly over time in response to economic conditions or are influenced by investor sentiment.

Stochastic models address this by explicitly modeling the inputs' randomness, not just the underlying asset price. This leads to more realistic representations of financial markets, especially under stress, uncertainty, or structural shifts.

One common application of the stochastic framework is in stochastic volatility models, where volatility can vary over time randomly. Instead of assuming a fixed level of volatility, these models describe it as following a separate process, potentially influenced by the asset price or other market factors. This approach captures the observed behavior that volatility often spikes during market downturns and tends to cluster over time. These features are not accounted for in the Black–Scholes framework.

Another significant extension is stochastic interest rate models, which allow interest rates to evolve unpredictably rather than staying constant. This is especially relevant for valuing interest rate derivatives, long-dated options, or any product whose cash flows are sensitive to changes in borrowing costs. In these models, the interest rate is given its dynamic process, such as mean reversion,[5] where rates tend to move back toward a long-term average over time.

Jump-diffusion models, which account for sudden and discontinuous changes in asset prices, further enhance the model. These models supplement the standard continuous movement of asset prices (as captured by Brownian motion) with occasional jumps, reflecting market events such as earnings surprises, economic announcements, or geopolitical shocks. The result accurately reflects the real-world behavior of asset returns,

---

[5]Mean reversion is the tendency of a variable, such as an interest rate, to drift back toward its long-term average over time. It reflects the idea that extreme values are unlikely to persist indefinitely.

which often exhibit sudden spikes or drops not captured by smooth diffusion models.

Stochastic models are distinguished from traditional models because they describe how asset prices evolve and how the inputs to the pricing model evolve over time. This produces a more flexible and nuanced understanding of market dynamics, capable of capturing complex features such as volatility smiles, the term structure of volatility, or yield curve movements. However, this added realism comes at a cost: Stochastic models are typically more mathematically sophisticated and often cannot be solved using simple formulas. Instead, they require numerical methods, such as finite difference techniques or Monte Carlo simulations, to approximate solutions.

In practice, stochastic models are essential tools in advanced financial modeling and risk management. Institutions use them to value complex derivatives, stress test portfolios, and understand how market variables interact in uncertain environments. While they introduce more computational complexity, they offer a richer framework for capturing the uncertainty that lies at the heart of financial markets.

20.4.4 *Machine learning framework* (*data-driven models*)

ML is a newer and increasingly influential approach. Unlike the frameworks above, which are based on explicit mathematical models, ML is non-parametric and data-driven.[6] It does not require return distributions, volatility, or market behavior data. Instead, it learns patterns directly from historical data.

ML models utilize features commonly employed in option pricing models. However, these models can capture complex, nonlinear relationships that traditional models cannot easily model. These models have been shown to perform well when pricing exotic options or when market dynamics are especially irregular.

[6]Commonly applied ML models used in option pricing models include neural networks (multilayer perceptrons, convolutional and recurrent architectures such as LSTM and GRU), decision trees, random forests, k-nearest neighbors (kNN), support vector machines, gradient boosting methods (XGBoost and LightGBM), logistic regression, and kernel-based models such as Gaussian processes.

That said, ML models have tradeoffs. First, they require large volumes of high-quality data to train effectively, and second, they often lack interpretability.[7] That is, they can provide predictions but don't offer much insight into why an option is priced in a certain way. Finally, they are not a replacement for traditional models but rather a complement in situations where the latter break down or cannot be used.

20.5 Summary

In this chapter, I explain the mathematical and conceptual groundwork needed to understand option pricing models. I introduce stochastic processes, particularly GBM, as the foundation for modeling the uncertainty of asset price movements. GBM offers a tractable way to model continuously evolving prices and underpins the Black–Scholes model, among others.

I then explain how modeling returns rather than prices leads to a lognormal distribution of prices, supporting key assumptions in closed-form pricing models. I also explain the cumulative normal distribution function, central to the Black–Scholes model, illustrating how it transforms model outputs into interpretable risk-neutral probabilities.

A central theme of the chapter is the role of volatility, both as an input and a conceptual driver of option value. I discuss the limitations of assuming constant fluctuations. I highlight empirical realities such as volatility clustering, fat tails, and skewness in return distributions, all of which challenge the assumptions of standard models.

The concept of risk-neutral valuation is then introduced as a unifying principle. It allows option prices to be derived without requiring knowledge of investor preferences by valuing future payoffs using adjusted probabilities and discounting at the risk-free rate. I also explain how risk-neutral valuation connects the two key approaches to pricing: replication and probabilistic valuation.

I conclude the chapter with an overview of multiple option valuation frameworks—analytical, numerical, stochastic, and ML approaches—each with its strengths and limitations. The discussion emphasizes that no

[7] In general, interpretability is crucial in financial modeling because decision-makers (e.g., portfolio managers, risk managers, and regulators) must understand not only what a model predicts but why. Transparent, interpretable models help build trust in the results, support regulatory compliance, and enable effective communication of risks and assumptions to interested parties.

single model is universally applicable and that each framework reflects a different trade-off between realism, tractability, and computational efficiency. Analytical models offer speed and clarity, numerical models offer flexibility, stochastic models provide realism, and ML models offer empirical adaptability, though often at the expense of interpretability.

Together, these quantitative foundations provide the tools necessary to understand how option pricing models operate, as described in the following two chapters, why they differ, and how to select among them in practice. The concepts presented in this chapter are essential for interpreting model behavior, assessing outputs, and adapting pricing methods to the complexities of real-world markets.

Chapter 21

The Lattice Option Pricing Model

The Black–Scholes–Merton framework for option valuation, presented in the following chapter, remains a foundational achievement in financial theory, offering a closed-form solution for European options in continuous time. Yet, its practical reach is constrained by simplifying assumptions: constant volatility, exercise only at expiration, frictionless markets, continuous trading, and stylized dividend/interest-rate treatments. Real contracts routinely depart from these conditions: Early-exercise rights, path-dependent payoffs, time-varying volatility and rates, and discrete dividends are common. Understanding these limitations is essential to appreciating why a more flexible approach is needed.

In this chapter, I describe lattice option pricing, a discrete-time framework that evolves asset prices step by step and values options by backward induction under no-arbitrage.[1] Lattice methods, most notably the binomial model of Cox, Ross, and Rubinstein,[2] and its trinomial extensions, handle what closed-form models do not: They evaluate early exercise at each node, incorporate discrete cash flows and changing parameters

[1] Some concepts introduced in earlier chapters, such as replication, no-arbitrage pricing, and option payoffs, are repeated here to ensure the chapter is fully self-contained and can be read independently.

[2] Cox, Ross, and Rubinstein introduced a general lattice-based pricing framework capable of handling American-style options and other features beyond the Black–Scholes scope. See John C. Cox, Stephen A Ross, and Mark Rubinstein, "Option Pricing: A Simplified Approach." *Journal of Financial Economics*, 7(3), 1979, 229–263.

over time, and accommodate path-dependent structures such as barriers and lookbacks.

Because calls and puts with the same strike and maturity are economically linked, I also introduce the put–call parity relationship and explain why it matters. Parity provides a model-agnostic, no-arbitrage connection between call and put values: It lets us infer the price of one from the other, check internal consistency across quotes and implied volatilities, and construct synthetic positions (for example, a synthetic forward from a call–put combination). I position this discussion immediately after the one-period example so I can obtain the put value from a known call without rebuilding the entire lattice, while also seeing how a put-specific lattice would deliver the same result.

These tools make the lattice model a flexible and computationally transparent approach to valuation, one that bridges classroom intuition and market reality.

21.1 Limitations of the Black–Scholes Model

As explained in the following chapter, the Black–Scholes model marked a significant step forward in financial theory, providing a clean and elegant formula for pricing European-style options under a set of simplified assumptions. By using continuous time and assuming frictionless markets, constant volatility, and no early exercise, the model laid the groundwork for modern arbitrage-free pricing methods. It transformed how traders, investors, and academics thought about options.

However, as noted in Chapter 20 and discussed further in the following chapter, the assumptions that make Black–Scholes analytically attractive often don't hold in practice. The model breaks down when applied to options that allow early exercise, depending on the historical path of prices, or involve changing volatility or discrete dividends. In these cases, the Black–Scholes formula becomes either inaccurate or unusable without significant adjustments or approximations.

Despite these limitations, the model is still widely used and forms the foundation of modern option pricing. Its basic intuition, replicating an option with a combination of the underlying asset and a risk-free bond, remains central to derivative valuation. But real-world options often require more flexible tools. That's where numerical models, especially lattice-based methods, come in. These models can handle early exercise, changing assumptions over time, and complex payoffs in ways that Black–Scholes simply cannot. This chapter introduces the binomial and trinomial lattice frameworks, extending the reach of arbitrage-free pricing to a broader range of securities.

This section describes situations where the Black–Scholes model runs into trouble. I look at several key categories of options and financial instruments that cannot be priced accurately and explain why more general frameworks are needed. These limitations are not merely theoretical; they show up routinely in practice, and understanding them is crucial for anyone working with options.

21.1.1 *American options and the problem of early exercise*

One of the most significant limitations of the Black–Scholes model is that it can only be used to value European-style options (i.e., contracts that may be exercised only at expiration). However, many real-world options, particularly those traded on U.S. exchanges, are American-style options (i.e., the holder has the right to exercise the option at any time before or at expiration). This seemingly minor contractual difference has substantial implications for valuation.

The flexibility of early exercise introduces what is known as an *optimal stopping problem*. At each point before expiration, the holder must decide whether exercising the option immediately yields a better payoff than continuing to hold it. This decision depends on the underlying asset's current price and the option's time value (i.e., the potential for future movements to increase its worth). The Black–Scholes model cannot handle this comparison. Because it operates in continuous time and provides a single terminal solution, it has no built-in mechanism to evaluate whether early exercise is optimal at any intermediate time.

The shortcomings of Black–Scholes in this context are most evident with deep in-the-money American put options, which may be exercised early to lock in the option's intrinsic value, especially when interest rates are high and time value is minimal. Similarly, for American call options on dividend-paying stocks, early exercise may be optimal just before the ex-dividend date, when the holder wants to capture the dividend payment. Since the Black–Scholes model assumes either no dividends or continuous dividend yields, it does not accurately capture this behavior.

Lattice models described in this chapter, especially the binomial option pricing model, are designed to address this problem. These models allow us to evaluate the option at every discrete time step, comparing the immediate exercise value to the continuation value (the value of holding the option rather than exercising it immediately, based on the discounted expected payoff at future nodes). The model calculates the option's value at each node using the backward induction method explained later in this chapter. This ensures that early exercise decisions are considered at every possible point along the tree. This makes binomial and trinomial models the standard choice for valuing American-style options in practice.

21.1.2 *Path-dependent options and exotic payoffs*

The Black–Scholes model is *path-independent*: It values an option solely based on the underlying asset's current price, the time to maturity, and volatility. However, many options have path-dependent payoffs. Three examples are (1) *Asian options*, whose payoff depends on the average price of the underlying over a period; (2) *lookback options*, which pay off based on the maximum or minimum price observed; and (3) *barrier options*, which activate or deactivate based on whether the underlying crosses a predetermined level.

For these options, the payoff is not determined solely by the underlying asset's price at expiration but depends on the path the price takes over time. Simply knowing the underlying asset's current price is not enough. One also needs to know how it got there. The Black–Scholes model, by design, uses only the current value of the underlying asset and the time remaining until expiration to determine an option's value. It does not track or store information about the sequence of prices that led to that point. As a result, it cannot handle options whose value is influenced by price history, such as the average price, the highest price, or whether a specific threshold was crossed during the option's life.

While a few closed-form solutions exist for specific exotic options under highly simplified assumptions, most path-dependent options cannot be priced accurately using analytic formulas such as Black–Scholes. Instead, they require numerical methods to account for the whole sequence of price movements over the contract's life. Lattice models are particularly well-suited for this task because they can be designed to track additional information at each node, such as the cumulative average of prices for Asian options, the running maximum or minimum for lookback options, or whether a barrier has been breached for barrier options. This flexibility makes lattice-based methods a natural and practical tool for valuing options where historical price behavior affects the final payoff.

21.1.3 *Volatility is not constant*

A central assumption of the Black–Scholes model is that the underlying asset's volatility remains constant over the option's life. This assumption makes the model mathematically tractable, but real-world data strongly contradict it. In practice, volatility is dynamic and exhibits several empirically observed behaviors undermining the constant-volatility framework.

One of the most well-documented patterns is *volatility clustering*, where periods of high volatility tend to be followed by periods of high volatility, and periods of low volatility tend to persist. This feature, observed across equities, currencies, and commodities, suggests that market volatility evolves over time and is often influenced by recent price behavior. Cont identified volatility clustering as one of the key stylized facts of asset returns, arguing that this behavior is statistically robust and incompatible with traditional constant-volatility models.[3]

Another important empirical feature of asset returns is the *leverage effect*.[4] The leverage effect refers to the observed tendency for volatility to increase as asset prices fall. This is especially pronounced in equity markets, where a drop in a firm's stock price increases its debt-to-equity ratio, making the firm more leveraged and riskier from the perspective of equity holders. As perceived risk rises, so does the stock's expected volatility. Importantly, this effect creates an asymmetric relationship between returns and volatility: Negative returns lead to rising volatility, but positive returns do not produce a similar decrease in volatility.

The Black–Scholes model cannot capture either volatility clustering or the leverage effect, which assumes a fixed volatility that does not respond to past price movements or asset-level changes. This leads to clear pricing errors, evident in the volatility smile observed in options markets. Under Black–Scholes, implied volatility should be flat across

---

[3] Rama Cont, "Empirical Properties of Asset Returns: Stylized Facts and Statistical Issues." *Quantitative Finance*, 1(2), 2001, 223–236.

[4] The leverage effect was first described in Fischer Black, "Studies of Stock Price Volatility Changes." In *Proceedings of the 1976 Meeting of the Business and Economic Statistics Section*, American Statistical Association, Washington, DC, 177–181.

strike prices. Implied volatilities vary by moneyness and maturity, reflecting market expectations of change or asymmetric risk.

Because the empirical features discussed above (such as volatility clustering and leverage effects) are inconsistent with the constant-volatility assumption of GBM, option-pricing models often incorporate state-dependent or time-varying volatility to match observed market behavior. Lattice models offer a flexible way to capture changing volatility. Although a basic binomial or trinomial tree assumes a constant level of volatility, the framework can be adapted to reflect shifts over time and across price levels. In a local-volatility approach, volatility is specified to depend on the current price and time and is calibrated so the tree matches the market's implied-volatility surface. In a stochastic-volatility approach, volatility itself is treated as an uncertain quantity that evolves over time. Both methods can be implemented by allowing the tree's up-and-down movements and the likelihood of those movements to vary from point to point and from one time step to the next. These adjustments help the lattice better reflect observed market behavior and produce option values that align more closely with traded prices.[5]

21.1.4 *Changing interest rates and discrete dividends*

The Black–Scholes model assumes a constant risk-free interest rate and either no dividends or a continuous dividend yield. These assumptions allow for analytical simplicity, but they often fail to reflect the reality of financial markets, particularly for long-dated options or options written on dividend-paying stocks.

In practice, interest rates fluctuate over time and are shaped by macroeconomic forces such as inflation, central bank policy, and changes in credit conditions. For example, an increase in the risk-free rate raises the present value of expected returns on call options by reducing the discounted value of the strike price. Conversely, falling rates tend to decrease the value of call options. Since Black–Scholes assumes a fixed rate, it cannot dynamically adjust option values in response to shifts in the yield curve or incorporate a term structure of interest rates across maturities.

A similar disconnect appears in the model's treatment of dividends. The continuous dividend yield assumption is a convenient abstraction,

[5] Steven L. Heston, "A Closed-Form Solution for Options with Stochastic Volatility with Applications to Bond and Currency Options." *Review of Financial Studies*, 6(2), 1993, 327–343.

especially when working with index options, but most companies pay discrete cash dividends at known intervals. These lump-sum payments affect the expected future price of the underlying stock and thus the value of any options written on it. In particular, to capture the dividend, American call options on dividend-paying stocks may be optimally exercised early, just before the ex-dividend date. The Black–Scholes model, which does not natively handle discrete cash flows, fails to account for this early exercise behavior, which can result in pricing errors for both puts and calls.

Lattice models, however, can incorporate non-constant interest rates by allowing the discount factor used at each time step to reflect a time-varying rate or a forward rate curve. Tree models can be adjusted for dividends to reflect known dates and amounts, typically by reducing the underlying asset's value by the dividend amount at the appropriate node. This flexibility enables lattice-based models to better match real-world conditions without needing ad hoc corrections or approximations.

This adaptability is why lattice models are often preferred for pricing options in environments with scheduled dividend payments or interest rate uncertainty, such as callable securities or employee stock options. The ability to integrate term structures and event-based price changes makes lattice methods an indispensable tool in applied option valuation.[6]

21.2 Foundations of Lattice Models

Lattice models provide a powerful and intuitive framework for valuing options and other contingent claims in discrete time. Unlike the continuous-time assumptions of the Black–Scholes model, lattice approaches divide the time to expiration into a finite number of time steps, with the underlying asset price evolving through a structured sequence of potential outcomes at each step. This structure creates a tree, most commonly a *binomial tree*, representing the range of possible price paths an asset can take. Although practitioners often refer to the diagram as a "tree," the formal name for the framework is a lattice.

A lattice is a discrete-time, discrete-state structure in which the underlying asset can move to a finite set of possible values at each time step. Because these values are connected across time in a branching pattern,

---

[6]Paul Wilmott, Sam Howison, and Jeff Dewynne, *The Mathematics of Financial Derivatives: A Student Introduction*. Cambridge: Cambridge University Press, 1995. See also John C. Hull, *Options, Futures, and Other Derivatives* (11th ed.). Boston, MA: Pearson, 2022.

the diagram visually resembles a tree, with nodes and branches showing the evolution of possible price paths. For this reason, the terms "lattice" and "tree" are used interchangeably in practice.

In this chapter, the underlying mathematical object is a lattice, but for ease of visualization, I will refer to the diagram as a tree when discussing its graphical representation.

21.2.1 *Discrete-time framework*

At its core, a lattice model is built on a *discrete-time, discrete-state process*. The option's life is divided into a number of equally spaced intervals (e.g., daily, monthly), and at each step, the underlying asset price can move to one of a finite number of possible states.

In the classic binomial model developed by Cox, Ross, and Rubinstein, the asset price is assumed to move up by a factor u or down by a factor d at each time step. This creates a *recombining tree*, meaning that different sequences of up and down moves can lead to the same asset price at a given point in time. For example, an up move followed by a down move result in the same price as a down move followed by an up move.

Because of this recombination, the tree does not branch out independently at each node but instead merges paths that lead to the same state. As a result, the total number of unique nodes at time step n is $n + 1$, rather than 2^n, which would occur in a *non-recombining* (*fully branching*) *tree*. This feature dramatically reduces computational complexity: While the number of nodes still increases as more time steps are added, it grows linearly, with $n + 1$ unique price states at time step n, rather than exponentially, which would produce 2^n nodes in a non-recombining tree. This means that the number of calculations required remains manageable even as the time horizon is broken into many steps, making the model efficient (i.e., fast to compute) and scalable (i.e., able to handle longer maturities or finer time intervals without overwhelming computational resources).

This discretization serves two purposes. First, it makes option valuation computationally feasible using simple backward induction. Second, it brings conceptual clarity: Rather than solving partial differential equations or applying stochastic calculus, the lattice model directly mirrors the no-arbitrage logic by evaluating option values step-by-step. Each node represents a possible state of the world, and the value of the option at that node is derived from the payoffs at the next time step.

21.2.2 *Risk-neutral valuation principle*

The binomial option pricing model is built on the risk-neutral valuation principle described in Chapter 20. Under this principle, the value of an option is equal to the expected value of its future payoffs, discounted at the risk-free interest rate, where the expectation is taken under a set of risk-neutral probabilities. These probabilities are not actual market beliefs but are adjusted so that all assets grow on average, at the risk-free interest rate without arbitrage. This approach transforms option pricing into a problem of computing discounted expected values, making the logic transparent and tractable, especially in a discrete-time lattice.

21.2.2.1 *Risk-neutral probability in the binomial model*

In the binomial model, over a single time step, denoted by Δt, the asset can move up by a factor u or down by a factor d. To ensure that the model is arbitrage-free and consistent with the risk-neutral framework, we assign a probability to the up-move and one minus that probability to the down-move, such that the expected value of the asset matches the return from investing in a risk-free bond. The convention used in the binomial model to denote the risk-neutral probability for an up move in the asset's price is q; therefore, for a down move, it is $1 - q$.

To derive the value of q, we start by equating the expected asset price under the risk-neutral probabilities to the forward price implied by risk-free compounding. This requires defining the following parameters to calculate q:

$$q = \frac{e^{r\,\Delta t} - d}{u - d} \tag{21.1}$$

where r is the risk-free interest rate and the symbol e is the base of the natural logarithm, approximately equal to 2.71828. In this context, $e^{r\Delta t}$ represents the future value of one dollar invested at a continuously compounded rate r over a time interval Δt. For example, if $= 0.05$ and $\Delta t = 1$, then $e^{0.05} \approx 1.0513$, meaning one dollar grows to approximately \$1.0513 in one year.

This ensures that when q is used to weight the possible up and down movements, the expected future value of the asset reflects the growth the asset's price would experience if it earned the risk-free interest rate over the period, increment t end superscript, is often referred to as the "forward price," the price the asset would be expected to reach in a frictionless market with no arbitrage, assuming continuous compounding at the risk-free interest rate.[7] This usage of *forward price* reflects a theoretical construct, not a traded forward contract, and should not be confused with the market price of a forward agreement. The binomial model maintains internal consistency with the no-arbitrage pricing framework by matching this value. Once q is determined, the option's value at each node in the tree can be calculated as the discounted expected value of the option's values at the next time step.

21.2.3 *One-period binomial option pricing*

With the risk-neutral probability q computed, it is now used to value options in the simplest version of the binomial model: a *one-period framework*. This setup involves only a single time step Δt, during which the underlying asset's price moves either up to $S{\cdot}u$ or down to $S{\cdot}d$.

Suppose we are valuing a European call option with a strike price K, as shown in Figure 21.1, which illustrates the basic one-period binomial tree structure and associated payoffs.

- If the asset moves up: $C_u = \max(S{\cdot}u - K, 0)$.
- If the asset moves down: $C_d = \max(S{\cdot}d - K, 0)$.

$C_u = \max(S{\cdot}u - K, 0)$ means that if the asset's price goes up to $S{\cdot}u$, the payoff of the call option is the difference between the new asset price and the strike price, but only if that difference is positive. The payoff is zero if the option is out-of-the-money (i.e., the asset price is below the strike price).

$C_d = \max(S{\cdot}d - K, 0)$ means that if the stock goes down to $S{\cdot}d$, the payoff of the call option is again the difference between the new stock price and the strike price, but only if it's positive. The option becomes worthless if the price drops enough (a zero payoff).

[7] The term "forward price" here refers to the theoretical future value of the asset assuming risk-free growth, *not* the quoted price of a forward contract.

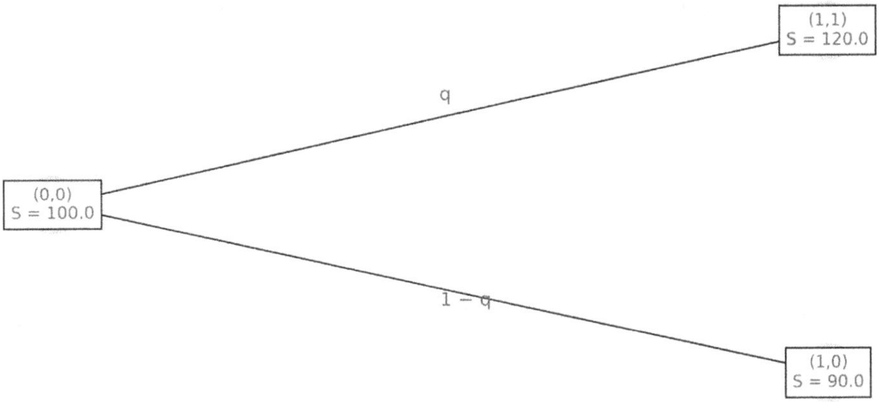

Figure 21.1. One-Period Binomial Tree for a European Call Option

The current value of the option, C, is the expected value of these two possible payoffs, weighted by the risk-neutral probabilities, and discounted at the risk-free rate:

$$C = e^{-r\,\Delta t}\,[q \cdot C_u + (1 - q) \cdot C_d] \tag{21.2}$$

This formula reflects the central principle of risk-neutral pricing: The option's current value is the present value of its expected payoff in a hypothetical world where the asset earns the risk-free interest rate, and probabilities have been adjusted accordingly.

As discussed in later sections, this one-period model provides the building block for more complex, multi-period lattice models that can handle American options and path-dependent payoffs.

To illustrate, suppose we want to value a European call option using a one-period binomial model. The parameters are as follows:

- current stock price: $S = 100$
- strike price: $K = 105$
- time to maturity: $\Delta t = 0.5$ years
- risk-free interest rate (continuously compounded): $r = 0.08$
- up factor: $u = 1.20$
- down factor: $d = 0.90$

Step 1: Compute the Risk-Neutral Probability: We use equation (21.2). First, calculate $e^{-r\,\Delta t}$:

$$e^{-0.08 \times 0.5} \approx 0.9608$$

Now, plug into equation (21.2):

$$q = \frac{0.9608 - 0.90}{1.20 - 0.90} \approx 0.2026$$

So, the risk-neutral probability of an up move is q approximately 0.2026, or 20.26%, and the probability of a down move is $1 - q$ or approximately 0.7974, or 79.74%.

Step 2: Compute the Option Payoffs at Expiration:

- If the stock goes up: $S{\cdot}u = 100{\cdot}1.20 = 120$. Therefore,

$$C_u = \max(120 - 105, 0) = 15$$

- If the stock goes down: $S{\cdot}d = 100{\cdot}0.90 = 90$. Therefore,

$$C_d = \max(90 - 105, 0) = 0$$

Step 3: Compute the Present Value of Expected Payoff: Using equation (21.2),

$$C = 0.9608\,[0.2026{\cdot}15 + 0.7974{\cdot}0] \approx 2.92$$

Therefore, the value of this European call option is approximately \$2.92.

21.2.4 *Put–call parity and the put value for European options*

We have obtained the value of the European call. How do we obtain the value of the corresponding put with the same strike and expiration? There are two equivalent approaches. First, we can build a lattice for the put using the same up/down moves, probabilities, and discounting and then apply backward induction to compute the put's value directly. Second, we can exploit put–call parity, a no-arbitrage relationship that links European calls and puts. Although risk-neutral probabilities are introduced later, put–call parity does not rely on them; it follows directly from no-arbitrage replication, which is why it can be presented at this stage.

For a non-dividend-paying underlying, put–call parity states that the value of a long call and short put equals the value of a long underlying financed by borrowing the present value of the strike price. In present-value terms,[8]

$$C - P = S - K\,e^{-rt} \tag{21.3}$$

where K is the strike price and P is the put price.

Rearranging gives the put value from a known call price,

$$P = C - S + K\,e^{-rt}$$

Using the call value $C \approx 2.92$ from above and the same parameters ($S = 100$, $K = 105$, $r = 8\%$, and $T = 0.5$), the discounted strike price is

$$K\,e^{-rt} = 105 \cdot 0.9608 \approx 100.88$$

Applying parity yields

$$P = 2.92 - 100 + 100.88 = 3.8$$

which matches the value that would have been obtained by valuing a put on the same lattice.

Exact parity holds for European options. With American options, early-exercise rights break the equality; only inequality bounds apply. And those bounds depend on dividends and financing friction.

Put–call parity follows directly from the arbitrage logic and the law of one price introduced in Chapter 19: When two positions deliver the same cash flow in every future state, they must carry the same cost today, or else a risk-free profit would be possible by buying the cheaper package and selling the dearer one. In the parity context, a call combined with appropriate financing (to cover the strike price at expiry) is economically equivalent to holding the underlying together with a put that protects the downside; because those two packages produce identical payoffs across states, competitive markets force their current values into alignment. This

[8] If the underlying pays known discrete dividends before expiration, subtract the present value of those dividends from the right-hand side. If the underlying carries a continuous yield (for example, an equity index dividend yield or a foreign interest rate in currency options), the parity becomes

$$C - P = S\,e^{-qt} - K\,e^{-rt}$$

is the same replication-and-no-arbitrage reasoning used to value forwards and futures, now applied to a pair of option portfolios rather than to a single contract. The result is a practical tool: From a listed call price one can infer the consistent put price (and vice versa), check quotes and implied volatilities for internal consistency, and construct synthetic exposures without building a separate pricing model. Framed this way, parity is not an isolated formula but a direct application of Chapter 19's core idea that replication plus the law of one price pins down fair values in arbitrage-free markets.

21.3 Multi-Period Binomial Option Pricing

The one-period binomial model introduced earlier provides a clear and intuitive foundation for understanding the core logic of risk-neutral valuation. However, it is far too limited for most real-world applications. In practice, options rarely have just one time interval to expiration, and valuation accuracy depends on modeling multiple stages of asset evolution. To address this, we now extend the binomial model to handle multiple periods.

A multi-period binomial model breaks the life of an option into a sequence of discrete time steps, allowing the asset to follow a branching path of possible price movements. This expanded framework will enable us to capture time-varying price behavior, evaluate early exercise decisions at multiple points, and approximate the results of continuous-time models, such as the Black–Scholes model. It also serves as the foundation for modeling more complex instruments such as American options, exotic payoffs, and derivatives with time-dependent features.

21.3.1 *Constructing the asset price tree*

We first construct the asset price tree to begin the multi-period valuation process. Suppose the option has N discrete time steps before expiration. At each step, the asset price can move up by a fixed factor u or down by a fixed factor d, just as in the one-period case. However, the key difference is that the tree now extends across several time layers, forming a recombining structure: Different sequences of up and down moves may lead to the same asset price at a given time step. This recombining property arises because the model uses multiplicative price changes, so an up-move followed by a down-move produces the same price as a down-move followed by an up-move.

The one-period binomial model is a helpful starting point for understanding the logic of risk-neutral valuation, but it is too simplistic for most real-world applications. To make the model more realistic, we extend it to multiple periods. In a multi-period binomial model, the option's life is divided into N equal time steps of length $\Delta t = T/N$, where T is the total time to maturity.

At this point, the asset price tree is constructed so that the number of distinct nodes at time step n is $n + 1$, reflecting the recombining structure that keeps the model computationally tractable as N grows.

In this framework, a *node* represents a specific point in the tree corresponding to a particular time step and price level. Let node (i, j) denote the point in the tree reached after i time steps and j upward movements in the asset price; the asset price at that node can be expressed as

$$S_{i,j} = S \cdot u^{j} \cdot d^{i-j}$$

This formula gives the asset price after i steps, of which j are up moves and $i - j$ are down moves.

Once the asset price tree is constructed, the option payoff is computed at each final node (at time T):

- *For a call*: $C = \max(S_{N,j} - K, 0)$ (21.4)
- *For a put*: $P = \max(K - S_{N,j}, 0)$ (21.5)

Then, we work backward through the tree using the risk-neutral expectation, discounted at the risk-free interest rate:

$$V_{i,j} = e^{-r\Delta t} \left[q \cdot \mathrm{V}_{i+1,j+1} + (1-q) \cdot V_{i+1,j}\right]$$

Here, $V_{i,j}$ is the option value at node (i, j), and q is the risk-neutral probability, calculated as in equation (21.1).

This backward induction process continues until we reach the present (time 0), where $V_{0,0}$ gives the option's value today.

The multi-period binomial model is powerful because of the following reasons:

- It allows for finer time resolution, improving accuracy.
- As the number of steps increases, the model converges to the Black–Scholes price for European options.
- It can be adapted for American-style options, allowing early exercise.
- It handles path-dependent payoffs and variable parameters more flexibly than closed-form solutions.

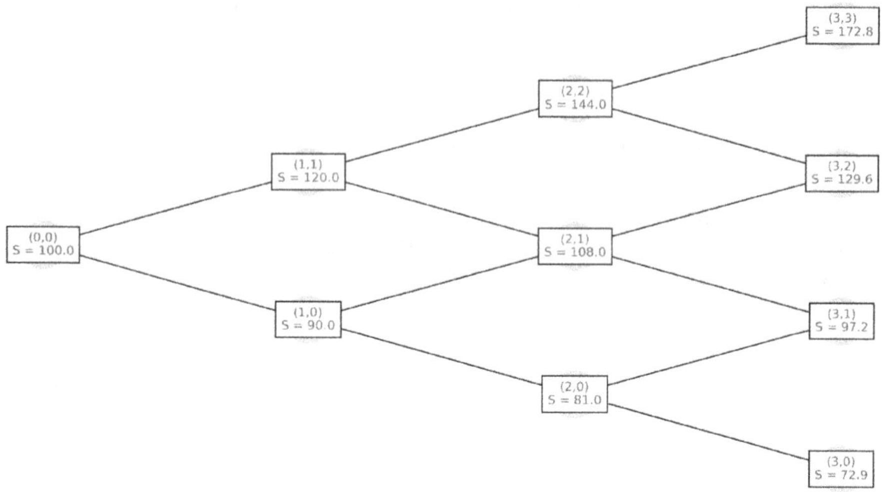

Figure 21.2. Three-Step Binomial Tree with Node Indices and Asset Prices

21.3.1.1 *Three-step binomial tree* (*asset price tree*)

With the multi-period structure in place, we now illustrate the evolution of asset prices using a three-step binomial tree. Consider a three-step binomial tree using simple assumptions to illustrate how asset prices evolve in a multi-period binomial model. This example computes the asset price at each node in the tree and demonstrates the lattice's recombining nature.

Suppose the current stock price is $S = 100$, the up factor is $u = 1.20$, and the down factor is $d = 0.90$. At each time step, the asset can either move up by 20% or down by 10%, and we track the possible prices over three time steps.

Each node in the tree represents the asset's price at a specific point in time, given a specific number of up and down moves. Figure 21.2 shows the three-step binomial tree with node indices and the corresponding asset prices, illustrating how price levels evolve over time. We denote each node by the pair (i, j), where:

- i is the time step (from 0 to 3 in this illustration),
- j is the number of upward price movements that have occurred by that time.

The asset price at node (i, j) is given by

$$S_{i,j} = S \cdot u^j \cdot d^{i-j}$$

This means the asset's price is scaled up j times and down $i - j$ times from the original price.

Let's walk through a few nodes:

- At time step $i = 0$, the price is just the starting price: $S_{0,0} = 100$.
- At time step $i = 1$, there are two possible outcomes:
  - (1, 0): the price goes down once → $100 \cdot d = 90$;
  - (1, 1): the price goes up once → $100 \cdot u = 120$.
- At time step $i = 2$, we have three possible outcomes:
  - (2, 0): two down moves → $100 \cdot d^2 = 81$;
  - (2, 1): one up and one down (in any order) → $100 \cdot u \cdot d = 108$;
  - (2, 2): two up moves → $100 \cdot u^2 = 144$.
- At time step $i = 3$, we compute similarly:
  - (3, 0): three down moves → $100 \cdot d^3 = 72.9$;
  - (3, 1): one up, two down → $100 \cdot u \cdot d^2 = 97.2$;
  - (3, 2): two up, one down → $100 \cdot u^2 \cdot d = 129.6$;
  - (3, 3): three up moves → $100 \cdot u^3 = 172.8$.

This structure is called a *recombining tree* because multiple paths through the tree can lead to the same price. For example, going up then down or down then up results in the same final price at node (2, 1). Thanks to this recombination, the total number of unique price outcomes at each time step is only $i + 1$, which keeps the model computationally manageable even as the number of steps increases.

Figure 21.3 displays the full three-step binomial tree with node indices and the option values that ultimately result from the backward-induction procedure. These values are shown here to provide a preview of the completed valuation tree; the step-by-step calculation of the node value is developed in the following section.

21.3.2 *Calculating payoffs at expiration*

In a multi-period binomial model, the final step in constructing the asset price tree is to compute the option's payoff at expiration; that is, at the

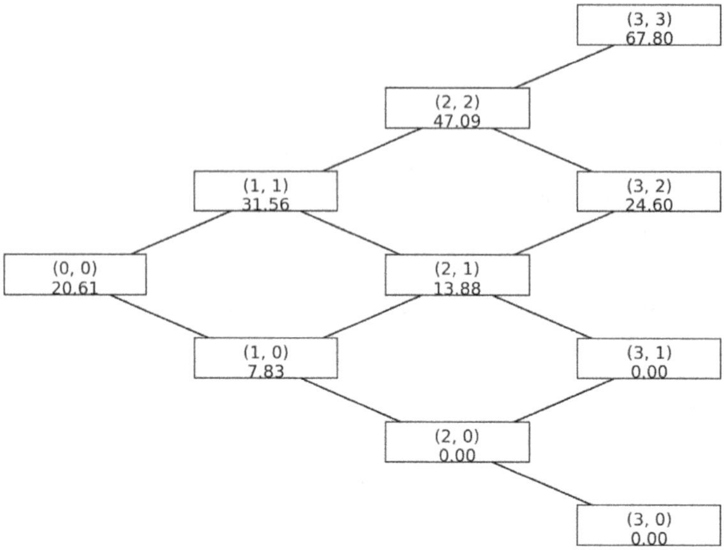

Figure 21.3. Backward-Induction Valuation on the Three-Step Binomial Tree

terminal nodes of the tree. For a European call option, the payoff at expiration is determined by applying (21.4):

$$C_{N,j} = \max(S_{N,j} - K, 0)$$

where:

- $C_{N,j}$ is the option value at time step N after j up moves,
- $S_{N,j}$ is the asset price at that node,
- K is the strike price.

I will continue using the following inputs from our earlier example: $S = 100$, $u = 1.20$, $d = 0.90$, $K = 105$, and $N = 3$ (three time steps). At time step 3 (expiration), we calculate the asset prices and then compute the corresponding call option payoffs at each node. Table 21.1 shows the illustration's call payoffs at expiration (time step 3).

These payoffs at expiration form the terminal values of the option price tree. Next, we work backward through the tree using the risk-neutral valuation formula to calculate the option's present value at earlier nodes, ultimately solving for its value today.

Table 21.1. Asset Prices and Call Payoffs at Expiration (Time Step 3)

Node (3, j)	**Asset Price $S_{3,j}$**	**Call Payoff max($S_{3,j}$ − 105, 0)**
(3, 3)	$100 \cdot u^3 = 100 \cdot 1.728 = 172.8$	max(172.8 − 105,0) = 67.8
(3, 2)	$100 \cdot u^2 \cdot d = 100 \cdot 1.44 \cdot 0.9 = 129.6$	max(129.6 − 105,0) = 24.6
(3, 1)	$100 \cdot u \cdot d^2 = 100 \cdot 1.2 \cdot 0.81 = 97.2$	max(97.2 − 105,0) = 0
(3, 0)	$100 \cdot d^3 = 100 \cdot 0.729 = 72.9$	max(72.9 − 105,0) = 0

21.3.3 *Backward induction and option valuation*

With the call option payoffs at expiration now determined, the next step is calculating the option's value at earlier points in the tree using backward induction. This method applies the risk-neutral valuation principle at each node, moving from the final time step back to the present. These risk-neutral probabilities serve the same role as state-price weights in no-arbitrage valuation, providing the relative weights used to compute the discounted expected value at each node.

At each node, the option's value is computed as the discounted expected value of the option's values at the two successor nodes in the next time step. The formula used is the appropriately modified equation (21.2) given by

$$C_{i,j} = e^{-r\,\Delta t}\,[q \cdot C_{i+1,\,j+1} + (1-q) \cdot C_{i+1,j}] \tag{21.6}$$

where $C_{i,j}$ is the option value at node (i, j).

The backward induction method involves starting with the payoffs at time step 3 (the option's expiration date shown in the last column in Table 21.1. Then, we compute the option values at time step 2 nodes using the formula given by (21.6) as follows:

- $C_{2,2} = 0.9231 \cdot [0.611 \cdot 67.8 + 0.389 \cdot 24.6] \approx 47.09$
- $C_{2,1} = 0.9231 \cdot [0.611 \cdot 24.6 + 0.389 \cdot 0] \approx 13.88$
- $C_{2,0} = 0.9231 \cdot [0.611 \cdot 0 + 0.389 \cdot 0] = 0$

Now the two values at time step 1 are computed:

- $C_{1,1} = 0.9231 \cdot [0.611 \cdot 47.09 + 0.389 \cdot 13.88] \approx 31.56$
- $C_{1,0} = 0.9231 \cdot [0.611 \cdot 13.88 + 0.389 \cdot 0] \approx 7.83$

Finally, the option value today (i.e., the value at the root of the tree) is

$$C_{0,0} = 0.9231 \cdot [0.611 \cdot 31.56 + 0.389 \cdot 7.83] \approx 20.61$$

This is the value of this European call option using a three-step binomial model.

21.3.4 *Demonstrating the flexibility of the lattice model: An American put option example*

One of the binomial (lattice) model's most powerful features is its ability to accommodate early exercise decisions. This flexibility is essential for valuing American-style options, which can be exercised at any point up to and including expiration. Unlike European options, whose valuation depends only on terminal payoffs, American options require that we evaluate, at every node of the tree, whether early exercise is preferable to holding the option for one more period.

The Black–Scholes model cannot directly handle this type of decision. It assumes continuous trading and excludes early exercise. In contrast, the binomial model handles this naturally through backward induction, comparing the intrinsic value (the payoff from immediate exercise) to the expected value of continuing to hold the option, discounted at the risk-free rate. To demonstrate this feature, we will value a three-period American put option using the same parameters as the earlier call option example.

We will use the parameters in our previous illustration for the European call option to compute the value of the American *put* by evaluating the option at each node in the binomial tree. At expiration, the value of the American option is the same as that of a European option because there is no time left to exercise early. We calculate the intrinsic value of the put at each terminal node by applying the formula given by (21.6):

$$P = \max(K - S, 0)$$

This yields the following values:

- At node (3, 3), the asset price is 172.8, so the payoff is max (105 − 172.8,0) = 0.
- At node (3, 2), the asset price is 129.6, and the payoff is again 0.
- At node (3, 1), the asset price is 97.2, yielding a payoff of 7.8.
- At node (3, 0), the asset price is 72.9, and the payoff is 32.1.

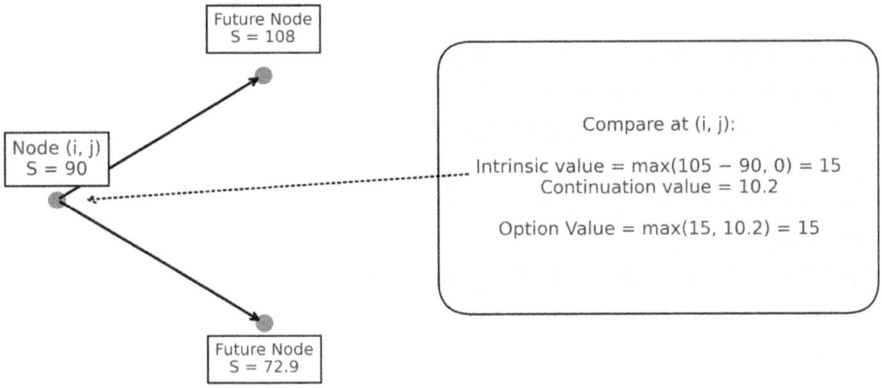

Figure 21.4. Early Exercise Decision at a Node in an American Option Tree

At each node prior to expiration, we must now compare two values: the intrinsic value from exercising the option immediately and the discounted expected value from continuing to hold the option.

Figure 21.4 illustrates the decision process at a single node when valuing an American option. At each step, the model compares the immediate exercise value with the continuation value and selects the greater of the two.

Let's examine each node:

- At node (2, 2), the asset price is 144, so the intrinsic value is $\max(105 - 144, 0) = 0$. The expected continuation value, using the two terminal values below it (both zero), is also zero. So, $P_{2,2} = 0$.
- At node (2, 1), the asset price is 108, so the intrinsic value is zero. The expected continuation value is $0.9231 \cdot (0.611 \cdot 0 + 0.389 \cdot 7.8) \approx 2.80$. Since this is higher than the intrinsic value, the put option is not exercised, and $P_{2,1} = 2.80$.
- At node (2, 0), the asset price is 81, so the intrinsic value is $105 - 81 = 24$. The continuation value is $0.9231 \cdot (0.611 \cdot 7.8 + 0.389 \cdot 32.1) \approx 15.94$.

Since immediate exercise is worth more than waiting, early exercise is optimal, and we set $P_{2,0} = 24$.

Next, we continue the backward deduction to time step 1:

- At node (1, 1), the asset price is 120, so the intrinsic value is zero. The continuation value is $0.9231 \cdot (0.611 \cdot 0 + 0.389 \cdot 2.80) \approx 1.01$. Since this is greater than the intrinsic value, the option is not exercised, and $P_{1,1} = 1.01$.

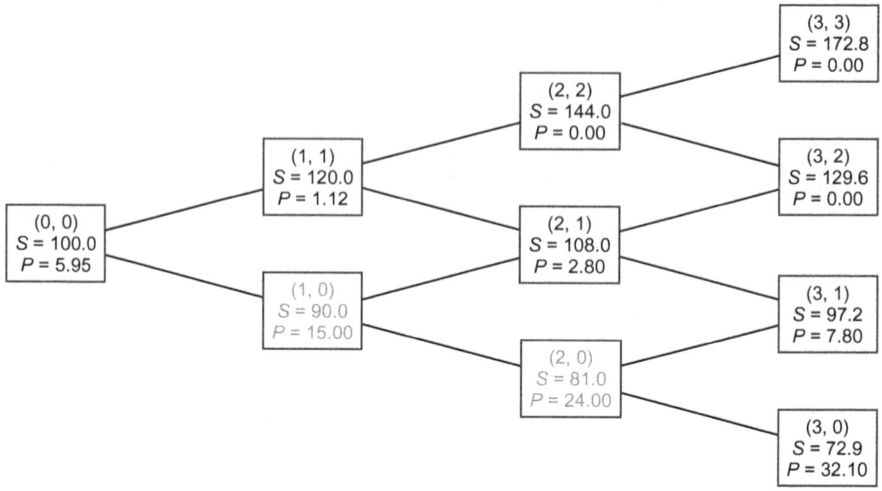

Figure 21.5. Full Binomial Tree Valuation of an American Put Option

- At node (1, 0), the asset price is 90, with an intrinsic value of 15. The continuation value is $0.9231 \cdot (0.611 \cdot 2.80 + 0.389 \cdot 24) \approx 10.21$. Since the intrinsic value is greater, there is an exercise early, and $P_{1,0} = 15$.

At the root node (0, 0), the asset price is 100, so the intrinsic value is $105 - 100 = 5$. The expected continuation value is $0.9231 \cdot (0.611 \cdot 1.01 + 0.389 \cdot 15) \approx 5.95$. Since the continuation value is greater than the intrinsic value, the option is not exercised, and the option value today is $P = 5.95$.

This illustration highlights one of the key advantages of the lattice model: its ability to evaluate early exercise decisions at every node. Figure 21.5 presents the full binomial tree for the American put example, including asset prices, option values, and early exercise decisions. In this case, the American put is more valuable than a European put with the same parameters, and we observe that early exercise is optimal at two nodes. The binomial model handles this naturally and efficiently through backward induction flexibility not available in closed-form models such as Black–Scholes.

21.4 Trinomial Trees and Extensions

Trinomial trees expand upon the basic binomial framework by introducing a third possible outcome at each node. In addition to the asset price moving up or down, it may also remain unchanged. This three-branch structure makes trinomial trees more flexible and often more accurate, especially when pricing complex options or when fewer time steps are desired for computational efficiency.

The key advantage of a trinomial tree is its ability to offer a more refined representation of how asset prices can evolve over time. By allowing the price to remain constant, in addition to moving up or down, the model can better approximate the behavior of continuous-time processes. This leads to more stable and faster convergence to theoretical values, such as those derived from the Black–Scholes model.

Trinomial trees are beneficial when (1) pricing American options, where early exercise is possible, (2) dealing with features such as discrete dividends or barriers, and (3) modeling derivatives under more complex conditions, such as stochastic interest rates or volatility.

At each point in the tree, the asset can take on three possible values in the next time step. As with the binomial model, the tree is built forward in time to determine all possible future asset prices and then worked backward to compute the present value of the option. Adding the third branch enhances the model's ability to handle scenarios where the asset price remains relatively stable over a short time interval, which is particularly important for capturing the behavior of certain financial instruments.

Trinomial trees often require fewer steps than binomial trees to achieve the same level of accuracy, making them more efficient for specific applications. They also reduce some of the directional bias seen in binomial models by offering a more symmetrical and realistic set of price movements.

For American-style options, the additional node in a trinomial tree, representing the possibility that the asset price remains unchanged during a time step, enhances the model's ability to identify optimal early exercise points, leading to more precise valuations.

The trinomial tree concept can be extended even further. In some advanced applications, non-recombining trees capture path-dependent behavior, though these come with increased computational demands. Trinomial trees also form the basis of more complex structures used in modeling interest rates or volatility, such as in the Hull–White or Heston models described in the following chapter.

Trinomial trees offer a natural and powerful extension to the binomial framework. Their ability to model a broader range of asset price behaviors makes them particularly valuable when precision, flexibility, or complex payoff features are required. For practitioners seeking to balance accuracy with computational efficiency, trinomial trees are a foundational tool in modern option pricing.

21.5 Lattice Models for Exotic and Path-Dependent Options

Standard lattice models, such as the binomial and trinomial trees, are powerful tools for pricing vanilla options. However, many real-world derivatives include more complex features, such as payoffs that depend on the path taken by the underlying asset or barriers that trigger or nullify the option based on price levels reached during the option's life. As explained in Chapter 8, these are known as *exotic* and *path-dependent* options. Adapting lattice models to handle such features requires structural modifications and careful implementation.

The following presents a purely descriptive overview of how lattice models can be adapted to price several common exotic and path-dependent options. The discussion avoids mathematical derivations and technical detail, focusing instead on the intuition and structural adjustments required.[9]

21.5.1 *Barrier options*

Barrier options are a class of options whose payoff depends not only on the final price of the underlying asset but also on whether the asset's price has crossed a pre-specified barrier during the option's life. For instance, a *knock-out* option becomes void if the barrier is breached, while a *knock-in* option only becomes active if the barrier is reached.

To price barrier options using a lattice, the tree must track whether the barrier has been crossed at any point along each possible price path. This often involves discarding or activating nodes based on whether they lie above or below the barrier. The challenge lies in ensuring that the tree

[9]A rigorous treatment, including formulas and computational methods, is available in Domingo Tavella, *Quantitative Methods in Derivatives Pricing: An Introduction to Computational Finance*. Wiley, 2003, and Espen G. Haug, *The Complete Guide to Option Pricing Formulas* (2nd ed.). McGraw-Hill, 2007.

correctly reflects the option's activation or deactivation status at every point in time.

21.5.2 *Asian options*

Asian options derive their value from the average price of the underlying asset over a specific period, rather than its price at maturity. This makes them less sensitive to extreme price movements and is useful for hedging purposes.

To incorporate this averaging feature into a lattice model, the tree must be expanded to account for both the current asset price and the cumulative or average price along each path. This introduces an additional state variable, which increases the tree's complexity. Nevertheless, lattice models remain practical for Asian options if the averaging mechanism can be discretized effectively.

21.5.3 *Lookback options*

Lookback options have payoffs that depend on the maximum or minimum price the underlying asset reaches during the option's life. These options offer the holder the benefit of hindsight and tend to be more valuable than standard options.

Modeling lookback options with a lattice requires tracking the highest or lowest price attained along each possible path through the tree. As with Asian options, this introduces a memory component into the model. The tree must be modified to retain information about historical extrema and current prices. This can be computationally intensive, but it allows for flexible modeling of these uniquely advantageous contracts.

21.5.4 *Modifications needed in the tree structure*

Adapting lattice models for exotic and path-dependent options requires structural changes beyond simple branching. One key modification is the introduction of path tracking. Because the payoff of these options often depends on the sequence of asset prices rather than just the final value, the model must retain historical information at each node. This could include the highest or lowest asset price reached so far, the running average of prices over time, or whether a specific price barrier has been crossed. Without this capability, the model cannot accurately reflect the path-dependent nature of the payoff.

Another critical adjustment involves node duplication. In standard lattice models, different paths that lead to the same current price are treated identically. However, for path-dependent options, two such paths may have very different implications for the payoff if their histories differ. To address this, the model must duplicate nodes to preserve distinctions between paths that result in the same asset price but differ in historical experience, such as whether a barrier was touched or the cumulative average.

Finally, these enhancements substantially increase the computational complexity of the model. To maintain tractability, it becomes necessary to implement memory-efficient algorithms. These algorithms are designed to handle the expanded state space without an unmanageable memory or processing time increase. They ensure that the model remains computationally practical, even as it tracks more information and manages a larger number of distinct paths.

21.6 Volatility and Interest Rate Considerations

In the basic formulation of lattice models, whether binomial or trinomial, both volatility and interest rates are usually assumed to be constant. Each node in the lattice applies the same volatility level and risk-free interest rate, regardless of the underlying asset's current price or the time period. This simplification makes the models more tractable and easier to implement. However, it does not accurately reflect the reality of financial markets, where volatility often depends on market conditions and interest rates vary across different maturities and periods. These limitations can lead to inaccurate pricing, particularly for complex derivatives, long-dated options, or instruments whose payoffs are sensitive to changes in volatility or interest rates over time.

Two major extensions are commonly employed to enhance the realism and flexibility of lattice models: *local volatility models* and the incorporation of a *term structure of interest rates*. These refinements enable the model to accurately reflect market-observed pricing behaviors and economic dynamics, allowing for a more precise valuation of options under varying conditions.

21.6.1 *Local volatility in lattice models*

Local volatility models allow volatility to vary across different states of the tree based on the asset's current price and the time period. Instead of assuming that volatility is fixed, these models recognize that in actual markets, implied volatility tends to differ across strike prices and maturities, a phenomenon known as the volatility smile or volatility skew, described in Chapter 11.

Incorporating local volatility into a lattice requires a more flexible structure, where the price movement ranges and transition probabilities are recalculated at each node based on local conditions. This dynamic structure enables the model to fit observed option prices more accurately and to account for the market's expectation of future volatility as a function of asset level and time. This is especially valuable in pricing path-dependent or exotic options, such as barrier or lookback options, which are highly sensitive to the variation of volatility along the entire path, not just at expiration.

While more computationally demanding, local volatility models greatly improve the alignment between the model and real-world pricing patterns. They also provide a richer framework for managing volatility risk and conducting scenario analysis in derivative portfolios.

21.6.2 *Term structure of interest rates in lattice models*

Just as volatility is not static, interest rates in practice vary across different maturities. This variation is captured by the term structure of interest rates, which refers to the yield associated with bonds or investments of differing time horizons. In standard lattice models, applying a single, constant interest rate ignores the reality that short-term rates and long-term rates can differ substantially and that these differences can have a meaningful impact on the present value of future option payoffs.

To incorporate a term structure into a lattice, the discounting process must be adjusted so that each cash flow is evaluated using the rate applicable to its specific time horizon. This can be achieved in two ways: by applying a static term structure derived from market data, such as Treasury or swap yield curves, or by modeling the interest rate itself as a stochastic process. In the latter case, a separate lattice is used to simulate the evolution of interest rates over time.

This extension becomes particularly important when pricing interest rate–linked derivatives, such as bond options, swaptions, and callable securities. In such cases, like the Hull–White model,[10] Black–Karasinski model,[11] and Kalotay–Williams– Fabozzi model,[12] are often used, as they allow interest rates to evolve in a mean-reverting fashion consistent with historical behavior. Even for equity or commodity options, interest rate term structure can matter for long-dated contracts, where slight differences in the assumed rate over multiple years can compound into significant pricing errors.

Incorporating a term structure enhances the realism of the lattice model and improves pricing accuracy, especially when aligning the model with instruments whose value is directly tied to yield curve dynamics.

21.7 Online Tools and Model Implementations

A number of interactive lattice pricing tools are available online to compute option values using binomial or trinomial frameworks. These tools offer user-friendly interfaces for specifying option parameters and observing tree construction, valuation steps, and payoff structures. However, it is important to note that such tools appear and disappear over time; they are often maintained by educators, researchers, or enthusiast developers rather than institutions. Some platforms support basic binomial pricing of European and American options, while others extend to trinomial trees or support pricing of barrier and Asian options that we describe in the following.

Table 21.2 summarizes currently accessible and reliable models as of mid-2025, focusing on lattice-based frameworks.

[10] John C. Hull and Alan White, "Pricing Interest-Rate-Derivative Securities." *Review of Financial Studies*, 3(4), 1990, 573–592.

[11] Fischer Black and Piotr Karasinski, "Bond and Option Pricing When Short Rates Are Lognormal." *Financial Analysts Journal*, 47(4), 1991, 52–59.

[12] Andrew J. Kalotay, George O. Williams, and Frank J. Fabozzi, "A Model for Valuing Bonds and Embedded Options." *Financial Analysts Journal*, 49(3), 1993, 35–46.

Table 21.2. Selected Online Tools for Binomial and Trinomial Option Pricing Models

Website/Tool	Model Type	Key Features	Access Link
FinTools OptionsCalc	Binomial (American/ European)	Supports early exercise, dividends, Greeks; Excel-based; part of professional analytics suite	https://www.fintools.com/products/fincalcs/optionscalc
Hoadley.net Calculator	Binomial and trinomial	Visual trees, American/ European exercise, discrete/continuous dividends, downloadable Excel tools	https://www.hoadley.net/options/calculators.htm
FinCalcs.net Binomial Tool	Binomial (American/ European)	Clean interface for calls/ puts; supports discrete dividends	https://fincalcs.net/OptionsBin
Macroption Excel Tool	Binomial (CRR, Jarrow-Rudd, Leisen-Reimer)	Offers Excel sheets for lattice modeling, with Greeks and model selection flexibility	https://www.macroption.com/binomial-option-pricing-excel/
Barchart.com Options Calc	Binomial (used for Greeks)	Greeks derived from binomial method; includes calls, puts, IV, and expiration analysis	https://www.barchart.com/options/options-calculator
WolframAlpha	Binomial via user input	Can solve discrete-time binomial models via structured query or interactive demo	https://www.wolframalpha.com/input/?i=binomial+option+pricing+model

21.8 Summary

In this chapter, I explain the lattice approach to option valuation as a discrete-time, no-arbitrage framework grounded in replication and why the simplifying assumptions of the foundational Black–Scholes–Merton option-pricing framework limit its practical reach. That discussion is important for appreciating the flexibility of lattice methods, which value options by stepping through time and pricing by backward induction.

Starting from the one-period binomial construction and extending to multi-period and trinomial trees, I show how the lattice accommodates features that closed-form models handle poorly: early exercise in American options, discrete dividends and other cash flows, path-dependent payoffs (such as barriers and lookbacks), and time-varying volatility and interest rates. Extensions that help align the tree with observed markets, such as state- and time-dependent volatility specifications, stochastic-volatility ideas implemented through node-by-node adjustments, and term-structure discounting, are explained, and how these choices can be calibrated in practice. While these enhancements increase computation, they preserve transparency and offer a helpful framework for analysis and instruction.

I also explain the usefulness of the put–call parity relationship for European options. Parity links calls and puts with the same strike price and maturity, allowing one to infer a put from a known call (or the reverse), check internal consistency across quotes and implied volatilities, and construct synthetic positions (for example, a synthetic forward from a call–put combination).

Taken together, these elements present the lattice model as a flexible and economically clear approach that connects no-arbitrage intuition to real-world contract features. With these foundations in place, the following chapter presents the continuous-time Black–Scholes–Merton solution and shows how its closed form emerges from the same underlying economics.

Chapter 22

The Black–Scholes–Merton Option Pricing Framework

In this chapter, I extend the analysis from the lattice framework of Chapter 21 to the continuous-time Black–Scholes–Merton option pricing model, which has become one of the most influential achievements in modern finance. Whereas the lattice framework values options by moving step by step in discrete intervals of time and applying backward induction, the Black–Scholes–Merton framework removes the step size entirely and models asset prices in continuous time. In *continuous time*, price changes are represented as an uninterrupted process, evolving smoothly at every instant rather than only at specific nodes of a tree. This shift allows the framework to capture market dynamics with greater mathematical precision and leads to a closed-form solution for option prices.

I begin by situating the model in its historical context, explaining how Fischer Black, Myron Scholes, and Robert Merton formulated it in 1973. I then focus on the broader economic logic that underpins the model, building directly on the replication and no-arbitrage reasoning introduced in the lattice chapter. The goal is not merely to present the formula but to highlight how the Black–Scholes framework generalizes discrete-time methods of binomial and trinomial lattices into a continuous-time setting. By doing so, it provides a common foundation for a wide range of valuation techniques, including analytical models such as the closed-form Black–Scholes formula itself, numerical methods such as Monte Carlo simulation, and extended lattice approaches. Rather than being an isolated result, the Black–Scholes model exemplifies how the principles of replication and risk-neutral valuation can be applied consistently across different modeling environments.

From there, I return to the assumptions that make the Black–Scholes model analytically tractable: frictionless markets, constant volatility, and no dividends. These assumptions were first discussed in Chapter 21 as limitations that motivate the use of lattice models; here, I review them again to show how they are embedded in the derivation of the closed-form solution. A step-by-step numerical illustration then demonstrates how the option price responds to changes in volatility, interest rates, and time to maturity. I also describe how practitioners use the model in reverse to compute implied volatility and visualize volatility surfaces. Finally, I highlight cases where the model breaks down, such as in bond options, and introduce several extensions that address these shortcomings, including dividend adjustments, stochastic volatility, and jump models.

22.1 Origins and Distinctions in the Black–Scholes–Merton Framework

Throughout this section, I use 'framework' to refer to the general continuous-time, risk-neutral valuation environment introduced by Black, Scholes, and Merton, and 'model' to refer specifically to the closed-form pricing formula derived under constant-volatility and no-dividend assumptions.

The development of the Black–Scholes option pricing model marked a turning point in modern financial theory. Introduced in 1973 by Fischer Black and Myron Scholes, the model provided the first closed-form solution for pricing European-style options under idealized market conditions.[1] That same year, Robert C. Merton offered an independent derivation, establishing the model's mathematical rigor and solidifying its foundational role in continuous-time finance.[2] Recognizing these contributions, the model is widely called the *Black–Scholes–Merton framework*.

---

[1]Fischer Black and Myron Scholes, "The Pricing of Options and Corporate Liabilities." *Journal of Political Economy*, 81(3), 1973, 637–654.

[2]Robert C. Merton, "Theory of Rational Option Pricing." *Bell Journal of Economics and Management Science*, 4(1), 1973, 141–183.

The Black–Scholes–Merton framework is a prime example of risk-neutral valuation, extending the discrete-time logic developed in Chapter 21 into a continuous-time setting. It shows that the same no-arbitrage principles used in the lattice model can be carried into continuous time to produce a closed-form solution for option values. It prices derivative securities not by appealing to real-world probabilities or individual preferences, but by relying on the idea of no arbitrage and the existence of a replicating portfolio. In such a setting, the value of an option is equal to the expected payoff under a risk-neutral probability measure, discounted at the risk-free rate. This framework enables pricing without requiring knowledge of the investor's utility function or risk preferences, as the replication and market structure capture all relevant information.

The Black–Scholes–Merton framework provides the foundational structure for modern derivative pricing. The specific model developed by Black and Scholes (and later Merton) under idealized assumptions is known as the *Black–Scholes model*. Throughout this chapter, we distinguish between the broader framework and this specific model where appropriate.

Black and Scholes approached the problem by showing that a dynamically adjusted portfolio of the underlying stock and a risk-free bond could perfectly replicate the payoff of a European option. They derived a partial differential equation (PDE) that governs the option's price. Solving this PDE yields the now-iconic pricing formula. Merton, by contrast, used Itô calculus and continuous-time stochastic processes to derive the same result, positioning the model squarely within the theory of stochastic differential equations and martingale pricing.

Despite their different mathematical routes, both approaches arrive at the same pricing expression. The formula connects the current value of an option to the underlying asset price, strike price, time to expiration, volatility, and the risk-free interest rate. Importantly, it assumes that asset prices follow a *lognormal diffusion process*, a condition justified by the assumption of continuous compounding and constant volatility. As explained in Chapter 20, this lognormality is essential to ensure that prices remain strictly positive and that returns are normally distributed over time.

What elevates the Black–Scholes–Merton framework beyond the specific pricing model is the structure of reasoning it represents. It synthesizes three quantitative foundations: stochastic modeling of asset prices, no-arbitrage valuation, and probabilistic pricing under a risk-neutral measure. This structure not only supports the derivation of the option formula but also unifies the logic behind analytical models, numerical methods such as Monte Carlo simulation, and lattice approaches described in Chapter 20. Even when newer or more realistic models are applied, they do so by relaxing one or more of these assumptions, rather than abandoning the underlying framework.

22.1.1 *Assumptions and limitations of the model*

The elegance and power of the Black–Scholes model stem from its ability to price options using a relatively compact set of inputs. However, this tractability comes at the cost of imposing a series of strong assumptions, each critical to the model's derivation and, ultimately, its conclusions. These assumptions are not incidental; they are structurally embedded in the logic of replication and risk-neutral valuation that underpins the entire framework.

First and foremost, the model assumes that the underlying asset follows a geometric Brownian motion with constant drift and volatility. This assumption is convenient and analytically tractable, but it does not align with empirical observations. Asset returns exhibit skewness, kurtosis, and occasional jumps, all features that violate the assumption of log-normality and constant volatility.

Equally important is the assumption that the risk-free interest rate remains constant over the option's life. In equity options, this simplification may be relatively benign over short horizons. However, as will be shown later when the model is applied to bond options, the assumption of a flat and unchanging interest rate structure can lead to economically implausible results. In fixed-income markets, interest rates are both stochastic and mean-reverting, and their volatility is a first-order consideration in pricing. When this assumption is violated, the Black–Scholes model may produce positive values for options that should have negligible or even zero value, especially when the price of the underlying bond caps the payoff.

Another critical assumption is that markets are *frictionless*: There are no transaction costs, taxes, or constraints on trading. Investors are assumed to be able to buy and sell any quantity of the underlying asset or risk-free bond continuously and without cost. Moreover, they are presumed to do so in infinitesimal increments over time, allowing for perfect dynamic replication of the option payoff. This assumption is indispensable for deriving the Black–Scholes PDE, which relies on the ability to rebalance the replicating portfolio to eliminate all risk continuously. Yet, in actual markets, trading is discrete, liquidity is variable, and transaction costs, however small, can significantly affect the viability of continuous rebalancing.

The assumption of no dividends during the option's life also plays a vital role in simplifying the model's mathematics. It allows the present value of the expected payoff to be calculated without adjusting for intermittent cash flows. In practice, however, many underlying assets pay dividends, and adjustments must be made by modifying the formula to include a dividend yield or by turning to more flexible models that accommodate discrete payments.

Finally, the model presupposes that arbitrage opportunities are absent and that the market is *complete,* meaning every option can be perfectly replicated by trading in available assets. This notion is central to risk-neutral valuation and the use of martingale measures. As emphasized in the earlier discussion of the no-arbitrage framework, this assumption is not merely a convenience but a condition that ensures the internal consistency of the pricing model. However, real-world markets often display *incompleteness*, especially when pricing complex or illiquid instruments, which makes exact replication infeasible and undermines the model's precision.

These assumptions, taken together, create a highly idealized representation of financial markets that is powerful for analytical purposes but vulnerable to practical misapplication. The limitations they impose are not just technical quirks; they shape the boundary between where the Black–Scholes model provides insight and where it risks producing misleading results. These assumptions will be further unpacked in the following sections, particularly through applications to interest rate instruments and extensions beyond the basic model. The goal is not to dismiss the model for its simplicity but to understand precisely how and where its simplifying assumptions begin to constrain its relevance.

22.2 The Replicating Portfolio: Economic Intuition Behind the Black–Scholes Model

Although the formal derivation of the Black–Scholes formula is not presented in this chapter, as it relies on advanced techniques from stochastic calculus and PDEs, it is still valuable to understand the economic reasoning behind the model. As introduced in Chapter 20, replication is the idea that a dynamic combination of the underlying asset and a risk-free bond can reproduce an option's payoff. The Black–Scholes framework extends this logic into continuous time, showing that dynamic replication underpins a unique, arbitrage-free option value.

This is known as a *replicating portfolio*, and the logic behind it is straightforward. Suppose you want to mimic the payoff of a European call option. The option gains value when the underlying stock rises, but not in a one-to-one relationship. To reproduce this nonlinear behavior, an investor can construct a portfolio with a fractional share of the underlying stock. This amount approximates the change in the option's value when the stock price moves, and the remainder is adjusted by borrowing or lending at the risk-free interest rate. The portfolio is rebalanced continuously as market conditions change, hence the term "dynamic replication." This reliance on the risk-free rate anticipates the risk-neutral valuation framework introduced later, in which all assets are priced as if they grow at the risk-free rate under the risk-neutral measure.

This approach has important implications. Suppose a replicating portfolio can be constructed to match the option's payoff perfectly in all future scenarios. In that case, the principle of no arbitrage requires that the option's current market price be equal to the cost of creating that portfolio. The principle of no arbitrage holds that in efficient markets, two assets with identical future payoffs must have the same price today; otherwise, traders could buy the cheaper asset and sell the more expensive one, locking in a risk-free profit. In the context of option pricing, if an option were priced higher than its replicating portfolio, investors could sell the option and buy the cheaper portfolio to earn a guaranteed profit. If it were priced lower, traders could do the reverse. Such opportunities would quickly be exploited, driving prices back into alignment. Therefore, replication leads directly to a unique, arbitrage-free value for the option.

In this sense, the Black–Scholes formula does not "assign" a price to an option. Instead, it reveals the cost of reproducing its future payoff using liquid, tradable instruments in a frictionless market. It transforms pricing from subjective estimation into a financial engineering problem: If you can replicate it, you can price it.

This intuitive foundation sets the stage for the formal model. In the following section, I present the Black–Scholes pricing formula for European call and put options and apply it to a numerical example.

22.3 The Black–Scholes Formula: Structure and Components

Having established the economic intuition behind the model, namely, that the value of an option reflects the cost of dynamically replicating its payoff using a combination of the underlying asset and a risk-free bond—I turn to the formula that results from this logic. The Black–Scholes model provides a closed-form solution for valuing European-style options, which can only be exercised at maturity. This pricing formula links observable market inputs to a theoretically consistent estimate of option value, under the idealized conditions described in the previous section. It remains one of the most celebrated results in financial economics.

22.3.1 *The Black–Scholes formula for European options*

The Black–Scholes model translates the intuition of replication into a formal pricing tool. Under idealized assumptions, such as continuous trading, frictionless markets, and constant volatility, the model produces a closed-form expression that prices a European-style option based on observable market variables. Here, I present the mathematical formula for a European call option and explain each component.

For a European call option, the Black–Scholes formula is as follows:

$$C = S_0 N(d_1) - Ke^{-rT} N(d_2)$$

where the variables are defined as

$$d_1 = \frac{\ln\left(\frac{S_0}{K}\right) + \left(r + 0.5\sigma^2\right)T}{\sigma\sqrt{T}}$$

and

$$d_2 = d_1 - \sigma\sqrt{T}$$

where:

- C = price of the European call option,
- S_0 = current price of the underlying asset,
- K = strike price (exercise price),
- T = time to maturity (in years),
- r = constant risk-free interest rate (continuously compounded),
- σ = volatility of the underlying asset's returns,
- $N(\cdot)$ = cumulative distribution function (CDF) of the standard normal distribution.[3]

[3]The CDF is explained and illustrated in Chapter 20.

The formula for a European put option can be derived separately or, as explained in Chapter 21, obtained using put-call parity. In the Black–Scholes framework, this relationship does not establish the principle itself but serves as a convenient way to move between call and put valuations.

These expressions are valid only under the assumptions discussed in the previous section. The CDF, $N(d)$, represents the probability, under the risk-neutral measure, that a standard normal variable is less than or equal to d. As explained in Chapter 20, this function is central to translating stochastic processes into probabilistic expectations.

22.3.2 *Numerical illustration: Applying the Black–Scholes formula*

Complementing the discrete, step-by-step lattice illustration in Chapter 21, which valued an otherwise identical option via backward induction, this example shows the closed-form route in continuous time. The aim here is not to re-derive concepts such as replication, put-call parity, or risk-neutral valuation (already developed in Chapter 21) but instead to demonstrate how those same building blocks feed into the Black–Scholes formula and to foreground sensitivity to volatility, interest rates, and time to maturity.

The example walks through the calculation of each formula component, including the cumulative normal distribution values that translate risk-neutral probabilities into option prices. By presenting the steps explicitly, the illustration underscores how the closed-form model embodies the same no-arbitrage logic as the lattice approach while making the formula's dependence on key inputs transparent. As in the lattice framework, volatility and time to maturity emerge as especially important drivers, helping to explain why practitioners pay such close attention to these variables when interpreting market prices.

To illustrate, consider the following set of inputs: Suppose the current stock price is $S_0 = 100$, the strike price is $K = 100$, the time to expiration is $T = 1$ year, the risk-free interest rate is $r = 5\%$, and the volatility is $\sigma = 20\%$.

We first compute

$$d_1 = \frac{\ln\left(\frac{100}{100}\right) + \left(0.05 + 0.5 \cdot 0.2^2\right) \cdot 1}{0.2\sqrt{1}} = 0.35$$

$$d_2 = 0.35 - 0.2 = 0.15$$

Next, using values from a cumulative normal distribution table or calculator,

$$N(d_1) = N(0.35) \approx 0.6368$$
$$N(d_2) = N(0.15) \approx 0.5596$$

Now, compute the present values:

$$C = 100\,(0.6368) - 100\,(e^{-0.05})\,(0.5596) = 10.46$$

Thus, the fair value of the European call option is approximately \$10.46. This value represents the amount a prospective buyer should be willing to pay today for the right to purchase the stock at \$100 in one year, assuming the model's inputs and assumptions are met.

22.3.3 *Parameter sensitivity: Illustrating the impact of key inputs*

While the Greeks (discussed in Chapter 11) provide local measures of how option values change with small parameter shifts, it is also helpful to see how the closed-form Black–Scholes formula responds to broader input changes. In Chapter 21, the lattice example showed how volatility, time to maturity, and interest rates affect option values step by step in a discrete setting. Here, I revisit the same drivers in a continuous-time framework to highlight how the Black–Scholes model encodes these sensitivities directly in its pricing expression.

The following tables show full Black–Scholes revaluations as each parameter varies, holding all others constant. This complements the lattice results: Whereas the binomial model's adjustments accumulate node by node, the closed-form solution summarizes the effect of each input instantaneously. By comparing the two, it can be seen how volatility, time, and interest rates influence option values under both discrete and continuous approaches, reinforcing the central role of these factors in option pricing.

22.3.3.1 *Effect of volatility*

As shown in Table 22.1, increasing the underlying asset's volatility raises the call option's value. This effect was already visible in the lattice framework of Chapter 21, where higher volatility widened the distribution of possible outcomes across the tree. The same logic applies in the

Table 22.1. Black–Scholes Call Option Prices for Varying Volatility Levels

Assumptions

- Current price (S) = \$100
- Strike price (K) = \$100
- Risk-free interest rate (r) = 5%
- Time to maturity (T) = 1 year

Volatility (σ)	**Option Price**
10%	\$6.80
15%	\$8.52
20%	\$10.45
25%	\$12.52
30%	\$14.68
35%	\$16.88
40%	\$19.10

continuous-time Black–Scholes model but is embedded directly into the closed-form formula: Greater volatility increases the likelihood of finishing in the money, while downside exposure remains capped at zero.

22.3.3.2 *Effect of time to maturity*

Table 22.2 shows that extending the time to maturity increases the option's value. As in the lattice example from Chapter 21, more time expands the range of possible outcomes, thus raising the likelihood of a profitable payoff. The Black–Scholes formula captures this time value directly: The longer the horizon, the greater the cumulative probability mass in the favorable distribution tail, translating into a higher option premium.

22.3.3.3 *Effect of risk-free interest rate*

Table 22.3 shows that increasing the risk-free interest rate raises the value of call options and lowers the value of put options. The lattice results in Chapter 21 illustrated the same pattern, where the discounting of the strike value played a central role. In the Black–Scholes framework, this effect is

Table 22.2. Black–Scholes Call Option Prices for Varying Time to Expiration

Assumptions

- Spot price (S) = \$100
- Strike price (K) = \$100
- Risk-free interest rate (r) = 5%
- Volatility (σ) = 20%

Time to Maturity (Years)	Option Price
0.5	\$6.80
1.0	\$10.45
1.5	\$13.37
2.0	\$15.74
2.5	\$17.78
3.0	\$19.58
3.5	\$21.22
4.0	\$22.74

Table 22.3. Black–Scholes Call Option Prices for Varying Risk-Free Rates

Assumptions

- Spot price (S) = \$100
- Strike price (K) = \$100
- Time to maturity (T) = 1 year
- Volatility (σ) = 20%

Risk-Free Rate (r)	Option Price
3%	\$9.66
4%	\$10.07
5%	\$10.45
6%	\$10.80
7%	\$11.12
8%	\$11.42

expressed directly in the closed-form solution: A higher rate reduces the present value of the strike price while leaving the spot price unchanged. The result is consistent with the economic intuition behind rho, the Greek that measures interest-rate sensitivity.

22.4 Interpretation and Intuition: A Weighted Expectation of Payoff

The Black–Scholes formula is often presented as a difference between two adjusted quantities:

$$C = S_0\, N(d_1) - Ke^{-rT}\, N(d_2)$$

While this form is analytically elegant, it can obscure the underlying intuition. A more revealing perspective comes from rearranging the terms to highlight the probability-weighted nature of the option's value:

$$C = N(d_2) \cdot \left(S_0 \cdot \frac{N(d_1)}{Nd_2} - Ke^{-rt} \right)$$

This expression frames the option's value as a risk-neutral, probability-weighted net payoff. $N(d_2)$ can be interpreted as the risk-neutral probability that the option will finish in the money (i.e., the stock price will exceed the strike at expiration). Likewise, $N(d_1)$ represents the option's hedge ratio (delta), indicating how much the option's value is expected to change for a small change in the underlying stock price under the risk-neutral measure. The expression in the parentheses represents the expected value of the asset conditional on exercise minus the discounted strike price. In other words, this formulation interprets the call price as

Probability of exercise × (Expected payoff given exercise)

This view reinforces the idea that the value of a call option comes not from its intrinsic value today but from the *weighted average of future outcomes*, where the weights are derived from the *risk-neutral stock price distribution*. Importantly, this distribution reflects a world where all investors are indifferent to risk, not because they are irrational but because risk has been hedged away through replication.

The rearranged form also clarifies why the Black–Scholes model is sensitive to volatility: As volatility increases, tail probabilities in the distribution spread out, increasing the chance that the option ends up in the money at the expiration date, thus raising the weighted expected payoff.

To visualize this, consider Figure 22.1, which displays the standard normal distribution and the shaded areas corresponding to $N(d_1)$ and $N(d_2)$. In the figure, the darker-shaded region under the curve represents $N(d_1)$,

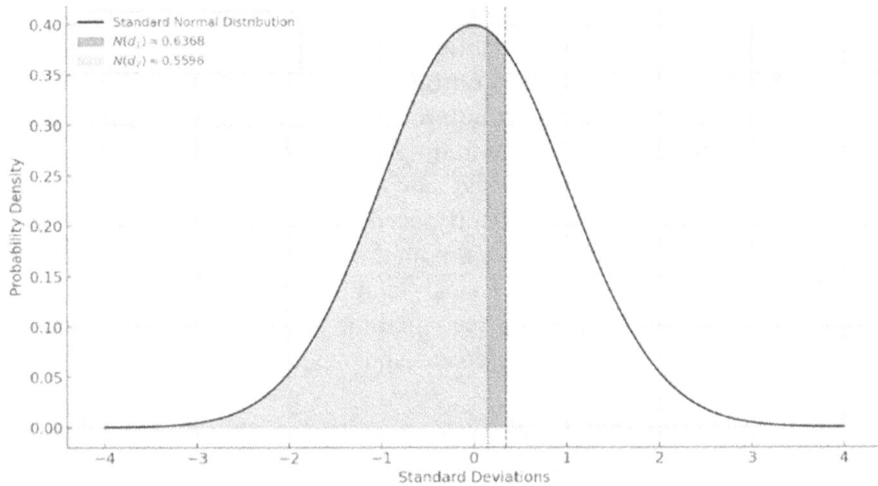

Figure 22.1. Cumulative Normal Distribution with $N(d_1)$ and $N(d_2)$ Shaded

approximately 0.686. This is linked to the option's sensitivity to the stock price, often interpreted as the option's delta. The lighter-shaded region represents $N(d_2)$, approximately 0.5596. This reflects the risk-neutral probability that the option will finish in the money at the expiration date. The difference in shading distinguishes these two cumulative probabilities and highlights their distinct roles in the Black–Scholes valuation. Together, they illustrate how the formula balances potential reward with likelihood, forming a pricing mechanism rooted in replication and probability.

This framing also clarifies how the Black–Scholes model captures the tradeoff between potential gain and the likelihood of realizing that gain, which depends on key market variables such as the underlying price, volatility, time to maturity, and interest rates. Far from being a mere computational convenience, the formula encapsulates a disciplined, probabilistic view of option value grounded in financial replication and risk-neutral logic.

22.5 Using the Model in Practice: Online Tools and Implied Volatility

Although developed in the early 1970s, the Black–Scholes model remains widely used in academic settings and market practice, particularly due to its simplicity and analytical tractability. One of the most accessible applications for practitioners is the use of online Black–Scholes calculators, which allow users to input the basic parameters (current price, strike price, time to maturity, volatility, and the risk-free interest rate) to compute the theoretical price of a European call or put option. These tools are widely available and serve as helpful pedagogical aids, benchmarking devices, and sanity checks in live trading environments.

Importantly, the model is used not only to generate a price from assumed inputs but is also frequently used in reverse to extract market-implied volatility. Traders observe the market price of an option, input all other known parameters into the Black–Scholes formula, and solve for the volatility that makes the model price equal the market price. This *implied volatility* represents the market's consensus expectation of future volatility over the option's life.

From these implied volatilities, practitioners construct volatility surfaces, which plot implied volatility against strike price and time to maturity. Figure 22.2 illustrates a typical volatility surface, revealing that implied volatility is neither flat nor constant as the Black–Scholes model assumes, but varies systematically with strike price and time to maturity. These variations give rise to well-known phenomena, such as the *volatility smile* and the *term structure of volatility*, which reflect market risk expectations and potential price fluctuations. The surface often slopes

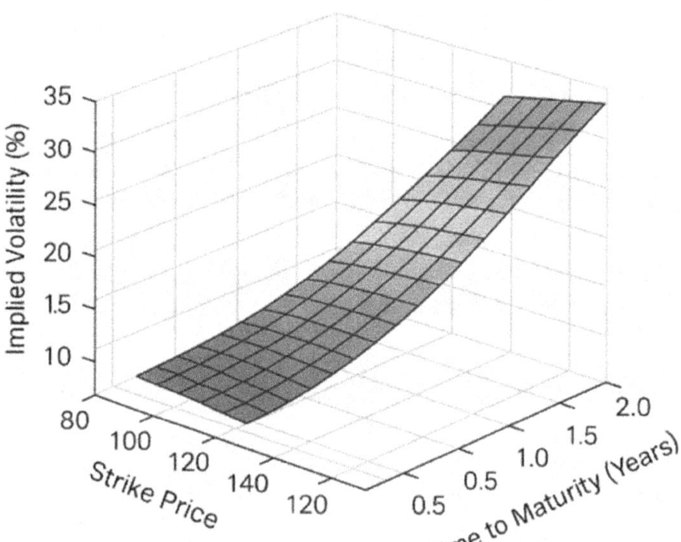

Figure 22.2. Implied Volatility Surface Across Strike Prices and Time to Maturity

upward for deep, out-of-the-money options or long-dated maturities, capturing risk premiums or uncertainty not accounted for in the basic model. The volatility surface has thus become a foundational element in modern derivatives pricing, hedging, and risk management, serving not only as an input to more advanced models but also as a diagnostic tool for identifying market anomalies, liquidity gaps, and stress conditions.

Yet, practitioners are mindful of the model's sensitivity to inputs, especially volatility. Small changes in the assumed volatility can lead to significant shifts in the option value, particularly for out-of-the-money or long-dated options. This highlights both the model's practical utility and limitations.

22.5.1 *The importance of assumptions: A bond option illustration*

While the Black–Scholes model is widely used for pricing options on equities and equity indices, its extension to fixed-income instruments, such as bond options, requires careful attention to the underlying assumptions. In this section, I apply the Black–Scholes framework to a simple option on a zero-coupon bond and illustrate why the model can yield distorted results when key assumptions are violated.

Unlike a stock, a zero-coupon bond has a well-defined upper bound on its price: the present value of its face value discounted at the risk-free interest rate, assuming interest rates are positive or zero. It does not pay dividends or generate cash flows before maturity. In theory, this superficially makes it look like a non-dividend-paying stock, for which Black–Scholes was initially developed. However, several fundamental differences disrupt the assumptions embedded in the model. This mismatch between the lognormal Black–Scholes assumption and the empirically mean-reverting nature of interest rates is precisely why short-rate models such as Vasicek and Cox–Ingersoll–Ross were developed.

First, consider the assumption of constant volatility. For equity options, the underlying asset can, in principle, exhibit constant or at least persistent volatility over time. But for zero-coupon bonds, volatility typically decays as the bond approaches maturity. This is especially true under mean-reverting interest rate models. As time progresses, there is less uncertainty about the bond's final value; it will pay its face value with certainty, assuming no credit risk. As a result, applying constant volatility in the Black–Scholes formula overstates the option value, particularly for shorter maturities.

Second, the assumption of constant interest rates is unrealistic in the fixed-income context. Bonds are defined by their sensitivity to changes in interest rates, and options prices should reflect the term structure of interest rates and their volatility. A single, constant rate fails to capture the curvature of the yield curve or the richness of real-world interest rate dynamics. This can lead to a mispricing of deep out-of-the-money or long-dated bond options, especially sensitive to shifts in yield curve expectations.

Third, and most critically, the price of the underlying bond is bounded above, something the Black–Scholes model fails to recognize. This can result in options that are logically mispriced. For example, under Black–Scholes, an out-of-the-money call option on a zero-coupon bond (with a strike price above the bond's maximum possible price) can still be assigned a positive value, even though the bond can never reach the strike price. This is not only a numerical error but also a logical breakdown. No rational investor would pay a positive premium for an option that cannot finish in the money.

To illustrate these distortions, see Figure 22.3, which plots the Black–Scholes value of a European call option on a zero-coupon bond under different volatility and interest rate assumptions. The implied price distribution exceeds the upper bound on the bond price, highlighting the model's failure to respect bond-specific constraints.

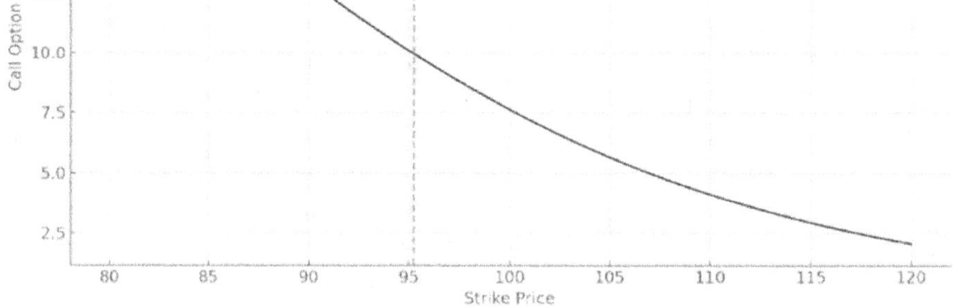

Figure 22.3. Logical Inconsistencies in Black–Scholes Pricing for Zero-Coupon Bond Options

In practice, bond options are more appropriately modeled using interest rate models that account for the stochastic nature of rates and the bounded behavior of bond prices, such as those discussed later in this chapter. These models abandon the constant volatility assumption and incorporate the dynamics of the yield curve, offering more consistent and logically sound valuations.

22.6 Extensions of the Black–Scholes Model for Stocks and Equity Indices

The foundational Black–Scholes model makes several simplifying assumptions that limit its accuracy when applied to real-world financial markets. In the context of stocks and equity indices, four major modifications have been developed to address key empirical shortcomings: incorporating dividends, allowing for stochastic volatility, including price jumps, and calibrating local volatility. These adjustments aim to align the model more closely with observed market behavior while preserving as much analytical tractability as possible. Together, these four extensions form the core tools for adapting the Black–Scholes model to the realities of equity and index options. They provide greater flexibility and improved empirical performance while maintaining a connection to the original model's analytical structure.

22.6.1 *Incorporating dividends*

The original Black–Scholes model assumes that the underlying asset pays no dividends, which is unrealistic for most individual stocks and all major equity indices. When an asset pays dividends, its expected future value is lower than that of a non-dividend-paying asset, reducing the value of a call option.

To incorporate the effect of dividends, the Black–Scholes formula is modified by introducing a continuous dividend yield q. The call option price becomes

$$C = S_0\, e^{-qT}\, N(d_1) - Ke^{-rT}\, N(d_2)$$

Here, d_1 and d_2 are adjusted accordingly.

This dividend-adjusted version is widely used for equity index options, representing the average dividend yield across index constituents. For individual stocks with known dividend amounts and dates, discrete dividend adjustments are often made by subtracting the present value of dividends from the spot price before applying the standard formula.

22.6.2 *Stochastic volatility*

The Black–Scholes model assumes constant volatility over the option's life. However, empirical evidence shows that volatility is neither constant nor deterministic. It tends to cluster and vary with market conditions. To address this, stochastic volatility models, such as the Heston model, allow volatility to fluctuate randomly over time rather than fixing it. These models introduce a second source of uncertainty, governing the behavior of volatility itself.

The *Heston model*,[4] in particular, assumes that volatility tends to revert to a long-run average over time, which helps it capture the dynamics seen in real-world markets. This additional flexibility allows the model to better fit market prices for options, particularly the implied volatility "smile" and "skew" patterns described earlier in this chapter, which the original Black–Scholes model cannot account for.

22.6.3 *Jump-diffusion models*

Asset prices often experience sudden, discrete jumps due to earnings surprises, economic announcements, or geopolitical events. These jumps are abrupt price changes that cannot be captured by the continuous movement assumed in the Black–Scholes model. To incorporate such behavior, *jump-diffusion models* introduce an additional mechanism into the price process that allows for infrequent but significant shifts in asset values.

Merton's jump-diffusion model is one of the most influential models in this category.[5] In this framework, asset prices evolve according to a standard diffusion process, as in Black–Scholes, but are also subject to occasional random jumps. A Poisson process governs these jumps, a statistical model used to describe the occurrence of events that happen

---

[4] Steven L. Heston, "A Closed-Form Solution for Options with Stochastic Volatility with Applications to Bond and Currency Options." *Review of Financial Studies*, 6(2), 1983, pp. 327–343.

[5] Robert C. Merton, "Option Pricing When Underlying Stock Returns Are Discontinuous." *Journal of Financial Economics*, 3(1–2), 1976, pp. 125–144.

independently and at a constant average rate over time. In the context of financial markets, this means jumps arrive randomly but with a predictable long-run frequency.

Each jump changes the asset price by a random amount, typically modeled as a lognormally distributed percentage change. The combination of continuous price movement and discrete jumps allows the model to capture the so-called "fat tails" observed in empirical return distributions, where extreme events happen more frequently than the normal distribution would predict.

Jump-diffusion models are handy for pricing options sensitive to the probability of large price movements, such as deep out-of-the-money put and call options. They help explain why such options often trade at prices higher than those implied by the Black–Scholes model, which underestimates the likelihood of extreme outcomes.

Merton's model marked a significant advance in option pricing by introducing a more realistic representation of asset dynamics while retaining analytical tractability. It remains a cornerstone in studying asset price behavior and option valuation.

22.6.4 *Local volatility models*

While stochastic volatility and jump-diffusion models introduce randomness to better match observed option prices, *local volatility models* aim for exact calibration to market data by assuming that volatility is a deterministic function of both the underlying asset's price and time. The most well-known example is the *Dupire local volatility model*,[6] which reverses the Black–Scholes formula to infer a surface of volatilities from observed option prices across strike prices and maturities.

This model can be expressed as

$$\sigma^2_{\text{local}} \cdot (S,t) = \text{Function from market option prices}$$

Because it fits the implied volatility surface exactly, the local volatility model is a valuable tool in the equity options market, particularly for exotic option pricing and model validation. However, its assumption of deterministic volatility can lead to implausible dynamics and hedging issues, especially during volatile markets.

[6]Bruno Dupire, "Pricing with a Smile." *Risk*, 7(1), 1994, 18–20.

22.7 Extensions to Other Asset Classes

While the Black–Scholes model was originally developed for pricing options on non-dividend-paying stocks, its core framework has been extended to other asset classes, such as foreign exchange (FX), commodities, and interest rate derivatives. Each asset class has unique characteristics that require specific adjustments or alternative models to accurately reflect market dynamics.

22.7.1 *Foreign exchange options*

For FX options, the Black–Scholes framework is adapted into what is known as the *Garman–Kohlhagen model*,[7] which incorporates both domestic and foreign interest rates. This model treats the foreign interest rate analogously to a dividend yield. This modification enables the pricing of European-style FX options and is widely used in practice. The Garman–Kohlhagen model is essential for managing currency exposure and pricing cross-currency options.

22.7.2 *Commodity options*

Commodities such as oil, natural gas, and gold often serve as the underlying assets for options. Since these are typically traded via futures contracts, the *Black model* (also known as *Black'76*) is commonly used. In contrast to the Black–Scholes model,[8] which prices options on spot assets, the Black model prices options on forward or futures contracts. The model discounts the expected future payoff of the option using the risk-free interest rate. It is especially suitable for exchange-traded commodity options and is utilized by exchanges such as the Chicago Mercantile Exchange and the Intercontinental Exchange.

The Black model is straightforward and widely used. Still, it does not directly account for features such as storage costs, convenience yields, or seasonal effects unless these are embedded in futures prices. More

---

[7] Mark B. Garman and Steven W. Kohlhagen, "Foreign Currency Option Values." *Journal of International Money and Finance*, 2(3), 1983, 231–237.

[8] Fischer Black, "The Pricing of Commodity Contracts." *Journal of Financial Economics*, 1–2, 1976, 167–179.

advanced models, such as the *Schwartz model*[9] or models with stochastic convenience yield, are used when these characteristics are significant.

22.7.3 *Interest rate derivatives*

Interest rate options such as interest rate caps and floors, as well as swaptions (i.e., options on interest rate swaps), require models that can handle the stochastic nature of the entire yield curve. As demonstrated earlier in this chapter, the Black–Scholes model is unsuited for this task because it assumes a single, constant interest rate. Instead, models such as Black's model for interest rate derivatives, the model developed by Hull and White,[10] and the Morton–Heath–Jarrow[11] model are employed.

Black's model prices interest rate options, such as caplets and swaptions, by treating the forward rate as the underlying. The Hull–White model introduces mean-reverting dynamics for the short rate, allowing for a better fit to the observed term structure. The Morton–Heath–Jarrow framework generalizes these approaches by modeling the entire forward rate curve as a stochastic process.

These models reflect the complexity of interest rate markets and allow for more accurate pricing and risk management of instruments sensitive to the evolution of interest rates over time.

22.8 Summary

In this chapter, I introduce the Black–Scholes–Merton model, emphasizing both its theoretical significance and practical applications. I outline the historical contributions of Black, Scholes, and Merton, and explain why the model is widely seen as a milestone in modern finance. I then frame the model as part of a larger, risk-neutral valuation framework that relies on replication and no-arbitrage logic.

---

[9]Eduardo S. Schwartz, "The Stochastic Behavior of Commodity Prices: Implications For Valuation and Hedging." *Journal of Finance*, 52(3), 1997, 923–973.

[10]John Hull and Alan White, "Pricing Interest-Rate Derivative Securities." *Review of Financial Studies*, 3(4), 1990, 573–592.

[11]Andrew Morton, David Heath, and Robert Jarrow. "Bond Pricing and The Term Structure of Interest Rates: A New Methodology For Contingent Claims Valuation." *Econometrica*, 60(1), 1992, 77–105.

After presenting the intuition behind dynamic replication, I walk through the Black–Scholes pricing formula for European call options and explain the meaning of each component. I use a numerical example to illustrate the mechanics of the model and explore how key inputs such as volatility, interest rates, and time affect the option's value. I also show how the model is used inversely to infer implied volatility and construct volatility surfaces.

I highlight the assumptions underlying the model and its limitations. I introduce model extensions incorporating dividends, stochastic volatility, price jumps, and local volatility calibration to address these shortcomings. These enhancements reflect how practitioners adapt the original Black–Scholes–Merton framework to real-world markets.

Chapter 23

Framework for Valuing Swaps

As I explained in Chapter 4, certain swaps are risk-sharing derivatives—contracts designed to transfer specific financial risks, such as interest rate, equity market, or currency risk, between two parties. In this chapter, I present a valuation framework for equity swaps, total return swaps (TRSs), interest rate swaps, and currency swaps. While each swap type may differ in contractual structure and underlying asset exposure, they all share a common valuation principle.

Each risk-sharing swap consists of two sides: a *receiver leg*, representing the stream of payments a party receives, and a *payer leg*, representing the stream of payments that party is obligated to make. Except in the case of currency swaps, which may involve exchanging notional principal amounts as well as periodic interest payments, the valuation task consists of determining the present value of the cash flows associated with each leg and then computing their difference:

Value of swap = PV of payments received – PV of payments made

If this difference is positive for a party, the swap is an asset on its balance sheet; if negative, it is a liability.

This chapter establishes a consistent framework for estimating cash flows, selecting discount rates, and valuing the various types of swaps encountered in practice. I also include illustrations and a discussion of risks that influence the mark-to-market value of a swap over its life.

23.1 Valuation Logic and Financial Reporting Implications

The valuation of a swap reflects the economic difference between what a party expects to receive and what it expects to pay as of the date of valuation. Each leg of the swap, whether fixed, floating, or total return based, can be interpreted as a series of future cash flows. The fixed leg usually involves known, contractually specified amounts. The floating leg, in contrast, depends on an index or asset performance, such as an interest rate benchmark, equity return, or foreign exchange rate. Importantly, even though future floating payments are unknown at the time of valuation, they can be estimated using market instruments such as forward or futures contracts. These instruments effectively allow the floating leg's value to be "locked in" based on observable market prices, rather than forecasts.

The discounting step is crucial. Future payments must be converted to present value terms using appropriate discount factors derived from the prevailing yield curve and adjusted for counterparty risk. In practice, discounting often uses overnight indexed swap (OIS) curves for collateralized swaps or funding curves adjusted for counterparty risk. The OIS is an interest rate swap in which one party pays a fixed rate and the other pays a floating rate linked to a compounded overnight index over the payment period.[1] An OIS curve is built from fixed-for-floating swaps where the floating leg is tied to a daily overnight rate (such as the Secured Overnight Financial Rate, SOFR[2]). Because overnight rates reflect very short-term, low-risk funding costs, the OIS curve has become the standard benchmark for discounting collateralized derivatives.

For currency swaps or other structures that involve notional exchanges, the same valuation convention applies—"PV of what you receive minus PV of what you pay"—with the exchanged notionals simply treated as additional cash flows included in the valuation.

Swaps are zero-sum instruments: The value one party gains is lost by the other. As calculated above, the swap's net value becomes a mark-to-market value recorded on the firm's balance sheet. Depending on the type of swap, this value can fluctuate significantly over time with changes in

---

[1]The widespread adoption of OIS discounting followed the 2007–2008 Global Financial Crisis, when market participants recognized that OIS rates better reflected the true cost of collateralized funding than traditional LIBOR-based curves.

[2]SOFR is the U.S. overnight risk-free rate, based on Treasury repurchase (repo) transactions. SOFR replaced USD LIBOR as the main reference rate for U.S. derivatives and loans.

interest rates, credit spreads, equity performance, or foreign exchange (FX) rates.

23.1.1 *Numerical example: Valuing a total return swap*

To illustrate the general procedure, consider the following simplified TRS between two parties, where the reference rate is SOFR:

- *Notional amount*: $100 million
- *Payment frequency*: Semiannual
- *Time to maturity*: 1 year (two payments remain)
- *Party A pays*: SOFR + 100 basis points
- *Party A receives*: total return on an equity index (assumed at 5% per six-month period)
- *Forward SOFR rates*: 4.2% for both upcoming periods
- *Day count fraction*: 0.5 (semiannual)
- *Discount factors*: 6 months 0.98 and 12 months 0.95

The first step is to estimate the cash flows. For the floating leg (paid by Party A):

$$\begin{aligned}\text{Payment} &= \$100{,}000{,}000 \times (0.042 + 0.01) \times 0.5 \\ &= \$2{,}600{,}000 \text{ (each period)}\end{aligned}$$

The total return leg (received by Party A):

$$\text{Payment} = \$100{,}000{,}000 \times 0.05 \times 0.5 = \$2{,}500{,}000 \text{ (each period)}$$

Given the cash flows, the present values must be computed. Here is where the discount factors are used. The present value of the payments received (total return leg) is

PV for first payment received = $2,500,000 × 0.98 =	$2,450,000
+ PV for second payment received = $2,500,000 × 0.95 =	$2,375,000
PV of total payments received	$4,825,000

The present value of the payments made (floating leg):

PV for first payment paid = $2,600,000 × 0.98 =	$2,548,000
+ PV for second payment paid = $2,600,000 × 0.95 =	$2,470,000
PV of total payments paid	$5,018,000

The swap value is

PV of total payments received	\$4,825,000
– PV of total payments paid	\$5,018,000
Value of swap	– \$193,000

Thus, Party A has a mark-to-market liability of \$193,000, while Party B has a corresponding asset.

The present value of each leg is shown in two steps (one for each cash-flow date) to make the mechanics transparent; aggregating them at the end is simply a presentation choice and yields the same result.

23.2 Cash Flow Calculations

As discussed above, the valuation of any risk-sharing swap begins with estimating the future cash flows exchanged by each party. Depending on the structure of the contract, swaps may fall into one of the following three types: (1) fixed-for-floating swap, (2) fixed-for-fixed swap, and (3) floating-for-floating swap. Each swap type requires a distinct approach for determining cash flows, though the valuation logic remains the same: Calculate each leg's cash flows, discount them to present value, and compute the difference.

23.2.1 *Fixed-for-floating swaps*

Fixed-for-floating swaps are the most common swap structure across asset classes. One leg pays a fixed rate (based on a predetermined contractual rate r), and the other pays a floating rate (based on a reference index such as SOFR, an equity index return, or an FX rate change).

For a fixed payment, the formula is

$$\text{Fixed payment} = \text{Notional principal} \times \text{Fixed rate} \times \left(\frac{\text{Days in period}}{\text{Days in year}}\right) \quad (23.1)$$

Note that the last term (i.e., Days in period/Days in year) reflects the day count convention[3] used in financial markets. While it might seem

[3] A day count convention is a market rule that specifies how the number of days between two dates is measured and how those days are translated into a fraction of a year for the purpose of calculating interest, accrued interest, or discount factors.

intuitive to use 365 days in a non-leap year, market conventions may specify 360 (actual/360), actual/365, or other systems, depending on the asset class and currency. Likewise, the number of days in the period may be based on actual calendar days or a convention (e.g., 30/360). These day-count conventions determine how interest is accrued for the period and vary across fixed-income markets. Under Actual/360, the accrual factor uses the actual number of days in the period divided by 360, the standard for most money-market rates and many floating-rate legs. Under 30/360, each month is treated as having 30 days and the year 360 days, a convention frequently used for fixed-rate instruments. Actual/365 is common in certain government bond and loan markets. These conventions do not change the economic value of the swap; they simply ensure that cash-flow calculations conform to market standards for the underlying rate.

For a floating payment, there are two general cases: (1) when the floating leg is linked to a reference rate (such as an interest rate or FX rate) and (2) when the floating leg is linked to a reference asset return (such as an equity or commodity return).

Floating leg linked to a reference rate:

$$\text{Floating rate payment} = \text{Notional principal} \times \text{Reference rate} \times \left(\frac{\text{Days in period}}{\text{Days in year}}\right) \tag{23.2}$$

Floating leg linked to a reference asset return:

$$\text{Floating return payment} = \text{Notional principal} \times \text{Asset return} \times \left(\frac{\text{Days in period}}{\text{Days in year}}\right) \tag{23.3}$$

Note that total return swaps vary in how the floating return is accrued. Some TRS contracts apply the full percentage return over the period without prorating by days, while others follow the interest-rate swap convention shown here. The formulation in equation (23.3) reflects the day-count approach, but both conventions are used in practice depending on the asset class and negotiated terms.

23.2.2 *Fixed-for-fixed swaps*

In a fixed-for-fixed swap, both legs involve known payment streams. This structure is typical in currency swaps, where parties exchange interest payments in two different currencies at fixed rates. Each leg's payment is calculated using equation (23.1); however, the notional principal and fixed rate may differ, and each leg is denominated in a different currency. That is,

$$\text{Fixed payment (Currency } i) = (\text{Notional } i) \times (\text{Rate } i)$$

Since the two legs are in different currencies, each leg is discounted using the relevant domestic yield curve. If necessary, one leg is converted to a common currency using the prevailing or forward FX rate. In many currency swaps, the notional principals in each currency are exchanged at maturity, and in some structures also at initiation, although other swaps omit notional exchange altogether. The specific convention depends on the contract's hedging purpose and negotiated terms. Unlike interest rate swaps, the notional principal may be exchanged at maturity (and sometimes at initiation), adding an additional payment to the cash flow stream.

23.2.3 *Floating-for-floating swaps*

In this structure, both legs involve payments that depend on a floating reference rate or asset returns. Floating-for-floating swaps are often used to swap exposure between two benchmark interest rates, swap equity index returns versus total return on a single stock, or swap returns on two different currencies or indices. Each payment is calculated using equation (23.1) or (23.3), depending on whether the leg is tied to a rate or return. For example, a currency basis swap might involve receiving three-month SOFR on a U.S. dollar notional and paying three-month EURIBOR on a euro notional.

The challenge is estimating future floating payments at each reset date. Fortunately, market instruments (e.g., interest rate futures, FX forwards, or equity futures) can be used to lock in or imply these future values, allowing the swap to be valued today.

23.3 Discounting and the Choice of Interest Rate Curve

Once the future cash flows for each leg of a swap are estimated using the formulas above, the next step is to calculate their present value. This involves discounting future cash flows using appropriate discount factors derived from the prevailing term structure of interest rates. The selection of the discount curve is a critical and sometimes complex decision, depending on factors such as collateralization, counterparty risk, and market conventions.

23.3.1 *Discounting fixed and floating cash flows*

Each payment amount, whether fixed or floating, is discounted using a formula of the form

$$\mathrm{PV} = \sum_{i=1}^{n} CF_i \times Z(t_i)$$

where:

- CF_i is the cash flow (payment) at period i;
- $Z(t_i)$ is the discount factor for time t_i, derived from the discount curve;
- n is the total number of payment periods remaining.

The discount factor $Z(t_i)$ represents the present value of $1 received at future time t.

23.3.2 *Choosing the right discount curve*

A discount curve is a term structure of interest rates used to determine the present value of future cash flows. It shows the market-implied rates for borrowing or lending money over different time horizons. From this curve, discount factors are derived (i.e., the present values of receiving $1 at various future dates). In the context of swap valuation, the discount curve plays a crucial role, as it determines the present value of each future payment.

When valuing a swap, getting the cash flows right is only half the job. You also need to know how to discount those cash flows properly. And that's where things get a bit more complicated. Selecting the appropriate discount curve is a critical, and sometimes complex, decision. It depends on several important factors:

- Is the swap collateralized, and if so, what type of collateral is posted?
- Are the payments in different currencies, requiring different interest rate environments?
- What is the credit risk of the parties involved?
- What are the prevailing conventions in the market for valuing similar contracts?

Using the wrong discount curve can significantly misstate the value of a swap. It can lead to over- or underestimations of exposures, incorrect risk measures, and even flawed hedging or pricing decisions.

In practice, the choice of curve depends on the characteristics of the swap, particularly how it's funded and what risks are embedded in its structure. The following section describes how to select the appropriate curve for several common swap scenarios.

23.3.2.1 *Collateralized swaps: Use the OIS curve*

Many swaps are collateralized, meaning that both parties agree to post collateral, typically cash or high-quality securities, to protect against the risk that one party might default on its obligations. This practice is widespread for swaps that are cleared, which means they are processed through a central clearinghouse. A clearinghouse acts as an intermediary between the two original parties, becoming the buyer for every seller and the seller for every buyer. Its role is to guarantee performance, reduce counterparty risk, and enforce strict margin requirements. Cleared swaps, along with many over-the-counter swaps that are not cleared but are still governed by bilateral agreements, often require regular margin posting to reflect changes in the contract's value over time.

Because collateral usually earns overnight interest, payments in these swaps are effectively funded at the overnight rate. So, the discount curve that best reflects these economics is the OIS curve. This curve is built from overnight lending rates, which are considered low-risk and closely tied to the real cost of money in these arrangements.

Consequently, if a swap is collateralized, use the OIS curve to discount the cash flows.

23.3.2.2 *Uncollateralized swaps: Adjust for credit and funding*

Some swaps (especially between banks and corporate clients) are not collateralized. In these cases, there is more credit risk involved. Each party must worry about the other's ability to pay, and there is no daily margining to protect against market movements.

In such swaps, it is sensible to use a discount curve that reflects the cost of unsecured funding, which varies among different lending institutions. This is often referred to as a *funding curve* and is typically based on the institution's cost of borrowing in the market. If a bank needs to borrow at $x\%$ to fund its positions, then future payments that the bank expects to receive should be discounted at something close to $x\%$, not at a risk-free rate.

Additionally, since the other party may default, a credit adjustment may be added to the discount rate to reflect this risk.

Therefore, a discount curve that reflects the party's funding costs and credit risk should be used in uncollateralized swaps.

23.3.2.3 *Currency swaps with two currencies*

A currency swap involves exchanging payments in two different currencies (e.g., Japanese yen and U.S. dollars). Because each leg of the swap is tied to a different currency, each side needs to be valued using the interest rates appropriate for that currency.

One way to do this is, in the case of a swap involving the Japanese yen and U.S. dollars, to first value the yen leg using a yen discount curve and the dollar leg using a U.S. dollar discount curve. Then, convert one leg into the same currency as the other using forward exchange rates so that you are comparing apples to apples.

Alternatively, some practitioners convert both legs into a single currency using forwards first and then discount using a single curve. Either way, currency swaps require you to think in two interest rate worlds at once.

23.3.2.4 *Equity and total return swaps: Use the market's expected return*

An equity swap or TRS is a bit different. It's not about interest rates so much as it is about asset performance. These swaps typically exchange a fixed or floating interest payment for the return on a stock, equity index, or specified equity portfolio.

The floating return leg (i.e., the leg linked to an equity or asset return) is often valued using futures prices or other market-based indicators that reflect the return implied by current prices. These instruments enable the estimation of the return leg's value without relying on forecasts, as the necessary return information is embedded in observable market data. The fixed or interest-based leg is then discounted using an appropriate curve, such as a risk-free rate (like the U.S. Treasury or OIS curve) or, if there is some credit exposure, an adjusted curve that reflects that risk.

Accordingly, market data should be used to estimate the return leg for equity or return-based swaps, while the fixed leg should be discounted using a risk-free or credit-adjusted curve.

23.3.3 *Locking in future floating cash flows using market instruments*

A critical challenge in valuing a swap is estimating future floating payments, as these depend on variables that have not yet been realized, such as interest rates, equity returns, or foreign exchange rates. Because future cash flows are unknown, valuation must rely on market-implied expectations, which can be "locked in" using observable prices of derivative instruments. This approach eliminates the need to forecast future rates or returns, thereby maintaining swap valuation as arbitrage-free and market-consistent.

By using market-based instruments, such as interest rate futures, equity futures, or FX forwards, the valuation of floating cash flows avoids subjective forecasting. Instead, each floating payment is based on replicable, tradable prices, consistent with the arbitrage-free pricing principle.

23.3.3.1 *Forward rates for interest rate and currency swaps*

For swaps involving floating interest rate legs, such as those linked to SOFR or other benchmarks, future payments can be estimated using forward rates implied by the current yield curve. These forward rates reflect the market's consensus of future short-term rates and are derived using interest rate futures contracts or forward rate agreements or by bootstrapping zero-coupon yield curves.[4]

These instruments enable the extraction of forward rates for any future period. For example, if the forward SOFR for a six-month period starting in three months is 4.1%, then a floating leg payment over that period would be valued using this implied rate, not a forecast.

23.3.3.2 *Equity and total return swaps: Using futures prices*

For equity and total return swaps, the floating leg is tied to the return of a reference asset (such as an equity index, single stock, or a specified basket of stocks). Since actual returns are unknown at valuation time, they can be estimated using equity futures contracts on the reference asset.

For example, the value of a floating payment linked to the S&P 500 index return can be locked in by using the price of a futures contract

[4] Bootstrapping is a method used to construct a zero-coupon yield curve (i.e., a curve that shows the interest rate applicable to a single payment made at a future date). For an illustration of how this is done, see Chapter 7 in Frank J. Fabozzi and Francesco A. Fabozzi, *Bond Markets, Analysis, and Strategies*, MIT Press, 2026.

that matures on the same date as the swap payment. The implied return is

$$\text{Implied return} = \frac{F_t - S_0}{S_0}$$

where F_t is the futures price with maturity t and S_0 is the asset's spot price.

This return can be used in equation (23.3) to estimate the floating leg cash flow:

$$\text{Floating return payment} = \text{Notional principal} \times \left(\frac{F_t - S_0}{S_0}\right) \times \left(\frac{\text{Days in period}}{\text{Days in year}}\right)$$

23.3.3.3 *Currency swaps: Forward FX rates*

In currency swaps, one leg typically involves future payments in a foreign currency. To value the swap in a single currency, forward FX rates are used to convert the foreign-currency leg into domestic currency terms at each payment date. Forward FX rates are derived using the interest rate parity relationship[5]:

$$F_t = S_0 \times \left(\frac{1 + t\,r_{\text{domestic}}}{1 + t\,r_{\text{foreign}}}\right)$$

where:

- F_t is the forward exchange rate,
- S_0 is the spot exchange rate,
- r_{domestic} is the domestic interest rate,
- r_{foreign} is the foreign interest rate,
- t is the time in years to maturity.

[5] Interest rate parity is the principle that the difference between forward and spot exchange rates reflects the interest rate differential between two currencies. In other words, if an investor were to borrow in one currency, convert it into another currency at the spot rate, and invest at the corresponding foreign interest rate, then the return from this strategy should equal the return from investing domestically once the FX rate is used to convert back. This relationship ensures that no arbitrage opportunities exist between domestic and foreign money markets.

These forward rates are then used to project domestic-currency equivalents of foreign cash flows for present value calculations.

23.4 Valuation Examples by Swap Type

Having outlined the principles of swap valuation—estimating cash flows, discounting with appropriate curves, and considering the structure of each leg—we now turn to practical illustrations of how these steps are applied. While the valuation process is conceptually similar across all swap types, the details can vary depending on the underlying reference (interest rate, equity, or currency) and the payment structure. The examples that follow illustrate how the general valuation framework is applied to three commonly encountered swap types: an interest rate swap, an equity TRS, and a currency swap. Each example walks through the process of determining future payments, selecting the appropriate discounting method, and computing the net present value of the contract from the perspective of one party.

23.4.1 *Interest rate swap (fixed-for-floating)*

Let's begin with an interest rate swap, the most widely used and conceptually foundational of all swap structures. The following example illustrates how to value a plain-vanilla fixed-for-floating interest rate swap using forward rates and discount factors. The swap terms in our example are as follows:

- *Notional*: $100 million
- *Tenor remaining*: 2 years
- *Payment frequency*: semiannual (4 periods left)
- *Fixed leg*: 3.0% annually
- *Floating leg*: 6-month SOFR
- *Day count*: Actual/360

To value future cash flows, both legs of the swap must be discounted to the present using discount factors. These discount factors reflect the current market interest rates for risk-free borrowing over various time horizons. As explained earlier, in practice, they are obtained from a zero-coupon yield curve, which is built using observable market instruments such as Treasury securities, interest rate swaps, or futures contracts. The values below are illustrative and represent the present value of $1 received at each payment date.

Discount factors:

- 6 months: 0.985
- 1 year: 0.96
- 1.5 years: 0.94
- 2 years: 0.915

Forward SOFR rates:

- 4.2%, 4.3%, 4.5%, 4.6%

First, the cash flows are calculated. For the fixed leg (semiannual payments),

$$\text{Payment} = \$100{,}000{,}000 \times 0.03 \times \frac{180}{360} = \$1{,}500{,}000 \text{ (each period)}$$

For the floating leg (using forward SOFR rates),

- *Period 1*: $\$100{,}000{,}000 \times 0.042 \times \frac{180}{360} = \$2{,}100{,}000$
- *Period 2*: $\$100{,}000{,}000 \times 0.043 \times \frac{180}{360} = \$2{,}150{,}000$
- *Period 3*: $\$100{,}000{,}000 \times 0.045 \times \frac{180}{360} = \$2{,}250{,}000$
- *Period 4*: $\$100{,}000{,}000 \times 0.046 \times \frac{180}{360} = \$2{,}300{,}000$

The present value for each leg must be calculated. For the fixed leg, the present value is

$$\$1{,}500{,}000 \times (0.985 + 0.96 + 0.94 + 0.915) = \$5{,}700{,}000$$

For the floating leg, the present value is

$$(\$2{,}100{,}000 \times 0.985) + (\$2{,}150{,}000 \times 0.96) + (\$2{,}250{,}000 \times 0.94) + (\$2{,}300{,}000 \times 0.915) = \$8{,}352{,}000$$

The value of the swap is

$$\$8{,}352{,}000 - \$5{,}700{,}000 = \$2{,}652{,}000$$

This is a positive asset value for the floating-rate receiver.

23.4.2 *Equity total return swap*

Equity TRSs allow one party to gain exposure to the performance of an equity or equity index without actually owning the underlying asset. These swaps are often used to take synthetic equity positions, hedge existing holdings, or manage balance sheet exposures. In this example, one party agrees to pay a floating interest rate and receive the total return on a broad equity index. The swap terms in our example are as follows:

- *Notional*: $50 million
- *Payment frequency*: quarterly
- *Tenor remaining*: 1 year (4 payments)
- *Party A receives*: total return on S&P 500
- *Party A pays*: SOFR + 100 bps
- *Day count*: Actual/360 (use 0.25 for simplicity)

To estimate the value of the floating return leg, expected returns on the S&P 500 are inferred from market instruments, such as equity index futures, which reflect the market's view of forward returns over various horizons. The floating-rate payments are based on forward-looking SOFR rates, which can be implied from short-term interest rate futures or constructed from the yield curve. All future cash flows are discounted using discount factors derived from the relevant risk-free curve:

- *Quarterly forward S&P 500 returns*: 3.0%, 2.5%, 2.0%, 2.0%
- *Forward SOFR*: 4.2%, 4.3%, 4.4%, 4.5%
- *Discount factors*: 0.99, 0.975, 0.96, 0.945

Given the swap term and other data, let's estimate the cash flows. The amount received for the total return leg for each of the four quarters:

Quarter 1: $\$50{,}000{,}000 \times 0.030 \times 0.25 = \$375{,}000$
Quarter 2: $\$50{,}000{,}000 \times 0.025 \times 0.25 = \$312{,}500$

Quarter 3: $50,000,000 × 0.020 × 0.25 = $250,000
Quarter 4: $50,000,000 × 0.020 × 0.25 = $250,000

For the payments that must be made (SOFR + 1%) for the four quarters, the payments are

Quarter 1: $50,000,000 × 0.052 × 0.25 = $650,000
Quarter 2: $50,000,000 × 0.053 × 0.25 = $662,500
Quarter 3: $50,000,000 × 0.054 × 0.25 = $675,000
Quarter 4: $50,000,000 × 0.055 × 0.25 = $687,500

The present value of the cash flows for each quarter for each leg must now be computed. For the payments received, it is

$$(\$375{,}000 \times 0.99) + (\$312{,}500 \times 0.975) + (\$250{,}000 \times 0.96) + (\$250{,}000 \times 0.945) = \$1{,}152{,}188$$

The present of the amount paid is

$$(\$650{,}000 \times 0.99) + (\$662{,}500 \times 0.975) + (\$675{,}000 \times 0.96) + (\$687{,}500 \times 0.945) = \$2{,}587{,}125$$

The value of the swap is then

$$\$1{,}152{,}188 - \$2{,}587{,}125 = -\$1{,}434{,}937$$

Since the swap's value is negative, Party A has a mark-to-market liability of $1,434,937.

23.4.3 *Currency swap* (*fixed-for-fixed*)

Currency swaps differ from other types of swaps in that they involve the exchange of both interest payments and principal amounts in two different currencies. These swaps are often used by institutions seeking to manage exposure to foreign interest rates or to hedge currency risk in long-term financing. In a typical fixed-for-fixed currency swap, each party agrees to pay fixed interest in one currency while receiving fixed interest in another. Because each leg is denominated in a different currency, valuation requires discounting cash flows using the appropriate yield curve for each currency and converting values to a common currency using FX rates. The following example illustrates how this valuation process works in practice.

We use as our swap for this illustration one with the following terms:

- *Tenor remaining*: 1 year
- *Party A pays*: $100 million at 2.5% U.S. dollar fixed rate
- *Party A receives*: €90 million at 3.0% euro fixed rate
- *Annual payments*: notional exchanged at maturity
- *Spot FX rate*: 1.10 USD/EUR

The discount factors, derived from the respective zero-coupon yield curves for each currency, are as follows: 0.94 for the 1-year U.S. dollar discount factor and 0.935 for the 1-year euro discount factor. To convert the euro-denominated cash flows into U.S. dollars for comparison, we apply the 1-year forward exchange rate, which reflects the interest rate differential between the two currencies over the contract term. The 1-year forward FX rate used in this example is 1.12 USD/EUR.

Because the two legs of the swap are in different currencies, we also need to express them in a common currency for comparison. This is done using the forward exchange rate, which reflects the market-implied conversion rate for one currency into another at a future date. In this example, the 1-year forward exchange rate is 1.12 USD per EUR, meaning that one euro is expected to be worth 1.12 U.S. dollars in one year, based on current interest rate differentials between the two currencies:

- U.S. dollar discount factor (1 year): 0.94
- EUR discount factor (1 year): 0.935
- Forward FX rate (1 year): 1.12 USD/EUR

The cash flow for the payment for the USD leg is

- *Interest*: $100,000,000 × 2.5% = $2,500,000
- *Principal*: $100,000,000
- *Total PV in U.S. dollars*: ($2,500,000 + $100,000,000) × 0.94 = $96,350,000

For the EUR leg (received),

- *Interest*: €90,000,000 × 3% = €2,700,000
- *Principal*: €90,000,000
- *Total PV in euros*: (€2,700,000 + €90,000,000) × 0.935 = €86,674,500

Now, it is necessary to convert to U.S. dollars using the 1-year forward rate:

$$\text{USD value} = €86{,}674{,}500 \times 1.12 = \$97{,}075{,}440$$

The swap is then

$$\$97{,}075{,}440 - \$96{,}350{,}000 = \$725{,}440$$

Party A has a mark-to-market asset of $725,440.

23.5 Risk Considerations in Swap Valuation

Calculating the present value of a swap provides a snapshot of the contract's worth at a given point in time. But that valuation is only part of the story. The value of a swap can fluctuate significantly over time due to changes in market conditions, evolving credit profiles, or operational events. Understanding the risks that drive these changes is essential for anyone using swaps for hedging, investment, or balance sheet management.

The discussion that follows highlights the key types of risk that affect swaps during their life cycle—risks that can influence not only the value of the instrument but also the decision of whether and how to use it.

The most prominent risk is market risk, which arises from movements in the financial variables the swap is designed to exchange. For example, an interest rate swap is sensitive to changes in both short- and long-term interest rates. An equity TRS is affected by fluctuations in the price of the underlying equity or index. Currency swaps are driven by movements in exchange rates as well as shifts in domestic and foreign interest rates. Even if a swap has zero value at initiation, market changes can cause one leg of the contract to become more valuable than the other, altering the mark-to-market value and potentially triggering margin requirements or affecting financial statements.

Another important consideration is basis risk. This occurs when the cash flows from the swap do not perfectly match the exposure they are intended to hedge. For instance, a swap linked to the return on a broad equity index may not fully offset the risk of a portfolio concentrated in specific stocks. Similarly, a currency swap tied to a particular benchmark rate might diverge from the actual borrowing or lending costs incurred by the user. Even minor mismatches can create unintended gains or losses, making swaps imperfect hedging tools in certain situations.

Swaps also expose parties to counterparty risk, which is the risk that the counterparty may fail to fulfill its obligations. In a bilateral swap, if one party defaults while the contract has a positive value to the other party, the non-defaulting party may suffer a loss. This risk is mitigated when swaps are subject to collateral arrangements, such as those governed by Credit Support Annexes (CSAs), which require counterparties to post cash or securities to reflect changes in the contract's value. In the case of centrally cleared swaps, a clearinghouse assumes counterparty risk and enforces stringent collateral and margining rules to reduce the likelihood of a default-related loss.

Liquidity risk presents another challenge in valuation. This refers to the possibility that a swap cannot be easily unwound, transferred, or repriced without incurring significant costs. Some swap markets, such as cleared interest rate swaps referencing SOFR, are highly liquid, while others, such as bespoke equity swaps or customized TRSs, may be thinly traded. In illiquid markets, exiting a position early or obtaining reliable valuations can be difficult, leading to pricing uncertainty and wider bid–ask spreads.

While valuation tells us what a swap is worth today, risk analysis tells us how and why that value might change tomorrow. Incorporating both perspectives is essential for prudent swap use in practice.

23.6 Summary

In this chapter, I introduce a unified framework for valuing the four most common types of risk-sharing swaps: interest rate swaps, equity swaps, total return swaps, and currency swaps. After defining the general valuation logic, based on the difference in present value between the two legs, I explain methods for calculating swap cash flows across fixed-for-floating, fixed-for-fixed, and floating-for-floating structures.

I also explain the selection of appropriate discount curves depending on whether a swap is collateralized, uncollateralized, denominated in multiple currencies, or tied to an asset return. The chapter also emphasizes how forward rates and futures contracts are used to lock in floating payments, allowing for arbitrage-free valuation without relying on subjective forecasts.

Illustrative examples are provided for each swap type, showing how to compute projected payments, apply discount factors, convert foreign currency legs, and determine mark-to-market swap values. The final section identifies and explains key valuation risks—market risk, basis risk, counterparty risk, and liquidity risk—offering a more complete picture of what it means to assess a swap's value in real-world settings.

Author Index

Subject Index

C

E

H

I

www.ingramcontent.com/pod-product-compliance
Lightning Source LLC
Chambersburg PA
CBHW070228010526
43978CB00004B/67